CAMBODIA

The **Institute of Southeast Asian Studies (ISEAS)** was established as an autonomous organization in 1968. It is a regional centre dedicated to the study of socio-political, security and economic trends and developments in Southeast Asia and its wider geostrategic and economic environment. The Institute's research programmes are the Regional Economic Studies (RES, including ASEAN and APEC), Regional Strategic and Political Studies (RSPS), and Regional Social and Cultural Studies (RSCS).

ISEAS Publishing, an established academic press, has issued more than 2,000 books and journals. It is the largest scholarly publisher of research about Southeast Asia from within the region. ISEAS Publishing works with many other academic and trade publishers and distributors to disseminate important research and analyses from and about Southeast Asia to the rest of the world.

CAMBODIA

PROGRESS AND CHALLENGES SINCE 1991

EDITED BY

POU SOTHIRAK

GEOFF WADE

MARK HONG

INSTITUTE OF SOUTHEAST ASIAN STUDIES

Singapore

First published in Singapore in 2012 by
Institute of Southeast Asian Studies
30 Heng Mui Keng Terrace
Pasir Panjang
Singapore 119614

E-mail: publish@iseas.edu.sg
Website: http://bookshop.iseas.edu.sg

All rights reserved. No part of this publication may be reproduced, stored in a retrieval system, or transmitted in any form or by any means, electronic, mechanical, photocopying, recording or otherwise, without the prior permission of the Institute of Southeast Asian Studies.

© 2012 Institute of Southeast Asian Studies, Singapore.

The responsibility for facts and opinions in this publication rests exclusively with the authors and their interpretations do not necessarily reflect the views of the policy of the publishers or their supporters.

ISEAS Library Cataloguing-in-Publication Data

Cambodia : progress and challenges since 1991 / edited by Pou Sothirak, Geoff Wade and Mark Hong.
1. Cambodia—Politics and government—1979–
2. Cambodia—Economic conditions—20th century.
3. Cambodia—Social conditions—20th century.
4. Cambodia—Foreign relations—20th century.
5. Cambodia—Foreign relations—Southeast Asia.
6. Southeast Asia—Foreign relations—Cambodia.
7. United Nations. Transitional Authority in Cambodia.
8. International police—Cambodia—History.
9. Mekong River.
I. Pou Sothirak.
II. Wade, Geoff.
III. Hong, Mark.
DS554.842 C97 2012

ISBN 978-981-4379-82-3 (soft cover)
ISBN 978-981-4379-83-0 (e-book, PDF)

Typeset by Superskill Graphics Pte Ltd
Printed in Singapore by Markono Print Media Pte Ltd

CONTENTS

FOREWORD

When I was requested to draft a foreword for this book, I inquired into the origins of the book proposal, and was immediately struck by its timeliness, as 2011 is the 20th anniversary of the 1991 Paris Peace Conference which brought about a diplomatic resolution of the protracted Cambodia conflict. I also liked the way it focused on the future prospects of Cambodia, looking ahead and putting past acrimony behind, which is in tune with the concept of national reconciliation, which we practice in Cambodia. Thirdly, I was amazed by the appropriate nationalities of the three scholars from ISEAS, who are the co-editors of this book. One is a Cambodian, another is Singaporean and the third is Australian. Those who know the history of the diplomatic efforts to help resolve the Cambodian conflict will recognize that these were the three countries intimately involved in bringing the conflict to a negotiated settlement. Let me express my appreciation for the hard work, organization and initiative of the three co-editors who guided this useful book to fruition.

2011 is also the year in which Singapore's Minister Mentor Lee Kuan Yew's thoughts, recorded through interviews by a team of journalists from the Singapore *Straits Times*, were published in a book entitled: *Lee Kuan Yew: Hard Truths to Keep Singapore Going*. What struck me most was a quotation from Mr Lee, who said: "Singapore is my concern till the end of my life." (*Straits Times*, 22 January 2011) When I read it, I was impressed by the dedication and passion of Mr Lee, whom we all know as the Father of Modern Singapore. I have been lucky to meet Mr Lee, and also know that it was his strong support for King Sihanouk and for Free Cambodia that kept the efforts going for over ten years.

What I wish for my Cambodian compatriots is that same patriotism and drive to make our country a modern, peaceful, prosperous and forward-looking country. After all the terrible conflicts, killings, sufferings and turmoil, all Cambodians would surely share my wishes for our beloved country. In a sense, I wish to dedicate this book to our two great leaders, HM King Sihanouk and to MM Lee Kuan Yew, and their ministers and officials, who achieved peace and freedom for democratic Cambodia. Now we need to draw some lessons in economic development from the Little Red Dot. After all, if even great China can learn from Singapore, why not Cambodia?

Lastly, in regard to the future of Cambodia, let me touch upon the three principles which may guide our nation-building, just as the French have chosen: Liberté, Egalité and Fraternité, for their founding principles. I suggest Buddhism, Education and National Unity as our guiding principles. Every one will have their own mix, but bearing in mind our tragic history, our culture and the need to build knowledge for our future, these three principles seem as appropriate as any. Let this timely book serve as a foundation and compass for future generations of Cambodians, who need to look back at our history, and forwards towards a glorious future: we who are the children of Great Angkor.

HRH Norodom Sirivudh
Phnom Penh, Cambodia
June 2011

MESSAGE

This timely book commemorates the Twentieth Anniversary of the October 1991 Paris Peace Agreement on Cambodia. The Paris Conference on Cambodia itself was the high-water achievement and culmination of a long and determined campaign by the ASEAN countries to bring about a peaceful and negotiated settlement of the Cambodian conflict. It succeeded where previous attempts had failed, primarily because the international, regional and domestic Cambodian parties were now supportive of a negotiated peace settlement. Various papers in this book describe how the various factors fell into place, which enabled the many participants to be ready to accept an UN-organized, Permanent Five UNSC members-brokered, Cambodian factions-accepted peace settlement.

Cambodia was one of the first major challenges confronting the decade-old ASEAN, to test how it would face up to the question of whether ASEAN could countenance the overthrow of a small state in its region by armed force. What about its hallowed principles, such as the non-use of force to settle disputes; of respect for the territorial integrity, sovereignty and independence of all states; of the use of consultation, consensus and dialogue to settle disputes? It was because of these deeply-held principles that ASEAN decided to oppose the foreign invasion and occupation of Cambodia for over a decade, until the conditions were ripe for a peaceful settlement.

Now that the UNTAC PKO and UN-supervised general elections of 1993 have peacefully come and gone, key questions remain, such as: what is the state of Cambodia today, eighteen years later, and after millions of dollars in ODA by various countries and generous assistance by numerous NGOs have been provided to Cambodia to recover and reconstruct its economy and society? What will be the future of Cambodia in the 21st Century? The various papers in this volume seek to address these complex issues of socio-economic development, of human resource development, of good governance, and of Cambodia's foreign relations. The story of the liberation and reconstruction of Cambodia is one of the noblest achievements of the international community and one of ASEAN's finest successes, and it is a story well told within this book.

That is not to say, however, that there are no difficulties or that all sides are happy with the current situation within the Kingdom of Cambodia.

The centralised power which is often advantageous during a period of reconstruction at times results in the exclusion of some groups from development and the stilling of alternative voices within the social milieu. Cambodia certainly still has many issues with which to grapple and we hope that this volume will provide the background for more people to understand the history of Cambodia over the last 20 years and the potentials yet to be realized. I commend the great efforts by the many paper writers and the three co-editors for a job well done.

K. Kesavapany
Director
ISEAS Singapore
6 June 2011

CONTRIBUTORS

HRH Prince Norodom Sirivudh was born in 1951. He graduated with a Master's Degree in Economics at Paris IX of Dauphine University in 1976. He began his political career in 1971 when he joined the Paris-based royalist movement, GRUNC/FUNK. In 1981, he joined the National United Front for an Independent, Neutral, Peaceful and Cooperative Cambodia (FUNCINPEC), and he was the Chief Representative of Prince Norodom Ranariddh (who assumed the leadership of the FUNCINPEC Party in 1983). In 1988, he was appointed as Chief of FUNCINPEC's Humanitarian Department and was designated Secretary-General of the FUNCINPEC-Kampuchea from 1989 to 1990. At the Cambodian Peace talks in Jakarta, Indonesia in 1988, Prince Norodom Sirivudh was one of FUNCINPEC's delegates until the final agreements were signed in Paris on 23 October 1991. On 7 November 1991, Prince Norodom Sirivudh returned to his beloved motherland Cambodia for the first time in 20 years. He laid the groundwork for FUNCINPEC's participation in the electoral process, mandated under the Paris Peace Agreement. He was the FUNCINPEC's Bureau Chief in Phnom Penh during the United Nations-Administered Elections. Prince Norodom Sirivudh was elected to the Parliament in 1993 as a representative of Kampong Cham Province. Following the 1993 Elections, Prince Norodom Sirivudh was appointed Co-Deputy Prime Minister and Minister of Foreign Affairs of the Royal Government. In late 1993, the Prince was also appointed as Secretary-General of the FUNCINPEC Party. In 1994, the Prince was appointed as Chairman of the Cambodian Institute for Cooperation and Peace (CICP), a non-government Phnom Penh-based research and policy organization. In October of the same year, the Prince resigned from the post of Co-Deputy Prime Minister and Minister of Foreign Affairs. In April 1999 he was nominated as Supreme Privy Counsellor to His Majesty the King. On 5 July 2001, Prince Norodom Sirivudh was reappointed for the second time as Secretary-General of the FUNCINPEC Party. And in August 2001, Prince Norodom Sirivudh was elected as Senator. In the July 2003 General Elections, Prince Norodom Sirivudh was elected as Member of Parliament for Kandal Province and became Deputy Prime Minister and Co-Minister of Interior of the Royal Government until March 2006. From March 2006, Prince Norodom

Sirivudh has been Privy Counsellor to His Majesty the King and Member of Parliament.

K. Kesavapany has been ISEAS Director since 1 November 2002. Prior to his appointment, Ambassador Kesavapany was Singapore's High Commissioner to Malaysia. In his 30-year career in the Foreign Service, he served as Permanent Representative to the United Nations in Geneva (December 1991–March 1997) and held key staff appointments in the Ministry of Foreign Affairs of Singapore. Ambassador Kesavapany was an active participant in the final phase of the Uruguay Round negotiations and was the first Chairman of the WTO's General Council in 1995.

Sok An is the Deputy Prime Minister and Minister in charge of the Council of Ministers of Cambodia. He graduated from the Royal University of Phnom Penh with a Bachelor's degree in Geography, History and Sociology in 1972. In 1981, he was the Chief of Cabinet of HE Samdech Hun Sen, the Minister of Foreign Affairs and later on in 1988, the Secretary General of the Ministry of Foreign Affairs. In 1983, he was the Secretary General of the Cambodian National Peace Committee. In 1985, he was Ambassador Extraordinary and Plenipotentiary of Cambodia to India. In 1988, he was Secretary of State of the Ministry of Foreign Affairs and in 1991, Secretary of State of the Ministry of Interior. Vice Minister of Foreign Affairs and in 1990, Vice Minister of Interior. In 1991, he was the Supreme National Council representative and also the Head of the Central Cabinet of the Cambodian People's Party. In 1993 he was elected as Member of Parliament of the Takeo Constituency of the National Assembly and nominated as the Co-Minister in Charge of the Office of the Council of Ministers of the Royal Government of Cambodia. In 1996, he was awarded the Honorary Degree of Doctor of Laws by Wesleyan College, Iowa. His other positions include Chairman of the Council for Public Administrative Reform, Chairman of the Cambodian National Petroleum Authority (CNPA) and Chairman of the Khmer Rouge Tribunal.

Tommy Koh is Ambassador-at-Large at the Ministry of Foreign Affairs, Chairman of the Centre for International Law at the National University of Singapore (NUS), and Special Adviser to the Institute of Policy Studies. He had served as Dean of the NUS Faculty of Law, Singapore's Permanent Representative to the United Nations in New York and was Ambassador to the United States of America, Canada and Mexico. He was President of the

Third UN Conference on the Law of the Sea and chaired the Earth Summit. He served as the UN Secretary General's Special Envoy to Russia, Estonia, Latvia and Lithuania. He was Singapore's Chief Negotiator for the U.S.-Singapore Free Trade Agreement. He had chaired two dispute panels for the WTO. He acted as the agent of Singapore in two legal disputes between Singapore and Malaysia, which were adjudicated by the ICJ and ITLOS. He chairs three committees for the National University of Singapore (NUS) relating to law, Asia research and environmental management. He was the founding Chairman of the National Arts Council; founding Executive Director of the Asia-Europe Foundation; and Chairman of the National Heritage Board. He was recently appointed Rector of a new College at NUS, the Tembusu College, and Chairman of the SymAsia Foundation of Credit Suisse.

Mark Hong is a Visiting Research Fellow, ISEAS. He obtained a Bachelor of Arts degree in Economics from Cambridge University, UK in 1969 and a Master of Science degree in International Relations from Georgetown University, Washington DC in 1982 on a Fulbright Scholarship. He served in the Singapore Foreign Ministry from October 1969 to March 2002, with postings in Cambodia, Hong Kong, Paris, New York as Deputy Permanent Representative to the UN, Russia and Ukraine. He has edited five books, two on energy issues, two on ASEAN-Russia relations and one on Southeast Asia, with chapter contributions to each.

Rodolfo C. Severino is the head of the ASEAN Studies Centre at the Institute of Southeast Asian Studies in Singapore and a frequent speaker at international conferences in Asia and Europe. Having been Secretary-General of the Association of Southeast Asian Nations from 1998 to 2002, he has completed a book, entitled *Southeast Asia in Search of an ASEAN Community*. His views on ASEAN and Southeast Asia have also been published in *ASEAN Today and Tomorrow*, a compilation of his speeches and other statements. He has co-edited two books: *Whither the Philippines in the 21st Century?* and *Southeast Asia in a New Era*. Before assuming the position of ASEAN Secretary-General, Severino was Undersecretary of Foreign Affairs of the Philippines, the culmination of 32 years in the Philippine Foreign Service. He twice served as ASEAN Senior Official for the Philippines and is one of the Philippines' Experts and Eminent Persons for the ASEAN Regional Forum. Severino has a Bachelor of Arts degree in the humanities from the Ateneo de Manila and a Master of Arts degree in international relations from the Johns

Hopkins University School of Advanced International Studies. He is a member of the Advisory Board of *The Fletcher Forum of World Affairs*, the journal of the Fletcher School of Tufts University.

Benny Widyono holds an M.A. and Ph.D. in Economics and served as a United Nations diplomat in Bangkok, Santiago, New York, and Cambodia, 1963 to 1997. He was a peacekeeper in Cambodia with the United Nations Transitional Authority in Cambodia, from 1992 to 1993, and then returned to Cambodia as the UN Secretary-General's Representative from 1994–97. His recently published book, *Dancing in the Shadows: Sihanouk, the Khmer Rouge, and the United Nations in Cambodia* was written while Dr Widyono was a visiting scholar at Cornell University. He is currently adjunct professor of economics at the University of Connecticut in Stamford, Ct., a board member of CKS and PIO, and an adviser to Leopard Cambodia enterprises.

Carlyle A. Thayer is Emeritus Professor, University of New South Wales at the Australian Defence Force Academy in Canberra. He was educated at Brown University, holds an M.A. in Southeast Asian Studies from Yale and a Ph.D. in International Relations from The Australian National University. He was a United Nations-accredited observer for the May 1993 elections in Cambodia. He is the author of over 400 publications dealing with the domestic politics, foreign policies and security issues of Southeast Asia including *Southeast Asia: Patterns of Security Cooperation* (ASPI 2010).

Julio A. Jeldres is a Ph.D. Candidate and an Adjunct Research Fellow at Monash University in Australia. He served as Senior Private Secretary to King Norodom Sihanouk of Cambodia and has been since 1993 his Official Biographer. He is a graduate of Swinburne University in Melbourne and has published three books on the Cambodian Royal Family and the Cambodian Monarchy as well as translating the Memoirs of King Sihanouk from French into English. He has been a Visiting Research Fellow at Chulalongkorn University in Thailand and a Guest Lecturer at CASS (Beijing) and ISEAS (Singapore). He was awarded the rank of Ambassador of Cambodia (Honorary) in June 1993 by the King of Cambodia. His Ph.D. research proposal is entitled: "Norodom Sihanouk Charismatic Authority and Cambodia's Foreign Policy". He has published numerous articles about Cambodian politics, human rights, democracy development, relations with China and the monarchy. He has also worked as a consultant with several UN agencies in Bangkok, mostly on human rights issues.

Lam Peng Er is a Senior Research Fellow at the East Asian Institute, National University of Singapore. He obtained his Ph.D. from Columbia University. A Japan specialist, his latest single-authored book is *Japan's Peacebuilding Diplomacy in Asia: Seeking a more active political role* (2009). Lam's forthcoming books are: *Japan's Relations with Southeast Asia: The Fukuda Doctrine and Beyond*, (co-edited with Victor Teo), *Southeast Asia between China and Japan*, *Japan Chronicles: 2001–11 — A Second Lost Decade?* (co-edited with Purnendra Jain), *Japan's Strategic Challenges in a Changing Regional Environment* and (co-edited with Qin Yaqing and Yang Mu), *China and East Asia in the Post-Financial Crisis World.* Lam has the vision to build a school for young children in Cambodia.

Yukio Imagawa was born in 1932 in Tokyo. In 1955, he graduated from Waseda University, Faculty of Political Science. In 1956, he entered the Ministry of Foreign Affairs (MOFA). Besides serving at MOFA in Tokyo, he served in foreign countries such as Cambodia, France, Laos, Vietnam (Hanoi), Algeria. In 1985, he served as Consul General of Japan at Marseille and in 1988 as Minister of Japanese Embassy in France. From 1989–99, he was appointed as Co-Chairman of the third committee of Paris International Conference on Cambodia. In 1990, he was appointed as Minister of Japanese Embassy in Thailand and from1991–96 as Ambassador of Japan to Cambodia. In 1996, Ambassador IMAGAWA retired from MOFA. In 1996 he took up a position as Professor of Faculty of Law, Kanto-Gakuen University, Gunma Japan. From 2005, he is serving as Professor Emeritus of Kanto-Gakuen University.

Yasushi Akashi graduated from the University of Tokyo in 1954. Mr Akashi then studied as a Fulbright Scholar at the University of Virginia, and later at the Fletcher School of Law and Diplomacy and Columbia University. He became the first Japanese citizen to join the United Nations Secretariat in 1957. He served as Ambassador at the Permanent Mission of Japan to the United Nations, United Nations Under-Secretary-General for Public Information, Under-Secretary-General for Disarmament Affairs, Special Representative of the Secretary-General for Cambodia and later for the Former Yugoslavia. He was Under-Secretary-General for Humanitarian Affairs until the end of 1997. He is currently Representative of the Government of Japan on Peace-Building in Sri Lanka, Chairman of the International House of Japan, and President of the Japanese Organization for International Cooperation in Family Planning (JOICFP), Vice-President of the United

Nations Association of Japan and Visiting Professor at Ritsumeikan University. Author of many books including Memoirs (2001), *The United Nations — Its History and Prospects* (2006), and *In the Valley of War and Peace — Personalities I met* (2007).

Son Soubert was born on 20 June 1942 in Phnom-Penh, Cambodia; H.E. Son Soubert is currently High Privy Councillor to His Majesty King Sihamoni, as from May 2010. He received Master Degree in Classics (French, Latin and Greek Literatures; Grammar and Philology) from La Sorbonne — Paris University, Paris France. H.E. Son Soubert was appointed Member of the Constitutional Council, appointed by His Majesty the King of Cambodia from 1998–2010. He was Professor at the Faculty of Archaeology of the Royal University of Fine Arts, Phnom Penh and served as Vice-President of Cambodian Red Cross from 1993 to 2008. He was appointed Second Vice-President of the National Assembly from May 1993–July 1998. He was elected by the Congress of the Party as President of the SON SANN Party from March 1998. He was then elected as Member of Parliament during the UNTAC supervised and organized elections from May 1993. He was elected as Secretary General of the Buddhist Liberal Democratic Party by its Congress from May 1993. From 1982–91, he served as Assistant to the Prime Minister of the Coalition Government of Cambodia (recognized by the United Nations), in charge of Diplomatic Relations and participating in the Human Rights Commission of the UN every year from 1983 to 1990. From 1982-91, he served as Second Vice-President of the Khmer People's National Liberation Front and from 1979–82 as Member of the Khmer People's National Liberation Front of Humanitarian Affairs, in charge of supplying food and medicine to the Cambodian refugees at the Thai-Cambodian borders. From1974–79, he was General Manager of a Chain of Grocery Shops (Superettes) in Nice, France. H.E. Son Soubert has set up various Children's homes in Cambodia and served as Member of the Board of the Khmer Institute of Democracy and Member of the Board of the Centre for Khmer Studies in Siem-Reap. He received numerous awards, including a French Order des Palmes Académiques: Chevalier, for Culture and Several Khmer Orders and Medals.

Ken Berry was legal adviser to the Australian Task Force on Cambodia (1990–93) and participated in all negotiations leading to the signing of the Paris Agreements. He is the author of *Cambodia From Red to Blue: Australia's Initiative for Peace* (1997). He subsequently became chief of staff of then

Australian Foreign Minister Gareth Evans, Australian Ambassador to Chile, Peru and Bolivia, and Assistant Secretary for Arms Control and Disarmament. After leaving the Foreign Ministry in 2000, he became Executive Assistant to the Co-Chairs, International Commission on Intervention and State Sovereignty (2000–01), Legal Adviser to the International Crisis Group, Brussels (2002–08), and Research Coordinator of the International Commission on Nuclear Non-Proliferation and Disarmament (2008–10). He then retired to live in New Zealand.

Jean-Marc Lavergne completed his higher education at the Clermont-Ferrand Law School, and received his Masters in Private Law and Public Notary Certification in 1983. In 1982 he has been admitted to the Clermont-Ferrand Lawyers Training Centre (Centre de Formation Professionnelle des Avocats de Clermont-Ferrand). In 1988 after completing his magistracy studies, he was appointed to the High Civil Court of Angers as Parole Judge (Juge de l'application des Peines au Tribunal de Grande Instance). In 1997 he was appointed to the Appeals Court of Rennes as judge (Conseiller), where he has acted in particular as Presiding Judge of the Court of Assizes of Loire Atlantique and Morbihan. From 2001 to 2007, he served as Vice-President of the High Civil Court of Le Mans. In 2007 he was appointed as Conseiller at the Court of Appeal of Angers where he has also acted as Presiding Judge of the Court of Assizes of Sarthe and Maine et Loire. In 2006 he was appointed as International Judge at the Extraordinary Chambers in the Court of Cambodia (Trial Chamber). Since 2008 he serves on a full time basis as resident Judge in Phnom-Penh. Under the terms of Agreement between the United Nations and the Royal Government of Cambodia, the Extraordinary Chambers have jurisdiction to bring to trial senior leaders of Democratic Kampuchea and those who were most responsible for the crimes and serious violations of Cambodian penal law, international humanitarian law and custom, and international conventions recognized by Cambodia, that were committed during the period from 17 April 1975 to 6 January 1979.

Phoak Kung is a Harvard Yenching Institute Doctoral Scholar, and a Ph.D. Candidate in the Department of Politics and International Studies at the University of Warwick. He is also doing research in the Department of Government and Southeast Asian Program at Cornell University. He earned a master's degree in Public Policy from Crawford School of Economics and Government at the Australian National University. He was Assistant Dean (2008–10) in the Faculty of Social Sciences and International Relations at Paññāsātra University of Cambodia.

Wolfgang Sachsenröder is a German European, born in Brussels. He finished his studies of political science and public law with a Ph.D. from Bonn University. After some years in academic exchange he worked as a political science practitioner with the German Friedrich Naumann Foundation. Postings in Asia (11 years), the Middle East (6 years) and the Balkans (3 years) gave him the opportunity to work with numerous political parties. Since 2008 he is back in Singapore where he joined the Institute of Southeast Asian Studies as a visiting fellow. His current research is focusing on political parties in the ASEAN member countries.

Hang Chuon Naron is Secretary of State of the Ministry of Finance and Economy of the Royal Government of Cambodia since 2010 and the Permanent Vice Chairperson of the Supreme National Economic Council of Cambodia. Previously, he was Secretary-General of the Ministry of Economy and Finance. He is also a Member of the Government Committee for the Preparation of the National Strategic Development Plan. He had served as the Director, Economic and Financial Policy Planning and Monitoring Unit in the Ministry of Economy and Finance, responsible for coordinating fiscal reform programmes with international financial institutions (ADB, IMF, World Bank). He was also Assistant to the Eminent Person Group for the ASEAN Charter in 2006. He was previously consultant for the World Bank (1999–2000) and the International Union for the Conservation of Nature (IUCN) (2001). Dr Hang Chuon Naron received his Ph.D. in Economics from the Moscow State Institute for International Relations, Russia. In 2004 and 2008, he attended the Executive Programme at the JF Kennedy School of Government, Harvard University and the National School of Administration (ENA) in France respectively.

Ing Kantha Phavi was reappointed Minister for Women's Affairs in September 2008. She is responsible for the management and leadership of the Ministry of Women's Affairs. Prior to becoming Minister in 2004, Dr Ing served five years as Secretary of State of Women's and Veterans' Affairs. In addition to her ministerial post, she was appointed in 2004 as Chairwoman of the Cambodian National Council for Women. Dr Ing was an active architect to levy Gender on the agenda of the national development (National Poverty Reduction Strategy, Cambodian MDGs, National Strategic Development Plan, UNDAF 2011–15) and was instrumental in developing an effective mechanism of gender mainstreaming at national and sub-national levels. Under her supervision, the Ministry of Women's Affairs succeeded to integrate the gender issues in the laws such as the Land law, the Decentralization and Deconcentration organic laws, the new anti- trafficking of human beings and sexual exploitation law, and got the law on domestic violence and protection of the victim adopted in 2005. She continues to advocate for gender in ongoing state reforms and actually is promoting economic empowerment and increasing role in public decision making for women. In the 1990s, Dr Ing worked in France, as a private medical doctor then as director of the drugs trials department at ABR, a French enterprise involved in marketing and research for medical drugs. Dr Ing also served as Deputy Secretary General in a medical NGO, Association des Medecins Cambodgiens (AMC) which provides medical and social assistance to Cambodia. From 1995 to 1997, Dr Ing worked in Cambodia as technical adviser to the Ministry of Rural Development where she was responsible for community health and rural economic development programmes including micro-credit. Dr Ing holds a Doctorate of Medecine from Saint Antoine University, Paris with a specialty in nutrition and tropical diseases and a Brevet in Public Administration from Ecole Nationale d'Administration (ENA) Paris.

Winta Ghebreab is Technical Assistant to the Ministry of Women's Affairs in Cambodia.

Pou Sovachana holds a Bachelor of Arts degree (Mathematics) from the University of Oregon, USA. After a career in hospitality business and as a National Consultant at the Ministry of Tourism in Cambodia, he changed his focus and completed Advanced TESOL (Teacher of English to Speakers of Other Languages) certification in 2006 from Global TESOL College at Portland (USA). As a volunteer in Cambodia in the summers of 2005, 2006, and 2007, he taught and advised teachers and monks' on education issues. He also taught English Language and Khmer culture to vulnerable children. He graduated with a Master of Arts in Curriculum and Instruction in July 2008 from Portland State University (USA). In 2009, he volunteered teaching English language to the poor children at Wat Unnalum for Buddhism Education for Peace Centre. He has written many articles on the education progress and challenges in Cambodia. Currently, he is an Academic Lecturer on Introduction to Ethics, Cultural Anthropology, Fundamentals of Communication, and English Reading and Writing Compositions at Paññāsātra University of Cambodia and serves as an Advisor for Buddhism Education for Peace Centre at Wat Unnalum and Bamboo Shoot School in Steung Mean Chey.

Ian Harris is Professor Emeritus at the University of Cumbria and Tun Lin Kok Yuen Distinguished Visiting Professor in Buddhist Studies at the University of Toronto for 2011–12. He has held previous visiting positions at the University of Oxford, the University of British Columbia, the National University of Singapore, and the Documentary Centre of Cambodia in Phnom Penh. Initially a student of Buddhist philosophy, his current academic interests focus on the modern and contemporary history of Cambodia, Buddhism and politics in Southeast Asia, Buddhist environmentalism, and landscape aesthetics. His most recent books are *Cambodian Buddhism: History and Practice* (2005), *Buddhism Under Pol Pot* (2007), and an edited volume entitled *Buddhism, Power and Politics in Southeast Asia* (2007). A new work, *Buddhism in a Dark Age: Cambodian Monks under the Khmer Rouge* will appear in early 2012. He is currently engaged in research on Buddhism and political conflict in Cambodia, 1940–75.

Pou Sothirak was born in Phnom Penh, received secondary school education in France from 1973–75 and settled in America from 1975–86. He received a Bachelor Degree in Electrical and Computer Engineering from Oregon State University in 1981 and worked as an engineer at the Boeing Company in Seattle Washington from 1981 to 1985. Mr Pou Sothirak joined the crusade to safeguard Cambodian from foreign occupation and internal conflict from 1986–92 serving as Humanitarian Coordinator at one of the refugee camp on the border between Thailand and Cambodia where over 60,000 displaced Cambodian resided. He had worked also in the field of education and community development program for the Cambodian refugees, under USAID programme. He was elected as Member of Parliament twice during the general election in Cambodia in 1993 and 2003. He had served as Minister of Industry Mines and Energy of the Royal Government of Cambodia from 1993 to 1998. He was appointed as Cambodian Ambassador to Japan from April 2005 to November 2008. He joined the Institute of Southeast Asian Studies in Singapore in 2009 as Visiting Senior Research Fellow.

Milton Osborne has been associated with Southeast Asia for more than fifty years since being posted to the Australian Embassy in Phnom Penh, Cambodia, in 1959. A graduate of Sydney and Cornell Universities, he has held academic positions in Australia, the United Kingdom, the United States and Singapore. In 1980–81 he was a consultant to the United Nations High Commissioner for Refugees in relation to the Cambodian refugee problem, working along the Thai-Cambodian border. In 1982 he returned to Australian government service as Head of the Asia Branch of the Office of National Assessments, remaining in that position for eleven years. Since 1993 he has been an independent writer and consultant on Asian issues based in Sydney, and has been an Adjunct Professor and Visiting Fellow at the Australian National University, Canberra. He is currently a Visiting Fellow at the Lowy Institute for International Policy, Sydney. He is the author of ten books on the history and politics of Southeast Asia, including, *Southeast Asia: An Introductory History*, now in its tenth edition; *River Road to China: The Search for the Source of the Mekong*; *The Mekong: Turbulent Past, Uncertain Future*; and *Phnom Penh: A Cultural and Literary History*. His most recent monographic publication for the Lowy Institute is, *The Mekong: River Under Threat*.

Geoffrey Wade is a Visiting Senior Research Fellow at the Nalanda Sriwijaya Centre at ISEAS. Dr Wade is a historian with interests in Sino-Southeast Asian historical interactions and comparative historiography. He has worked on a range of other related issues including early Islam in Southeast Asia, Chinese expansions, Asian commercial networks, Chinese textual references to Southeast Asia and the Cold War in Southeast Asia. His online database, *Southeast Asia in the Ming Shi-lu: An Open Access Resource* (http://epress.nus.edu.sg/msl/) provides in English translations of 3,000+ references to Southeast Asia as extracted from the Ming imperial annals, while his most recent edited work *China and Southeast Asia* (2009) comprises a six-volume survey of seminal works on Southeast Asia-China interactions.

TIMELINE OF RECENT CAMBODIAN HISTORY

1953.11.9	Cambodia gains independence from France.
1954.2.21	Diplomatic relations established between Cambodia and Japan.
1962.3.27	Diplomatic relations established between Cambodia and Indonesia.
1965.8.10	Diplomatic relations established between Cambodia and Singapore.
1967.6.24	Diplomatic relations established between Cambodia and Democratic Republic of Vietnam.
1969–73	Republic of Vietnam and United States air forces bomb Cambodia to disrupt Viet Cong and Khmer Rouge.
1970.3	General Lon Nol leads coup against Prince Norodom Sihanouk with backing of United States.
1975.4	End of Indochina War with fall of Saigon to Viet Cong forces.
1975.4.17	Khmer Rouge capture Phnom Penh.
1975.5	Chinese embassy reopens in Phnom Penh.
1978.12.25	Vietnamese forces invade Cambodia.
1979.1.7	Vietnamese-backed People's Republic of Kampuchea established, with Heng Samrin as the Chief of State. Khmer Rouge's Democratic Kampuchea continues to be recognised by the United Nations.
1979.2	China attacks Vietnam as punishment for Vietnam invasion of Cambodia.
1979.10.9	Inception of Khmer People's National Liberation Front (KPNLF).
1981.2	FUNCINPEC established in Paris by Norodom Sihanouk.

1982.6.22	Coalition Government of Democratic Kampuchea (CGDK), comprising FUNCINPEC, Khmer Rouge and KPNLF, established.
1985.1.14	Hun Sen appointed as prime minister of PRK.
1985.8	Meetings in France between Hun Sen and KPNLF.
1987. 7	Vietnam accepted idea of informal meetings to resolve Cambodia issue.
1987.12 – 1988.1	Prince Sihanouk of CDGK and Hun Sen of PRK have two meetings at Fère-en-Tardenois, a village northeast of Paris to discuss peace.
1988. 7	First Jakarta informal meeting between CGDK and the PRK to discuss peace.
1989.4.29	Name of Cambodian state changed from People's Republic of Kampuchea to State of Cambodia (SOC).
1989.7.30 – 1989.8.30	Peace discussions held in Paris between representatives of 18 countries, the four Cambodian parties, and the UN Secretary General.
1989.7.30 – 1989.8.30	Paris Peace Conference held but inconclusive.
1989.9	Vietnam concludes withdrawal of forces from Cambodia.
1990	CGDK renames itself the National Government of Cambodia.
1990.2 & 1990.9	Informal Meetings on Cambodia (IMC) held.
1990.9.10	Supreme National Council (SNC) established in Cambodia.
1991.10.23	Paris Conference convened and a comprehensive settlement is signed giving the UN full authority to supervise a ceasefire, repatriate the displaced Khmer along the border with Thailand, disarm and demobilize the factional armies, and prepare the country for free and fair elections.
1991.11.14	Prince Sihanouk, President of the Supreme National Council of Cambodia (SNC), and other members of the SNC, including Khmer Rouge representatives return to Phnom Penh.
1992.1.18	Diplomatic relations re-established between Cambodia and Singapore.

1992.3.16	The UN Transitional Authority in Cambodia (UNTAC) arrived in Cambodia to commence implementation of the UN Settlement Plan
1992.3	The UN High Commissioner for refugees begins full-scale repatriation of Khmers on the Thai border
1993.5	Elections held throughout Cambodia, with 4 million people participating. FUNCINPEC (58 seats), Cambodian People's Party (51 seats) and Buddhist Liberal Democratic Party (10 seats) form coalition government, with Norodom Ranariddh(FUNCINPEC) as First Prime Minister and Hun Sen (CPP) as Second Prime Minister. Khmer Rouge outlawed.
1993.9.23	Cambodia restores monarchy and King Norodom Sihanouk resumes position as head of state.
1993.9.24	Royal Government of Cambodia established on basis of elections. New Constitution promulgated.
1996.7.18 – 1996.7.23	Hun Sen visits China.
1997.7.5	Showdown between CPP and FUNCINPEC. Hun Sen achieves victory. Prince Ranariddh goes into exile in Paris. Ung Huot elected as new First Prime Minister.
1997.7.23	Taiwanese diplomats expelled from Phnom Penh.
1997.8.2	Hun Sen meets with ASEAN Troika mediators and agrees on election in 1998.
1998.7.26	Second National Assembly elections. CPP obtains 64 seats while FUNCINPEC obtains 43 seats and Sam Rainsy Party 15 seats.
1998.11.30	CPP and FUNCINPEC form another coalition government, with Hun Sen as sole prime minister and Prince Norodom Ranariddh as Head of the National Assembly.
1999.4.30	Cambodia admitted to ASEAN.
2002.2	First commune elections held.
2003.6	Agreement reached between Cambodia and United Nations on Extraordinary Chambers in the Courts of Cambodia for the Prosecution of Crimes Committed during the Period of Democratic Kampuchea.

2003.7.27	Third National Assembly Elections held. CPP captures 73 seats, FUNCINPEC 26 seats, and Sam Rainsy Party 24 seats.
2004	Coalition government formed between CPP and FUNCINPEC.
2004.10.13	Cambodia joins World Trade Organization.
2004.10.7	King Sihanouk announces his abdication from throne. Replaced by his son King Sihamoni.
2005.8	US lifts ban on US military assistance.
2008.7.27	Fourth National Assembly elections after Paris Agreement. Cambodian People's Party wins 90 of 123 seats. Hun Sen remains Prime Minister. Sam Rainsy Party win 26 seats, Human Rights Party win three seats, Norodom Ranariddh Party win two seats, FUNCINPEC win two seats and League for Democratic Party wins one seat.

CAMBODIA AND SINGAPORE

1

FORGING CLOSER BILATERAL RELATIONS BETWEEN CAMBODIA AND SINGAPORE

Sok An

HISTORICAL TIES BETWEEN CAMBODIA AND SINGAPORE

Historically, Singapore has been a time-tested friend of Cambodia. Diplomatic relations between our two countries were established on 10 August 1965 — a day after Singapore became independent, thus making the Kingdom of Cambodia one of the very first countries to recognize the independent Republic of Singapore.

The diplomatic ties were cut in 1975, but were resumed on 18 January 1992. However, during this interregnum, Singapore maintained trade relations with Cambodia. In the 1980s, Cambodia had to endure an economic embargo following the demise of the Khmer Rouge regime. The trade and economic relations with Singapore provided crucial support to Cambodia during this difficult period. The timely humanitarian assistance that was provided to Cambodia and channelled through Singapore during the 1980s allowed Cambodia to embark on rehabilitation and reconstruction activities in key economic sectors.

Singapore and Cambodia have enjoyed excellent bilateral relations, strengthened over the years through exchanges of state visits between Heads of State and government leaders of the two countries. The foundation of our close relationship was shaped by His Majesty King-Father Norodom Sihanouk and His Excellency Minister Mentor Lee Kuan Yew. The then Prime Minister Lee was a frequent visitor to Cambodia and was conferred a doctorate *honoris causa* by the Royal University of Cambodia in December 1967 for his contributions to strengthening Cambodia-Singapore relations. Cambodian Prime Minister Hun Sen officially visited Singapore in 2000, while Singaporean Prime Minister Goh Chok Tong paid an official visit to Cambodia in May 2001. Mr Goh's visit resulted in: i) The promotion of Singapore foreign direct investment to Cambodia, ii) The enhancing of human resource development in Cambodia and iii) The Provision of a Tourism Development Master Plan for the Cambodian government. His Excellency Singapore President S. R. Nathan paid a state visit to Cambodia in February 2003 at the invitation of His Majesty King-Father Norodom Sihanouk. His Majesty King Norodom Sihamoni paid a state visit to Singapore in March 2006. In March 2005, Singapore Prime Minister Lee Hsien Loong paid a visit to Cambodia. Frequent exchanges of visits by the leaders of Cambodia and Singapore have helped further solidify the already excellent bilateral relations between the two countries and their people.

Singapore's contributions to Cambodia's human resource development in the last decade are particularly noteworthy. Singapore has provided training to Cambodian officials in diverse fields including civil aviation, economic analysis, English language, finance, information technology and trade promotion. The Civil Service College of Singapore has signed an agreement with the Royal School of Administration in Cambodia to help strengthen Cambodia's capacity in public administration. More recently in March 2010 Singapore's Ministry of Finance signed a Memorandum of Understanding with the Cambodian Ministry of Economy and Finance to share Singapore's experience in public finance management by conducting study tours, training courses, seminars and workshops.

The Government of Singapore has also provided scholarships to bright Cambodian students at the secondary school, undergraduate and post-graduate levels in Singapore's prestigious schools and higher educational institutions. Cambodia is among the top 10 recipient countries under the Singapore Cooperation Programme. Singapore's schools and universities could further assist Cambodia by increasing the admission of Cambodian students and providing them with the necessary support to carry out their studies and research in the disciplines of their choice. Singapore has indeed made a significant contribution to the long-term development of Cambodia by enhancing its human resources.

CAMBODIA'S RECENT DEVELOPMENT AND PROSPECTS

Cambodia has made rapid strides since the early 1990s in establishing a firm foundation for sustained development. Since 1993, the Cambodian economy has undergone a dramatic structural transformation. The rudiments of a market economy and a financial sector have been established, and the private sector is now a key player in many aspects of the economy. Economic growth traditionally based on agriculture is now driven increasingly by the industrial and the services sectors.

One of the outstanding achievements of Samdach Akka Moha Sena Padei Techo Hun Sen, Prime Minister of the Kingdom of Cambodia, is the implementation of the *win-win policy* that has resulted in the return of full peace in Cambodia after more than three decades of internal strife. Under this policy, the political and military organization of the Khmer Rouge was dismantled and Khmer Rouge forces were successfully integrated into the mainstream of our society. A sense of confidence and pride pervades the country which bodes well for the future of the economy.

The return of full peace, political stability and complete national unity after more than five centuries since the fall of the Khmer Empire has created an unprecedented opportunity for economic reform and social progress. Cambodia regained international recognition and was formally admitted to ASEAN in April 1999. Since then, Cambodia has embarked on wide-ranging reforms in areas such as public administration, public finance, and the legal and judicial systems. It has also reformed the Royal Cambodian Armed Forces, reformed public finances and macro-economic management, carried out decentralization and de-concentration, reformed the management of natural resources (water, forestry, fisheries, land and environment), and stepped up the fight against corruption. The reforms in public administration are particularly aimed at serving people better through institutions that are transparent, responsive and efficient and enhancing the values of motivation, loyalty, professionalism and a culture of service among civil servants. Moreover, in addition to other fundamental laws, such as the civil code, the criminal code, the code of civil procedure and the code of criminal procedure, an *Anti-Corruption Law* has recently been adopted. The improvement in the legal and physical infrastructure will win the confidence of private investors, improve domestic investment and attract international investors to do their businesses in Cambodia.

The Royal Government attaches great importance to private investment for laying the foundation for economic takeoff. The government aims to make Cambodia a focal point for foreign investment by dismantling the disincentives to the export of goods and services. Cambodia will shape its economic destiny by relying on market forces, macroeconomic reforms, an outward-looking growth strategy, and high quality of institutions. The focus will be on improving labour productivity and infrastructural development, enlarging foreign investment and more closely integrating Cambodia into the regional and global economy. With the restoration of peace, economic results have improved dramatically. During the last decade GDP has grown at an average annual rate of 9.3 per cent, thanks to prudent fiscal policy, conservative monetary management, and bold structural reforms. Though Cambodia has made much progress, the reform effort must be reinforced in key areas to sustain development.

Following the implementation of market reforms, Cambodia's GDP increased fivefold from US$1.27 billion in 1989 to US$10.3 billion in 2009. During this period per capita income also grew fourfold from US$152 to US$739. Mainly due to the sustained high growth, poverty incidence dropped from 50 per cent in 1994 to 30 per cent in 2007.

The recent global economic crisis has sharply curtailed Cambodia's economic performance. Growth slowed to 6.7 per cent in 2008 and is estimated at 0.1 per cent for 2009. Three of the four main growth-driving sectors — garments, tourism and construction — contracted during 2008–09. Private investment was also hit. More than 40,000 jobs in garment factories have been lost. Growth is projected to have picked up to 4.5 per cent in 2010. However, export performance continues to be vulnerable in view of the narrow commodity base and the high concentration of garment exports to the US market.

Cambodia's per capita GDP is expected to reach US$1,000 by 2015. However, the resumption of high growth will require more concerted action to strengthen competitiveness, improve the business climate and diversify the production base. Achieving full compliance with WTO requirements and lowering the cost of doing business will be crucial for enhancing competitiveness.

The high growth rates in the two decades preceding the global economic crisis were attributable to favourable internal and external factors. Internal factors include political stability, the existence of peace, stability of the macroeconomic environment, well-performing governmental institutions, and the adoption of a liberal policy towards foreign direct investment and international trade. The major favorable external factors in this period were the general robustness of the regional and global economy and the strong progress in globalization and regional cooperation. Such remarkable socio-economic achievements have provided excellent opportunities for Singapore-Cambodia economic relations.

SINGAPORE-CAMBODIA TRADE AND INVESTMENT RELATIONS

Singapore-Cambodia economic cooperation has been a significant factor in the economic success of Cambodia over the last two decades. Bilateral trade and investment between our two countries increased more than fourfold during the last decade. Our total bilateral trade is expected to exceed US$2 billion within the next few years, making Singapore one of the main trading partners of Cambodia. However, Cambodia has a large bilateral trade deficit with Singapore which needs to be addressed.

Bilateral business contacts have also expanded between the two countries. Singapore is one of major investors in Cambodia. According to the Council for the Development of Cambodia, Singapore invested in 106 projects in Cambodia during 1994–2009. The investment capital comprised of US$658 million and the investment covered several sectors including services and manufacturing, in particular garments.

The expansion of Singaporean direct investment in Cambodia is mainly attributed to the excellent relations between our political and business leaders, and also to the Royal Government's continued efforts to make Cambodia an increasingly attractive investment destination for international investors including Singaporean companies.

Several incentives have been provided to encourage foreign direct investment in Cambodia. The Investment Law of 1994 was amended in 2003 to greatly simplify the license application procedures. The amended law mandated the approval of an investment project within 31 working days after the receipt of the investment application by the Council for the Development of Cambodia. A Sub-Committee on Investment in Provinces-Municipalities of the Kingdom of Cambodia was also established by a sub-decree in 2005 to approve investment projects costing less than US$2 million dollars in the host province or municipality.

These important initiatives need to be followed up by other measures for boosting foreign investment. Special economic zones are high on the

Government's policy agenda for attracting foreign investment to Cambodia. The Royal Government of Cambodia has approved 21 Special Economic Zones (SEZs) to attract foreign direct investment and to diversify the Cambodian economy. These zones are managed by the private sector. Cambodia can learn from Singapore's vast experience in the management of Special Economic Zones.

Trade and investment activities are mutually beneficial and enhance welfare in the partner countries. All steps taken to promote trade and investment are therefore welcome and ought to be encouraged. Singaporean business leaders should explore opportunities for trade and investment in sectors in which Cambodia has comparative advantage. Cooperation with Singaporean partners is particularly welcomed in the more advanced technological sectors and technical education.

The open skies policy of Cambodia has been helpful in promoting tourism, trade and investment. With direct flights to Siem Reap from a number of regional destinations, particularly Singapore which is a prime international gateway, the number of tourist arrivals in Siam Reap has increased sharply, creating a new growth pole in Cambodia, in addition to Phnom Penh and Sihanoukville. Tourism has generated substantial employment and sparked trade and investment in a host of auxiliary activities. The liberalization of international travel has also facilitated business and commercial exchanges in addition to cultural exchanges. The number of Cambodian businessmen visiting Singapore and Singaporean entrepreneurs visiting Cambodia to explore business opportunities is steadily increasing. Strengthening business relations between our two countries has also helped foster a deeper appreciation of each other's culture.

REGIONAL AND INTERNATIONAL COOPERATION

Cambodia-Singapore relations are not limited to the bilateral level. The two countries are partners in global, regional and sub-regional cooperation initiatives and share several transnational concerns and aspirations. Cambodia and Singapore are both members of ASEAN. Cambodia's entry into ASEAN in 1999 was an important milestone in Cambodia's foreign policy evolution, as it marked the end of Cambodia's isolation in the region. Moreover, the admission of Cambodia into ASEAN helped unify all the ten countries of Southeast Asia under the ASEAN umbrella which was the vision of the ASEAN founding fathers.

The main goal of ASEAN is the establishment of *the ASEAN Security Community, the ASEAN Economic Community and the ASEAN Socio-Cultural*

Community. The Goals and Strategies for Narrowing the Development Gaps within ASEAN and the accompanying implementation mechanisms, is a key ASEAN initiative which will help bring forward the establishment of the ASEAN Community by 2015.

Cambodia values highly Singapore's role as an important partner in ASEAN. During the last decade of Cambodia's full-fledged membership in ASEAN, we have been able to balance our bilateral relationship with Singapore alongside our strong commitment to promoting regional cooperation under the ASEAN framework. In 2002, under the Initiative for ASEAN Integration (IAI), the Cambodia-Singapore Training Centre was established in Phnom Penh. The Institute has trained 4,534 Cambodian officials during 2002-2009. This has been a significant contribution to the improvement of the quality of public administration in Cambodia.

Cambodia and Singapore have closely cooperated on international issues of common concern. For instance, in 2005 Cambodia supported the establishment of the Information Sharing Centre in Singapore to fight piracy and sea-based terrorism. Singapore has supported Cambodia's early inclusion in the Asia-Pacific Economic Cooperation (APEC) initiative and its candidature for a non-permanent seat on the United Nations Security Council for the 2013–2014 session. This mutual support clearly reflects the ever deepening cooperation, friendship and understanding between our two countries.

Given Cambodia's small market size and per-capita income, the integration of the Kingdom's economy into the region and the world is necessary for market expansion. Therefore, Cambodia is committed to strengthening economic cooperation, both bilateral and multilateral, through regional and global initiatives. In particular strengthening economic cooperation with Singapore and other ASEAN members is high on the government's policy agenda. It has also signed a number of trade and investment agreements with various countries, including those in the ASEAN grouping.

Cambodia has also actively participated in other sub-regional, regional and global cooperation initiatives, including the Greater Mekong Sub-region (GMS) initiative, with important implications for Cambodia-Singapore relations. The proposed Singapore-Kunming rail-link, a major GMS undertaking, and the economic corridor projects of the GMS will improve connectivity and competitiveness of the Southeast Asian region, while accelerating the pace of economic growth and improving the welfare of the entire sub-region.

The Royal Government of Cambodia is committed to a proactive foreign policy, which is based on the following principles: neutrality, peaceful coexistence with all our neighboring countries, non-alignment, friendship and cooperation with all countries based on the principles of equality, mutual respect for independence, sovereignty and territorial integrity, and non-interference in each other's internal affairs.

CONCLUSION

Cambodia-Singapore relationships have blossomed rapidly in the last two decades both bilaterally and in the ASEAN framework. To forge closer bilateral relations in the coming years, cooperation between our two countries should be focused in the following key areas:

- Economic cooperation through accelerating bilateral trade between the two countries and enhancing Singapore's investments in Cambodia, mainly trade facilitation, port management, the financial and banking sectors, SMEs, industrial parks, and city and urban planning where Singapore has overseas success particularly in China and Vietnam;
- Education cooperation in order to promote human resource development and strengthen capacity and institutional building, and particularly strengthening bilateral cooperation in public administration through the Singapore Cooperation Programme;
- Good governance which is core to bilateral cooperation between Cambodia and Singapore, and an area where Cambodia can gain from the experiences of Singapore's success story;
- Enhancing cooperation in tourism sectors, particularly in promotion and marketing; and
- Close cooperation in multilateral diplomacy.

The well-informed government officials, scholars, researchers, and other participants gathered at the Cambodia Forum in Singapore in April 2010 had discussed the way forward in further improving mutual understanding between our two countries.

2

MY CAMBODIAN STORY

Tommy Koh

My Cambodian story begins in 1965, when Singapore suddenly found itself separated from the Federation of Malaysia and became a new sovereign and independent country. The Kingdom of Cambodia, headed by Prince Norodom Sihanouk, was one of the first countries to recognise Singapore's independence. A few months later, as a gesture of goodwill, the government of Cambodia invited the government of Singapore to send a goodwill delegation to visit Cambodia. As the newly established Ministry of Foreign Affairs was still finding its feet, the Singapore government turned to a nongovernmental organisation, the Singapore Institute of International Affairs (SIIA), to organize such a delegation.

GOODWILL DELEGATION TO CAMBODIA: 1965

The SIIA was founded by a group of like-minded friends, who were interested in international affairs, in 1961. I was one of the founding members. As the Honorary Secretary of the Institute, I had corresponded with the Royal Institute of International Affairs (Chatham House), to seek their guidance and advice. The President of the Institute was a Scottish colonial official, Mr G. G. Thomson, who was the Director of the Political Studies Centre, established by the PAP government to educate the civil servants on the political trends and developments of the region and the political agenda of the government.

A MAGICAL EVENING AT ANGKOR WAT

Mr Thomson and I organised a delegation of about 20 members, consisting mainly of members of the Institute. We were a motley crew, consisting of both locals and expatriates. We spent a week in Cambodia, visiting Phnom Penh and Siem Reap. Phnom Penh was, at that time, a small, beautiful and peaceful city. The war in South Vietnam seemed far away and we did not understand why the senior Cambodian officials we met had expressed the fear that Cambodia might be sucked into that conflict. In Siem Reap, we were treated to an unforgettable experience. We were invited to watch a performance by the Royal Cambodian Ballet, with Princess Bopha Devi as the prima ballerina, under a full moon, at Angkor Wat. It was a magical evening. Thus began my involvement with Cambodia, with eight encounters with this beautiful but tragic country.

LON NOL SEIZES POWER

My next encounter with Cambodia occurred five years later, in 1970. In that year, the Prime Minister, General Lon Nol, overthrew Prince Norodom Sihanouk and seized power. Unlike Samdech Sihanouk's stance of neutrality, Lon Nol supported the South Vietnamese and the Americans in their fight against the Viet Cong and North Vietnam. As a result, Cambodia was consumed by the Vietnam War.

CAMBODIA'S SEAT AT THE UN: 1970

In 1970, I was the Permanent Representative of Singapore to the United Nations. The issue at the UN was who should occupy Cambodia's seat. There were two contenders for that seat: Sihanouk's government-in-exile based in Beijing and the government of General Lon Nol. Singapore followed the British and mainstream views on recognition. Although our sympathies were with Sihanouk, we recognised the government of Lon Nol because it complied with the criteria prescribed by international law, namely, it was in occupation of the country's territory and enjoyed the obedience of the people.

CAMBODIA'S SEAT OCCUPIED BY KHMER ROUGE: 1975

My third encounter with Cambodia occurred in 1975. Following the fall of Saigon and South Vietnam, it was a matter of time before the two neighbouring states, Cambodia and Laos, would fall to the communists. Laos accepted the inevitable and the change of power took place peacefully. In the case of Cambodia, the regime of General Lon Nol fell to the forces of the Khmer Rouge, after several years of bloody civil war. Cambodia's seat at the UN was vacated by Lon Nol's representatives and occupied by representatives of the Khmer Rouge, which styled the country as "Democratic Kampuchea". The ASEAN countries were wary of the Khmer Rouge and kept their distance. Sihanouk had returned from exile as the nominal Head of State. The world knew little of what was going on inside Cambodia, although we heard unconfirmed stories of the horrors taking place inside that country.

SAVING CAMBODIAN LIVES

My fourth encounter with Cambodia occurred in late 1970s. After years of rumours about how the Khmer Rouge had turned Cambodia into a living hell, thousands of sick, desperate and starving Cambodians had fled to the Thai-Cambodian border. They had escaped their Khmer Rouge captors and trekked for days and weeks towards the border to seek refuge and succour. The UN Secretary General, Dr Kurt Waldheim; UN agencies, led by UNHCR; the ICRC; ASEAN countries, led by Thailand; and the international community, sprang into action. Huge refugee camps were built, inside Thai territory, to look after tens of thousands of Cambodians. I visited one such camp called Khao-I-Dang, and was very impressed by what I saw.

VIETNAM INVADES CAMBODIA: 1978

My fifth encounter with Cambodia began on Christmas Day 1978. Vietnam sent its armed forces into Cambodia, to overthrow its former ally, the Khmer Rouge, and to replace it with a Vietnam-backed regime headed by Heng Samrin. The ASEAN countries were faced with a moral dilemma. On the one hand, ASEAN, like the rest of the world, was relieved that the Khmer Rouge had been ousted from power. On the other hand, ASEAN regarded the precedent set by Vietnam as a danger to its own security. ASEAN decided that the Vietnamese invasion and occupation of Cambodia was the greater of the two evils. ASEAN, therefore, requested an urgent meeting of the UN Security Council to consider the situation and to demand a withdrawal of

Vietnamese forces from Cambodia. The Council voted on a draft resolution submitted by ASEAN. Although it received 11positive votes, it was vetoed by the Soviet Union.

ASEAN'S DIPLOMATIC OBJECTIVES

As part of my sixth encounter with Cambodia, I was involved in ASEAN's Cambodian diplomacy, from December 1978 until the signing of the Paris Agreement in 1991. During this long campaign, ASEAN's objectives were as follows:

(a) Prevent the Heng Samrin regime from occupying Cambodia's seat at the UN;
(b) Isolate Vietnam diplomatically and economically in order to pressure Vietnam to come to the negotiating table;
(c) Persuade the Khmer Rouge; the Cambodian resistance movement led by Sihanouk and his son, Ranariddh; and the resistance movement led by the nationalist, Son Sann; to form a coalition government;
(d) Help the armed resistance against the Vietnamese to gain traction and prevent the Vietnamese occupation of Cambodia from becoming a fait accompli;
(e) Work closely with the UN Secretary-General, the UN Security Council and the Non-Aligned Movement to persuade Vietnam, and its patron, the Soviet Union, that the only solution to the Cambodian conflict was a negotiated one; and
(f) Negotiate an international agreement to bring the Cambodian conflict to a peaceful conclusion, to accept the UN as the interim administration of Cambodia, to give the people of Cambodia the right to determine their own future and to restore Cambodia's sovereignty and independence in a free and fair election.

THE PARIS CONFERENCES OF 1989 AND 1991

In August 1989, France convened the first international conference on Cambodia, in Paris. The reason why the conference was convened by France and not by the UN was that Vietnam and the Phnom Penh regime would not attend a conference convened by the UN. We understood that Vietnam and Sihanouk had appealed to France to be the convener.

The Paris Conference was co-chaired by France and Indonesia. France invited Indonesia to be the co-chair because Indonesia had paved the way for the convening of the Paris Conference. It had done so by convening the first and second Jakarta Informal Meeting (JIM), which brought together the four Cambodian parties, Vietnam, Laos and the ASEAN countries. JIM I and JIM II had succeeded in defining the issues and narrowed the gap between the two sides.

The 1989 Paris Conference failed. It failed because France had misjudged the timing. In the summer of 1989, Vietnam was not ready to compromise. It had still hoped for victory on the battle field.

The Cold War ended in 1991 with the collapse of the USSR and, with it, the Soviet empire was dissolved. Vietnam lost its patron, the Soviet Union. In 1991, France re-convened the conference. This time, all the parties were ready to settle and to compromise. It was a very happy day for me to be present at the signing of the Paris Agreement, putting an end to a conflict which had lasted over twenty years. Thus ended my seventh encounter with Cambodia.

UNTAC

My eighth encounter with Cambodia was to help the UN Transition Authority in Cambodia (UNTAC) succeed in its mission. The UN Secretary-General had chosen Japan's most senior UN official, Yasushi Akashi, as his Special Representative and head of UNTAC. I was serving as Singapore's Ambassador to the United States at that time. The Chairman of the Sub-Committee on East Asia and the Pacific of the Committee on Foreign Affairs of the US House of Representative, Congressman Stephen Solarz, had asked for my opinion on who the UN Secretary-General should appoint to that post. I told Congressman Solarz that the UN should appoint a Japanese. Akashi was (and is) a close friend and I did everything I could to help him succeed in his difficult task. Singapore contributed a police contingent to help keep the peace. When Akashi wanted to start a UN radio in Cambodia, he asked me to help him recruit a competent Singaporean. I managed to find Ms Zhou Mei, who did a very good job. The UN radio played an important role in persuading the Cambodian people not to be afraid of the Khmer Rouge and to go and cast their ballots.

MISSION IMPOSSIBLE

The Khmer Rouge had refused to lay down their arms and to participate in the UN-supervised elections. One day, I received a telephone call from the UN Secretary-General, Dr Boutros-Ghali. He asked me to undertake a secret mission on his behalf. The mission was to see the Khmer Rouge leader, Pol Pot, and to persuade him to participate in the elections. I told the Secretary-General that it was a mission impossible as the UN did not know where to find Pol Pot. I urged him to speak to China and Thailand, and to ask for their assistance. In the end, the Khmer Rouge boycotted the elections and tried unsuccessfully to intimidate the Cambodian people to do the same.

UNTAC: LESSONS LEARNT

In 1994, Dr Marcel Boisard, the Executive Director of UNITAR, and I, as Director of the Institute of Policy Studies (IPS), co-convened an international conference on UNTAC, to review its successes and failures and to seek lessons to be learnt. The conference was co chaired by Boisard, me and Hisashi Owada, currently the President of the International Court of Justice. The conference also led to the publication of a book in 1995, edited by Nassrine Azimi of UNITAR, entitled "The United Nations Transitional Authority in Cambodia (UNTAC): Debriefing and Lessons". The conference was the first opportunity for those involved in UNTAC to debrief their experiences. The conference also paved the way for the establishment of the Lessons Learned Unit, in the UN Department of Peacekeeping Operations.

REFLECTIONS

I wish to conclude with three reflections.

First, the Paris Agreement of 1991 represents, for the world, the victory of international law and the rule of law over military might. It was also a victory for diplomacy and negotiations. During the debate in the UN Security Council, in early 1979, the Permanent Representative of Vietnam to the UN told me that the situation in Cambodia was irreversible. He also said that the world would soon come to accept the fait accompli. ASEAN refused to be intimidated by the so-called reality on the ground. We persisted in our mission because we believed that our cause was just and that we would eventually succeed in helping Cambodia to recover its independence and, at the same time, to be liberated from the terror of the Khmer Rouge.

Second, the ASEAN diplomacy on Cambodia was the most important diplomatic battle which ASEAN has fought since its founding. In the beginning, the odds against us were formidable. Vietnam enjoyed the support of the Soviet bloc as well as the pro-Soviet wing of the Non-Aligned Movement, including such influential countries as India and Cuba. ASEAN diplomacy succeeded because the ASEAN team of five was united, tireless and skilful.

A whole generation of ASEAN diplomats forged their skills in the decade-long campaign. Our success at the UN put ASEAN on the map as a diplomatic player of substance and significance.

Third, twenty years have passed since the signing of the Paris Agreement in October 1991. Fifty-six years have passed since my first visit to Cambodia. When I look back to the past and reflect on the present, I feel both sad and optimistic. I feel sad because I have seen so much suffering, mass killing and destruction in Cambodia. I feel optimistic because in the past twenty years, Cambodia has, like the proverbial phoenix, emerged from the ashes of war. Cambodia has made enormous progress in the last twenty years, in nation-building and in becoming a contributing member of the ASEAN family. In 2005, I led a delegation from the National Heritage Board of Singapore to visit Cambodia. Our mission was to make friends with the Cambodian officials in charge of culture and their museums and to offer Singapore's friendship and help. I wish Cambodia, a country I love, continued success in its journey to a bright future.

3

CAMBODIA-SINGAPORE SYNERGY
A Paradigm for Cooperation and Connectivity

Mark Hong

INTRODUCTION

When I reflected upon my links with Cambodia and my credentials for writing this essay, I realised that I had spent one third of my working career in the Singapore Ministry of Foreign Affairs (1969 to 2002) concentrating on Cambodian issues. Firstly, I was sent on my initial field posting to Phnom Penh (1974–75). It was an introduction to diplomatic operations in the midst of war, in a collapsing nation run by an ineffectual leader, General Lon Nol. Months later, I became the last Charge d'Affaires of Singapore as our mission had to be closed down and evacuated in March 1975, through the kindness and cooperation of the Australian government, via a military plane, as by then no civilian flights were available.

Secondly, when Vietnam invaded Cambodia in December 1978, this event triggered off a decade-long diplomatic struggle by Singapore and other ASEAN countries to find a peaceful diplomatic solution to the Cambodian problems. Whether in my postings in New York or in Paris, as the Deputy Permanent Representative of Singapore to the United Nations or Counsellor in Paris, the Cambodia issue dominated our work and efforts at lobbying, information-seeking, reporting, conferring, speech writing, etc. The long awaited resolution came in the Paris Peace Conference on Cambodia, in October 1991. By then, the international situation was conducive to an international solution: first, the collapse of the USSR, the backer of Vietnam, had convinced Hanoi that there was no longer any economic or diplomatic support available from Moscow; Hanoi was motivated to seek rapprochement with China, and began some troop withdrawals from Cambodia; France began to see diplomatic opportunity and signs of hope for successful diplomatic negotiations to the Cambodian problems, and the US supported UN involvement, which eventually became the UNTAC mission in 1993, to supervise general elections in Cambodia.

Thirdly, Cambodia has now in the twilight of my life, again resurfaced in the context of my research work at the Institute of Southeast Asian Studies in Singapore. The issue that I now wish to discuss in 2011 is how Cambodia can tap the developmental experience of Singapore, via connectivity and synergy, so as to catalyze Cambodian socio-economic development. Within 20 years, by 2030, hopefully, Cambodia will have developed enough to attain the level of a mid-level developing country, with GDP per capita around US$3,000.

The paradox we face is that Cambodia is surrounded by neighbours, such as China, Vietnam and Thailand, which have all reached out to Singapore and requested its assistance in their development. Thailand, for instance, has engaged Singapore in assisting their civil service to improve in efficiency and productivity; Vietnam requested former Prime Minister and current Minister Mentor Mr Lee Kuan Yew, to be their economic adviser, and also requested Singapore to help set up an industrial park named the Vietnam-Singapore Industrial Park (VSIP). This project was so successful that it has expanded to two other provinces.

CHINA LEARNS FROM SINGAPORE

China has also asked Singapore to assist, starting with the visit by Mr Deng Xiaoping in 1978. He was so impressed by what he saw and witnessed in Singapore that when he returned to China, he instructed his officials to visit Singapore and learn two main lessons from it: rapid economic development and social discipline. Thereafter, there was a whole stream of Chinese officials, from the central, provincial and municipal governments, who came to visit and learn from Singapore. One thing led to another, resulting in the launch of the giant Suzhou Project, then a further and increasing number of requests from other provinces and cities for similar projects. Now, Singapore is embedded in 8 mega-projects in China, in Suzhou, Hangzhou, Nanjing, Guangzhou, Tianjin, Chengdu, Liaoning, and Wuxi; perhaps there will be other Singapore projects in China as well. Meanwhile, in Singapore itself, two of Singapore's universities, Nanyang Technological University and the National University of Singapore (Lee Kuan Yew School of Public Policy) run MBA programmes for Chinese senior officials. By these links, Singapore acts as a catalyst for Chinese economic development, sharing and transferring software and knowledge in good governance, socio-economic development, innovation, creativity and entrepreneurship, as well as other aspects of modernization. There has been a string of visits by Chinese party officials to Singapore in the past 10 years; a total of 22,000 Chinese officials have visited Singapore to study the ruling People's Action Party's techniques, management and philosophy in nation-building and party renewal, in particular in fighting corruption and achieving clean government.

CHINA AND SINGAPORE: LEARNING FROM EACH OTHER

One of the biggest problems facing countries with authoritarian political systems, massive corruption and under-development is how to resolve these problems. Could it be that Singapore has found effective solutions to these problems? From the detailed attention that it pays to Singapore via numerous study visits, China apparently feels that there are worthwhile lessons to be learnt from this Little Red Dot. One big focus is the political lessons for China from the Singapore system.

Since the Dengist reforms started in 1978, China has been studying economic & political systems in various countries, including Singapore. Since then, Chinese CCP officials have started visiting Singapore, looking for the mirror image of the CCP, but Singapore civil servants could only discuss economic policies or governance matters, but could not answer questions about Singapore's general ideological approach. (Actually Singapore's ideology is pragmatism: it adopts whatever works.) Hence after Mr Li Yuanchao — the Chinese Minister of the CCP Central Organization Department — visited Singapore in April 2010, he proposed that both sides should intensify party to party meetings yearly.

From the Singapore side, the ruling PAP interest is to nurture and strengthen bilateral relations and to raise relations from G-to-G to party to party, as the CCP leaders form and run the Chinese government. Deng Xiaoping had changed party policies to be more flexible when dealing with parties of different ideological orientations-so by 1992, the CCP has set up relations with more than 400 parties in about 140 countries. It was thus possible for the non-communist PAP to work closely with the CCP. In general, about 80 per cent of party visits to the PAP come from China; the rest are from Malaysia, Indonesia, Kazakhstan, and S. Africa. For Singapore, one key objective is building guanxi or personal friendships; it is always good to have friends in senior positions.

The PAP-CCP relations began in 1992. The recent intensification of party ties result from a combination of factors, such as close bilateral ties; the 20th anniversary of diplomatic relations and the CCP's policy to transcend ideological differences through mutual cooperation. There has been a string of visits to Singapore by party officials in the past 10 years — a total of 22,000 Chinese officials have visited Singapore to learn the PAP's technical, management know-how and its philosophy in nation building and party renewal. The CCP see Singapore as an Asian society with a Chinese majority which has assimilated Chinese culture with western practices. It wants to know why and how the PAP has remained in power for over 50 years, whilst fighting general elections every 5 years. Maybe this is the political future road for China: the main CCP interest is to figure out what China should do to make their party relevant so that they have legitimacy to rule for a long time. Some Chinese officials have stressed the differences between China and Singapore — such as size differences. China also sends more officials to study the US than to Singapore, and also to Japan and to Britain.

The CCP can also learn from the PAP how to combine British parliamentary democracy, the mass line of being servants of the people, and the idea of letting meritorious performers implement unpopular policies for the good of the country, and in particular, about maintaining strict party management spirit and values training most of all. The CCP visiting delegations often observe how the PAP conducts the Meet the People sessions, and they are struck by how the attitude of doing things for the people without personal profit is maintained. The CCP is amazed that the PAP is absent everywhere but present everywhere. It is struck by how the party's manifesto and value system are operationalised in every part of the Government and society. One of the PAP's key lessons is the need to be relevant: in order to have the mandate to rule and to lead, you must be in touch with the ground and work for the interests of most people. One key difference is; China has a system of reporting to the top whilst the PAP has a system of reporting to the top and also of being responsible for the bottom.

In return, the PAP can learn from the CCP in theory building, party organization and talent nurturing — PAP talent is often dropped into electoral battles whilst CCP talents go through a steady training process from the grassroots and gaining through rich work experience. In September 2010, a PAP delegation visited China and observed a meeting in a Jiangsu village to elect one of two candidates to be the village party secretary. The group also visited Chinese community centres; it was struck by Chinese patriotism and nationalism, and how the CCP extended its influence to all stakeholders.

WILL CAMBODIA LEARN FROM SINGAPORE?

Could the ruling party of Cambodia be interested to learn some of the political lessons that China is absorbing from Singapore, about the need for the three types of legitimacy to rule: independence, economic development and performance legitimacy? But there is not much apparent interest from Cambodia about Singapore, lying merely two hours flying time away: how do we explain this? This is why we need to look at the future, in the hope that perhaps there might be some incipient possibilities for cooperation between two close neighbours. Singapore has not forgotten that Cambodia was amongst the first countries to recognize its independence, and remembered with appreciation that King Sihanouk offered the new and struggling state, an exile-government refuge in case of need. We need to understand that there should be **leaders on both sides** who understand the imperatives and mutual benefits for synergy and connectivity between both countries.

REASONS WHY SINGAPORE SHOULD ASSIST CAMBODIA

Singapore as a small state, constantly tries to maintain and expand its political space. This fundamental principle of its foreign policy now needs to be supplemented in the 21st Century by other important principles: the need to ensure food, water, resources and energy security. Cambodia is a relatively large but under-populated country with rich natural resources, such as oil and gas, fertile land to grow rice, vegetables, fruits, raise pigs and poultry. Cambodia is a natural partner for Singapore which totally lacks natural resources, including water, sand, minerals etc. Singapore has a rich developmental experience and knowledge, and has successfully developed its human resources through education and skills training. These are aspects which Cambodia needs and lacks. Again there is a natural fit between both countries in these aspects.

Singapore is a very small country of which no other state needs to fear or suspect of imperialism or aggression. In fact, Singapore frequently reiterates that we do not wish to export our systems and would prefer to concentrate on our own self-development, as we still have much to accomplish, few officials to do our own development work and no ideology to export. It is only when countries invite us to help, as China, India, Vietnam and others have expressly done so, that we have responded. Singapore offers a One-stop service for developmental advice, as when it was developing, Singapore had absorbed many best practices from many countries and adapted them to its needs. Now it too can assist other developing countries in its turn.

There are many reasons for the success of Singapore, and it is important for Cambodia to understand the context, principles, application and implementation of the Singapore systems. Otherwise the blind application of these systems and principles without adaptation to Cambodia's context, history and culture and specific need will result in failure. One key factor is leadership. A strong leader should ask himself: what is the purpose of my capture of power: is it a matter of personal enrichment or do I exercise power in order to benefit the people and deliver the goods and services they need?

ECONOMIC LINKS

What are the basic numbers of trade and investments between the two countries? Both Singapore and Cambodia enjoy excellent bilateral relations, strengthened over the years through the expansion of trade and business contacts. Trade volume between the two countries has been increasing steadily from US$237 million in 2006 to US$417 million in 2008. Singaporean investments has continued to flow into Cambodia and in 2005, Singapore was its sixth largest investor. With Cambodia's accession to the World Trade Organization and the Royal Cambodian Government's continued efforts to attract foreign investments, Cambodia is increasingly becoming a more attractive location for Singapore companies looking to expand overseas.

According to Cambodian Deputy Prime Minister Dr Sok An, Singapore-Cambodia economic cooperation has been a significant factor in the economic success of Cambodia in the last two decades. Bilateral trade and investment between the two countries increased more than fourfold during the last decade. The total bilateral trade is expected to exceed US$2 billion within the next few years, making Singapore one of the main trading partners of Cambodia. However, Cambodia has a large bilateral trade deficit with Singapore which needs to be addressed. Bilateral business contacts have also expanded between the two countries.

Singapore is one of major investors in Cambodia. According to the Council for the Development of Cambodia, Singapore had invested in 106 projects in Cambodia during 1994–2009. The investment capital comprised of US$658 million and the investment covered several sectors including services and manufacturing, in particular garments. Special economic zones are high on the Government's policy agenda for attracting foreign investment to Cambodia. The Royal government of Cambodia has approved 21 Special

Economic Zones (SEZs) to attract foreign direct investment and to diversify the Cambodian economy. These zones are managed by the private sector. Cambodia could learn from Singapore's vast experience in the management of Special Economic Zones. The open skies policy of Cambodia has been helpful to promote tourism, trade and investment. With direct flights to Siem Reap from a number of regional destinations, particularly Singapore, which is a prime international gateway, the number of tourist arrivals in Siem Reap has increased sharply creating a new growth pole in Cambodia, in addition to Phnom Penh and Sihanoukville.

In 2002, under the Initiative for ASEAN Integration (IAI), *the Cambodia-Singapore Training Centre* was established in Phnom Penh. The Institute has trained 4,534 Cambodian officials during 2002–09. This is a significant contribution to the improvement of the quality of Cambodian public administration. Cambodia and Singapore have also closely cooperated on international issues of common concern. For instance, in 2005 Cambodia supported the establishment of *the Information Sharing Centre* in Singapore to fight piracy and sea-based terrorism. In turn, Singapore has supported Cambodia's early inclusion in the Asia Pacific Economic Cooperation (APEC) initiative and its candidature for a non-permanent seat on the United Nations Security Council for the 2013–14 term. The proposed Singapore-Kunming rail-link, a major Greater Mekong Sub-region undertaking, and the economic corridor projects of GMS will improve connectivity and competitiveness of the Southeast Asia region, while accelerating the pace of economic growth and improving the welfare of Indochina.

These trends show that there is still much potential for future and further development.

Now since China, India and Vietnam can see the benefits of cooperating with Singapore, why not Cambodia? In fact, over 10,000 officials from over 100 countries have already learnt from Singapore in the transport sector, such as its excellent award winning, Singapore Airlines, Changi Airport and the Singapore Metro. *Cambodia can cooperate with Singapore, as Vietnam did, via a Connectivity Platform, or via a General Framework Agreement for Cooperation.*

THE CASE FOR SYNERGY

The case for synergy between Cambodia and Singapore is easily stated: that a developing country, like Cambodia, in need of investments, technological knowledge, advice on modernization and globalization, infrastructural development, markets etc should turn to the nearest Global City, Singapore, for connectivity to the external world, whilst a compact city state, Singapore, lacking a Hinterland, should cooperate with Cambodia, rich in resources, energy, water, foodstuffs and economic opportunities. Both sides will of course maintain their independence and sovereignty: we are not discussing neo-colonialism here, merely synergy and cooperation for mutual benefits.

THE STATE OF CAMBODIA TODAY

Cambodia today has achieved remarkable progress in peace, prosperity, stability and development. People who remember and understand the recent history of Cambodia are best placed to appreciate how much progress Cambodia has attained. Briefly stated, Cambodia's history since 1970, when General Lon Nol overthrew King Sihanouk by a coup d'état, included: a civil war between the Khmer Rouge and the Government, during which Cambodia became a sideshow to the Vietnam War, and suffered saturation bombing of suspected areas used by the Vietcong, by US B52s planes; the capture of power and subsequent lunatic policies of the KR regime, such as the genocide of up to one million Cambodians, including the elimination of the educated and intellectual classes — via mass murders, exile, torture; invasion and occupation by Vietnamese forces and setting up of a puppet Heng Samrin regime; the arrival of UN Peace keeping UNTAC forces and UN-supervised general elections, a two-Prime Ministers led Government and political instability; membership in ASEAN in 1999 and integration into regional affairs, and since year 2000, gradual and increasing peace, prosperity and stability. But we should remember the deep poverty, the millions of mines and the victims of such mines, the need for education, jobs, housing, infrastructure, and good governance. Such problems still persist and trouble Cambodia today. These are huge problems and obstacles facing nation building in Cambodia.

THE DEBATE OVER OFFICIAL DEVELOPMENT AID (ODA)

Cambodia, like many other least developed countries, is heavily dependent on Official Development Aid (ODA).

In 2005, 90 per cent of Cambodian budget resources came from ODA, amounting to US$610m., whilst 10 per cent came from domestic sources, totalling US$79m. The apparent danger for Cambodia is that it has become over-dependent on ODA, with all its dangers.

There are a great number of aid agencies and NGOs doing many aid projects in Cambodia, performing many positive and praise-worthy activities, such as de-mining, helping women and children, in education and health projects. A significant percentage of the national budget comes from ODA funds. But I wonder if the fate of many African countries, which have received ODA for over 50 years, and which are still poor and under-developed and heavily indebted, might similarly befall Cambodia. To escape the Aid Trap, Cambodia might envisage an end-date to aid, via a gradual phase-out of aid, say over 10 years, with its own oil and gas revenues replacing aid. Many analysts argue that ODA is a trap, in which much of the funds revert to the donor country, because of conditionalities, expensive consultants and political influence. Aid is not cost free, unless given as grants, and it causes indebtedness. These arguments are laid out in works such as: William Easterly's *The White Man's Burden* (2006); Dambisa Moyo's book entitled *Dead Aid* (2009), and Paul Collier's *The Bottom Billion* (2007).

Many observers have stated that there are net annual transfers of millions of dollars from poor countries to the donor countries. Dr Moyo noted that an estimated $300 billion in aid had been provided to African countries since 1970. She argued in her book that African countries are poor precisely because of this aid. Aid had caused to make the poor poorer, and growth slower. In her book, she asked key questions, such as, over 50 years, Africa had received $1 trillion in ODA, yet Africa remains mired in poverty, corruption, aid -dependency and under-development: why was this? She concluded that ODA actually retards African development, acting like a resource curse, sparking conflicts over control and access to aid funds, corruption and retarding entrepreneurship. She argued that ODA makes the poor even poorer and growth slower: over past 30 years, most aid-dependent countries growth declined by minus 0.2 per cent per annum. ODA is *the disease that pretends to be the cure. Over 30 years from 1970, African poverty rates rose from 11 per cent to 66 per cent.* Aid creates a vicious cycle of: aid-corruption-dependency-debt-poverty. ODA creates 4 problems for economies: 1.reduction of domestic savings and investments, in favour of consumption; 2. Inflation; 3. decreasing exports; 4. difficulty in absorbing large cash inflows.

Conditionalities are seen as a major factor why ODA is not working properly; there were 3 reasons:

- Aid is tied to procurement from the donor country;
- Donors reserve the right to pre-select the sector or project to support;
- Recipients must agree to a favoured set of policies — such as privatization, democracy and governance

Dr Moyo's valuable insight is that aid is like a resource curse that encourages corruption and conflicts, whilst discouraging free enterprise. She stressed that

FDI and rapid growing exports, not ODA, were the keys to China's economic success; Africa should learn these lessons from Asia. She proposed a radical suggestion for shock therapy: cut off aid within 5 to 10 years. Countries which rejected ODA have prospered; countries which accept ODA become trapped in corruption, market distortions, poverty, debts, and no growth. To make Development happen, Moyo advised that the following steps be taken: First, draw up an economic plan to reduce ODA dependency year by year; rely more on trade, attract FDI, capital markets, remittances, micro-finance, savings — use market-based approach. Secondly, enforce Rules of Financial Prudence-save for rainy days and do not spend beyond means. Thirdly, strengthen Institutions: enhance accountability, transparency, integrity and anti-corruption amongst leaders and civil servants; promote good governance, rule of law and respect property rights.

What are the implications of her arguments for Cambodia? Another huge problem facing Cambodia is the resource-curse: that Cambodian oil and gas revenues will be stolen via corruption, like in Nigeria and other oil-rich countries.

If poor developing countries are advised to shun ODA, then they rightly ask: where should we get the funds for socio-economic development? Are there sources of funds which are not punitive in high interests, which are relatively selfless and do not have political agendas? The answer lies in Foreign Development Investments (FDI) provided by international companies, which seek to enter foreign markets, make and repatriate profits, but in the process, they create jobs, set up marketing networks for the goods and services they produce, transfer technology, train managers and workers, and if they pursue good corporate management, which involves helping local communities, they will generally be helpful in assisting the host country.

This approach of working with MNCs and attracting FDI was the one adopted by Singapore. It did not have an American Santa Claus, which showered US aid to Japan, South Korea, and Western Europe via the Marshall Plan. So Singapore devised its own alternatives: make itself attractive to MNCs and FDI via many incentives; secondly, empower itself to be a worthwhile partner to MNCs by eliminating corruption, which increases transaction costs for international business and drains away revenues into the bank accounts of corrupted people. MNCs could not exploit Singapore because the government was clean, efficient and competent. In the 1960s and 1970s, Singapore was quite alone in this field of working with MNCs and FDI, because other developing countries were suspicious of these companies. The timing was also lucky for Singapore, as then the Cultural Revolution scared off MNCs and FDI from China and Hong Kong, India was enclosed in Nehruvian socialism, and Japan was beginning to export entire factories to counter the rising yen, reduce Japanese trade surpluses in view of American pressures. In the 21st century, the situation is not so propitious for developing countries struggling to develop and to modernize: there are huge competitors such as India and China; markets are beginning to close under increasing protectionism in OECD countries; weakening world trade, global financial crises and a declining Anchor Economy, the USA, which built the global institutions: one wonders what happens when the Centre cannot hold together what it helped to create, such as the Bretton Woods Institutions: IMF, World Bank, the WTO.

Therefore Cambodia is emerging at a very difficult time in world history. It needs all the help it can get, but this help should aim to make Cambodia self-sustaining and not dependent eternally on ODA nor fall under foreign political influence. Singapore's economic development was guided by Minister Mentor Lee Kuan Yew. Long ago, he taught our people and emphasized: **The world does not owe you a living**". He also advised: Avoid the 3 traps: foreign aid; foreign debts; welfarism. Mr Lee laid down Six Principles of Good Governance:

- Send clear signals;
- Set consistent policies;
- Maintain a clean government;
- Win respect, not popularity;
- Spread benefits to the people;
- Strive to succeed.

Led by Mr Lee Kuan Yew and the First Generation of Singapore leaders, the ruling People's Action Party, since independence in 1965, gained three types of legitimacy to rule the country: first, **independence legitimacy**: as the leaders who fought for independence from the British; secondly, **economic legitimacy**: by achieving high-level economic development over 45 years; thirdly, **performance legitimacy** — delivering the goods and services which the people wanted and needed: jobs; public housing, education, healthcare, peace, prosperity and stability, law and order, justice. It is noteworthy that the Housing & Development Board (HDB) has built one million public housing flats from 1965 to 2010 in Singapore.

THE SINGAPORE STORY

One big development secret of Singapore is that instead of creating zaibatsus or chaebols, it first focused on creating systems, institutions and conditions needed for rapid economic development-known as the eco-system — such the EDB, (Investment Attraction & Management); DBS (Development Finance), JTC (Setting up & Managing Industrial Estates), MAS (Central Bank), MoE (Ministry of Education — a key agency in human resource development), HDB (Public housing), SAF (Singapore Armed Forces, to protect the country and to assure foreign investors) etc. — these are the boosters and catalysts which enhance rapid growth. Once these pro-business eco-systems are created, the foreign MNCs are easily attracted. Then Singapore moved on to create its own national champion companies, known locally as Government-linked companies, such as SIA (Singapore Airlines for air connectivity), PSA (to provide excellent port services and maritime connectivity and logistics support), etc which are later privatized. The many systems in Singapore reinforce each other, so that there is **systems synergy**, and government agencies do not work at cross-purposes. There is a whole-of-government approach to solving problems. All these wonderful assets, systems and institutions are great, but do they last? What happens when they are tested by a great crisis, like the 2008–09 Global Financial Crisis? Answer: the Singapore economic system passed the crisis test by growing at around 15 per cent in 2010, a sharp recovery from the minus 1 per cent decline in 2009. Lastly, we should note the importance of political stability and good governance in socio-economic development. It also reminds us of the lessons that Mr Lee Kuan Yew noted in his Six Principles of Good Governance.

Development is like a marathon and all policies geared toward it must be sustainable and continuous.

Quote from Dr Robert Klitgaard, Harvard professor in the *Straits Times* (21 December 2010, speaking of Singapore: "*I am so astonished to see such a knowledge-based society. There are few places in the world where the mind is the primary emphasis of government policy, and the future is seen in terms of leapfrogging other countries at the highest end of intellectual achievement.*"

Despite the lack of the 3 traditional factors of production, namely, land, labour and capital, how did Singapore disprove traditional development theory? Perhaps because Singapore was given by God, as compensation for all the lack of natural resources, a brilliant team of political and economic leaders and master-minds, led by Mr Lee Kuan Yew. He said: *What a country needs to develop is discipline, more than democracy*. Westerners will of course dispute this, but we note that many disciplined East Asian countries, like China, South Korea, Taiwan, Vietnam and Singapore, have all achieved rapid economic growth, and democracy came later.

When Singapore became independent in 1965, its per capita GNP was \$500; by 2009, it had grown to \$37,300 and it had overtaken Japan, UK and many other OECD countries. Its GNP in 2009 was 50 times the GNP of 1965.The main point to learn is the *importance of choosing the right systems from the beginning*. Singapore chose the democracy-free market system from independence whilst some other countries chose the Soviet model of central planning and the command economy; after the collapse of the USSR, these countries had to adopt painful economic reforms, as Vietnam and China have already done. In fact, it was because Deng Xiao-ping on his visit to Singapore in 1978 saw that it had already achieved the dream of China — rapid economic growth with social discipline — that he adopted Singapore-styled economic model via the SEZs model. It was no coincidence that China invited Dr Goh Keng Swee, Singapore's Master Economist, to be Economic Advisor to China's SEZs.

Singapore is ranked No. 20 in GDP per capita, in nominal terms. In PPP terms, it ranks No. 4 in the world. It has the world's second busiest port after Shanghai, best airport and Public housing, which has won UN awards. Average manufacturing foreign investment into Singapore is US$8 bn per year. Inflation is annually below 3 per cent; unemployment stands at about 3 per cent with one million foreigners working in Singapore. Poverty has been in effect abolished, with residual poverty at 4 per cent of the population, as there are always uneducated, old and sickly people in any society who cannot work. Singapore ranks as one of the most competitive, least corrupt and business-friendly economies in the world. Another good indicator of the Rise of Singapore is that according to a Gallup poll held in November 2010, if people were allowed to freely migrate anywhere, Singapore was ranked No. 1 destination ahead of NZ, Canada and Switzerland. Then its population would swell by 219 per cent, and it was the top choice for the young and educated would-be migrants. Its attractions include: located in booming Asia, whilst also offering the comfortable life-style of a developed country, besides being safe, English-speaking, having an active and rich culture, a good education and health system. The Gallup poll covered 350,000 adults in 148 countries.

So how did Singapore become such a world leader in so many areas? One answer is Human Resource Development (HRD), which includes education, skills training and worker orientation. Singapore spends 4 per cent of its GDP on education; now 95 per cent of its people are literate — the 5 per cent left are mainly the very old who missed out their education because of WW2 and poverty. Since people are the only resource of Singapore, it makes sense to nurture the human resource. More importantly, knowledge is the only resource which never depletes, unlike minerals or fossil fuels. Those countries which invest in HRD enjoy the highest growth rates. It is not surprising therefore that Singapore continuously sets up new universities, such as the Yale-NUS Liberal Arts College in 2011; the Singapore University of Technology and Design in partnership with MIT and Zhejiang University; the Singapore Institute of Technology; the Medical School jointly set up by Imperial College of London and the Nanyang Technological University.

Singapore is host to various international agencies such as Interpol, World Bank and the IMF. The IMF cites Singapore as a model for economic development and has published a case study on Singapore. Both cooperate with the Singapore Government to run training programmes. For instance, the Bank and Singapore have set up a Regional Infrastructure Finance Centre of Excellence, under the World Bank-Singapore Urban Hub. Indonesia and Vietnam have signed MoUs with this Centre for development projects. Unilever has set up in Singapore a training centre for its regional managers, whilst UBS bank of Switzerland has set up a wealth management training academy in Singapore.

There are probably around 9,000 international MNCs in Singapore. These are huge foreign companies which put their money where their mouth is. For instance, a Norwegian company called REC had opened a US$6 billion factory in Singapore in 2010, which is the world's biggest solar panel manufacturing factory. One reason why these MNCs invest in Singapore is its great infrastructure, besides other reasons. Perhaps Cambodia might wish to learn this competitive business of how to attract foreign investors from an experienced practitioner.

Singapore consistently ranks very highly in all sorts of surveys by the IMF, World Bank, World Economic Forum, IMD, PERC and other ratings agencies. For instance, Transparency International ranks Singapore amongst the top 5 least corrupt countries; the World Bank ranks Singapore as No. 1 for ease of doing business for several years in a row. The IMD based in Switzerland ranked Singapore the most competitive economy in 2010, beating Hong Kong and USA. Singapore also enjoys a high international respect, shown for instance, by its leaders being able to access the leadership of great powers, and ordinary Singaporeans being able to visit over 100 countries without needing a visa. Singapore is also consistently ranked as one of the most liveable cities in Asia. It is recognized as very successful in maintaining racial and religious harmony, and in building a strong national identity in 4 decades. Its two sovereign wealth funds are recognized as second most transparent in the world, after Norway, in 2010.

THE TEN WONDER MACHINES

Over 45 years, Singapore has gradually developed a number of critical systems in its governance and socio-economic development. Due to lack of space, these are briefly mentioned, with short comments:

1. Political leadership: talent spotting, selection, training, exposure, crisis handling testing; this is done systematically and implemented carefully so that there is a gradual handover and turnover of new blood. It is also applied to the Civil Service and the Armed Forces. The stress is on competence, talents, people skills, integrity, honesty, and compassion.
2. Multi-racial and Multi-Religious Tolerance and Harmony: because Singapore by its diverse population and religious composition is obliged to stress mutual tolerance, respect and harmony, this principle is very carefully implemented;
3. Education and Human Resource Development: since Singapore has no natural resources, only its people, it was obliged to focus on education and skills training, which has proven to be a correct strategy, especially since Singapore is now building a Knowledge Economy; in dealing with modernization, urbanization and globalization, HRD is a necessity, to cope with modern science and technology; Singapore was "*renowned for its long-term investment in science and technology, for its commitment to nurturing exceptional talent, and also for encouraging students to study abroad — well before it became fashionable.*"
4. Sustained & High Economic growth over 45 years, with shared Benefits for the People: via bonuses for the people in high growth years; public housing, good and affordable health care & excellent educational system, socio economic benefits such as jobs — but no social welfare, in order to avoid a dependency syndrome.
5. Democracy, Rule of law, social cohesion and discipline, integrity of systems and personnel, protection of property rights and the sanctity of contracts, protection of peoples' rights; strong institutions: these are basic rights and fundamental freedoms which help ensure a more just and equal society.
6. Anti-corruption, Long term Planning, Anticipation, Prudent Financial management: the leadership must set personal examples of honesty, excellence
7. Tripartite cooperation between Government, Labour & Management: to ensure labour peace & to share the profits in good times and the sacrifices (pay cuts) in bad times;
8. Good governance. In an era of failed states and increased global competition, this aspect gives competitive and comparative advantage.
9. Pragmatism; Open-minded; Connectivity: to be linked to Centres of Ideas, Knowledge, Finance, Hubs, to be willing to learn best practices from others, accepting and embracing Change and Foreign Talents: be plugged into the world and be humble to learn from others. Strive for

Excellence: if Singapore cannot be better, it will not survive against giant competitors such as India and China (a stress on vulnerability; a degree of paranoia is needed to maintain a constant drive to succeed).

10. A strong, clean, pro-people and pro-development ruling party and civil service: without these as instruments of planning and implementation, no country will progress, develop and modernize.

In case readers might doubt and wonder if the above really constitute Singapore's policies, the *Straits Times* (17 December 2010) reported that for the first time, the Singapore Government has publicly spelt out six broad goals to enable the country to progress further in the future, and how ministries and agencies work together to achieve these six goals, which are:

- Sustainable economic growth: this includes identifying engines of growth, creating job opportunities and creating a globally competitive workforce;
- Creating a strong social security framework: this includes ensuring financial security and providing good, affordable healthcare and public housing (Note: the Housing Development Board has built its one millionth public apartments in December 2010; the HDB has won UN awards for its achievements)
- Creating and maintaining world class environment and infrastructure: this involves maintaining Singapore as a vibrant global city, having goof transport infrastructure and a clean and green environment;
- Creating a secure and influential Singapore; this includes being prepared for crises (which means planning and anticipation) and creating a safe and secure home (which involves having strong defence and police forces);
- Having strong families and a cohesive society: this includes providing quality education, having locals as the core of the population and maintaining racial and religious harmony;
- Effective government: this includes having a forward-looking leadership rule of law; honest and committed civil servants and effective use of resources.

The Singapore Public Sector Outcomes Report stressed that every government has the responsibility for managing and allocating public money to achieve national goals. Singapore is no different. One defining trait of the Singapore government's approach to fiscal management is its commitment to prudence. Unlike many developed countries, it does not borrow to pay the bills. Instead, Singapore adheres to a policy of spending within its means, maintaining a stable and diversified base of revenues, and building up financial reserves to meet contingencies such as unexpected global shocks. Singapore's prudent approach means that it constantly faces two fiscal challenges, namely:

- Raise sufficient revenue to invest in the range of capabilities and infrastructure that Singapore needs to survive and succeed into the future, such as education, physical development and security.
- Allocate funds so as to achieve the best outcomes for Singapore as a whole. This requires the Ministry of Finance to assess outcomes holistically, not compartmentally by individual Ministries. The Ministries must also maximize value for Singapore when they use public funds.

THE NEED FOR WHOLE-OF-GOVERNMENT OBJECTIVES AND STRATEGIES

As the world becomes more globalised and complex, so will the business of governance. The national issues Singapore faces will transcend Ministry boundaries, and public agencies will increasingly need to work together to address any given issue effectively. In such a context, setting and monitoring outcomes of individual agencies, while useful, is insufficient. All Ministries have therefore worked to jointly establish whole-of-government outcomes along with suitable indicators to track the progress towards achieving them. The diagram below illustrates the holistic approach described above.

With regards to Cambodia, the approach described above might serve as useful examples to think about. Within a globalized world, competition has increased tremendously. The arrival of India, China and Eastern Europe has added 3 billion hardworking and driven workers to the global workforce. Not only individual workers but also companies and governments have to realize the need to be more productive and efficient, but also the need to work as teams, in order to enjoy and benefit from synergies and lessened red tape. Countries no longer exist in isolation, even countries which deliberately withdraw from the world and prefer to exist in autarchy. Such countries find themselves slipping backwards as others advance. Hence for Cambodia, it might be useful to think of the leaders and the people as one United Team Cambodia. After all, this was the approach which helped the Angkor Kingdom to build Angkor Wat, a magnificent monument built by millions of people. Similarly, to build modern and prosperous Cambodia will require a united leadership and people working within a holistic, whole-of-nation approach. (See Figure 3.1)

FIGURE 3.1
Whole of Government Strategy Outcomes Adopted by the Singapore Government, December 2010

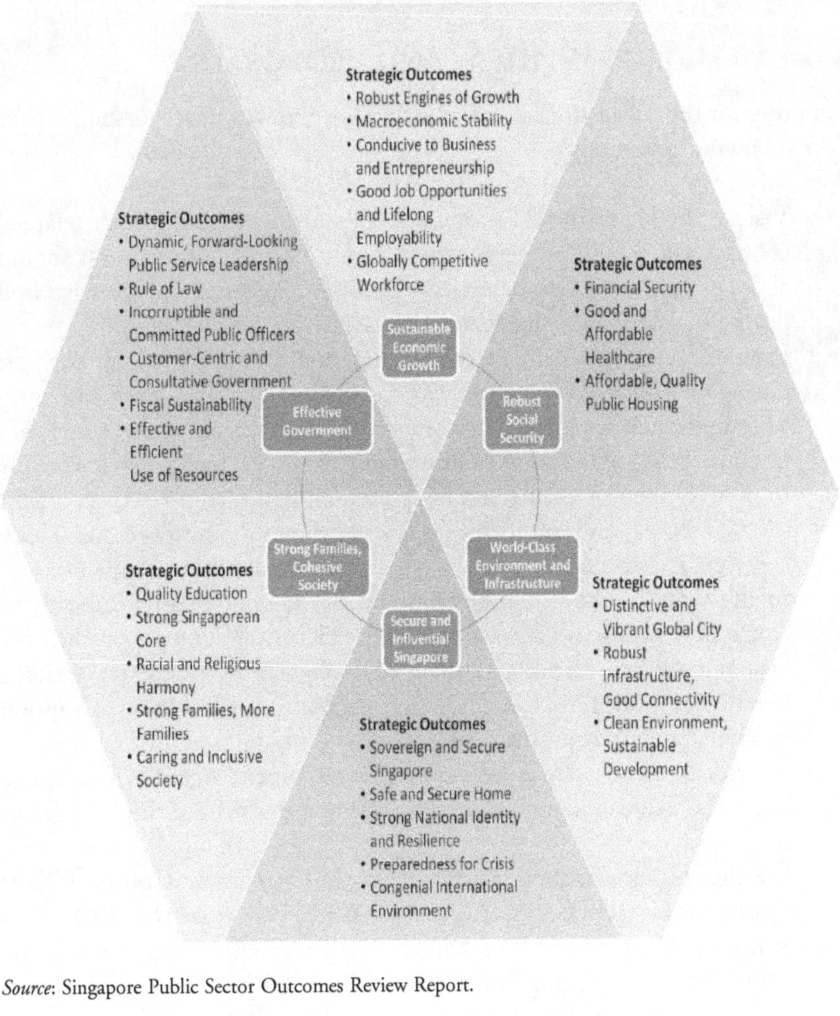

Source: Singapore Public Sector Outcomes Review Report.

A CAMBODIAN MANDALA FOR MODERNIZATION & PROGRESS

The above diagram spells out the plan and principles defining the approach taken by the Singapore Government towards future development. What might be a Cambodian Mandala towards a future planning? Some ASEAN countries might adopt certain key words, such as: King, Nation, and Religion. France has: liberty, equality and fraternity. It is up to the Cambodian leaders and people to decide on their own Vision Statement.

SOME IDEAS AND PROPOSALS

In order for the suggestions to be solid and have some impact, it should have the following qualities:

- Vision: the paper should propose a certain direction in which bilateral cooperation should proceed, which would benefit both sides; it should also lay out how Cambodia can become a modern, progressive and prosperous economy and society;
- Practical suggestions for projects which could be undertaken, such as: setting up a SEZ in Cambodia with assistance from Singapore; setting up a Sovereign Wealth Fund with some funds from the oil wealth which will be coming on stream soon in Cambodia; this SWF will generate revenue from investments which could be spent on human resource development for Cambodia and infrastructure development; Singapore has much experience with running its two SWFs, which should be tapped;
- Analysis of Cambodia's problems and needs which can be met with Singapore's assistance, for example: A) Leadership training — at the LKY School in NUS; Institutions such as EDB, Civil Service College, National Institute of Education, (Teachers Training body), CPIB (Anti-Corruption agency), port and airport assistance; Systems, such as E-Government, workers training such as Workforce Development Agency, Institute of Technical Education or ITE, NTUC (trade unions training) programs etc.
- Specific Singaporean institutions, such as the Civil Service College, ISEAS, Centre for Liveable Cities, Institute for Water Policy and the Water Hub, Singapore Cooperation Programme, Regional English Language Centre, Third Country Training Programme, Changi Airport, Port of Singapore Authority, etc could be approached to offer tailored programs to train Cambodians, and Singapore could offer attachments and scholarships to NUS, NTU, SMU (Singapore Management University), and various junior colleges and polytechnics.
- Any proposal for cooperation must be supported by political will from both sides. If the leaders have doubts or negative feelings, for whatever reason, then the proposals will remain academic ideas only.

- Cambodia's needs are immense, in order to become a modern, progressive, prosperous, more just and equal society; it has to: become an open economy to the outside world and be integrated to global systems; minimize, control and combat corruption; oil wealth can totally corrupt and destroy Cambodia, just like Nigeria has been severely affected by oil-wealth corruption. Cambodia can learn from how Norway has handled its oil wealth without abuses; develop its infrastructure, its human resources via education and skills training — herein, Cambodia should request Singapore's assistance; develop key institutions with Singapore's aid; adopt basic principles of development, such as meritocracy, discipline, pragmatism, anti-corruption, cronyism and nepotism, and good governance; ensure performance legitimacy — deliver what the people want — jobs, education, healthcare, housing, rule of law, peace and prosperity.
- The line of argument in the paper should be to match Cambodia's needs with Singapore's strengths and capabilities, for instance in good governance.

POSSIBLE AREAS OF COOPERATION

For the sake of brevity, the following is a simple list, which is my personal views, without elaboration:

Cambodia's Wish-List

1. Economic Development assistance
2. Human Resource Development
3. Education-Primary, secondary, university, Teacher-training; vocational education
4. Infrastructure: airport; sea-port, rail, airline
5. Civil service training and development
6. Finance and Banking
7. Development of Institutions
8. Anti-corruption
9. Leadership Development
10. Military training and Development
11. Tourism development

Singapore's Wish-List

1. Natural resources supplies: oil and gas, sand
2. Agricultural supplies
3. Space for military training
4. Water supplies
5. Joint tourism cooperation: marketing Angkor
6. Possible retirement homes

12. Information Technology & Connectivity
13. Investment Attraction & Promotion
14. Trade Promotion
15. ICT & E-Government

MODALITIES AND TIMEFRAME

Using already established examples as is done between China and Singapore, a High level Ministerial Joint Cooperation Committee — chaired by either Prime Minister or Deputy Prime Minister — consisting of relevant ministers, and supported by Working Groups, consisting of senior officials, Cambodia and Singapore could adopt this tried and true approach. The senior officials could draw up an overall master plan, which after discussion and scrutiny by the Governments and Parliaments could be formally adopted. The time frame should aim at the long term, about 20 ears, till 2030. Annual reviews will be held to check the state of progress and iron out problems.

CONCLUSIONS

A country like Cambodia is unique in its national story. Beginning with its Angkor civilization, its people have shown what they can achieve with excellent leadership, which can mobilize national energies in notable projects. Another great achievement in recent times is the ability of the Cambodian people to overcome national tragedies such as the KR genocide and the wiping out of the creative and the educated classes, foreign invasion and occupation, and gradually rebuild their country, society and economy. Perhaps the Buddhist faith of the people have helped them to meld culture and suffering, and become stronger. Many Cambodians have lost many relatives to the KR genocide. During the KR era, many families did not have children, as they saw no future. Today, Cambodia again has children, as the future is brighter and more peaceful. Cambodia is a brave, tragic nation which deserves the help of its ASEAN neighbours like Singapore and the rest of the world.

By the start of the 21st Century, Cambodia has achieved growth but not development. Its per capita in 2003 was US$300. Cambodian social indicators have worsened over the past 10 years — which means that the country is regressing. Weak governance is its Achilles heel, whilst Singapore is particularly strong in good governance. Cambodia remains a developing Country, one of the poorer members in ASEAN and is regarded by some observers as a failed state. (According to the Fund for Peace, Cambodia is ranked as No. 49 in its

List of 131 Failed States/At Risk. For comparison, Myanmar is listed as No. 13, Laos as No. 44. The UNDP Human Development Report of 2008 ranked Cambodia No. 131 out of 182 UN members, in its Human Development Index. For comparison, Singapore was ranked No. 23 in the 2009 UNDP Human Development Report.) These data demonstrates that Cambodia is still considered under-developed and would need much help.

It is obvious that Cambodia and Singapore are very different in land area, population, natural resources endowment, history, ethnic composition, levels of development, global status, institutions, economics and politics and society. The challenge is how to find a basis for two very different countries to establish a win-win, long-lasting, mutual benefit program of cooperation. One solution is for Cambodia to supply a resource which Singapore lacks totally, namely, a hinterland. Ever since Singapore separated from Malaysia in August 1965, and thus lost its natural hinterland, Singapore has been searching to replace this lost hinterland. Its solution was to evolve into a global city, and to regard the entire world as its hinterland. This approach created a different set of problems, such as the constant striving by Singapore to be competitive, productive, innovative, and relevant and to add value. For instance, Singapore sources for food as far away as Brazil. The latest Singapore food project is to develop the Singapore-China Modern Agricultural Food zone, comprising 1450 square km., which will produce pork, beef, dairy products, rice, strawberries and ginseng. This project has 3 phases and will be completed in 15 years at a cost of S$22.7 billion.

Cambodia might consider as a strategic move to offer to act as a hinterland for Singapore, by offering land for Singapore to set up farms to supply rice, fish, meat, as well as other important resources such as oil and gas, sand, minerals, military training areas, retirement homes for Singaporeans, on a commercial basis. This will also benefit Singapore as Cambodia is much nearer, thus transport costs are cheaper. Another advantage for Singapore is the diversification of supplies, thus enhancing food and resources security. Cambodia has a friendly attitude towards Singapore and will not issue threats to cut off supplies as some neighbours had done. As this role of hinterland is provided on a commercial basis, there is no threat to national sovereignty, as the resources and land remain under Cambodian control, using short term leases for example.

What does Cambodia get in return? Singapore will assure Cambodia of foreign investments; transfer of technology; assistance in economic development; assistance in helping Cambodia become a developed nation by 2030, in various sectors, such as human resource development, education and skills training, civil service training, development of a modern, effective civil service, infrastructure development-ports, airport, MRT, Information Technology, and other areas.

Can Singapore deliver such an ambitious programme? In China, for example, Singapore is building 8 replica-cities: they assume various forms, such as Eco-city, Knowledge-city and industrial cities, the most well-known model city being the Suzhou project, already completed. Singapore also assists India (Bangalore high-tech project, and other projects as well), Vietnam (the VSIP already expanded to two other sites), Russia (2 SEZs), Indonesia (Batam, Bintan and Karimun), Malaysia (the Iskandar project in Johor). If so many ASEAN and Asian countries, and great powers like China, India and Russia, have sought the assistance of Singapore in developmental projects, why not Cambodia?

The most important principle is synergy, namely that both sides benefit, and that their roles are complementary, and are built on trust and friendship, and sincere cooperation. Singapore has already shown its sincerity towards Cambodia by its decade-long diplomatic struggle to free Cambodia from foreign invasion and occupation. Cambodia showed true friendship towards Singapore by being one of the first to recognize Singapore's independence and to offer a place of refuge for a government-in-exile, at a time of peril for Singapore. As a fellow small state, Singapore does not pose a threat to Cambodia, and in fact by helping Cambodian development in many areas, will enhance Cambodian national resilience and strength

This paper has outlined some possible areas for further future bilateral cooperation. It provides a fascinating case study of how two small states can help each other, not just in diplomacy and rhetoric but with concrete assistance programs. *The winners in the future are those countries which are strong in SPICE (synergy, productivity, innovation, creativity & enterprise) and Good Governance.*

CAMBODIA AND SOUTHEAST ASIA

4

ASEAN AND THE CAMBODIA CAMPAIGN

Rodolfo C. Severino and Mark Hong

In the 44-year history of the Association of Southeast Asian Nations, the "Cambodia campaign" (December 1978 to October 1991) has been one of the most significant challenges to face the organization. ASEAN was only a little over 12 years old when the campaign began. It tested the mettle of ASEAN, whether it could stand by its principles — the non-use of force, non-interference in domestic affairs, and the peaceful settlement of disputes. ASEAN was also tested by the long duration of the diplomatic campaign to liberate Cambodia from foreign intervention and occupation. ASEAN's protracted diplomatic campaign, fought in various international fora, such as the United Nations General Assembly every year and the annual meetings of the Non-aligned Movement (NAM) and the Group of 77 developing countries (G77), also brought the young organization into the international public spotlight, and won it praise for its tenacity and principled stance. It was not an easy task to stand up against Vietnam, backed as it was by the Soviet bloc. But then ASEAN also had powerful supporters, including the United States, the West Europeans, China, Japan, Australia and other friends in the NAM and G77. ASEAN also received substantial support from friendly UN Secretariat officials, such as Under-Secretary General Rafeeuddin Ahmed and

Mr Hedi Annabi, who provided regular briefings on Cambodia. These information updates were useful in crafting and gaining support for the annual ASEAN UNGA resolutions on Cambodia.

THE VITAL ROLE OF NORODOM SIHANOUK

One of ASEAN's main assets in the diplomatic struggle to liberate Cambodia peacefully was Samdech Norodom Sihanouk, who, as once and future King and recognized and revered leader of the Khmer people, provided legitimacy for the diplomatic campaign. Samdech Sihanouk was a well-known figure in the Non-Aligned Movement, having been a key actor in the 1955 Bandung Conference that led to it. Thus, he lent his charismatic prestige to the Khmer resistance and to ASEAN's efforts. Every year at the UN General Assembly, Samdech Sihanouk would organize parties at the Waldorf Astoria Hotel in New York, and it became de rigueur for ASEAN representatives and other friendly supporters to gather there and to network.

At this point, it is appropriate to provide a short biographical sketch of Samdech Norodom Sihanouk. Born on 31 October 1922, he was the King of Cambodia from 1941 to 1955 and again from 1993 until his semi-retirement and voluntary abdication on 7 October 2004 in favor of his son, the current monarch, King Norodom Sihamoni. Since his abdication, Samdech Sihanouk has been known as the King-Father of Cambodia. Despite the great ritualism surrounding the Cambodian monarchy, he has always maintained close relations with the Cambodian people, who show deep respect and strong support for him, displaying his photographs in their homes. He has been called one of Southeast Asia's great survivors. He tried his best to keep Cambodia out of the Vietnam War, but the US supported a coup against him on 18 March 1970 whilst Samdech Sihanouk was travelling in Russia. We can trace many of the subsequent problems, including civil war, within Cambodia, to this coup.

After he was deposed, Samdech Sihanouk moved to Beijing, formed the National United Front of Kampuchea (Front Uni National du Kampuchea — FUNK) and began to support the Khmer Rouge in their struggle to overthrow the Lon Nol government. During the Lon Nol era, Samdech Sihanouk lived mostly in exile in North Korea, where a 60-room residence was built for him. When the Khmer Republic fell to the Khmer Rouge in April 1975, Samdech Sihanouk became the symbolic head of state of the new regime while Pol Pot remained in power. The Khmer Rouge has been blamed for the deaths of five of his 14 children. He was basically a captive of the KR until he escaped in 1978. We should note his patient biding of time during these three years awaiting a positive turn of events. In 1978, Samdech Sihanouk went to the UN General Assembly to deliver a speech against the Vietnamese invasion, and then sought refuge in China and North Korea.

In 1982, he opposed the Vietnam-supported puppet government, and became President of the Coalition Government of Democratic Kampuchea (CGDK), which kept the UN seat of Cambodia. After the 1991 Paris Peace Conference on Cambodia, Samdech Sihanouk returned to Phnom Penh in November of that year, following 13 years in exile. In 1993, Samdech Sihanouk once again became King of Cambodia. During the restoration, however, he suffered from ill health and traveled frequently to Beijing for medical treatment. Citing reasons of ill health, he announced his abdication of the throne on 7 October 2004. The Throne Council met on 14 October and appointed Prince Norodom Sihamoni as the new King. Whilst it may be premature to definitively assess the contributions of Samdech Norodom Sihanouk to Cambodia, many observers have noted the longevity of his stay in the spotlight of his country's history, his immense popularity amongst his people, and his great political skills, which enabled him to survive the many twists and turns of the turbulence of Cambodian politics.

Samdech Sihanouk was the key person in dealing at a strategic level with the PRC, who, while they backed their protégé, the KR, also invested time, funds and long-term patience in him for over 40 years. This strategic cultivation and long-sighted vision of China contrasts sharply with the US support of General Lon Nol over five years. In the end, the US had to bribe General Lon Nol with US$1 million to persuade him to leave Phnom Penh, so as to open the way for negotiations with the KR, who, sensing that victory was within their grasp, refused to negotiate with the US. Today, Chinese influence in Cambodia is strong, whilst the US is closer to Vietnam than to Cambodia. In the final analysis, we can consider Samdech Norodom Sihanouk to be one of the great leaders of Southeast Asia, who endured amazing twists of fate and lived to see an independent Cambodia.

On a personal note, when King Sihanouk was interviewed on 10 December 2003 in Phnom Penh, the King stated that if he had not cooperated with the Khmer Rouge, Cambodia would have disappeared as an independent country. He had refused to join the Khmer Rouge despite strong Chinese pressures to do so. As the KR had killed 2 million Cambodians, the King had refused to become a part of the organization, despite being the President of the CGDK. He had a personal dislike for the KR, which had killed five of his children. During the interview, Samdech Sihanouk added that from 1979 to 1981, he had written three letters to the

Vietnamese leader, Mr Pham Van Dong, asking the Vietnamese to withdraw their troops from Cambodia, but was unsuccessful.

ASEAN: UNITED BUT FLEXIBLE

One of aspects of the Cambodian campaign most commented upon was that it helped to solidify ASEAN as a cohesive regional association. This was so much so that, after the Cambodian issue ended in 1991 with the Paris Peace Conference and after the general elections that the UN Transitional Authority in Cambodia organised in 1993, some observers wondered whether there would be any future life for ASEAN. Now, in 2011, 18 years later, ASEAN is still alive, vigorous and very much at the centre of regional politics and economics. It has overcome various crises, such as the East Timor problem, the issues centred on Myanmar, the 1997–98 Asian financial crisis, the 2008–09 global financial crisis, SARS, terrorism attacks, disagreements attendant on the setting up of the ASEAN Regional Forum, the establishment of Asia Europe Meetings, ASEAN+3 (China, Japan and the Republic of Korea) and the East Asia Summit, the ASEAN Charter, the ASEAN Free Trade Area, the economic arrangements with China, India, Japan, South Korea, Australia-New Zealand, a number of border tensions, etc.

It is noteworthy that ASEAN adopted a solid and united front throughout the long Cambodian diplomatic campaign. But ASEAN was also flexible enough to allow member states like Indonesia to attempt some initiatives, such as the informal cocktail parties, known as the Jakarta Informal Meetings (there were two JIMs), in which the four Cambodian factions met in informal settings for dialogues. This process helped to pave the way for the later Paris Peace Conference, which in turn owed its success to the détente between Russia and the United States, after the collapse of the USSR in 1991. The motives for Indonesia to host such meetings were its concerns about Chinese influence, and thus its desire not to offend Vietnam, which it perceived to be a bulwark against China. In retrospect, it was the genius of ASEAN in being able to oppose Vietnam over its intervention and occupation of Cambodia, without offending Indonesia, thanks largely to the wisdom and forbearance of President Suharto, who understood the bigger picture. The Cambodian issue was the very first instance in which ASEAN took a definitive stand, despite differing views amongst the member states and thus was able to maintain its solidarity. ASEAN understood that Thailand was the frontline state, and that the Cambodian issue was as much about shoring up Thai security as about helping to liberate Cambodia. We might add that, for Singapore, the motives included the principle of no regime change by force.

THE ROLE OF THE PHILIPPINES

The Philippines' motive in supporting the common ASEAN position on Cambodia, like Singapore's, was based on the principle of no regime change by force. There were also Philippine concerns about Vietnamese actions helping to expand Soviet influence in East Asia. The Philippines and China were thus on the same side of the Sino-Soviet dispute. It was remarkable that ASEAN and China were working together to help resolve the Cambodia dispute from 1978 to 1993, whilst in the 21st century, China and the ASEAN claimant-states are on opposite sides in the South China Sea disputes.

During the long Cambodian struggle, the Philippines' Foreign Secretary, Carlos Romulo, in New York, refused to shake the "blood-stained hand" of Khieu Samphan, who was the KR head of State and its public face. When the Vietnamese leader, Prime Minister Pham Van Dong, visited Manila as part of his regional tour, he had neither consulted ASEAN members nor warned about Vietnam's intention to invade Cambodia. Singapore Prime Minister Lee Kuan Yew reportedly felt betrayed by Dong's actions. The Philippines' role in the lobbying for votes at the UN General Assembly in support of the annual ASEAN resolution was carried out mainly among the Latin American states, but its efforts were made easier by the American lobbying amongst the Latin states. In those days, the 1980s, the US had much influence in Latin America.

CONCLUSIONS

What held ASEAN together in the 1980s, during the long Cambodia struggle? Essentially it was a determination not to let Southeast Asia become the arena for proxy wars between the great powers. Later, in the 1990s, ASEAN was determined to integrate the region, thus extending membership to erstwhile opponents such as Vietnam; while in the post-2000 period, ASEAN has focused on strengthening itself as a political body and on the centrality of ASEAN in the regional efforts to build an Asian community.

5

CAMBODIA-INDONESIA RELATIONS

Benny Widyono

JAYAVARMAN II: THE PRINCE FROM JAVA

Diplomatic relations between Indonesia and Cambodia have been established in their contemporary form for only a few decades, but the ties between the peoples of Indonesia and Cambodia date back centuries.

"I wish to thank you, Excellency Mr Yasushi Akashi, for sending another prince from Java to help bring peace to Cambodia," quipped Prince Sihanouk, referring to me. It was August 1992. We were in the city of Siem Reap, six kilometres from the world-famous Angkor Wat temple for the official inauguration of the provincial headquarters of the United Nations Transitional Authority of Cambodia (UNTAC), established to implement the Paris Agreements for Cambodia. I had joined UNTAC from the United Nations in New York and was appointed the provincial director in Siem Reap, some sort of shadow governor to the de facto governor of the People's Republic of Cambodia (PRK), renamed the State of Cambodia (SOC) in 1991, which had remained unrecognized by the United Nations since its establishment in January 1979.

Sihanouk's witticism had its origin back in the year 802 CE, when a solemn ceremony was performed at Mahendraparvata, now known as Phnom Kulen, a sacred mountain top not far from where we were gathered that day in Siem Reap. At that ceremony, Prince Jayavarman II ostensibly was proclaimed a universal monarch.[1] According to some sources, King Jayavarman II had resided for some time in Java during the reign of the mighty Sailendras, or Lords of the Mountains.[2] Hence the concept of Devaraja, or God King (still often applied to Sihanouk), was ostensibly imported from Java.[3] This ceremony was also allegedly meant to free King Jayavarman II from the overlordship of the Sailendras of Java.[4] At that time, the Sailendras ruled over Java, Sumatra, the Malay Peninsula, and parts of modern Cambodia. Jayavarman II's inauguration in the year 802 CE gave birth to the Angkor period, a glorious Khmer civilization that dominated mainland Southeast Asia with ebbs and flows for the next six centuries. The Hindu-turned-Buddhist Angkor Wat temple in Siem Reap was built in the first half of the 12th century, during the reign of Suryavarman II (1113 – c. 1150). Incidentally, the famous Buddhist temple of Borobudur was built in the year 800 by the Sailendras. Sihanouk's quip had special significance for me as I, though not a prince was born in Magelang, six kilometres away from Borobudur.

DURING THE COLD WAR

In modern times, diplomatic relations between Indonesia and Cambodia were established on 27 March 1962 with the appointment of Indonesian ambassador to Cambodia, Abdul Karim Rasyid, and Cambodian ambassador to Indonesia Koun Wick.[5] However, close relations between the two countries were fostered before that, with the deep friendship between President Sukarno of Indonesia and Prince/King Norodom Sihanouk from Cambodia, the first leaders of the two countries since independence: Indonesia in 1945 and Cambodia in 1953. Sukarno and Sihanouk met for the first time at the Asia-African conference in Bandung, Indonesia in 1955. During the period 1959 to 1965, they visited each other's countries a total of five times and they called each other brothers. In 1960, the two leaders signed a Treaty of Amity which called for permanent peace and friendship between the two countries.

During the Cold War, Southeast Asia had, due to its geopolitical location, seen itself involved in the ongoing power struggles for hegemony in the region. During the 1960s, both President Sukarno of Indonesia and Prince Sihanouk of Cambodia expressed neutrality in the Cold War, while trying to maintain a political balance between a right-wing military and a growing Communist movement, the Partai Komunis Indonesia (PKI) and the Khmer Rouge in Cambodia.

At a lunch during the Asian-African Conference, Chinese Premier Zhou Enlai had assured Sihanouk that China respected Cambodia's neutrality.[6]

However, neutrality had not been acceptable to President Eisenhower of the United States and to the key US intelligence services, including the CIA, who were determined to support any anti-Communist Khmer they could find.[7] Both leaders were thus forced to turn to the Left as a result.

Ultimately both were overthrown by anti-Communist military elements close to the United States. The regime change from Sukarno to Suharto, precipitated by a failed coup d'etat by Leftist elements on 30 September 1965, had been accompanied by a massacre of some 700,000–800,000 suspected communists.[8] Sukarno died under house arrest ordered by his successor, Suharto, the anti-Communist general who would rule Indonesia for the next 32 years.

Meanwhile in Cambodia, two US actions — one overt, the other covert — indirectly fed the meteoric rise of the Khmer Rouge: U.S. President Richard Nixon's massive bombardment of Cambodia, 1969–73, and the overthrow of Sihanouk by rightwing General Lon Nol in 1970, patterned on Suharto's regime change from Sukarno, including the training of Cambodian military forces by American Green Berets in Bandung, Indonesia.[9] Enraged by the coup, in Beijing Sihanouk embraced Pol Pot and established a government in exile which was dominated by the Khmer Rouge. Sihanouk called for "Cambodians to struggle against US imperialism who have invaded our Indochina and are oppressing our peoples…."[10]

Both these actions radicalized the Cambodian youth and drove many of them into the ranks of the Khmer Rouge. A civil war ensued between Lon Nol, backed by the US, and the Khmer Rouge, backed by China. With massive Chinese help, now no longer bound by its respect for Sihanouk's neutrality, the Khmer Rouge triumphed in Cambodia in 1975, and massacred an estimated 1.7 million people. At first, Sihanouk was proclaimed head of the government by the Khmer Rouge but he was soon put under house arrest. The real leader of the Khmer Rouge was the secretive Pol Pot. But Sihanouk proved more resilient than Sukarno. He survived the Khmer Rouge massacre and continued to govern in various capacities during the subsequent tumultuous history of Cambodia.

Indonesia under Suharto immediately recognized Lon Nol's Khmer Republic which deeply hurt Sihanouk. On May 1970, Lon Nol wrote a letter to Suharto thanking him for his role in trying to bring peace in Cambodia.[11] At the Non-Aligned countries Summit in Guyana in 1972, Indonesian Foreign Minister Adam Malik objected to the recognition of the Sihanouk government in exile.[12]

Recently, Indonesian Foreign Minister Hasan Wirajuda summarized these developments as follows: Indonesia and Cambodia began to drift apart as a result of changes within Cambodia from 1970, and widened by the fall of General Lon Nol and the takeover of the country by the Democratic Kampuchea regime under the Khmer Rouge and Pol Pot [in 1975]. The rift remained even with the end of the Khmer Rouge regime in 1979. However, Indonesia, which was a founding member of the then anti-Communist Association of Southeast Asian Nations (ASEAN) in 1967, played an active and pivotal role in the Association's search for a just and comprehensive settlement of the Cambodia conflict during 1980-92.[13]

THE BATTLE SHIFTS TO NEW YORK

In 1978, Pol Pot's Khmer Rouge launched increasingly vicious attacks against Vietnam — their erstwhile strong supporter — and Pol Pot's paranoia subsequently caused him to massacre his own soldiers in the eastern zone bordering Vietnam. To escape these purges, many eastern zone Khmer Rouge soldiers fled to Vietnam, where their leaders, Heng Samrin and Hun Sen, raised a rebel army and formed a government in exile, the Renaksei Samaki Sangkruoh Cheat Kampuchea, or United Front for the National Salvation of Kampuchea (UFNSK), also known as the Salvation Front. The front vowed that it would "unite the entire people to topple the Pol Pot/Ieng Sary gang of dictators."[14]

On 25 December 1978, twelve Vietnamese divisions, totalling 100,000 troops, together with the UFNSK's rebel army of 20,000 men, entered Cambodia and liberated Cambodia from the Pol Pot regime. The UFNSK established the People's Republic of Kampuchea (PRK) led by Heng Samrin and Hun Sen. It soon gained control over 95 per cent of the country.

The battle shifted to the corridors of the United Nations in New York. Intense lobbying by the United States, China, and ASEAN portrayed the ouster of the Khmer Rouge as an act of aggression by Vietnam, and condemned the PRK. The Soviet Union, its allies and a number of non-aligned countries supported the PRK. In 1979, representatives of the two Cambodian governments, the Khmer Rouge and the PRK, jockeyed for Cambodia's UN seat. After intense debate, the General Assembly, spurred by China and the USA, voted on a resolution to continue to recognize the genocidal Khmer Rouge government in exile as the legitimate representative of the Cambodian people. The vote was 71 to 35, with 34 abstentions and 12 absentees.[15]

This resolution was repeated year after year for 11 years. In 1982, ASEAN, supported by the United States and China, pressed strongly for the formation of a Coalition Government of Democratic Kampuchea (CGDK) consisting of the Khmer Rouge and two newly-established anti- or non-

Communist resistance movements: the National United Front for an Independent, Neutral, Peaceful and Cooperative Cambodia (known by its French acronym FUNCINPEC) established by Prince Sihanouk in 1981 and the Khmer People's National Liberation Front (KPNLF) led by former Prime Minister Son Sann and made up mainly of remnants of Lon Nol's regime. Henceforth the CGDK held the Cambodian seat in the General Assembly. In the field, the CGDK received substantial assistance from China and the west to continue its low-intensity civil war against the PRK.

These sophisticated diplomatic manoeuvrings in the corridors of the UN had a harsh impact on ordinary Cambodians. The political ostracism and economic isolation imposed on Cambodia by the General Assembly's resolutions led to another 11 years of suffering for the Cambodian people after the ouster of the Khmer Rouge.

TWELVE YEARS OF NEGOTIATIONS LEADING TO THE PARIS AGREEMENTS

Given the international political divisions, it is not surprising that it took more than 12 years to bring the various Cambodian factions to the negotiating table. International meddling, outside the control of Cambodians, left them in a quagmire for much of the 1980s. The enormous suffering of the Cambodian people failed to generate the necessary urgency to break the deadlock.

I. Sihanouk-Hun Sen direct talks

A real breakthrough only became possible when the Cambodians judged themselves ready for it. In December 1987 and January 1988, Sihanouk and Hun Sen, together with leaders of the two opposing forces, the CGDK and the PRK, now renamed the State of Cambodia (SOC), came together for two historic meetings near Paris that finally broke the stalemate. After nearly two decades of warfare, they began for the first time a direct dialogue of reconciliation and consultation about peace in Cambodia.

II. An Indonesian cocktail party

The Sihanouk-Hun Sen rapprochement enabled ASEAN and particularly Indonesia to play a key role in helping to achieve a comprehensive settlement of the Cambodian conflict.

Ben Kiernan, a prominent scholar of Cambodia, has argued that Indonesia in particular played a crucial role in the resolution of the Cambodia problem. In this connection, he described an unobtrusive 1980 visit by two famous Indonesian journalists, Fikri Jufri of *Tempo* magazine and Sabam Siagian of the *Sinar Harapan* newspaper to the Noor Al-Ihsan mosque in Phnom Penh, one of the oldest buildings in the capital, built in 1813, to talk to Cham Muslim survivors of the Khmer Rouge genocide. He believed that their visit and reporting on the situation helped, in a small way, to pioneer a slow policy turnaround in Jakarta, which unfolded over the ensuing decade. That policy revision enabled Indonesia to play a major role in resolving the Cambodia conflict at the end of the 1980s.[16]

Earlier, in March 1980, Suharto had met with Malaysia's Prime Minister in the Malaysian town of Kuantan, and the two men came up with the "Kuantan principle." The Indonesian and Malaysian leaders expressed their concern over the USSR's role in Cambodia, through its ally Vietnam, but they balanced this with their concern over China's role.

In February 1984, dropping his previous preference for secret diplomacy, Indonesian Armed Forces chief Benny Murdani made an official visit to Hanoi, the first senior ASEAN figure to do so for 3 years. He declared that Hanoi posed no threat to Southeast Asia, and that its invasion of Cambodia had been undertaken in self-defence. Two weeks later, during a visit to Hanoi, Jusuf Wanandi, the head of Indonesia's influential semi-official think tank of the Foreign Ministry, the Centre for Strategic and International Studies, praised "Vietnam's heroic struggle for independence," and he recommended "cooperating with Vietnam if there is a willingness on Hanoi's part jointly to seek a compromise in solving the Cambodian conflict."[17]

Throughout the 1980s, although Indonesia continued to show its solidarity with frontline state Thailand, it began to see the prolongation of the war in Cambodia, the "bleeding Vietnam and Cambodia white" strategy, as not being in its or the region's interests. Indonesia actively sought to engage the Cambodians and Vietnamese and their external sponsors. By 1984, Indonesia was given the formal role of "interlocutor" in the Cambodian situation.[18]

Hanoi then made a new diplomatic proposal, which Indonesia's foreign Minister Mochtar Kusumaatmadja, called "a significant step forward."[19] The breakthrough came in July 1987, in the Mochtar Kusumaatmadja-Nguyen Co Thach (Indonesia's and Vietnam's Ministers of Foreign Affairs respectively) communiquè in which Vietnam accepted the idea of an informal meeting (or so-called cocktail party) held on the basis of equal footing, without preconditions and with no political labels, in two stages: first among the factions of the Cambodian people, and, at a second stage, other concerned countries, including Vietnam, would be invited to participate.[20]

In July 1988 the first round of the Jakarta Informal Meetings (JIMs) was convened in the Bogor palace, near Jakarta. It was attended by the six ASEAN countries, and the three Indo-Chinese countries, including all four of the Cambodian factions. This meeting was a major breakthrough in that for the first time, all four Cambodian factions, who were not talking to each other, met in a neutral setting. Hitherto each faction had insisted that it would negotiate only with the foreign backers of the other. Indonesia artfully broke the deadlock by having the Cambodians parties meet first with the Southeast Asian supporters of each faction, and then join the conference.[21]

The Jakarta informal meetings (JIMs) of July 1988 and February 1989 as well as the Informal Meetings on Cambodia (IMC) in February and September 1990 were chaired by internationally-acclaimed Indonesian Foreign Minister Ali Alatas, who skilfully steered the tense negotiations in the right direction for maximum results.

The Paris Agreements

After that, a confluence of favourable factors, including the end of the Cold War, brought a solution closer to reality. Vietnamese troops completed the final stage of their withdrawal from Cambodia in 1989. These meetings enabled the Paris Peace Conference of 30 July to 30 August 1989 to be convened and co-chaired by Foreign Ministers Ali Alatas from Indonesia and Roland E. Dumas from France. Unfortunately, the conference broke up without reaching final conclusion. It was dead-locked over the demand by the CGDK factions for interim power-sharing arrangements which were unacceptable to the Hun Sen government, which had de facto ruled the country since 1979, as well as on the future participation of the genocidal Khmer Rouge. With the adjournment of the Paris Conference, intensive efforts were made by all parties and meetings were held in Jakarta, Bangkok, Tokyo, Paris and New York.

The key conceptual breakthrough was an idea of Sihanouk, endorsed by US Congressman Stephen Solarz and officially proposed by Australian Foreign Minister Gareth Evans, in which, instead of the quadripartite power-sharing arrangement rejected by Hun Sen, the UN itself would take control of the administration of Cambodia, until it had successfully conducted elections for a new government. However, since the UN was banned by Article 78 of its Charter from placing a sovereign member state under trusteeship, on 9–10 September 1990, a Supreme National Council (SNC) would be established to serve as "the unique legitimate body and source of authority" in Cambodia throughout the transition period. It consisted of thirteen members, including six representatives of the PRK/SOC and two each from the Khmer Rouge, FUNCINPEC, and KPNLF, with Prince Sihanouk chairing and relinquishing his membership in FUNCINPEC. The SNC, which was largely a symbolic body, would delegate all powers necessary to UNTAC to implement the agreements. Both UNTAC and the SNC were novel concepts in international law.[22] Ultimately, all sides agreed to include the Khmer Rouge in the peace process.

A major breakthrough was achieved with the agreement reached by the Permanent Five Security Council members in New York 27–28 August 1990 on a framework document and key elements of a comprehensive settlement.[23] Subsequently, as their various foreign patrons all had agreed on a framework of peace, in the September 1990 IMC meeting in Jakarta convened by Indonesia and France, the four Cambodian factions agreed to accept the framework document in its entirety as the basis of settling the Cambodian conflict.[24] The IMC also agreed on the formation of the Supreme National Council.

The framework document became the Paris Agreements which were signed in the reconvened Paris conference co-chaired by Alatas and Dumas on 23 October 1991. UNTAC was created to implement the agreements.

Indonesia's role in UNTAC

On 9 November 1991, the United Nations Advance Mission in Cambodia (UNAMIC) was deployed in Cambodia, headed by Bangladeshi Mr Ataul Karim. The military component was headed by French Brigadier-General Jean Micheal Loridon, with Indonesia's Colonel Tinggogoy as his deputy.

On 15 March 1992, UNTAC started operating with the arrival in Phnom Penh of the United Nations Special representative of the Secretary General, Mr Yasushi Akashi and the Australian force commander, General John M. Sanderson. General Loridon became Sanderson's deputy and Indonesian Brigadier General Tamlicha Ali was made Chief of Staff.

The military component consisted of 15,991 personnel from 34 countries. Indonesia provided the largest component, consisting of two battalions of the Garuda XII contingent, totalling 1,904 soldiers. One battalion was based in the capital Phnom Penh and the other in Khmer Rouge-plagued Kompong Thom province. Everywhere they were stationed, the Indonesians were well-received by the Cambodian people, who could see similarities in culture between the two countries.

The civilian police component of UNTAC consisted of 3,359 officers from 32 countries. Indonesia contributed 224 police officers grouped in the Garuda XII contingent headed by Police Colonel Drs S. Tarigan.

In the civilian component of UNTAC consisting of around 5,000 personnel, no senior Indonesian official served at the director level. However, under the French Director of Civil Administration, Mr Gerard Porcell, two Indonesian UN officials served as provincial directors: Ahmad Padang in Takeo and as noted earlier, Benny Widyono in Siem Reap.

UNTAC faced the problems of dealing with the Khmer Rouge which violated all of UNTAC's provisions, often violently and together with the SOC which resented UNTAC control. Nevertheless, UNTAC fulfilled its major objectives successfully: the repatriation of 360,000 refugees from the Thai border and the elections in which 89.5 per cent of the eligible voters participated. FUNCINPEC won the elections with the Cambodian People's Party (CPP) the political party of SOC, coming second.

Indonesia and Cambodia in the Post-UNTAC era

The Royal Government of Cambodia, formed on the basis of the UNTAC-conducted elections, was established on 24 September 1993. King Norodom Sihanouk became the head of state that reigned but did not rule. The executive government was headed by two Prime Ministers of equal power, Prince Ranariddh of FUNCINPEC and Hun Sen of CPP. The Khmer Rouge was left intact after UNTAC attacked the new government incessantly. These unusual arrangements proved to be a recipe for disaster. The two Cambodian Prime Ministers went on a state visit to Indonesia from 20–22 June 1994, which was their first state visit abroad.

Taufik Soedarbo, the Indonesian ambassador to the SNC during UNTAC became the Indonesian ambassador to the royal government. After UNTAC left, the United Nations' political role was reduced to the appointment of a Representative of the Secretary General, Benny Widyono, to whom three military officers were assigned, from France, Malaysia and Belgium.

III. Political Developments

The persistent attacks by the Khmer Rouge complicated the situation for the new government. Also, after a brief honeymoon period, tensions between the two Prime Ministers with equal power, escalated relentlessly. This culminated in a final showdown between the two factions with fighting around Phnom Penh on 5–6 July 1997, resulting in a victory for CPP and the exile of

Ranariddh and a number of FUNCINPEC parliamentarians and government ministers. The international community, disturbed at what had happened, insisted that elections be held in which the exiles should be allowed to return and participate. Some donors suspended their aid.

The ASEAN Troika

Immediately after the July 1997 events, and following a decision adopted in a Special ASEAN Meeting in Kuala Lumpur in the same month, an ASEAN Troika consisting of Ali Alatas from Indonesia and the Foreign Ministers of the Philippines and Thailand met with Hun Sen in Phnom Penh. Hun Sen at first refused to accept ASEAN's mediation in the conflict, which he considered an internal affair. Alatas argued that as fellow Southeast Asian states, ASEAN did not want Cambodia to fend off external threats on its own, particularly as Cambodia had readied itself to become a member of ASEAN, along with Laos and Myanmar, in Kuala Lumpur in July 1997. Alatas also stated that under articles 5 and 29 of the Peace Agreements, the Indonesian Foreign Minister, as Co-Chair of the 1991 Paris Conference could engage in consultations in the event of any breach of the agreements.

After Alatas undertook extremely intensive and complex negotiations, Hun Sen quickly modified his position and expressed praise for Indonesia's role. On 2 August 1997, the ASEAN Troika met again with Hun Sen which proceeded in a positive atmosphere. Hun Sen agreed to hold elections in 1998, with the full participation of all political forces in Cambodia. Cambodia's entry into ASEAN was postponed because of the disturbances in the country.

After the 26 July 1998 elections, a new government was formed in November 1998 with Hun Sen as the sole Prime Minister. Subsequently, the ASEAN summit in Hanoi 1998 admitted Cambodia as a full member of ASEAN, fulfilling the dream of the founders of ASEAN to realise an "ASEAN Ten".

IV. Indonesia mediates in Preah Vihear dispute

The Preah Vihear temple was constructed by the Khmer kings Suryavarman I (1002 –1050) and Suryavarman II (1113–1150), who also built Angkor Wat. This temple was controlled by subsequent Khmer rulers until the late 18th century. It fell under Siam's (Thailand's) control around 1794 when Siamese rulers annexed a number of Cambodian provinces, including Siem Reap province which had administered the Preah Vihear temple. The 1907

Franco-Siamese Treaty required Siam (Thailand) to return Battambang and Siem Reap (including Preah Vihear) provinces to Cambodia, which became a French protectorate. In 1954, one year after Cambodia attained its independence, Thailand occupied Preah Vihear temple. Cambodia filed a complaint to the International Court of Justice (ICJ) in The Hague. On 15 June 1962, the ICJ awarded the ownership of Preah Vihear temple to Cambodia. However, in July 2008, the addition of the temple to a list of UNESCO World Heritage sites, and the rise of a nationalist royalist movement in Thailand called the People's Alliance for Democracy (PAD) — also known as the yellow shirts — reignited this longstanding border dispute between Thailand and Cambodia.

On 15 July 2008, Thailand sent its troops to the vicinity of the temple and this triggered a border conflict which is ongoing until today. On 4 February 2011, Thai troops started a strong border attack in the vicinity of Preah Vihear temple, and troops from both sides were locked in a border standoff, one that had led to skirmishes and killings since 2008. In February 2011, in the spirit of a United Nations resolution calling for restraint on both sides, Indonesian Minister of Foreign Affairs Marty Natalegawa hosted a meeting of ASEAN Foreign Ministers in Jakarta in which Thailand and Cambodia agreed to accept Indonesian observers and avoid further clashes over a border dispute. The agreement is a victory for ASEAN and its current Chairman, the Indonesian Foreign Minister Marty Natalegawa who, following in the footsteps of Indonesia as a peace-maker pioneered by his mentor, the late Ali Alatas, announced that a unique arrangement had been reached to end the violent clashes between the two countries, including an official ceasefire, the allowing in of unarmed Indonesian observers and the future holding of talks.

Cambodia swiftly accepted the terms of reference for unarmed Indonesian military observers to watch over a cease-fire. But Thailand, under pressure of the PAD — the yellow shirts — adopted a non-committal attitude to the proposed meeting, claiming that it needed more time to discuss the terms of reference.[25]

V. Military Cooperation

In 1995–96, 230 Royal Cambodian Armed Forces (RCAF) troops, comprising 180 commando and 50 territorial troops, received seven months of training at the Indonesian Special forces KOPASSUS training centre in Cilacap, Indonesia. They returned to Phnom Penh wearing the Indonesian special forces uniform and red beret and became known as Unit 911. This was followed by other training programs, including for RCAF officers and pilots. Subsequently, at the request of Hun Sen, since 2002, Indonesia's KOPASSUS has also trained officers and soldiers of Hun Sen's crack bodyguard regiment, many of whom are now serving at the Preah Vihear temple area. Such training is still continuing today.

ECONOMIC, SOCIAL AND CULTURAL COOPERATION

Since stability returned to Cambodia in 1998 and, especially since the beginning of the new century, Cambodia has fully entered the ranks of the Asian economic miracle. The economy grew at an average rate of 8 to 9 per cent until the global recession of 2008.

Indonesia has pioneered investment projects in the new Cambodia including: embassy properties, being the first to build a modern high-end apartment complex; Hotel Holiday International; Camintel, a joint venture between Indonesia's P.T. Indosat telecommunication company and Cambodia's Ministry of Post and Telecommunications, which rehabilitated the important Cambodian domestic telecommunications network long before the boom in mobile phones in the country; as well as Indonesian garment factories producing clothing for export. Other investments include President Airlines, KALBE Pharmaceuticals, car dealerships and a high-end restaurant.[26] In 2006, the first and biggest township development in Phnom Penh — Grand Phnom Penh International City, located at the north-western part of the city — was commenced by Indonesia's P.T. Ciputra. This project will be the first integrated city development in Cambodia that offers residential low-rises and high-rises, a commercial complex, educational institutions, a hospital, and an international standard 18-hole golf course.[27] Indonesia also assisted Cambodia in projects for the restoration of Angkor Wat from 1994 to 2000, rural development, education and other sectors.

CONCLUSIONS

Relations between Indonesia and Cambodia dates back for centuries and are based on deep cultural, social, economic, political and historical ties. It is for this reason that relations between the two countries, which understandably saw many twists and turns in intensity of engagement over the past few decades, especially during the Cold War, have consistently manifested their resilience against both time and events.

Notes

1. *Kamraten jagat ta Raja* in Cambodian, or God King (*Devaraja* in Sanskrit).
2. Actually, some sources trace Javanese influence over Kambuja from the beginning of the Eighth Century during the reign of King Sanjaya of Java over the Sailendra Empire. The Javanese influence over Kambuja was mentioned in his inscription dated CE 732. See Ramesh C. Majumdar, *Suvarnadvipa, Ancient Indian Colonies in the Far East*, vol. II, part II, "Cultural History", chapter 1, as quoted in Ramesh C. Majumdar, *Kambuja Desa, An Ancient Hindu Colony in Cambodia, Sir Williams Meyer Lectures, 1942–43*. Madras: University of Madras, 1944, reprinted by Philadelphia: Institute for the Study of Human Issues, 1980, 73 ff.
3. Majumdar, *Suvarnadvipa*, 77, footnote 3. According to an 11th-Century inscription, the cult was known as *kamraten jagat ta raja* in Khmer (universal Monarch) or *devaraja* in Sanskrit. G. Coedes and P. Dupont, "L'inscription de Sdok Kak Thom". *Bulletin de l'Ecole francaise d'Extreme Orient* (BEFEO), 43 (1943–1946): 57–134.
4. G. Coedes, *The Indianized States of Southeast Asia*, Honolulu: The East West Press of Hawaii, 1968, 97. Original French version: Paris: E. de Boccard, 1964. See also G. Coedes, *The Making of South East Asia*, Berkeley: Berkeley University of California Press, 1964, p. 97. Original French version: *Les Peuples de la Peninsule Indochinoise*, Paris: Dunod, 1962.
5. Nazaruddin Nasution et al., *Indonesia-Cambodia: Forging ties through thick and thin*. Unofficial translation of Pasang Surut Hubungan Diplomatik Indonesia Kamboja, Phnom Penh, Cambodia: Embassy of Indonesia, 2002, pp. 19 and 25.
6. George McT. Kahin, *Southeast Asia: A Testament*. London and New York: Routledge Curzon, 2003, pp. 260–61.
7. David Chandler, *The Tragedy of Cambodian History: Politics, War and Revolution Since 1945*. New Haven: Yale University Press, 1991, p. 81.
8. An extensive literature exists on this episode. On the coup and its aftermath, see, for instance, Benedict R. Anderson and Ruth T. McVey, *A Preliminary Analysis of the October 1, 1965 Coup in Indonesia*. Ithaca, NY: Cornell University, 1971; Harold Crouch, "Another Look at the Indonesian Coup," Indonesia, Cornell University, April 1972; and Robert Cribb, "The Indonesian Killings of 1965–1966". Centre of Southeast Asian Studies, Monash University, Clayton, Victoria, Australia, 1990.
9. For a well-documented and detailed account of U.S. involvement in Sihanouk's ouster, see George McTurnan Kahin, *Southeast Asia*, pp. 279–99.
10. "Message and Solemn Declaration by H. E. Samdech Norodom Sihanouk, Cambodian Head of Nation," Beijing, 23 March 1970 quoted in Benny Widyono, *Dancing in Shadows: Sihanouk, the Khmer Rouge and the United Nations*. Lanham, PA: Rowman Littlefield, 2007, p. 37.
11. Nazaruddin Nasution, op. cit, pp. 36 ff.
12. Ibid., p. 45.

13. Dr Hassan Wirajuda, Preface to Nazaruddin Nasution, p. xii.
14. Central Committee of the UFNSK, "Declaration of the Kampuchea National United Front for National Salvation," Kampuchean Liberated Zone, 2 December 1978. Benny Widyono, op. cit., p. 27.
15. UN documents A/34/PV.3 and A/34/PV.4, and Cor. 1, *Official Records*.
16. Ben Kiernan, "Foreword" to Benny Widyono, *Dancing in Shadows*, p. xix.
17. Ben Kiernan, "Foreword" to Benny Widyono, op. cit., citing *The Age* (Melbourne), 16 March 1984; Wilkinson, "Kampuchea: a Whiff". *National Times*, 6–12 April 1984.
18. Special meeting of ASEAN Foreign Ministers in Jakarta. UN document A/40/492, 17 July 1985.
19. Ibid., p. xxi.
20. Ali Alatas, Statement at the 42nd UN General Assembly, 13 October 1987 in Ali Alatas, *A Voice for a Just peace*. Jakarta, Gramedia Pustaka Utama, 2001, p. 265.
21. Ali Alatas, Opening remarks as Chairman of the Jakarta Informal Meeting (JIM), on Cambodia, Bogor Palace, July 25, 1988 in Alatas, op. cit., pp. 271–72.
22. Stephen R. Ratner, "The Cambodia Settlement Agreements", *American Journal of International Law*, vol. 87, no. 1, January 1993, p. 9. Actually the SNC was created by the Cambodian factions prior to Paris, but the concept was endorsed by Paris.
23. UN document A/45/472-S/21689, letter from the Permanent Five members transmitting a statement and framework document adopted by their representatives at a meeting in New York, 27–28 August 1990.
24. Ali Alatas, "Progress report to the ASEAN-EC Ministerial Meeting (AEMM) Luxembourg, 31 May 1991", in Alatas, op. cit., p. 291.
25. Pou Sothirak, "Preah Vihear Dispute puts ASEAN's Effectiveness to the Test", *Cambodia Daily*, 29 March 2011. http://web1.iseas.edu.sg/?p=2958.
26. Information provided by the Council for the Development of Cambodia (CDC).
27. Information provided in personal communication from P.T. Ciputra in Phnom Penh.

6

CAMBODIA AND VIETNAM
Good Fences Make Good Neighbours

Carlyle A. Thayer

INTRODUCTION

This chapter provides an overview of Cambodia's relations with Vietnam in the period following the 1991 political settlement of the Cambodian conflict. Particular attention is paid to the period since 2005, the year both sides adopted the guideline of "good neighbourliness, traditional friendship, comprehensive and long-term cooperation" for their bilateral relations.

The Kingdom of Cambodia and the Democratic Republic of Vietnam (DRV) formally established diplomatic relations on 24 June 1967. Since that time bilateral relations have reflected the vicissitudes of Cambodia's domestic politics. In 1970, for example, when Prince Norodom Sihanouk was deposed in a coup, the DRV granted recognition to his government-in-exile, the Royal Government of National Union of Kampuchea. In 1976, after the Khmer Rouge seized power and established Democratic Kampuchea, Vietnam (renamed the Socialist Republic of Vietnam, SRV) reopened its embassy in Phnom Penh.

As a result of mounting bilateral tensions and conflict along the border, Democratic Kampuchea severed diplomatic relations with the SRV on 31 December 1977. A year later Vietnam invaded Cambodia. The SRV granted recognition to its protégé, the People's Republic of Kampuchea (PRK, 1979–89), which renamed itself the State of Cambodia in 1989. As a result of an international agreement reached in Paris in October 1991, the SRV recognised the Supreme National Council and, following United Nations-sponsored elections in May 1993, subsequently recognised its successor, the Kingdom of Cambodia.

This chapter reviews Cambodia-Vietnam relations in four parts. Part one provides an overview of political relations. Part two discusses border issues, the most contentious aspect of bilateral relations. Parts three and four consider economic and defence relations, respectively.

POLITICAL RELATIONS

Vietnamese military forces invaded Cambodia in late 1978 and occupied the country until their unilateral withdrawal in September 1989. During this period, Vietnam's relations with the PRK were conducted under the framework of a 25-year treaty of friendship and cooperation. The restoration of the Kingdom of Cambodia in 1993 altered the framework of Cambodia-Vietnam bilateral relations. Under the new Constitution, Cambodia became a liberal democracy and a "permanently neutral and non-aligned country."[1]

United Nations-sponsored elections in May 1993 resulted in a coalition government comprising two main political parties, FUNCINPEC[2] and the Cambodian People's Party (CPP). In sum, Cambodia ceased being Vietnam's dependent ally and the ruling Cambodian People's Party, nurtured by Vietnam during its decade-long occupation, was now required to share power in a coalition government that contained political leaders who were hostile towards Vietnam. According to a veteran observer, "Hanoi's influence in Cambodia has been profoundly weakened and even relations with its former protégés are strained."[3] Two main issues have dominated Cambodia's relations with Vietnam since 1993 — Vietnamese residents and the land border (to be discussed in the following section).

Ethnic Vietnamese began settling in Cambodia during the French colonial era. Viet Minh forces operated in Cambodia during the anti-French War (1946–54) and communist Vietnamese forces established sanctuaries along the eastern border during the Vietnam conflict. Vietnamese communist sanctuaries became a political issue in 1970 and resulted in Khmer attacks on the ethnic Vietnamese community. Several thousand reportedly were killed and half a million fled to Vietnam. When the Khmer Rouge seized power in 1975 they expelled most of the Vietnamese. Those who remained were largely decimated by starvation and disease in the years that followed.[4]

During the period of Vietnamese occupation a large ethnic Vietnamese community re-emerged. They sought work in Phnom Penh, and settled in eastern Cambodia and in fishing villages around the Tonle Sap. The status of ethnic Vietnamese residents became a major political issue as negotiations for a comprehensive political settlement were completed. Under the terms of the United Nations-drafted Electoral Law, a qualified voter was defined as a Cambodian who was eighteen years or over, born in Cambodia, with a father or mother born in Cambodia, or a person outside Cambodia with a mother or father born in Cambodia.[5]

The three major anti-Vietnamese political parties — the Party of Democratic Kampuchea (Khmer Rouge), FUNCINPEC and the Khmer People's National Liberation Front (KPNLF headed by Son Sann) — alleged that there were one million illegal Vietnamese migrants who had come to colonise Cambodia and support the CPP in the forthcoming elections. These parties called for these Vietnamese to be disenfranchised and deported.

In this charged atmosphere over 30 Vietnamese were murdered in scattered incidents leading up to the May 1993 elections.[6] Vietnam lodged repeated protests. As pre-election violence mounted, tens of thousands of ethnic Vietnamese fled to Vietnam. Vietnam responded by sealing its border with Cambodia stranding an estimated 5,000 in no man's land.[7] Following the May 1993 elections and the formation of a coalition government, the status of these ethnic Vietnamese became the major irritant in Cambodia's relations with Vietnam.

In August 1993, the two co-prime ministers, Norodom Ranariddh and Hun Sen, visited Vietnam to reaffirm their commitment to improving bilateral relations. Their démarche was undercut when both King Sihanouk and Son Sann called for a review of border issues and redrawing of the boundary if necessary. In February 1994, Vietnam's Foreign Minister Nguyen Manh Cam visited Phnom Penh to discuss outstanding matters and to arrange for the visit by Prime Minister Vo Van Kiet. Kiet's trip in April of that year was the highest-level contact between Vietnam and the new Cambodian government. A joint communiqué stated that two commissions would be set up, one to discuss the status of ethnic Vietnamese and other to deliberate on border issues.[8]

The ethnic Vietnamese question nevertheless continued to surface as an irritant in bilateral relations particularly during national elections. In 1997, FUNCINPEC's campaign against ethnic Vietnamese drew Vietnamese diplomatic protests. Although the ethnic Vietnamese question was a major irritant in bilateral relations, this issue did not prevent the CPP-led government from developing close ties with Vietnam. Cambodia was slated to join the

Association of Southeast Asian Nations (ASEAN) in July 1997 but its membership was postponed due to a major domestic upheaval that resulted in the collapse of the coalition government and the exile of Norodom Ranariddh. These events strengthened the position of Prime Minister Hun Sen and the CPP. Vietnam strongly supported Cambodia's membership in ASEAN at this time.

Violence against ethnic Vietnamese, abetted by Cambodia's political parties, flared up in July 1998 during the election campaign, with the Cambodia-Vietnam friendship monument in Phnom Penh being vandalized during a demonstration. When the election results were announced, the CPP emerged as the winner. Vietnam, which had a strong stake in good ties with the CPP and in Cambodia's stability, lobbied strongly but unsuccessfully for Cambodia's admission at the informal ASEAN Summit held in Hanoi in December. Vietnam finally achieved success in April 1999 when consensus was reached on Cambodia's suitability and it was admitted as ASEAN's tenth member.[9]

After the 1998 elections the opposition parties continued to exploit the ethnic Vietnamese question. In June 1999, for example, anti-Vietnamese protests accompanied the visit of Vietnam Communist Party Secretary General Le Kha Phieu to Phnom Penh. Violence flared again in November when 200 Vietnamese residents were forcibly evicted from their homes in Phnom Penh. In November 2001, Vietnamese squatter settlements were set on fire during the state visit of President Tran Duc Luong.

During 2003, both FUNCINPEC and the Sam Rainsy Party once again adopted jingoistic anti-Vietnamese rhetoric and racial slurs during the election campaign. They charged the Vietnamese with threatening Khmer identity and national sovereignty. During the campaign Vietnamese residents were subjected to systematic violence. One analyst concluded, "Both ethnic Vietnamese and even mixed Vietnamese-Khmer are often subjected to evictions, extortion, and police brutality, as well as public discrimination by Khmer-language newspapers deploring 'invasions' by Vietnamese."[10] Despite the appeals to anti-Vietnamese sentiment by the opposition, the CPP strengthened its electoral margin over the 1998 election.

The consolidation of CPP rule from 1998 to 2003 set the stage for Cambodia and Vietnam to take their bilateral relations to the next level. In March 2005 the two countries agreed to guidelines for bilateral relations under the rubric of "good neighbourliness, traditional friendship, comprehensive and long-term cooperation."[11] This ushered in a period of sustained high-level interaction that broadened and deepened bilateral relations. (See Table 6.1)

TABLE 6.1
Cambodia-Vietnam High-Level Visits, 2005–2011

From Vietnam to Cambodia	From Cambodia to Vietnam
March/July 2006 Prime Minister Phan Van Khai	October 2005 Prime Minister Hun Sen
December 2006 Prime Minister Nguyen Tan Dung	March 2006 King Norodom Sihamoni
February 2007 President Nguyen Minh Triet	June 2006 President of the National Assembly Heng Samrin
April 2007 Chairman of the National Assembly Nguyen Phu Trong	June 2008 King Norodom Sihanouk
August 2007 Deputy Prime Minister and Minister for Foreign Affairs Pham Gia Khiem	November 2008 Prime Minister Hun Sen
December 2009 Secretary General Nong Duc Manh	November 2008 President of the Senate Chea Sim
August 2010 President Nguyen Minh Triet	January 2009 President of the National Assembly Heng Samrin
November 2010 Prime Minister Nguyen Tan Dung	December 2009 Prime Minister Hun Sen
April 2011 Prime Minister Nguyen Tan Dung	June 2010 King Norodom Sihamoni

Each Cambodian national election since 1993 has seen the CPP gain in electoral strength compared to its rivals. In 2008 the CPP won an absolute majority of the vote. The trend of CPP dominance has resulted in the lessening — but not ending — of the salience of the ethnic Vietnamese issue in domestic politics. Many ethnic Vietnamese remain stateless. In 2010, the U.S. State Department offered this assessment: "animosity continued toward ethnic Vietnamese, who were seen as a threat to the country and culture. Some groups, including political groups, continued to make strong anti-Vietnamese statements. They complained of political control of the CPP by the Vietnamese government, border encroachment, and other problems for which they held ethnic Vietnamese at least partially responsible".[12] The next section analyses the second major irritant in bilateral relations — border issues.

BORDER ISSUES

Border issues have featured prominently in Cambodia's relations with Vietnam since both countries gained independence from France. This section discusses border issues as an irritant in Cambodia's relations with Vietnam.

In the post-UN period, the activities of politically active anti-communist groups, or groups deemed hostile to the government in Hanoi, became a source of continuing concern to security authorities in Vietnam. In 1995, for example, several hundred personnel of the former Republic of Vietnam Army gathered in Cambodia and began acquiring weapons and conducting training programs aimed at the violent overthrow of the Vietnamese government. This group was funded by overseas Vietnamese in the United States. Their activities came to the notice of Cambodian authorities and in December six leaders were expelled.[13]

In November 2000, a group of 70 anti-communist Cambodian expatriates operating under the name Cambodian Freedom Fighters launched armed attacks on government buildings in Phnom Penh on the eve of a visit by President Tran Duc Luong. The Cambodian Freedom Fighters argued that the Hun Sen government lacked independence from Vietnam.[14] Cambodian security forces quickly dealt with the group but President Luong's visit was cancelled. In July 2001, Vietnam once again expressed its concern about the activities of anti-communist groups in Cambodia aimed at overthrowing the Vietnamese government.

In the first quarter of 2001 unrest broke out among the Degar people, an ethnic minority group living in Vietnam's Central Highlands.[15] The Degar claimed they were subject to religious persecution and loss of land. Vietnamese authorities accused them of trying to set up an autonomous state with financial backing from compatriots living in the United States. When Vietnamese authorities attempted to restore order an estimated 1,000 Degar crossed into Cambodia and sought sanctuary. Some were reportedly forced back into Vietnam by local authorities. As a result of this incident Vietnam's Minister for Public Security and Cambodia's Co-Minister for the Interior met and reached agreement on future border security arrangements.

In 2005 the United Nations High Commissioner for Refugees (UNHCR) brokered a five-year agreement with Cambodia and Vietnam. The UNHCR agreed to set up a processing camp where the Degar asylum seekers would be given the choice of resettlement in a third country or voluntary repatriation to Vietnam. By the end of 2010, 932 Degars were given refugee status and resettled. In early 2011, a further 55 Degar were resettled and ten were repatriated to Vietnam. Ten Degars are still awaiting a determination of their status.[16]

In June 2007, a Buddhist monk living in Vietnam, a member of the Khmer Krom ethnic minority, fled to Cambodia to escape what he claimed was religious persecution. Sympathetic Buddhists staged public protests outside the Vietnamese Embassy in Phnom Penh over what they alleged was mistreatment of ethnic Khmer monks in Vietnam.[17] The Cambodian government responded by banning the protests.

In addition to cross-border security issues, the borderline between Cambodia and Vietnam emerged as a contentious issue in Cambodian domestic politics following UN-sponsored elections in 1993. FUNCINPEC, the KPNLF and the Sam Rainsy Party rejected all border agreements and treaties signed between the People's Republic of Kampuchea and Vietnam on the basis that the PRK was a Vietnamese client, its independence was not recognised by the United Nations, and the border agreements favouring Vietnam were illegal.

The PRK and Vietnam have signed three major border agreements. The first agreement, signed in July 1982, delineated the historical waters between Cambodia and Vietnam. Cambodia's historical waters included the coast of Kampot province and Poulo Wai islands. Vietnam's historical waters included the coast of Kien Giang province and Phu Quoc and Tho Chu islands. The 1982 agreement did not establish a maritime boundary and overlapping claims remain unresolved to this day.[18]

In 1983 Cambodia and Vietnam signed a land boundary treaty that recognized the border as defined on a 1:100,000 scale map published by the Geographic Service of Indochina. In 1985, Cambodia and Vietnam adopted and ratified the Treaty on the Delimitation of the Vietnam-Kampuchea Frontier. This treaty accepted the border demarcation line at the time of Cambodia's independence. Between 1985 and 1988 the two sides erected seventy-two markers along a 200-kilometre stretch of their 1,137 km border.[19]

After the formation of a coalition government in 1993, both King Sihanouk and Prime Minister Ranariddh publicly rejected the treaties signed by the PRK. In 1996, King Sihanouk accused Vietnam of nibbling away Cambodian territory by moving border markers 300 to 400 metres into Svay Rieng province. Prime Minister Ranariddh went further and called Vietnamese encroachments a full invasion and threatened to use force.

In April 1996, Prime Minister Vo Van Kiet led a delegation to Phnom Penh for border discussions with Co-Prime Ministers Ranarridh and Hun Sen. Kiet proposed the creation of a formal mechanism to deal with border issues at local, provincial, and central levels. The following month Cambodia rejected Kiet's proposals.[20] During the 1998 election campaign, Prince Ranariddh accused Hun Sen of inaction in the face of Vietnamese encroachments. At the next election in 2003, the Sam Rainsy Party criticised Hun Sen for not standing up to Vietnam on border issues and promised to recover lost territories.

In response to domestic pressures, Cambodia (now firmly under the leadership of Hun Sen) and Vietnam negotiated and signed a "Supplementary Treaty to the Treaty on the Delimitation of the State Border of 1985" on 10 October 2005 in Hanoi.[21] The text of the 2005 treaty was virtually identical with the text of the 1985 treaty. The 2005 treaty resulted in the adjustment of six border markers in the Central Highlands because of mapping errors in the earlier treaty.

The 2005 border treaty has done much to defuse the borderline as an irritant in bilateral relations. Both Cambodia and Vietnam set up their respective Commissions on Border Demarcation and Marker Planting. The first meeting was held in Hanoi in May 1996 where agreement was reached to plant markers at six border gates by the end of the year and to mark the entire border by the end of 2008. The national border commissions continue to meet regularly alternating between Cambodia and Vietnam.

In September 2006, on the first anniversary of the 2005 border treaty, Prime Ministers Hun Sen and Nguyen Tan Dung attended the inauguration ceremony of border marker no. 171 at the Moc Bai-Bavet international border gate, the main crossing point between Cambodia and Vietnam. However, the border issues as an irritant in bilateral relations did not disappear entirely. Opposition leader Sam Rainsy continued to claim that Vietnam was using the border demarcation process to encroach on Cambodian land. In December 2009, Sam Rainsy and a group of supporters removed border posts in protest. Rainsy was convicted in court for his actions; he fled abroad to escape imprisonment.[22]

In March 2009, the joint Cambodia-Vietnam Commission on Border Demarcation and Marker Planting held its third meeting in Ho Chi Minh City and drew up a plan on border demarcation covering the period 2009–12. In April 2011, Cambodia and Vietnam signed a Memorandum of Understanding on demarcating the remaining area of the land boundary before the end of 2011 (a deadline since extended to the end of 2012).

ECONOMIC RELATIONS

The development of Cambodia-Vietnam economic relations reflects the improvement in managing cross-border security issues as well as progress in physically demarcating the border itself. Economic relations are managed through a Cambodia-Vietnam Joint Commission for Economic, Cultural, Scientific and Technological Cooperation. In November 2001, during the visit of President Tran Duc Luong, Cambodia and Vietnam codified their economic relations in a Joint Declaration on the Framework for Bilateral Cooperation. A major turning point was reached in September 2006 when Prime Ministers Hun Sen and Nguyen Tan Dung met and agreed to increase two-way trade to US$2 billion by 2010 and to facilitate cross-border investment. They also assigned their respective ministries of transport to develop cross-border road and rail routes.[23]

The 2005 border treaty laid the foundation for Cambodia to promote the development of Special Economic Zones on its border with Vietnam. These special zones were designed to attract investment through tax breaks and special services. The special zones also took advantage of cheaper electricity provided by Vietnam to boost competitiveness and encourage development beyond Phnom Penh.[24] Since 2007, Cambodia has licensed six Special Economic Zones, two of which have been set up and four of which are in the development stage, including a special zone for agricultural processing valued at US$100 million and due for completion by 2015.

In 2006 two-way trade stood at US$950 million. As a result of the Cambodia-Vietnam bilateral trade agreement reached in 2007, Vietnamese investments in the special economic zones and a downturn in Cambodia's trade with Thailand following a border dispute in 2008, Cambodia-Vietnam two-way trade increased steadily from US$1.2 billion (2007) to US$1.7 billion (2008). In 2008 and 2009 Cambodia and Vietnam adopted a number of measures to facilitate trade.[25] In November 2008 they signed five agreements including: visa exemption, goods transit, railway linkages, information exchanges between ministries and national radio stations. The following year Cambodia and Vietnam signed a treaty on cross-border navigation on the Mekong River.

The tenth Cambodia-Vietnam Joint Commission for Economic, Cultural and Scientific Technological Cooperation, which met in October 2008, set a target of US$2 billion in two-way trade by 2010. Due to the global financial crisis this target was not achieved. Two-way trade fell to US$1.3 billion in 2009 before rising to US$1.8 billion in 2010. Vietnam's major exports to Cambodia include agricultural machinery, pesticides, farm produce, seafood and petrol, while Cambodia's exports to Vietnam comprise grains, tobacco, cassava and wood products. Vietnam ranks third among Cambodia's ASEAN trading partners and sixth overall.[26] Bilateral trade is expected to reach US$6.5 billion by 2015.

Cambodia and Vietnam have also promoted trade through the development of cross-border linkages between provinces. In May 2010, for example, Cambodia's Minister of Commerce and his Vietnamese counterpart, the Minister of Industry and Trade, co-hosted a conference in Long An province attended by officials and businessmen from the border provinces.

This meeting agreed to simplify administrative procedures at border gates and upgrade technical infrastructure. The meeting also called for increased investment in services, the special economic zones and border markets over the next decade.

Vietnamese investment in Cambodia picked up as a result of the general improvement in bilateral relations after 2005 and due to a downturn in Thai-Cambodian relations in 2008–09. In November 2008, for example, Prime Minister Hun Sen paid an official visit to Vietnam and requested increased Vietnamese investment in Cambodia's rubber, oil and gas, electricity, and post and telecommunications sectors.[27] His counterpart, Prime Minister Nguyen Tan Dung, responded affirmatively.

According to Vietnam's Ministry of Planning and Investment, in 2009 Vietnamese entrepreneurs had invested in 63 projects with a combined total registered capital of over US$900 million of which US$400 was invested in 2009 alone. In December 2009, the two prime ministers co-hosted the first investment promotion conference in Ho Chi Minh City.[28] A Memorandum of Understanding was signed to facilitate increased Vietnamese investment in Cambodia including electricity generation, fertilizer production, rubber plantations, and bauxite mining. It was estimated that there was a potential for US$12 billion in investments from Vietnam.[29]

In August 2010, Prime Minister Hun Sen announced that feasibility studies would be carried out for two hydroelectric power projects to be undertaken by Vietnam. He also stated that Cambodia would allocate 100,000 hectares to a Vietnamese firm to plant and harvest rubber.[30] By the end of 2010 Vietnamese investors were involved in nearly ninety projects in Cambodia embracing agriculture, forestry, rubber, minerals and mining, oil and gas exploration, electricity generation, aviation, telecommunications, finance, insurance and banking. The combined total capital of these projects was estimated at more than US$2 billion.

Cambodian-Vietnam economic relations received a fillip in November 2010 when the two prime ministers met in Phnom Penh.[31] Prime Minister Nguyen Tan Dung asked for more cooperation in aviation, banking, rubber, customs procedure facilitation and greater encouragement for Vietnamese investors and businessmen. Dung also sought approval for a Vietnamese company to explore for oil and gas in Cambodia. Prime Minister Hun Sen, for his part, asked Vietnam to provide at least 170 MW of power from the end of 2010. At the conclusion of their talks, the prime ministers reached agreement to boost trade and investment in banking, power generation, mining, oil and gas, industrial crops and transport by encouraging cooperation between provinces. Hun Sen also agreed to accelerate formalities to enable Vietnamese companies to build the second Se San hydropower dam.

In April 2011, Prime Minister Nguyen Tan Dung returned to Cambodia to attend the second Cambodia-Vietnam Investment-Commerce-Tourism Promotion Forum co-hosted by Prime Minister Hun Sen.[32] This event witnessed the signing of cooperation agreements covering aviation, banking, telecommunication, hydroelectricity, mining, rubber, and sugarcane. Of particular note was the signing of the amendment to the agreement on the establishment of Cambodia Angkor Air to encourage tourism. Cambodia Angkor Air is a joint venture between the Cambodian government, which holds a fifty-one per cent share, and Vietnam Airlines, which has invested US$100 million. Both prime ministers also attended the opening of the Cambodia-Vietnam Securities Joint Stock Co. and ceremonies in which investment licenses were handed over to Vietnamese businesses.

DEFENCE RELATIONS

Vietnam created the PRK armed forces during its decade-long occupation. When the comprehensive political settlement on Cambodia was reached in 1991, Vietnam like all other signatories was required to cease providing military assistance. Vietnam complied with its international requirements. Indeed, in 1994, after the formation of the first coalition government when Cambodia approached Vietnam for military assistance to defeat Khmer Rouge remnants it was turned down.[33]

Defence relations between Cambodia and Vietnam were gradually restored after the 1998 elections. This section highlights three aspects of Cambodia-Vietnam defence relations: repatriation of the remains of Vietnamese combatants, high-level exchanges, and joint naval patrols. (See Table 6.2)

In 2000, Cambodia and Vietnam signed an agreement to cooperate in the recovery of the remains of an estimated 19,500 Vietnamese combatants from Cambodia.[34] In 2001, both sides established their respective State Committee for the Repatriation of Remains of Vietnamese Army Volunteers in Cambodia. These committees continue to meet on an annual basis to review past efforts and to agree on a work program for the following year. In May 2001, for example, the Cambodian and Vietnamese State Committees agreed on an action plan and two months later recovery teams from the military commands of Vietnam's Tay Ninh, Long An and Binh Phuoc provinces began joint excavations with their Cambodian counterparts. By the end of 2002 the remains of nearly 4,000 troops had been repatriated, a figure that rose to 6,569 by the end of 2004 and 10,000 by the end of 2007.[35]

In August 2002, Vietnam's Defence Minister, Lt. General Pham Van Tra, and Cambodia's Co-Ministers of National Defence General Tea Banh

TABLE 6.2
High-level Defence Exchanges, 2005–2011

Vietnamese Delegations to Cambodia	Cambodian Delegations to Vietnam
May 2005 Lt. Gen. Phung Trung Kien, Deputy Minister of National Defence	March 2005 General Ke Kim Yan, Commander in Chief Royal Cambodian Armed Forces (RCAF)
January 2006 Vice Admiral Nguyen Van Hien, Commander Vietnam People's Army (VPA) Navy	December 2005 General Tea Banh and General Nhek Bunchhay, Co-Ministers of National Defence
September 2006 Lt. Gen. Nguyen Khac Vien, Chief of the General Staff	June 2007 General Neang Phat, Secretary of State, Ministry of National Defence
January 2007 Lt. Gen. Pham Hong Thanh, Vietnam People's Army	October 2007 General Ke Kim Yan, Commander in Chief RCAF
March 2007 General Phung Quang Thanh, Minister of National Defence	October 2007 General Pol Saroeun, State Committee for the Repatriation of Remains of Vietnamese Army Volunteers in Cambodia
June 2007 Lt. Gen. Le Van Dung, Director, VPA General Political Department	March 2008 General Tea Banh, Minister of National Defence
January 2008 Lt. Gen. Bui Van Huan, State Committee for the Repatriation of Remains of Vietnamese Army Volunteers in Cambodia	March 2009 General Pol Saroeun, Commander in Chief RCAF
March 2008 Maj. Gen. Pham Ngoc Hoa, VPA General Staff	June 2009 General Neang Phat, Minister of State, Ministry of National Defence
February 2009 General Phung Quang Thanh, Minister of National Defence	September 2009 Ministry of National Defence, General Department of Logistics and Finance
September 2009 Maj. Gen. Nguyen Phuoc Loi, Deputy Commander VPA Border Guard	February 2010 General Dien Sarun, Deputy Chief of Staff, High Command Guards
August 2010 General Le Van Dung, Director, VPA General Political Department	February 2010 General Tea Banh, Minister of National Defence
September 2010 Lt. Gen. Nguyen Chi Vinh, Deputy Minister of National Defence	August 2010 Maj. Gen. Sam Sarin, Commander, RCAF Artillery High Command
March 2011 General Phung Quang Thanh, Minister of National Defence	October 2010 General Tea Banh, Minister of National Defence

and Prince Sisowath Sereyrath, signed a Memorandum of Understanding (MOU) on defence cooperation. The MOU provided for future high-level exchanges (see Table 6.2), military technical cooperation and exchanges of experience in the role of the military in national construction and defence.[36]

With the step-up in political relations in 2005, the Cambodian and Vietnamese defence ministries initiated the practice of signing annual protocols on defence cooperation.

In December 2005, Cambodia's Co-Ministers of National Defence visited Hanoi for discussions with their Vietnamese counterpart. The agenda for this meeting covered repatriation of Vietnamese remains, border demarcation and border security, and future defence cooperation activities (high-level visits, cooperation between general staffs, military education and training).[37] Both sides also agreed that their respective defence ministries should cooperate in implementing programs to alleviate poverty for people living in border areas.[38] In 2008, defence cooperation was expanded to include exchanges between military hospitals and research institutes.

Three issues have become standard agenda items at all high-level discussions. For example, at the most recent meeting between defence ministers held in Siem Reap in March 2011, Generals Tea Banh and Phung Quang Thanh discussed the repatriation of the remains of fallen soldiers, border demarcation and border security, and defence cooperation activities. The two defence ministers signed an MOU outlining future activities including Vietnamese training for RCAF personnel.[39]

Cooperation between the Royal Cambodian Navy and the Vietnam People's Army Navy commenced in September 2002 with the visit of the Cambodian naval commander to Vietnam at the invitation of his counterpart. In December 2005, during the visit to Vietnam by Cambodia's Co-Ministers of National Defence, Vietnam proposed that the two sides conduct joint naval patrols at sea. In January the following year, Vietnam donated two patrol boats to the Royal Cambodian Navy.[40]

In March 2008, the Cambodian and Vietnamese defence ministers agreed to conduct joint maritime patrols and to exchange information on search and rescue at sea.[41] By the end of the year it was announced that combined naval forces had conducted three patrols in the waters of the Gulf of Thailand. These patrols were aimed at providing security for fishermen as well as search-and-rescue training and cultural and sport exchanges. The Cambodian and Vietnamese naval commands set up a communications channel to exchange information and "jointly address issues as they arise."[42] In September 2010, two VPA naval ships paid their first port call to Cambodia since the end of the Cambodian conflict.[43]

CONCLUSION

Two major issues — the status of ethnic Vietnamese residents and border demarcation issues — have bedevilled bilateral relations between Cambodia and Vietnam since 1991. Both issues were seized upon by political parties in Cambodia for domestic advantage and this opportunistic posturing exacerbated their resolution. Both issues affected political, economic and defence relations.

As the political balance of power in Cambodia shifted towards the consolidation of CPP rule under the prime ministership of Hun Sen, the Cambodian government was empowered to address these issues. A major turning point came in 2005 when Cambodia and Vietnam adopted the expression "good neighbourliness, traditional friendship, comprehensive and long-term cooperation" as the framework for bilateral relations. In 2005, Cambodia and Vietnam signed a supplementary border treaty that gave legal status to previous agreements and which laid the basis for the physical demarcation of their common border. In the meantime, the ethnic Vietnamese question has receded in importance as a domestic issue. Cooperation in the recovery and repatriation of the remains of fallen Vietnamese combatants will soon close this chapter in bilateral relations.

After 2005 Cambodia and Vietnam began to develop extensive economic and defence relations. Vietnam is one of Cambodia's major trade and investment partners. Defence cooperation has contributed towards creating an environment conducive to economic development by stabilising the border and contributing to good order at sea. Even after the last border marker is laid the management of cross-border issues will still demand continuing attention by both Cambodia and Vietnam. Whereas in the past an ill-defined border contributed to insecurities on both sides, an agreed border will demonstrate Robert Frost's adage that "good fences make good neighbours".

Notes

1. The Constitution of the Kingdom of Cambodia, 21 September 1993 <http://www.embassy.org/cambodia/cambodia/constitution.htm>.
2. *Front Uni National pour un Cambodge Indépendant, Neutre, Pacifique, et Coopératif* (National United Front for an Independent, Neutral, Peaceful, and Cooperative Cambodia).
3. Dorothy R. Avery, "Vietnam in 1992: Win Some; Lose Some". *Asian Survey* 33, no. 1 (January–February 1993): 73.
4. Ramses Amer, "Cambodia and Vietnam: A Troubled Relationship". In *International Relations in Southeast Asia: Between Bilteralism and Multilateralism*, edited by N. Ganesan and Ramses Amer (Singapore: Institute of Southeast Asian Studies, 2010), p. 105.
5. Gary Klintworth, "Cambodia 1992: Hopes fading". In *Southeast Asian Affairs 1993*, edited by Daljit Singh (Singapore: Institute of Southeast Asian Studies, 1993), p. 124.

6. Frederick Z. Brown, "Cambodia in 1992: Peace at Peril". *Asian Survey* 33, no. 1 (January–February 1993): 89.
7. Frank Frost, "Cambodia: From UNTAC to Royal Government". In *Southeast Asian Affairs 1994*, edited by Daljit Singh (Singapore: Institute of Southeast Asian Studies, 1994), p. 97.
8. Frederick Z. Brown and Laura McGrew, "Cambodia: The Royal Government on Trial". In *Southeast Asian Affairs 1995*, edited by Daljit Singh and Liak Teng Kiat (Singapore: Institute of Southeast Asian Studies, 1995), p. 138.
9. Carlyle A. Thayer, "Southeast Asia: Challenges to Unity and Regime Legitimacy". In *Southeast Asian Affairs 1999*, edited by Daljit Singh and John Funston (Singapore: Institute of Southeast Asian Studies, 1999), pp. 11–12.
10. Robert B. Albritton, "Cambodia in 2003: On the Road to Democratic Consolidation". *Asian Survey* 44, no. 1 (January–February 2004): 106.
11. "Vietnam-Cambodia Relations", Socialist Republic of Vietnam, Ministry of Foreign Affairs, December 2009 <http:www.mofa.gov.vn> (accessed 12 April 2011).
12. U.S. Department of State, "Cambodia". *Country Reports on Human Rights 2010*.
13. Nick J. Freeman, "Vietnam: Better Managing Reform". In *Southeast Asian Affairs 1996*, edited by Daljit Singh and Liak Teng Kiat (Singapore: Institute of Southeast Asian Studies, 1996), p. 399.
14. Irene V. Langran, "Cambodia in 2000 New Hopes Are Challenged". *Asian Survey* 41, no. 1 (January–February 2001): 157 and John Marston, "Cambodia: Transitional Pressures and Local Agendas". In *Southeast Asian Affairs 2002*, edited by Daljit Singh and Anthony J. Smith (Singapore: Institute of Southeast Asian Studies, 2002), pp. 100–02.
15. Marston, "Cambodia: Transitional Pressures and Local Agendas", pp. 104–05 and Ang Cheng Guan, "Vietnam: Another Milestone and the Country Plods on". In *Southeast Asian Affairs 2002*, edited by Daljit Singh and Anthony J. Smith (Singapore: Institute of Southeast Asian Studies, 2002), p. 351.
16. Associated Press, "UN Refugee Site in Cambodia Closes", 15 February 2011.
17. Caroline Hughes, "Cambodia in 2007: Development and Dispossession". *Asian Survey* 48, no. 1 (January–February): 74.
18. Ramses Amer, "The Border Conflicts Between Cambodia and Vietnam". *Boundary and Security Bulletin* 5, no. 2 (1997): 80.
19. Vu Le Thai Hoang, "Vietnam's Quest for Influence and Its Implications for the Management of Border Disputes with Laos and Cambodia". *Journal of Current Southeast Asian Affairs* 26, no. 2 (2007): 7.
20. Sorpong Peou, "Cambodia: A New Glimpse of Hope?". In *Southeast Asian Affairs 1997*, edited by Daljit Singh (Singapore: Institute of Southeast Asian Studies, 1997), pp. 96–97.
21. Oskar Weggel, "Cambodia in 2005: Year of Reassurance". *Asian Survey* 46, no. 1 (January–February 2006): 159–60.
22. Caroline Hughes, "Cambodia in 2009: The Party's not over yet". In *Southeast*

Asian Affairs 2010, edited by Daljit Singh (Singapore: Institute of Southeast Asian Studies, 2010), p. 98 and Steve Heder, "Cambodia in 2010: Hun Sen's Further Consolidation". *Asian Survey* 51, no. 1 (January–February 2011): 212.
23. "Vietnam and Cambodia inaugurate border marker No. 171". *VietNamNet Bridge*, 28 September 2006.
24. Hughes, "Cambodia in 2007: Development and Dispossession", pp. 69–70.
25. Carlyle A. Thayer, "Cambodia: The Cambodian People's Party Consolidates Power". In *Southeast Asian Affairs 2009*, edited by Daljit Singh (Singapore: Institute of Southeast Asian Studies, 2009), p. 96 and Alexander L. Vuving, "Vietnam: A Tale of Four Players". In *Southeast Asian Affairs 2010*, edited by Daljit Singh (Singapore: Institute of Southeast Asian Studies, 2010), p. 385.
26. "Vietnam-Cambodia Relations", and "PM Nguyen Tan Dung visits Cambodia", *Saigon Daily*, 24 April 2011.
27. Thayer, "Cambodia: The Cambodian People's Party Consolidates Power", p. 96.
28. "Conference to boost investment in Cambodia". Vietnam News Agency, 21 December 2009.
29. Jared Ferrie, "A thin line between Cambodia and Vietnam". *Asia Times Online*, 28 January 2010.
30. David Chandler, "Cambodia in 2009: Plus C'est la M'me Chose". *Asian Survey* 50, no. 1 (January–February 2010): 234.
31. Agence Kampuchea Presse, 15 November 2010.
32. Vietnam News Agency, 22 April 2011 and Voice of Vietnam, 24 April 2011.
33. "Request to Replenish Stockpile Rejected". *Bangkok Post*, 31 March 1994; Reuters, "Vietnam Rules out Military Aid for Cambodia", 10 June 1994; and "Minister Rules Out Military Aid to Cambodia", Voice of Vietnam External Service, 11 June 1994.
34. Associated Press, 26 December 2002 and Agence France Presse, 27 January 2005.
35. Agence France Presse, 19 July 2001, 25 August 2002 and 27 January 2005; Associated Press, 26 December 2002; and *Nhan Dan Online*, 8 January 2008.
36. Vietnam News Agency, 22 August 2002.
37. "Cambodian PM receives Vietnam's general staff chief". *VietNamNet Bridge*, 2 October 2006; and Vietnam News Service, "VN, Cambodia boost national defence co-operation". *Viet Nam News*, 11 March 2011.
38. *Nhan Dan Online*, 22 December 2005; *Thanh Nien News*, 22 December 2005; and Vietnam News Agency, 24 December 2005.
39. Vietnam News Agency, *VietNamNet Bridge*, 11 March 2011; Voice of Vietnam News, 11 March 2010; and Vietnam News Service, "VN, Cambodia boost national defence co-operation". *Viet Nam News*, 11 March 2011.
40. Vietnam News Agency, 11 January 2006.
41. Vietnam News Agency, "President reiterates good ties with Cambodia". *VietNamNet Bridge*, 26 March 2008.
42. *Quan Doi Nhan Dan Online*, 28 November 2008.
43. *Quan Doi Nhan Dan Online*, 5 September 2010.

CAMBODIA AND OTHERS

7

CAMBODIA'S RELATIONS WITH CHINA

A Steadfast Friendship

Julio A. Jeldres

On 14 November 1991, a Chinese VIP Boeing 707 left Beijing airport carrying the former Cambodian King and Head of State, Norodom Sihanouk, back to his homeland after more than twelve years of exile in China. Also making a return to Cambodia was China's newly-appointed Permanent Representative to the Supreme National Council of Cambodia (SNC),[1] Ambassador Fu Xuezhang.[2] Widely recognized as one of China's foremost Cambodia specialists, Fu had been appointed Special Counsellor to the Chinese Embassy when it re-opened in Phnom Penh in May 1975, a month after the victory of the Khmer Rouge. Fu's return trip to Cambodia, after an absence of almost thirteen years, was emotional for him, as he had been forced to evacuate the Chinese Embassy in Phnom Penh in January 1979, following the Vietnamese invasion of Cambodia. Fu had assisted Ambassador Sun Hao in moving the Chinese mission to the Cardamom Mountains at the request of the about-to-be overthrown Democratic Kampuchea regime. The embassy became "a mobile embassy" until 11 April 1979, when the Chinese Foreign Ministry had ordered the Chinese diplomats to withdraw to Thailand.[3]

The Chinese embassy in Cambodia had been the first fully functioning embassy to re-open in Phnom Penh after the Khmer Rouge's victory. China was given that special honour because it was the strongest foreign ally of Democratic Kampuchea.[4]

Fu Xuezhang was now returning to Phnom Penh in his new role as China's principal representative in Cambodia. His instructions were to quickly recover the ground lost during China's absence from Phnom Penh. The Chinese diplomats dispatched to Phnom Penh to take care of the re-opening of the embassy immediately made their presence felt. They moved into their old embassy compound, which had been used as a guesthouse by the Cambodian Ministry of Defence, rather than staying at a hotel.[5]

CHINA AS PROTECTOR AND FRIEND OF CAMBODIA

Since Cambodia gained its independence in 1953, Cambodia's relations with China had been based on the long-held premise by Cambodian leaders that China could act as a protector and friend of Cambodia, when the latter faced its rapacious neighbours, Thailand and Vietnam. Norodom Sihanouk initiated Cambodia's modern relationship with China in July 1958 when it recognized Beijing against the advice of the Western world. Later, Sihanouk elaborated that China was "the explanation and the cause of our survival because of a balance of menaces between China and hostile Vietnam and Thai troops who wanted to kill Cambodia",[6] while telling a US reporter that "the influence of France and the United States may come and go, but China was a constant factor in Southeast Asia".[7] China remained a staunch ally of Sihanouk and after his overthrow in 1970; it closed its embassy in Phnom Penh.

China's reappearance on the Phnom Penh diplomatic scene in November 1991 was the result of calculated diplomatic actions which began in the framework of the Jakarta Informal Meeting on Cambodia in September 1990, when Phnom Penh representatives and a Chinese Vice-Foreign Minister met. Hun Sen, who had become Prime Minister following Vietnam's invasion of Cambodia, had written in 1988 a long essay suggesting that China was the root of everything that was evil in Cambodia, and had never visited China until July 1991, when Norodom Sihanouk in his capacity as SNC chairman organized a meeting of the SNC in Beijing.[8]

The arrival of the Chinese diplomats in Phnom Penh coincided with moves by Cambodian authorities to provide the local Chinese community with restored freedoms such as the right to re-open Chinese schools, to celebrate the Chinese New Year and to follow religious practices such as ancestor worship, which had been prohibited since the Khmer Rouge takeover of the country. The efforts by the Cambodian authorities were aimed at improving their own dialogue and ties with China as well as to try to detach Beijing from its Khmer Rouge protégées.[9]

The first challenge posed to the re-established Cambodia-China relationship was the attack against Khmer Rouge leaders and members of the SNC, Khieu Samphan and Son Sen, on 27 November 1991 upon their return to Phnom Penh. China was still the leading foreign supporter of the Khmer Rouge and Ambassador Fu hastily left Phnom Penh and established himself at the Chinese Embassy in Bangkok to observe developments in Cambodia. At the same time, the official visit to Cambodia by Foreign Minister Qian Qichen, originally scheduled for 5–6 December 1991 was postponed "for technical reasons".[10] According to Agence France-Presse, a commentary in the People's Daily of 29 November 1991, "strongly suggested the attack was premeditated, saying that "the Phnom Penh authorities (meaning the State of Cambodia), had an unshakable responsibility with regards to it".[11]

At a meeting in the Thai resort of Pattaya, Ambassador Fu informed Sihanouk of the postponement of the Chinese Foreign Minister's visit and of China's anger over the attacks on the two Khmer Rouge members of the SNC. Sihanouk told Fu that the invitation was open- ended and the Chinese Foreign Minister could visit at any time. He further reassured Ambassador Fu that he had received formal assurances that the safety of the Khmer Rouge representatives at the SNC would be properly assured by the Cambodian authorities. Sihanouk was in Pattaya for an emergency meeting of the SNC with the co-presidents, France and Indonesia, of the Paris International Conference on Cambodia and the United Nations, to discuss the attack on the Khmer Rouge members of the SNC and actions to prevent the recurrence of such attacks. Sihanouk also accepted a letter of accreditation from Ambassador Fu and urged him to begin his official role as China's envoy right away.[12]

Ambassador Fu joined the crisis meetings taking place in Pattaya among the representatives of the five permanent members of the UN, known as the P-5, which were empowered to ensure that the Paris Agreements on Cambodia were implemented, and also the meetings between the P-5 and the four Cambodian factions.

Throughout the transitional period, from November 1991 to September 1993, the Chinese diplomats maintained a robust, yet discreet, presence, attending and actively participating in all meetings of the SNC and keeping regular contacts with all the SNC members. Ambassador Fu forthrightly urged the four Cambodian factions "to exercise military restraint to implement the Paris Peace Accords, so as to resume peace in their country."[13]

In February 1992, Foreign Minister Qian Qichen's visit took place, and during a meeting with the SNC, the Chinese Foreign Minister told them that "The present world situation favours the settlement of the Cambodian issue and that despite the various differences among the Cambodian factions, it is the trend and the desire of the people that the factions realize national reconciliation."[14]

Just before the UN-supervised parliamentary elections in Cambodia, China made it known that it would not support any Cambodian party which resumed the civil war,[15] while using its veto powers at the UN Security Council both to warn its Khmer Rouge protégés and to encourage national reconciliation among the Cambodian factions. According to a Chinese diplomat, when the Khmer Rouge nominal leader, Khieu Samphan, visited Beijing in May 1993, he was warned by Chinese officials "not to disrupt the elections."[16]

The year 1992 saw also the first official visit to China of a delegation of the Cambodian People's Party, the successor to the People's Revolutionary Party of Kampuchea, led by its Chairman, Chea Sim, who was also President of the National Assembly of the State of Cambodia (SOC).[17] Chea Sim's visit established the first party-to-party contact between the Cambodian People's Party (CPP) and the Chinese Communist Party. Until the Chea Sim visit, China had shunned the CPP. However, in spite of these new contacts with the CPP, China and its leaders were still supporting the national reconciliation policy of Samdech Norodom Sihanouk which according to the then Chinese Prime Minister, Li Peng "was the most prudent policy for Cambodia to follow."[18]

Sihanouk's policy of national reconciliation included the participation of Khmer Rouge personalities in a new government formed after general elections had been held. This was not a premise agreeable to the CPP, which preferred no Khmer Rouge participation in any future government of Cambodia. This Chinese support of Norodom Sihanouk's policy of national reconciliation would remain in force, at least publicly, until the death of paramount leader Deng Xiaoping in 1997.[19]

Once a National Assembly was elected, a provisional government was put in place and Cambodia became again a monarchy in September 1993. China moved to formalize its diplomatic relations with Cambodia by elevating Ambassador Fu to the rank of Ambassador Extraordinary and Plenipotentiary to the Kingdom of Cambodia, while exchange visits between officials of the two countries became regular occurrences. At the same time, Cambodia sent a new Ambassador to China, who took over the diplomatic mission which had for more than 15 years been in the hands of Khmer Rouge diplomats.

At about this time also there was an important yet little-noticed, change in China's attitude towards Cambodia. This was that from there on the relationship was based on the higher interests of the two countries and not any longer on the privileged rapport of its leaders at a personal level. China, therefore, maintained even-handed relations with the winner of the national elections, the royalist FUNCINPEC party, as well as with the losers, the Cambodian People's Party and other minor parties, not only because of the prestige of the role retained by FUNCINPEC's founder and former president, King Sihanouk, but also because of the royalist party's capacity to counterbalance Hun Sen's dominant role, about which China was not yet certain.[20]

Another significant change in China's attitude was that, henceforth the Cambodian royal family would no longer be the privileged interlocutors of Chinese leaders in their relations with Phnom Penh, and China began cultivating other actors in the Cambodian political scene. The often edgy relations between Hun Sen and King Sihanouk, after the latter's coronation could not but lead Beijing to Hun Sen, particularly after the difficult days of July 1997, when many royalists, well-known to China, were killed often in atrocious circumstances. Indeed, King Sihanouk could no longer rely on his personal rapport with this so-called fourth generation of Chinese leaders, even during his extended stays in the Chinese capital for medical treatment.[21]

China, while reiterating that it did not interfere in other countries internal affairs, also made it known when necessary that it did not agree with legislation or measures adopted by the Cambodian government. For instance, when Cambodia outlawed the Khmer Rouge and all its political institutions in July 1994, China felt that the Royal Government had made a mistake as this would keep the armed conflict between the Royal Government and the Khmer Rouge going for years, preventing the reconstruction, rehabilitation and development of Cambodia.[22]

Similarly, during a meeting between Cambodian Foreign Minister, Prince Norodom Sirivudh and Chinese Foreign Minister, Qian Qichen, in Bangkok on 24 July 1994, Qian, speaking English, reiterated that China supported the policy of national reconciliation of King Sihanouk, including the participation of the Democratic Kampuchea (Khmer Rouge) Party in some governmental positions.[23]

The Chinese Embassy was extremely well-informed, relying in particular on a newly-established network of Sino-Khmer businessmen who had returned home to Cambodia from Australia, France, Hong Kong, Macau and the United States. They had exiled themselves prior to the Khmer Rouge takeover of Cambodia, and now upon their return to Cambodia they had started profitable businesses, while the UN was administering Cambodia, thus providing the Embassy with a wide network of information.

However, some of these Chinese merchants developed a close relationship with the Cambodian People's Party and provided the party with generous financial grants for its political activities. In fact, they had no alternative, as the Cambodian People's Party tightly controlled the administration, police and army and never allowed the United Nations to take over the five principal ministries of the government, as stipulated in the Paris Agreements. As a result, the Chinese Embassy began to develop good contacts among CPP cadres and officials, which in turn antagonised the royalist FUNCINPEC party.[24]

TAIWAN FACTOR

Incensed by China's new-found friendship, FUNCINPEC officials began to court pro-Taiwan Chinese in Cambodia while pushing for some kind of official relationship with the island. In September 1994, Cambodia and Taiwan signed a memorandum of understanding, paving the way for the opening of representative offices in Phnom Penh and Taipei. Then in March 1995, the deputy major of Phnom Penh, Khau Meng Hean, a confidant of Prince Ranariddh, the first Co-Premier[25] in the FUNCINPEC-CPP coalition government, became the first Cambodian official to visit Taipei since 1975, where he made some disparaging remarks that offended China.[26]

In October 1995, the Cambodian Ambassador in Beijing wrote to the two Co-Premiers, Prince Ranariddh and Hun Sen, warning that China was "furious about the presence of the Governor of Phnom Penh, the Vice-Ministers of Agriculture and Environment and other senior Cambodian officials, mostly from FUNCINPEC at the reception hosted by the Taiwan Commercial and Cultural Office in Phnom Penh to commemorate Taiwan's National Day on 10 October 1995." The ambassador reported that the Chinese ambassador in Phnom Penh had called on the Cambodian Secretary of State for Foreign Affairs to protest about this matter, but the latter had told the Chinese envoy that "she could do nothing about it as no one listened to her.[27] The ambassador went on to say that "China was willing to sacrifice everything, even billions of dollars and go as far as breaking diplomatic relations on issues concerning national sovereignty and in particular that of Taiwan".[28]

As the relationship between the two co-premiers deteriorated, the relationship between China and FUNCINPEC Party deteriorated as well. FUNCINPEC officials continued to place quick monetary gains before principles and embarked on a series of ties with Taiwan. China's attitude towards the royalist party was not helped by the consensus existing among other diplomats in Phnom Penh that the FUNCINPEC-CPP coalition government was an impediment to progress. Hun Sen was seen as someone that "we can do business with, who wants to develop the country".[29]

The year 1996 was to see a change in the nature of the relationship. In April of that year, a senior Chinese military delegation led by Chief of the General Staff, General Zhang Wan-Nian, visited Cambodia and signed a US$1 million aid package to the Royal Government to provide training and equipment to the Royal Cambodian Armed Forces (RCAF).[30] While the aid package was not large, the composition of the delegation was impressive. It led, later on, to the increase of the staff at the Chinese Embassy's Defence Attaché office to more than 30, the largest in Cambodia at the time.[31]

Also in 1996, the Chinese Embassy in Phnom Penh reported with concern on an incident which involved the sudden cancellation by the Cambodian Ministry of Industry of a contract between the Guangdong Engineering Industries Co. and the Cambodian Cement Co., a company owned by Sino-Khmers based in Hong Kong with close links to FUNCINPEC and the Royal Palace. The Chinese company had fallen out with its local partner over finances. The contract, signed in 1992 provided for the two companies to repair and up-grade the State Cement Factory at Chakrey Ting in Kampot province. This factory was a highly emotional matter for both the Cambodian and Chinese governments, as it has been given to Cambodia by China during the Sangkum Reastr Niyum (Popular Socialist Community)[32] period under Norodom Sihanouk. It had begun production in 1964 but had been in disrepair since the Khmer Rouge regime had been overthrown.

The Cambodian Ambassador in Beijing was summoned to the Foreign Ministry and was told that China was very unhappy about the cancellation of the contract, and that if the matter was not reconsidered by the Cambodian government, it would have "negative consequences on the relationship between the two countries."[33] However, Cambodia did not re-consider the matter, and a contract was awarded to a Swiss company, even though the Chinese partner had already invested US$10 million in ongoing repair work at the factory. The Chakrey Ting factory affair triggered a change in China's perception on whom to deal with in Cambodia. China was eager to re-establish itself in Cambodia and needed to make a choice. This had been made easier by FUNCINPEC's active courtship of Taiwan and would lead to rapid changes in Chinese policy towards Cambodia, which would favour the Cambodian People's Party.

CHINA WARMS TO HUN SEN

China began cultivating closer links with Hun Sen, even though the latter had received a lukewarm reception during a previous trip to China with Prince Ranariddh in 1993, the first trip he had made in his official capacity as co-Premier. China also changed its Ambassador in Cambodia, as Madame Xie Yue'e, the Ambassador since 1993, was not well-liked in CPP circles because she had been closely linked with the Khmer Rouge regime in her work as a translator and diplomat.[34]

Hun Sen's 18–23 July 1996 visit to China was "royal" in everything but name. The Chinese hosts sent a special plane to pick him up. Before leaving Phnom Penh, Hun Sen said that his visit to China would help end "the suspicion of the past."[35] His visit included meetings with President Jiang Zemin and Premier Li Peng. He also witnessed the signing of pacts on trade and investment protection. An accord for exchanges between the CPP and the Communist Party of China was also signed. Significantly, the delegation which was touted as a delegation of the Royal Government of Cambodia included only CPP officials, suggesting that China having observed for years the developments in Cambodia, had been offended by FUNCINPEC's flirtations with Taiwan and its incapacity to govern, and had finally decided to deal with Hun Sen.

The year 1996 was also important because Hun Sen obtained the defection of Ieng Sary, a deputy Prime Minister in charge of Foreign affairs of the Khmer Rouge regime, to the government, following the defeat of the KR in Pailin. According to a former Democratic Kampuchea minister, China negotiated the defection, as the Khmer Rouge movement began disintegrating within itself, with different factions manoeuvring to take power.[36] Ieng Sary was given a royal amnesty by King Sihanouk, upon the request of the two Co-Premiers and the National Assembly.[37]

When Hun Sen overthrew Prince Norodom Ranariddh in July 1997, China saw an opportunity to regain influence in Cambodia, as the international community reacted over the political killings that followed, and relations cooled with most of the country's Western donors, which suspended almost all but humanitarian assistance to Cambodia. Investors pulled out, scared by the killings but also concerned over the regional economic crisis of mid-1997. The Association of Southeast Asian Nations (ASEAN) denied Cambodia membership within the organization.[38]

INCREASING CHINESE INFLUENCE

Hun Sen moved quickly to gain China's trust, and on 23 July 1997, after accusing the Taiwan representation in Phnom Penh of helping FUNCINPEC to purchase arms, he shut down the Taiwan Economic and Cultural Representative Office in Phnom Penh, and expelled all the Taiwanese diplomats. Then, on 25 July 1997, joined by the new Chinese Ambassador, Yan Ting Ai, Hun Sen addressed the Chinese community in Phnom Penh in a talk that aimed to restore their confidence in the Cambodian government, now strongly under his control.[39]

Immediately after the coup, the Chinese schools, which had been granted permission to operate again in Cambodia in 1990, began opening up, with the assistance of the Chinese Embassy which provided grants, teacher training, visits to China, curriculum and technical visits from China as well as funding the re-purchasing of the former schools which had been confiscated by previous regimes. From thirteen Chinese schools operating in Cambodia in 1995, the number reached over 60 by 1999.[40]

Hun Sen denied playing the "China card" against his critics in Western countries. In a wide-ranging interview, soon after deposing Prince Ranariddh, he stated: "I would also like to affirm that China is not a card for any country to play. China has its own sovereignty and independence and also has a seat in the UN Security Council. So, China would not allow itself to be a card to be played by any country."[41]

Yet, Hun Sen's actions endeared him to Beijing and opened the door once again for Chinese influence in Cambodia. China was the first country to recognize the change of regime, after the July 1997 coup. China also opposed the imposition of international sanctions against Phnom Penh and admonished Western countries to stay away from the country's internal affairs. In December 1997, China delivered 116 military cargo trucks and 70 jeeps valued at $2.8 million, offsetting the cessation of military aid by Australia and other countries after the coup.

As China's influence increased in Cambodia, China would make more demands from its new protégé on such issues as the Khmer Rouge tribunal, Taiwanese businesses operating in Cambodia, Chinese members of Falun Gong under the protection of the UN High Commissioner for Refugees in Cambodia (who were deported back to China) and not allowing the Dalai Lama to attend the Third World Buddhist Summit in Cambodia in 2002.[42] Chinese diplomats had been angered by unfriendly reports about Chinese interests in the local, Malaysian-owned Chinese language *Sin Chew Daily* newspaper and had complained to the Cambodian Ministry of Information.[43] Since 2006, the Cambodian Ministry of Interior has established a regulation by which any Taiwanese citizen wishing to marry a Cambodian citizen needs to have his/her identity certified by a document issued by the Chinese Embassy in Phnom Penh. In response to this regulation, Taiwan no longer recognizes marriages certified in Cambodia.[44]

In 2003, after anti-Thai riots in Phnom Penh and the burning of the Thai Embassy, tensions between the two neighbours almost escalated into war, and China assumed the role of a broker through a statement by the Chinese Ambassador in Phnom Penh asking Cambodia and Thailand to cool relations down. Then, Chinese Vice-Foreign Minister Wang Yi, summoned the Cambodian and Thai ambassadors in Beijing and suggested to them that a way should be found to resolve their grievances but he also warned that the two neighbours should normalize relations as soon as possible, or risk angering China.[45]

Regarding the Khmer Rouge Tribunal, a Western diplomat in Phnom Penh was quoted by the *Far Eastern Economic Review* as saying that "Chinese diplomats tried to block the passage of legislation by the Cambodian National Assembly to establish a tribunal to try leaders of the former Khmer Rouge regime in meetings with senior Cambodian leaders over the 2000/2001 New Year weekend."[46] According to a highly-placed US diplomat in Phnom Penh, "Chinese diplomats had been literally following in American footsteps to prevent the bill from reaching the signing stage."[47] Prime Minister Hun Sen has stated that as far as his relationship with China was concerned "there is one taboo, and that is that we never bring up for discussion the topic of the Khmer Rouge."[48]

CHINESE ODA

In December 2007, China joined the Cambodia Development Cooperation Forum (CDCF), which gathered all the countries and international agencies providing assistance to Cambodia, and immediately became the largest donor. At the December 2008 CDCF pledging session, China committed a package worth US$257 million out of a total of US$951.5 million while China's investment in Cambodia reached US$4.3 billion or almost 40 per cent of the total Foreign Direct Investment (FDI) received by Cambodia.[49] According to data from the Council for the Development of Cambodia (CDC), China, as well as being the largest donor to Cambodia, has also become the largest investor with US$892.7 million of approved projects. Chinese investment in Cambodia for 2009 accounted for more than 15 per cent of all approved projects according to CDC data.[50]

Cambodia welcomed Chinese Vice President Xi Jinping in December 2009. The visit was hailed as a landmark in Cambodia's relations with China because of the extensive package of grants and aid given by the Chinese amounting to US$1.2 billion. Just before his arrival in Phnom Penh, the Cambodian government deported back to China 20 ethnic-minority Uighurs seeking refugee status in the country. By so doing, Cambodia was in breach of the 1951 Refugee Convention that it had ratified as well as several other International Conventions to which Cambodia is a party.[51]

China has also embarked on a crusade to promote Chinese studies, language and cultural programs among Cambodians. The launching of the China-Cambodia Friendship Radio in December 2008 and the opening of the Confucius Institute in Phnom Penh have enhanced China's cultural presence in the country. At the launching of the first Chinese-language class for public servants on 21 January 2010, Chinese Ambassador, Madame Zhang Jinfeng, told 50 students from the ministries of interior, defence, education, information and the Council of Ministers, that: "The Chinese government never took part in or intervened into the politics of Democratic Kampuchea. The Chinese did not support the wrongful policies of the regime, but instead tried to provide assistance through food, hoes and scythes. If there were no food assistance, the Cambodian people would have suffered more famine."[52] This was, of course, an outrageous statement, as military aid was hardly "hoes and scythes."

China's recent involvement in Cambodia has been positive to the extent that it has contributed to the construction, for instance, of up to 1,500 kilometres of roads and bridges[53] in a country whose infrastructure was extensively destroyed after years of civil strife, foreign occupation and further civil disruptions. The training of Cambodian officials will also contribute to the rehabilitation of Cambodia's administrative institutions.

However, specialists are divided on whether China's involvement in Cambodia is constructive. Ralph Wrobel, an economics professor at the West Saxon University of Applied Sciences of Zwickau, in Germany feels that Chinese investment "risks sending Cambodia towards a socialist market economy that benefits the elite," adding that the "socialist market economy in China is a system of exploitation of the people."[54] Francoise Mengin of France's Centre for International Studies and Research (CERI) feels that Chinese aid and investment "help to consolidate a political economy based on arbitrariness, increased inequalities and violence, as well as the overlapping of positions of power and accumulation."[55]

Cambodia's closeness to China is causing a lot of concern among ASEAN with former Singapore Prime Minister Lee Kuan Yew suggesting that everything that is discussed at ASEAN meetings is immediately known in Beijing because of China's close links with Myanmar, Cambodia and Laos.[56] US Secretary of State, Hillary Clinton, during a visit to Cambodia in 2010 counselled for balance in Cambodia's foreign policy adding that "You don't want to become too dependent on any one country."[57]

Furthermore, in 2010, Cambodian exports to China were valued at US$56.68 million while Chinese exports to Cambodia were US$1.07 billion, creating a huge gap in the commercial relationship between the two countries, even after ASEAN, of which Cambodia is a member, and China signed a free-trade agreement which came into force on 1 January 2010.[58]

When it comes to Cambodian relations with China, most contemporary Cambodian leaders have courted the People's Republic of China for different reasons: Norodom Sihanouk used China as a safety net against Cambodia's neighbours; Pol Pot employed it for ideological reasons, as a counterweight to Vietnam and to achieve revolution in Cambodia, while Hun Sen initially embraced China because Western and certain Asian powers did not like his undemocratic ways of holding onto power. Sihanouk stood up for China when it was necessary at a time when Beijing was isolated and needed Cambodia's friendship. Today's China is a different power with its own economic and strategic needs. Cambodia by following China's path helps Beijing to achieve its economic and strategic aims in Southeast Asia.

The danger for Cambodia is that it certainly loses its independence in foreign relations by agreeing to all of China's demands, such as in the affair of the deportation of the twenty Uighur refugees. What is particularly worrisome is that Cambodia is a country where many of its citizens have been refugees. It is a matter of concern that it should deport these refuge-seekers to China, a country that bears a great responsibility for the policies of Pol Pot and associates which caused so many Cambodians to become refugees!

Notes

1. SNC or Supreme National Council of Cambodia was a largely ceremonial body recognized by the international community as the unique legitimate body and source of authority in Cambodia in which, throughout the transitional period, national sovereignty and unity were enshrined, and which represented Cambodia externally. The SNC worked together with the United Nations Transitional Authority (UNTAC) during the period November 1991 to September 1993, when Cambodia became once again a constitutional monarchy, with King Norodom Sihanouk as Head of State.
2. Fu is fluent in Khmer and his diplomatic career had been dedicated wholly to Cambodia. He had joined the Foreign Ministry as Khmer translator and served in different posts in the Cambodian section of the Asia Division of the Foreign Ministry. In 1983, he was posted as Counsellor to the Chinese Embassy in Thailand in charge of relations with the three factions composing the Coalition Government of Democratic Kampuchea (CGDK). In 1985, Fu returned to the Foreign Ministry where he served as liaison officer in the residence of Norodom

Sihanouk, who was then living in exile in Beijing. Additionally, he served as Counsellor for Cambodian affairs and as deputy director of the Asian Division in the Chinese Foreign Ministry and as such he participated in all the meetings on Cambodia at which China was represented.

3. See Yun Shi "An Account of Chinese Diplomats accompanying the government of Democratic Kampuchea's move to the Cardamom Mountains" in "Chinese Diplomats in International Crisis situations" (*Guoji Fengyunzhongde Zhongguo Waijiaoguan*, Beijing, World Knowledge, 1992) pp. 85–112, translated by Paul marks, *Critical Asian Studies* 4, no. 34 (2002).
4. The other countries to be allowed to open embassies in Phnom Penh were: Albania, Cuba, Egypt, Laos, North Korea, Romania, Yugoslavia and North Vietnam.
5. *The Nation*, Bangkok, 20 November 1991, p. A8.
6. See "Cambodia's Best Friend Now is Communist China". *The Washington Post*, 23 November 1993, p. C15
7. Greenway H D S, "Report from Cambodia: The Tiger and the Crocodile". *The New Yorker*, 17 July 1989, pp. 72–83.
8. See Note for the Press from the Secretariat of Samdech Norodom Sihanouk of Cambodia, Beijing, 12 July 1991.
9. Author's discussion with a Chinese diplomat, Phnom Penh, 31 October 1992.
10. Agence France Presse, Hong Kong, English report, 30 November 1991.
11. Ibid.
12. New China News Agency-Xinhua in English, Beijing, 30 November 1991.
13. New China News Agency-Xinhua, Beijing, 29 December 1992.
14. FBIS-Daily Report-China, New China News Agency — Xinhua, Domestic service in Chinese, 12 February 1992.
15. *International Herald Tribune*, Paris, 23 April 1993, p. 2.
16. Author's discussion with a Chinese diplomat posted in Phnom Penh, 29 May 1993.
17. The State of Cambodia was the successor regime to the People's Republic of Kampuchea (1979–89).
18. New China News Agency-Xinhua, Beijing, 10 April 1992
19. Deng Xiaoping passed away on 17 February 1997.
20. Chinese diplomat, op. cit.
21. Ibid.
22. As recounted to me by a Cambodian Ambassador who visited Beijing in late October 1994.
23. Author's discussion with the Cambodian Under Secretary for Foreign Affairs, Marina Pok, who had been present at the meeting, Phnom Penh 25 July 1994.
24. Author's discussion with Prince Norodom Ranariddh, Bangkok, 16 April 1993, and with other FUNCINPEC officials in July/August 1993 in Phnom Penh, after the provisional coalition government had been established.
25. The Second Co-Premier was Hun Sen of the Cambodian People's Party.

26. See my article "Taipei office plan strains China-Cambodia ties". *The Bangkok Post,* 25 April 1995.
27. Memorandum from Ambassador Khek Sysoda to the two Co-Premiers, Prince Norodom Ranariddh and Samdech Hun Sen, Beijing, 23 October 1995. Copy in the author's possession.
28. Ibid.
29. Author's discussion with a European diplomat in Phnom Penh, December 1997.
30. Michael Hayes "Watching Beijing playing its cards". *The Phnom Penh Post,* issue 5/17, 23 August 1996.
31. Ibid.
32. The Sangkum Reastr Niyum was a political movement which gathered politicians from all the existing political parties in Cambodia, after they had renounced their political affiliations. The SRN ruled Cambodia from 1955 to 1970.
33. Report No. 129/MD/96 from the Cambodian Ambassador in Beijing to the Cambodian Minister of Foreign Affairs, 12 July 1996.
34. Author's discussion with a senior royal palace official, Phnom Penh.
35. Khmer Press Agency, Daily Bulletin in French, 18 July 1996.
36. Personal communication, 24 April 2003.
37. The royal amnesty concerned only the 1979 international tribunal organized by the pro-Vietnamese regime established in Phnom Penh.
38. See for instance, Sorpong Peou, "Diplomatic pragmatism: ASEAN's response to the July 1997 coup", London, Conciliation Resources, November 1998 and my "Cambodia: Anatomy of a Coup". *The Bangkok Post,* 7 September 1997.
39. "Japan and China up their stakes". *Daily Yomiuri,* 7 August 1997.
40. Author's discussion with the late Tol Lah, Deputy PM and Minister of Education, Bangkok, 3 November 1999.
41. "Premier Denies Playing China card, Backs IMF Prescriptions". *The Cambodia Daily,* 30 October 1997.
42. See my article "China's growing influence in Cambodia". *AFRICANA: Rivista di Studi Extraeuropei.* University of Pisa (Italy), No. VIII, 2002, pp. 7–11.
43. David Fulbrook, "China's growing influence in Cambodia". Hong Kong, *Asia Times Online* <http://www.atimes.com>, 6 October 2006.
44. Statement of the Ministry of Foreign Affairs of Taiwan, 29 June 2006.
45. Joshua Kurlantzick (Visiting Scholar, Carnegie Endowment for International Peace), New York. Testimony before the US-China Economic and Security Review Commission, 18 March 2008, p. 6. This information was also confirmed to the author by a Thai diplomat posted previously in Beijing, at a discussion in Bangkok on 15 November 2009.
46. Nayan Chanda, "Justice Delayed". *Far Eastern Economic Review,* 18 January 2001, p. 30.
47. Author's discussion with a senior US diplomat in Phnom Penh, May 2002.
48. Interview with Kyodo News Agency, Phnom Penh, 17 August 1999.
49. Donald E. Weatherbee, "China's activities in Southeast Asia and the Implications

on U.S. interests". Testimony before the US-China Economic and Security Review Commission", 4 February 2010, p. 7.

50. Simon Marks, "Chinese Growth Reverberates across Cambodia". *The Cambodia Daily*, 13 January 2010, pp. 1 and 32 and "Foreign Investment Down by half in 2009". *The Cambodia Daily*, 14 January 2010, pp. 25–26.
51. Christophe Peschoux, "Deporting Uighur potential refugees sets a terrible precedent". *The Phnom Penh Post*, 22 December 2009. Peschoux was the Director of the Cambodia Office of the UN High Commissioner for Human Rights from 2007 until April 2011.
52. Kong Sothanarith, Voice of America in Khmer, 22 January 2010.
53. Number given by Prime Minister Hun Sen in a speech at the inauguration of the Prek Tamak Bridge, Kandal province on 24 January 2011. Available at <http://www.cnv.org>.
54. "Experts debate China's role in Cambodia". *The Cambodia Daily*, 15 March 2011.
55. Francoise Mengin, "La presence Chinoise au Cambodge: Contribution a une economie politique violente, rentire et inegalitaire". Paris, CERI study No. 133, February 2007, p. 2.
56. US Embassy Singapore to State Department, No 529, 4 June 2009, released by Wikileaks on 29 November 2010. Available at <http://www.wikileaks.org>.
57. See "Clinton Presses Cambodia on China". New York, *The Wall Street Journal*, 1 November 2010.
58. "Trade with China improved during 2010". *The Cambodia Daily*, 17 January 2011.

8

CAMBODIA-UNITED STATES RELATIONS*

Carlyle A. Thayer

The United States first opened diplomatic relations with the Kingdom of Cambodia in 1950 when Cambodia became an associated state within the French Union. US-Cambodia relations have experienced abrupt changes and reversals since 1950. Political relations deteriorated in the early 1960s as a result of US military involvement in South Vietnam and Cambodia breaking diplomatic relations in May 1965. Diplomatic relations were resumed in July 1969, severed again after the Khmer Rouge seized power in April 1975 and re-established in 1991.

This chapter explores the impact of domestic and international factors on US relations with Cambodia in the period after 1991 when an international settlement brought an end to the decade-long conflict and Vietnamese occupation.[1] Bilateral interstate relations between the US and Cambodia comprise multiple dimensions including, but not limited to, diplomatic-political, economic, defence-security and humanitarian-development assistance. This chapter illustrates that the pace and scope of the bilateral relationship varied across these dimensions over time. Progress or setbacks in one area spilled over and affected relations in other areas.

BACKGROUND

Between 1975 and 1991 the United States withheld diplomatic recognition from both Democratic Kampuchea (under the Khmer Rouge) and the People's Republic of Kampuchea/State of Cambodia (a regime set up during the Vietnamese occupation). The US reopened its diplomatic mission in Phnom Penh in November 1991 following the comprehensive international political settlement of the Cambodian conflict in Paris a month earlier. The US ambassador was accredited to the Supreme National Council, a grouping of all the warring Cambodian parties under the auspices of the United Nations (UN).[2] Following UN-supervised elections in May 1993 and the subsequent formation of the Royal Government of Cambodia, the United States immediately extended diplomatic relations and the US Mission was upgraded to an Embassy.[3]

As a result of domestic political turmoil in 1997,[4] the US suspended aid to the central government led by Prime Minister Hun Sen, terminated all military assistance and opposed loans by international financial institutions with the exception of funds for basic humanitarian needs. US political relations with the Hun Sen regime deteriorated sharply during this period. A decade elapsed before US sanctions were lifted. During this period, the pace and scope of rapprochement varied across political-diplomatic, economic, military and aid dimensions. For example, military ties were restored in 2004, but it was not until early 2007 that the United States resumed direct foreign assistance. Political and defence relations peaked later, highlighted by the visits of Deputy Secretary of State John Negroponte to Phnom Penh in 2008 and Cambodia's Minister of Defence Tea Banh to Washington in 2009.

When the US Congress suspended delivery of direct aid to Cambodia's government it exempted assistance in a number of areas such as counter-narcotics, public health and law enforcement. The United States channelled its development assistance through foreign and local non-governmental organizations and provincial authorities. As a matter of practicality, however, US aid officials continued to liaise with their counterparts in the central government.[5]

The US Congress subsequently reversed its suspension of aid as a result of positive domestic political developments. In 1998 and 2003, Cambodia held flawed but generally free and fair national elections that confirmed Hun Sen's grip on power. Following each election Hun Sen formed a coalition government with the main opposition party. This lent Hun Sen's government international respectability. For example, Cambodia's membership in ASEAN, scheduled for mid-1997, was postponed following the outbreak of political violence.[6] But once a coalition government was formed after the 1998 elections Cambodia was admitted to ASEAN the following year. Nonetheless, Hun Sen has continued to promote a culture of impunity. For example, no-one has been tried for the dozens of extrajudicial killings that took place in 1997. Hun Sen routinely uses his parliamentary majority to strip opposition deputies of their immunity and bring defamation proceedings against them in courts under his political control.[7]

The Hun Sen government's record of persistent human rights abuses since 1997, and procrastination in setting up a tribunal to try Khmer Rouge leaders for crimes against humanity, aroused antipathy in the United States among influential lawmakers. According to one analyst, the US Congress adopted a partisan approach by taking sides in Cambodia's domestic politics while the Administration preferred to remain neutral.[8] Congressional views have constrained the process of political rapprochement.

TRADE RELATIONS

The United States is Cambodia's largest trading partner and textiles and garments make up 97 per cent of US imports from Cambodia.[9] Cambodia's textile and garment industry employs 330,000 people and in 1998 it accounted for 80 per cent of export revenue or US$2.5 billion. The influence of the domestic textile industry on the Cambodian government provided a powerful impetus for maintaining and developing trade relations. Cambodia's textile exports to the US were not targeted for sanctions during the decade of political estrangement primarily because Cambodia, at the urging of American trade unions, was compliant with international labour standards. American trade unions successfully lobbied against sanctions as long as Cambodia met its international obligations.

Under the terms of the 1996 trade agreement with the United States, Cambodia's garment industry was accorded preferential access to the US market in exchange for Cambodia's compliance with international labour standards. US preferential quotas on textile imports from Cambodia expired at the end of 2005. Cambodia joined the WTO in October 2004 and its market share of textile sales in the US was expected to come under threat by Chinese exports when the WTO Multi-Fibre Agreement expired on 1 January 2005. Cambodia and other developing countries lobbied the United States to give their exports preferential treatment,[10] and the US responded by imposing safeguards on the import of Chinese textiles until the end of 2008. During this period Cambodian textile and garment exports to the US increased by

20 per cent. In July 2006, Cambodia signed a bilateral Trade and Investment Framework Agreement (TIFA) with the United States. In subsequent years TIFA has provided a forum to discuss bilateral trade and investment issues such as enforcement of intellectual property rights, customs, banking and financial services and US assistance to Cambodia to meet WTO commitments and domestic economic reforms.

COUNTER-TERRORISM COOPERATION

In the wake of the 9/11 terrorist attacks, the US declared that Southeast Asia was the "second front" in the global war on terrorism. Cambodia was not immediately perceived as a priority. But a regional approach to counter-terrorism dictated that the US needed to improve relations with all Southeast Asian countries. Analysts pointed to Cambodia's porous borders, weak law enforcement capacity and the availability of small arms and light weapons as factors that might encourage Jemaah Islamiyah (JI) to set up a base of operations there. Small arms from Cambodia had already been smuggled to conflict areas in Sri Lanka and the Philippines.[11]

US concerns were well-founded when it was revealed that Hambali (Riduan Isamuddin), a chief planner of the 2002 terrorist outrage on Bali, took refuge in Cambodia for several months after the attacks. In 2003, Cambodian security authorities arrested four foreign members of JI who were allegedly planning a terrorist attack in Phnom Penh.[12]

The formation of a coalition government in Cambodia in 2004, after a hiatus of a year following the July 2003 elections, provided an opportunity for the Bush Administration to assuage critics in the US Congress and step up cooperation with Cambodia, including counter-terrorism. The Hun Sen government responded positively. In 2004, Cambodia accepted US assistance to destroy 233 Soviet-era surface-to-air missiles to prevent them from falling into the hands of terrorists.[13] Cambodia was pleased when US authorities arrested and charged a leader of the Cambodian Freedom Fighters group implicated in inciting sporadic acts of violence in Cambodia since late 2000. The Cambodian government argued that the Cambodian Freedom Fighters constituted a terrorist organization.

In August 2005, responding to positive political developments in Cambodia as well as the government's demonstrated willingness to cooperate with the US on security matters, the Bush administration lifted its 1997 ban on US military assistance. This decision enabled funds from the Foreign Military Financing Programme to be used to assist Cambodia in border control and counter-terrorism.[14] Prime Minister Hun Sen willingly agreed to exempt Americans working in Cambodia from prosecution by the International Criminal Court.

The lifting of the ban immediately led to a spike in security cooperation.[15] Between 2004 and 2006, Cambodia received US$4.5 million in military equipment and technical assistance. In 2005, over 40 Cambodian officials participated in US-funded training and Cambodia hosted three US military delegations. Cambodia also became a participant in the Regional Defence Counter Terrorism Fellowship Program that financed English language teaching at the Royal Cambodian Armed Forces (RCAF) English Language Centre. US Special Forces provided assistance for humanitarian mine action, while US Army ordnance disposal personnel taught safety and handling procedures. Cambodia became eligible for IMET funding at the start of FY2006.

In 2005, US-Cambodian political relations went into a temporary tailspin as a result of Hun Sen's heavy-handed treatment of opposition leader Sam Rainsy and civil society activists.[16] In late October 2005, the US House of Representatives formally expressed its concern about the attack on human rights and liberties in Cambodia. Congressman Jim Leach, chairman of the House International Relations Committee, strongly criticized Hun Sen for violating human rights and press freedom.

In mid-January 2006, Assistant Secretary of State Christopher Hill was dispatched to Phnom Penh to make an assessment. On the eve of Mr Hill's visit, Hun Sen presented what he called "a gift to the United States" by releasing several human rights and civil society activists.[17] Cambodia's aim in this was not only to improve relations with the US but also to forestall any cuts in aid by foreign donors who were about to hold their annual meeting. At this time foreign aid accounted for half of Cambodia's budget. Sam Rainsy was pardoned by King Norodom Sihamoni at the request of Prime Minister Hun Sen and permitted to return home in February 2006. Cambodia's National Assembly unanimously reinstated Sam Rainsy and two other opposition deputies who had been expelled from the legislature in 2005. Hun Sen's actions precipitated a quiet re-evaluation of US sanctions policy by the State Department and Congress.[18]

The upturn in US-Cambodia political relations was mirrored by progress in defence ties. In 2006, Cambodian's defence chief visited Pacific Command (PACOM) in Hawaii to request assistance to build up the RCAF.[19] PACOM Commander Admiral William Fallon paid a return visit in July. Admiral Fallon met with Defence Minister Tea Banh who requested US training for the RCAF, which he identified as a top priority.[20] A US military team was sent later to assess Cambodia's training needs.

Steady progress in trade relations, counter-terrorism cooperation and military-to-military ties, combined with positive domestic political developments, and led the US government in February 2007 to resume direct aid to the Cambodian government after a ten-year hiatus.[21] At that time the United States was the only major donor country that continued to impose sanctions as a result of the 1997 political upheaval. By the end of 2007 Cambodia had become the third largest recipient of US foreign assistance in East Asia and the Pacific after Indonesia and the Philippines,[22] with US foreign assistance totalling $62 million. Opposition leader Sam Rainsy applauded the change in US policy because he argued it would provide Washington with greater leverage to promote democracy and human rights and provide balance in Cambodia's external relations. Rainsy argued: "China does not pay any attention to human rights. We cannot leave our country to Chinese influence alone."[23]

RAPPROCHEMENT

The resumption of direct aid from the US to Cambodia in 2007 signalled the commencement of deeper rapprochement between Washington and Phnom Penh in a number of areas. For example, military relations took a step forward when Cambodia agreed to the first visit by a US naval ship in over 30 years. In February 2007, the USS *Gary* paid a port visit to Sihanoukville and crewmen provided goodwill medical care for villagers living near the port. In August, PACOM Commander Admiral Timothy Keating visited Phnom Penh and offered military training and other assistance. In November, US Marines began a training programme for Cambodia's National Counter-Terrorism Task Force and the USS *Essex* called in at Sihanoukville for the second US port visit in a year. The crew conducted medical and dental clinics for the local population.

Trade relations continued their upward trajectory. In February 2007, the Trade Act of 2007 was introduced into the US Congress with a provision extending trade preferences to 14 developing countries including Cambodia. At the same time, Cambodia and the US held their first round of discussions under TIFA in Phnom Penh. These talks focused on expanding and deepening bilateral trade and investment. The United States offered support for domestic economic reforms and assistance in Cambodia's efforts to implement its WTO commitments.

In mid-2009, the Obama administration also lifted restrictions on finance from the US Export-Import Bank for American companies operating in Cambodia. Cambodia and the United States amended their bilateral trade agreement in September 2009 to include provision for US support for Cambodia's economic priorities. The United States committed US$7.79 million in funds to expand USAID's Micro, Small and Medium Enterprises and Business Enabling Environment programme and support for increasing productivity of rural family businesses as a means of reducing poverty.[24]

US-Cambodia rapprochement also opened up new areas of interaction. In April 2007, the Peace Corps programme officially commenced in Cambodia with the arrival of 28 English teachers. Further, in June, the State Department's *Trafficking in Persons Report* concluded that Cambodia was making significant efforts to comply with minimum international standards. Despite improvements, however, Cambodia was retained on the Tier 2 Watch List.

US political rapprochement with Cambodia reached a peak in September 2008 when Deputy Secretary of State John Negroponte visited Phnom Penh and announced that the US would provide US$24 million in aid targeted at improving public health.[25] Negroponte also announced a reversal of US policy towards the Khmer Rouge tribunal. Up until 2008 the US had declined to contribute directly to the tribunal because of concerns over its independence and ability to meet international standards of justice. According to a US Embassy spokesperson, Negroponte's visit demonstrated Washington's direct interest in engaging with Cambodia's leaders and civil society.[26]

DEFENCE COOPERATION

In 2008–09, US-Cambodia defence relations expanded considerably as the US increased financial assistance and the scope of its training programmes.[27] In 2008, the US provided US$4 million to assist in demining activities, and offered loans and training to increase the RCAF's capacity to participate in UN peacekeeping operations.[28] In June 2008, the US donated 31 trucks to the RCAF and also provided assistance to enable Cambodian troops to participate in multinational exercises. In March–April 2009, US and Cambodian navy divers conducted their first joint rescue and salvage exercise. In May, US Marines and RCAF personnel conducted a medical and dental capabilities exercise. In September of the same year, the US donated twenty containers of excess military equipment (including Kevlar helmets, field packs and camouflage uniforms) valued at US$6.5 million.

The highpoint in US-Cambodia military rapprochement was reached in 2009 with the opening of the Cambodian Defence Attaché's office in the United States and the visit of Defence Minister Tea Banh to Washington. Tea Banh was received separately by Defence Secretary Robert Gates and Deputy Secretary of State James Steinberg.[29] Gates reaffirmed America's commitment to enhancing the capabilities of the RCAF in peacekeeping, maritime security and counter-terrorism. He also invited Cambodia to participate in a future Defence Policy Dialogue and identified defence sector reform as a new area for cooperation.

Steinberg and Tea Banh discussed bilateral security cooperation, Cambodia's role in ASEAN, human rights and Cambodia's participation in international peacekeeping operations. Of particular importance was Cambodia's decision to join the Global Peace Operations Initiative (GPOI), a global programme to train and equip 75,000 peacekeepers by 2010. The GPOI was a Group of 8 initiative funded by the US. In December 2009, Cambodia began construction of a Peacekeeping Demining Centre of Excellence under the auspices of the GPOI.

In late 2009, Cambodia-US defence relations hit a speed bump when the Hun Sen government repatriated twenty Uighur asylum-seekers to China despite diplomatic intervention by Secretary of State Hillary Clinton. In March 2010, the US suspended the delivery of 200 vehicles under the Excess Defence Articles programme in protest.[30] Within a short space of time, however, defence relations continued their upward trajectory. In June, Cambodia participated in Cooperation Afloat Readiness and Training (CARAT) programme for the first time and received a port visit by the USS *Tortuga*. And in July, Cambodia and the United States co-hosted the GPOI capstone exercise, Angkor Sentinel, involving 1,000 peacekeeping personnel from more than 20 countries who participated in field and command post exercises in Cambodia.

FUTURE TRAJECTORY

Rapprochement between the US and Cambodia is likely to continue on its present trajectory because a self-sustaining momentum in the areas of defence and counter-terrorism cooperation appears to have been built up. The involvement of US companies in the exploitation of Cambodia's recently discovered offshore oil and gas reserves will contribute to broadening the bilateral economic relationship. A further factor contributing to rapprochement is the new found interest of the Obama administration in assisting the countries of the Lower Mekong (Laos, Cambodia, Vietnam and Thailand) to develop this sub-region. In 2009, Secretary of State Hillary Clinton launched the Lower Mekong Initiative to promote environmental, education and infrastructural development. She has met twice with the foreign ministers of Thailand, Laos, Cambodia and Vietnam to advance development projects. The most recent visit was in November 2010 when Secretary Clinton travelled to Phnom Penh.

Human rights and democratic governance issues are likely to remain the main impediments to rapprochement due to Hun Sen's autocratic tendencies. Hun Sen's massive electoral victory in the 2008 general election, coupled with support from China, and the expected financial windfall from oil and gas reserves, will serve to buffer him from domestic pressure by domestic civil society groups and external pressure from the United States (and other like-minded states) to address deficiencies in democracy promotion and human rights.[31]

Cambodia's expulsion of the Uighur asylum-seekers and acceptance of loans from China has aroused the ire of several American congressmen. On 20 May 2010, they attached a provision to the Cambodia Trade Act of 2010 (H.R. 5320) that would prohibit the US government from reducing or forgiving "any debt owed by Cambodia to the United States". This refers to outstanding Cambodian debts of over US$440 million dating back to the Lon Nol era (1970–75).[32] What was once a minor irritant could become a major sticking point.

CONCLUSION

This review of US-Cambodia has explored the domestic and international factors that have influenced decision-makers in Phnom Penh and Washington to seek rapprochement through engagement across multiple dimensions. In the future, bilateral relations will be influenced by regional multilateral engagement. ASEAN has embarked on the process of creating an ASEAN Community based on three pillars — political-security, economic and socio-cultural. The Obama administration has clearly signalled its willingness to engage with ASEAN (by signing the Treaty of Amity and Cooperation) and regional institution-building (by joining the East Asia Summit). These two developments will create a framework for US relations with Cambodia. For example, in 2009 President Obama met with Southeast Asian leaders for the first time on the sidelines of the APEC Summit. There ASEAN leaders made clear they would like to reschedule future leadership meetings so that Cambodia and Laos, which are not members of APEC, can attend. President Obama hosted the second US-ASEAN Leaders Meeting in the United States in September 2010.

ASEAN is promoting a new process involving discussions between its defence ministers and some of its dialogue partners, known as ASEAN Defence Minister Meeting plus Eight (ADMM Plus Eight). The inaugural meeting was held in Hanoi on 12 October 2010 with the participation of the United States as one of the eight dialogue partners. This framework too will shape the contours of US relations with Cambodia by providing a multilateral framework for future practical defence cooperation activities

The United States is also promoting regional multilateral cooperation to address non-traditional security challenges such as humanitarian assistance and disaster relief, pandemics and infectious diseases, counter-narcotics, trafficking in persons, counter-terrorism etc. Transnational challenges are best addressed by multilateral rather than bilateral responses and this too will positively influence US relations with Cambodia.

Finally, United States relations with Cambodia will be shaped by the prospect of bilateral free trade agreements and the Obama administration's initiative to assist the states of the Lower Mekong in sub-regional development. In July 2010, the United States committed US$187 million to address water resources, food security and public health issues in this sphere. The Lower Mekong Initiative will provide incentives for Phnom Penh to work more closely with the United States to achieve its goal of economic development through sub-regional integration.

Notes

* This chapter is a revised version of "US Rapprochement with Laos and Cambodia". *Contemporary Southeast Asia* 32, no. 3 (December 2010): 442–59. It is republished with permission.

1. For background see Carlyle A. Thayer, "The UN Transitional Authority in Cambodia". In *A Crisis of Expectations: UN Peacekeeping in the 1990s*, edited by Ramesh Thakur and Carlyle A. Thayer (Boulder: Westview Press, 1995), pp. 121–40 and Viberto Selochan and Carlyle A. Thayer, editors, *Bringing Democracy to Cambodia: Peacekeeping and Elections* (Canberra: Regime Change and Regime Maintenance in Asia and the Pacific Project, Research School of Pacific and Asian Studies, The Australian National University and Australian Defence Studies Centre, 1996).
2. Carlyle A. Thayer, "The United Nations Transitional Authority in Cambodia: The Restoration of Sovereignty". In *Peacekeeping and Peacemaking: Towards Effective Intervention in Post-Cold War Conflict*, edited by Tom Woodhouse, Robert Bruce, and Malcolm Dando (London: Macmillan Press Ltd., and New York: St. Martin's Press, 1998), pp. 145–65.
3. US Department of States, Bureau of East Asian and Pacific Affairs. *Background Note: Cambodia*, January 2010. <http://www.state.gov/r/pa/ei/bgn/2732/htm>.
4. Carlyle A. Thayer, "Cambodia Continues Course of Political Violence". *Asia-Pacific Defence Reporter Annual Reference Edition*, 24, no. 1 (January–February 1998): 16–17.
5. Thomas Lum, *Cambodia: Background and U.S. Relations*. Washington, D.C.: Congressional Research Service Report for Congress, 18 July 2007, p. 10.
6. Carlyle A. Thayer, *Cambodia and Regional Stability: ASEAN and Constructive Engagement*. The CICP Distinguished Lecture Series Report Issue no. 14 (Phnom Penh: Cambodian Institute for Cooperation and Peace, June 1998).

7. Carlyle A. Thayer, "Cambodia Power Play". *The Wall Street Journal*, 4 December 2009, p. 11.
8. Sheldon W. Simon, "Military Support and Political Concerns". *Comparative Connections* 9, no. 1 (April 2007). The archive for this publication is located at <http://csis.org/program/comparative-connections>.
9. Lum, *Cambodia*, op. cit., p. 8 and Khatharya Um, "Cambodia: A Decade After the Coup". *Southeast Asian Affairs 2008*, edited by Daljit Singh and Tin Maung Maung Than (Singapore: Institute of Southeast Asian Studies, 2008), p. 111.
10. Lum, *Cambodia*, op. cit., p. 8.
11. Ibid., p. 13.
12. Ibid., pp. 13–14.
13. Ibid., p. 13.
14. Ibid., p. 10.
15. Embassy of the United States, Office of Defence Cooperation, "ODC Mission", 2005. <http://cambodia.usembassy.gov/defence_cooperation_office.html>.
16. Sheldon W. Simon, "Military Relations Restored with Indonesia; while U.S. Passes on the First East Asian Summit". *Comparative Connections* 7, no. 4 (January 2006). The archive for this publication is located at <http://csis.org/program/comparative-connections>.
17. Ibid., electronic version.
18. Ibid., electronic version.
19. Simon, "U.S. Pushes Security and Trade Interests in Southeast Asia". *Comparative Connections* 8, no. 2 (July 2006). The archive for this publication is located at: <http://csis.org/program/comparative-connections>.
20. Sheldon W. Simon, "U.S. Strengthens Ties to Southeast Asian Regionalism". *Comparative Connections* 8, no. 3 (October 2006). The archive for this publication is located at: <http://csis.org/program/comparative-connections>.
21. Lum, *Cambodia*, op. cit., p. 1.
22. Ibid.
23. Simon, "Military Support and Political Concerns", op. cit., electronic version.
24. Embassy of the United States in Cambodia, Press Release, 22 September 2009. <http://cambodia.usembassy.gov/sp_092209.html>.
25. "Remarks by Deputy Secretary Negroponte in Cambodia". U.S. Department of State, 16 September 2008. <http://www.state.gov/s/d/2008/109787.htm>.
26. "Remarks by Charge d'affaires Piper Wind Campbell on America's Role in Asia". Embassy of the United States, Speeches, 12 January 2009. <http://cambodia.usembassy.gov/sp_011209.html>.
27. This section draws on Carlyle A. Thayer, *Southeast Asia: Patterns of Security Cooperation*, ASPI Strategy Report (Canberra: Australian Strategic Policy Institute, September 2010), pp. 45–46.
28. Cambodia sent demining specialists to UN peacekeeping missions in Sudan in 2006, and in September 2009 agreed to send demining specialists to Chad and the Central African Republic.

29. Embassy of the United States, Press Release, 23 September 2009. <http://cambodia.usembasy.gov/pr_092309.html>.
30. In June 2010, Assistant Secretary of State for the Bureau of Population, Refugees and Migration, Eric Schwartz, visited Cambodia (and Laos) for discussions with government officials.
31. Carlyle A. Thayer, "Cambodia: The Cambodian People's Party Consolidates Power". In *Southeast Asian Affairs 2009*, edited by Daljit Singh (Singapore: Institute of Southeast Asian Studies, 2009), pp. 85–101.
32. Scot Marciel, Deputy Assistant Secretary for East Asian and Pacific Affairs, "The United States and Cambodia: Bilateral Relations and Bilateral Debt". Testimony Before the Subcommittee on Asia, the Pacific, and the Global Environment, House Foreign Affairs Committee, Washington, D.C., 14 February 2009.

9

JAPAN'S ROLES IN CAMBODIA
Peace-Making, Peace-Building and National Reconciliation

Lam Peng Er

Japan's various roles in the past decades in Cambodia may be underestimated and underreported, as Japan remains relatively low-profile and quiet about its activities. Stated briefly, Japan's roles in Cambodia include the following:

- Peace-Building: through its efforts in UNTAC
- Peace-Making: through its roles in organizing the Tokyo Informal meetings; reaching out to the Heng Samrin regime; and its participation in the 1991 Paris Peace Conference on Cambodia;
- National Reconciliation: Through its efforts to achieve reconciliation between Hun Sen and Prince Ranariddh in the July 1997 power struggle.

JAPAN'S PEACE BUILDING EFFORTS IN CAMBODIA

Peace-building efforts in Cambodia were Japan's first foray in this area, and also served as a model for Japanese efforts to address other domestic conflicts in various parts of Asia. It was in Cambodia that Japan gained valuable experience, national self-confidence and institutional knowledge in the whole range of inter-related areas of peace-building: diplomatic negotiations to achieve a peace agreement; operationalising the peace agreement through the dispatch of Japanese personnel (including sending Self Defence Forces personnel abroad for the first time since WW2) to support UNTAC; the provision of funds and personnel for socio-economic reconstruction in Cambodia; and critical mediation in the July 1997 crisis caused by a power struggle between Cambodian factions. Three key components of Japanese peace-building efforts were: ODA; Japanese diplomacy, and unprecedented participation in UN peace-keeping operations. Cambodia also saw the first instance of Japanese pro-active diplomacy in the 1990s. According to the Japanese Foreign Ministry, Cambodia was the first full-scale peace-building assistance program undertaken by Japan.

The Japanese Foreign Ministry considered the Cambodian experience to be successful in three aspects, namely:

- Firstly, Japan showed tenacity, patience and determination from 1978 to 1991, to help address the Cambodia conflict, which was the greatest challenge facing Southeast Asia, and contributed greatly to the implementation of the political solution via the 1991 Paris Peace Conference and UNTAC;
- Secondly, tackling the Cambodian conflict successfully was a demonstration of how the Fukuda doctrine should operate, as it envisaged an active Japanese role in bridging the gap between the non-Communist ASEAN member states, and the Indochinese states, and thus promoting regional peace, stability and prosperity.
- Thirdly, the Japanese involvement in Cambodian peace-building marked a critical turning point in the post WW2 era: Japan shed its low profile and embarked on an active and respected role in regional and international affairs, starting with its helpful role in Cambodia. The positive role in Cambodia helped the Japanese public to overcome its allergy to international peaceful cooperation, especially UN Peacekeeping. This further opened the way for public acceptance of Japanese support for US operations in Iraq and Afghanistan.

How successful has been Japanese and international assistance to Cambodia, which some observers assess as still not fully democratic, and which remains mired in poverty and corruption? This is the classic glass half-full or half-empty problem: much depends on how the observer views Cambodia and from which view point? In some ways, Cambodia has made much progress as measured from the dark and terrible years of the Khmer Rouge era. If measured according to Western developed country standards, then obviously

Cambodia still has a long way to go, and progress is slow and halting. While Cambodia today is not a full, Western-styled liberal democracy, it has political order and stability and has held periodic elections, in which members of the Opposition do capture a considerable number of seats in the Parliament.

It would be overly harsh to condemn Japan and the international community for failing to create a liberal democracy in Cambodia, via the peace-building process, because genuine democracy cannot be imposed from the top and from outside the country. Genuine democracy must be developed in-country, and can best grow under optimum conditions, such as where there are educated and sophisticated voters who understand the way democracy works, where there are institutions and processes — such as an independent judiciary, a free and responsible press, and honest and dedicated politicians who work for the people's benefit and the national good — which nurture and support democracy. In Cambodia, the conditions for democratization are lacking in such a poor country with weak democratic institutions and norms amongst its elite and the masses.

This paper argues that Japan's peace-building efforts in Cambodia have been its most successful and impressive example of conflict resolution and peace-building. Although the United States played a pivotal diplomatic role as one of the Five Permanent UNSC members with the veto, in negotiating for an Agreed Framework for a Cambodia Settlement, it appears to have "exited" before the hard work of UN peace-keeping began. Japan soldiered on with manpower and financial contributions, which were critical and helpful to UNTAC, and the socio-economic re-construction of Cambodia.

Less well-known but arguably Japan's finest diplomatic achievement was its successful arrangement of a deal between the two rival Cambodian factions in July 1997, which paved the way for a national election in 1998, and which was conducted in an acceptable way for the international community. Had Cambodia disintegrated into another civil war, this would have destroyed the hard-won achievements of UNTAC, wasted the great resources spent on Cambodian reconstruction, and damaged the reputation of UN peace-keeping and peace-building. In addition, persistent political violence in Cambodia would also have delayed or blocked ASEAN's aspirations for all 10 Southeast Asian countries to join ASEAN, and negated the outlook for the region as a stable, peaceful and progressive region.

HISTORICAL BACKGROUND: JAPAN'S ROLE IN THE 1980s–1990s

As early as 1980, two years after the Vietnamese invasion of Cambodia, Japan hosted a small conference in Tokyo, with the aim of persuading

Vietnam to withdraw its troops from Cambodia. In 1984, then Japanese Foreign Minister Abe Shintaro at the ASEAN Post-Ministerial Conference (AMC), proposed that Japan would support the consolidation of peace by providing financial and humanitarian assistance, and it would also provide economic and technical cooperation for the reconstruction of Indochina. Similar pledges were made by Japan throughout the 1980s, but these were not taken up. Only towards the end of the 1980s did the drying up of Soviet foreign aid to Vietnam, as a result of the poor economic conditions of the USSR, coupled with Vietnam's desire to mend fences with China in order to defuse Chinese pressure and to concentrate on its own domestic economic reforms, create opportunities for the international community to successfully push for a peace settlement for Cambodia.

The initial efforts to promote a peace settlement for Cambodia did not succeed because the conditions were not yet right. Neither the Jakarta Informal Meeting in July 1998, nor the First Paris International Conference in July 1999 could succeed due to disagreements over various issues, such as the power-sharing formula amongst the Cambodian factions. The focus then shifted to the Permanent Five in the UNSC. Meanwhile, Vietnam withdrew its troops in September 1998. This factor resulted in the political and power games surrounding Cambodia diminishing and turned the problem into an essentially local dispute among the Cambodian factions. It also removed the main sticking point between China and Vietnam, and lessened Thai and ASEAN concerns about a Vietnamese-controlled Cambodia. Thus the Cambodian problem became ripe for the international community to successfully push for a settlement. For Japan, it became an opportunity to play an active political role in regional affairs.

JAPAN ESTABLISHES DIRECT CONTACTS WITH HENG SAMRIN REGIME

In order to play a successful role, Japan as an interlocutor needed open channels with all the Cambodian factions. This included the ruling Heng Samrin regime. In February 1990, Japan's MOFA officials from its Asia Bureau sent a fact-finding team to Phnom Penh. MOFA was not monolithic in its views about the wisdom of sending this team and putting out feelers to the Heng Samrin regime. MOFA's UN Division believed that the Cambodian problem should be best resolved within the UN framework, and its North America Division was concerned that such a move would invite criticisms from Washington. Indeed, the USA had reservations about the dispatch of the Japanese team because it could undermine the Perm Five's role in resolving the Cambodian problem and also send conflicting signals to Phnom Penh. Despite such concerns, the Asia Bureau succeeded in obtaining support from the Japanese leadership and proceeded on the visit. This move demonstrated resolve to break away from the passive Japanese support for ASEAN's position in isolating the Heng Samrin regime. In any case, the fact-finding mission reported that the political reality was that the Heng Samrin regime was strongly entrenched and could not be ignored if there was to be peace in Cambodia.

Facilitating Japan's role in Cambodia was its strategic partnership with Thailand. In January 1990, Japanese Foreign Minister Nakayama Taro had visited Bangkok and forged a common understanding on Cambodia with Thailand. It was fortunate for Japan that the new Thai civilian Prime Minister Chatichai Choonhavan had rejected the previous Thai military government's hard-line approach towards Cambodia, and was now advocating a new policy: "From Battlefield to Marketplace". The new Thai government knew that it was necessary to tap Japanese cooperation and assistance to translate its new policy into reality. Thailand did not have sufficient resources to rebuild Cambodia, and given the historical suspicions of Cambodians towards Thailand, it was better for Thailand to forge a partnership with a neutral, non-threatening and affluent Japan than go it alone. Thailand understood that a stable and peaceful Cambodia as a neighbour was preferable to a neighbour in turmoil. At their meeting in Tokyo in April 1990, Prime Ministers Chatichai Choonhavan and Japanese PM Kaifu Toshiki agreed to persuade Prince Sihanouk and Hun Sen, the real strongman in Phnom Penh, to hold talks in Tokyo in June 1990.

THE TOKYO CONFERENCE ON CAMBODIA

At the June 1990 Tokyo Conference, which had expanded to include all four Cambodian factions, Hun Sen and Prince Sihanouk held a signing ceremony, which was widely covered by the Japanese media. It was a historical moment showcasing Japan's first instance of post-war diplomacy as a peacemaker. The most important result of this conference was that it paved the way for a shift in the power-sharing formula from an equal sharing amongst the four factions to one of 50-50 between the Heng Samrin regime and the other three, comprising Prince Sihanouk, Son Sann and the Khmer Rouge. This formula was a better reflection of political reality, showing the effective political control of the Heng Samrin regime over Cambodia, as well as helping to dilute and isolate the genocidal KR faction.

Despite this triumph, Japan's diplomacy towards Cambodia was subsequently troubled by four difficulties. First, Japan was excluded whenever the UNSC Perm Five discussed the Cambodia issue, as Japan was not part of the Perm Five. Secondly, the US continued to have misgivings that Japanese diplomacy towards Cambodia might undermine the Perm Five's efforts to reach a Cambodia settlement. Thirdly, the First Gulf War erupted in January 1991, and overshadowed the Cambodian issue. During the Gulf War period, Japan suffered an image problem of being a free-rider, engaging only in chequebook diplomacy. Fourthly, the Thai military coup which toppled PM Chatichai's government in February 1991 was a blow to Japan, because his government had been most cooperative with Japan over Cambodia.

JAPAN WOOS CAMBODIAN LEADERS

Despite these setbacks, Japan tenaciously and creatively sought to establish closer personal ties and rapport with the four factional leaders. In March 1991, Japan invited Son Sann to visit Tokyo to hold talks with PM Kaifu and Foreign Minister Nakayama, followed by a visit to the historic city of Nikko, where Son Sann stayed at a traditional inn or ryokan and enjoyed a hot spring or onsen and karaoke facilities. The next month, Japan conducted medical diplomacy by inviting Hun Sen for an unofficial visit cum medical check-up. In November 1990, Hun Sen had suddenly collapsed whilst discussing with French Foreign Minister Roland Dumas in Paris. After a thorough medical check-up by Japanese doctors, Hun Sen was given a clean bill of good health. According to MOFA officials, this medical diplomacy with Hun Sen was very important for Hun Sen personally, for Japan and the Cambodian peace process, as it established good rapport. By extending warm hospitality and personal attention to both Hun Sen and Son Sann, Tokyo sought to set up direct contacts and win the trust of both leaders. Apparently, none of the Perm Five, with the exception of China, which wooed and supported Prince Sihanouk, Son Sann and the KR, but not the Heng Samrin group, had showered Hun Sen and Son Sann with such personal attention. Moreover, Japan kept the momentum going in the Cambodian peace process, during this period when the Perm Five were pre-occupied and distracted by the Gulf War and its aftermath.

To allay the concerns of the Heng Samrin regime over the Perm Five's Framework document of August 1990 and the Perm Five's Proposed Structure of November1990, which had argued for an interim UN Authority for Cambodia and the demilitarization of all Cambodian factions, Japan proposed that the UN peace-keeping operation in Cambodia should verify the military de-mobilization, and that UN-related agencies should be set up to prevent the return of genocide. The Phnom Penh regime was fearful that its administrative apparatus would be dismantled, that the KR would not disarm, and that the proposed Supreme National Council, which included all four Cambodian factions might even legitimize the KR. Japan sounded out both China and Vietnam and the four factions on its proposals. Its medical diplomacy towards Hun Sen might have helped to make the Phnom Penh regime more accommodating towards the Japanese proposals, but of course the last word lay with Vietnam. Rather than undermining the Perm Five's role in arranging a Cambodian settlement, perhaps we might state that the Japanese role actually supplemented that role by Japan working to gain the confidence and cooperation of the Heng Samrin regime for the UN role.

In October 1991, at the Second International Conference on Cambodia in Paris, all four factions signed the peace agreement. The formal composition of the Supreme National Council would comprise individuals and not factions. In this way, the KR as an organization was kept out of a symbolic body representing Cambodians during the UNTAC interregnum.

JAPAN AND UNTAC

Japan's participation in UNTAC was a milestone in its international relations for three reasons. First, Mr Akashi Yasushi, a senior UN bureaucrat, was appointed Special Representative of UNTAC in January 1992. The choice of a Japanese person to lead UNTAC reflected international expectations of considerable Japanese financial support for UN efforts in Cambodia. Secondly, a law permitting the dispatch of Japanese Self Defence Forces for UN PKO under stringent conditions was passed in June 1992, after an intense and acrimonious domestic debate on whether such a commitment was constitutional or not, given the pacifist sentiments of the main opposition Japan Socialist Party and the general public. The Japanese actions thus went significantly beyond the previous chequebook diplomacy, including manpower contributions of the Japanese SDF for logistics support, including highway construction, truce and election monitoring and police officers. The Japanese SDF comprised over 600 personnel out of an international combined force of about 22,000 personnel.

Thirdly, the steadfastness of Japan in not withdrawing from Cambodia despite public disquiet after two Japanese — a UN civilian volunteer and a policeman — were killed, apparently by the KR in April and May 1993, was significant. Not surprisingly, there was controversy and trepidation within Japan whether a precondition to the dispatch of the SDF had been broken when the KR engaged in acts of violence and disruption. These preconditions included: that all parties to the internal dispute must accept the presence of the SDF; and there must be an agreement for a cessation of hostilities by the parties involved. However, to withdraw the SDF from Cambodia in the wake of two Japanese casualties surely would have undermined the UNTAC and subjected Japan to ridicule once again as a passive state with a low threshold for casualties, following its Gulf War debacle. Domestic public opinion had to be convinced by the argument that most of Cambodia was not in the hands of the KR, and therefore the SDF was not exposed to imminent danger. Moreover, Mr Akashi, cognizant of public opinion sensitivities, had withdrawn the Japanese police to safer areas, even though this was not fair to the other peacekeepers.

JAPAN'S MEDIATION IN THE JULY 1997 CRISIS

After the successful UNTAC-supervised 1993 general elections, Cambodia had a period of uneasy calm when FUNCINPEC, led by Prince Norodom Ranariddh, forged a coalition with Hun Sen's CPP, at the request of Samdech Sihanouk. Even though the FUNCINPEC had won the election with 45 per cent of the votes, Hun Sen, who won 38 per cent, controlled the state and military apparatus and refused to give up power. As a compromise, both leaders agreed to become Co-Prime Ministers. Both of them competed for power, with the absence of threats from a weakened KR, and both leaders tried to cultivate residual KR forces. Their tensions were increased by a forthcoming election. In June 1997, the troops of both sides clashed violently. At the G8 Denver Summit in June 1997, both France and Japan were tasked to try and defuse the tensions in Cambodia. Thus Japanese diplomats met with both Prime Ministers and urged restraint, but in July 1997, the forces of both parties clashed again, with the routing of Ranariddh's forces by Hun Sen's troops. Despite the personal efforts of Japanese Ambassador Naito Shohei to arrange a ceasefire by interceding with Hun Sen, the end result was the escape of Ranariddh overseas. The US condemned Hun Sen's coup, but interestingly, Japan adopted a different line from the US, which urged Japan to suspend aid to Cambodia. The Japanese advice was to maintain a democratic situation in Cambodia to ensure the flow of aid from the international community. Japan also urged Ranariddh to negotiate with Hun Sen. It also carefully refrained from calling the coup a coup in order to avoid antagonizing Hun Sen, and Japan sought to broker a deal. The Japanese plan included: to have Ranariddh cut all military ties with the KR; an immediate ceasefire; the trial of Ranariddh and his pardon by King Sihanouk; to have Hun Sen's government guarantee the safety and security of Ranariddh on his return to Cambodia, and for him to take part in the subsequent elections. This deal paved the way for the Cambodian national elections in July 1998, which was accepted by the outside world as relatively fair and cleanly conducted. Hun Sen's party won this election with 41.1 per cent against Ranariddh's party's 31.7 per cent. The 1998 elections restored normalcy to Cambodia, a precondition for Cambodia to join ASEAN, which it did later. By helping to restore peace in Cambodia, and thus paving the way for Cambodian membership in ASEAN, Japan fulfilled its longstanding vision spelt out in the Fukuda Doctrine, namely, that Japan would help to build a cohesive, stable and prosperous Southeast Asia.

JAPAN'S PEACE-BUILDING AFTER THE 1998 CAMBODIAN ELECTIONS

To further peace and stability in Cambodia after the 1998 elections, Japan organized and hosted the Third Consultative Group meeting on Cambodia in February 1999, under the World Bank's auspices, in Tokyo. Japan pledged new assistance measures totalling about US$100 million. Japanese aid to Cambodia included not just infrastructural projects, but also clearing of land mines, the collection of small arms and light weapons, and sponsorship of a draft agreement concerning cooperation between the Cambodian Government and the UN for the KR Trials. Cambodia agreed to appoint Professor Noguchi Motto (Senior Prosecutor) of the UN Asia and Far East Institute for the Prevention of Crimes and the Treatment of Offenders, as an international judge of the Supreme Court Chamber of the KR Trials, in May 2006.

JAPANESE OFFICIAL DEVELOPMENT AID TO CAMBODIA

Japan has been the top contributor of ODA to Cambodia, which has been dependent on the international community for half its annual state budget. Besides its financial and manpower contributions to UNTAC, Japan also successfully convened an International Conference on the Reconstruction of Cambodia in Tokyo in June 1992, with representation from 33 countries and 12 international organizations. Marshalling international financial and technical assistance to Cambodia was critical for nation-building after decades of violence. Some US$800 million was pledged towards reconstruction, with Japan leading with a contribution of US$150–200 million.

According to the Japanese embassy in Phnom Penh, since the first loan was provided for the development of Prek Tonot in 1968, and despite the interruption during the Lon Nol-Khmer Rouge eras from 1970 to 1978,

Japan has consistently supported Cambodia and the welfare of its people. Japan has given a considerable portion of its ODA resources to support the physical and social rehabilitation of war-torn Cambodia. Its ODA accounts for 20 per cent of the total ODA received by Cambodia, making Japan the biggest donor to Cambodia. In 1999, after about a 30-year interval, Japan decided to extend to Cambodia a loan of up to 4 billion yen for the rehabilitation and renovation of the antiquated and deteriorating Sihanoukville Port. This decision was taken in view of the fact that Sihanoukville Port is Cambodia's only deep-sea port and is considered vital for the country's restoration. Japan's policy is to provide assistance that contributes to Cambodia's sustained economic growth and poverty reduction, and is in line with the Cambodian Socio-Economic Development Plan (SEDPII) and Cambodia's Poverty Reduction Strategy Paper (PRSP), through closer consultations with the Cambodian government in policy dialogues.

Japanese ODA supports the following objectives:

- Development of social and economic infrastructure;
- Improvement of basic social services;
- Promotion of agriculture and rural development;
- Human resource development.

The Japanese Ministry of Foreign Affairs noted that Tokyo has provided financial assistance amounting to approximately US$1.76 billion (1992–2010) under Japan's ODA bilateral grant aid for the peace process, and the rehabilitation and development of Cambodia. Japan's ODA to Cambodia included yen loans of approximately US$289 million (1968–2009).

Japan's economic rehabilitation aid for Cambodia included the following: rural development projects, building a friendship bridge across the Tonle Sap River; and the construction of power plants and hospitals. Japanese aid programs were also driven by Japanese civil society, with volunteers and youths who dug wells and built schools.

Since the February 1999 Cambodia Consultative Group (CG) meeting in Tokyo, Japan has also made positive contributions in the areas of administrative and fiscal reforms, the demobilization of the armed forces, and forest preservation (natural resources management), spheres which have been identified as priorities by donor countries and by the Cambodian government. Japan has more recently later assisted Cambodia with social services improvement and training in good governance. Because of security concerns, Japan's assistance has been concentrated so far in the region of Phnom Penh, which has a population of around one million. To promote balanced development, it is important to strengthen ODA support for the rural areas where many poor people live. The expansion of support to the rural areas is particularly needed in sectors such as agriculture and rural development, basic human needs (BHN), and de-mining, with due consideration of the security situation in each region.

CONCLUSIONS

Japan's peace-building role in Cambodia was indeed comprehensive in scope, duration and purpose: first, by searching for a peace settlement from the late 1980s; secondly, holding various conferences in Tokyo for peace talks and to discuss economic reconstruction; thirdly, engaging in UN PKO in 1992–93; fourthly, by brokering a peace deal to help resolve the July 1997 crisis; fifthly, by the consolidation of peace by collecting weapons, clearing mines, and by helping to strengthen the Cambodian legal system, especially in helping the tribunal to put on trial the surviving KR leaders.

A noticeable feature of Japan's sustained peace-building efforts in Cambodia has been its will and drive to succeed as an active political actor on the world stage. Despite initial doubts from certain Asian neighbours that the dispatch of the Japanese SDF personnel for UNTAC in Cambodia was merely a prelude to the return of Japan as a military power, the SDF's professionalism and cooperation in Cambodia proved that such misgivings were misguided.

Have Japan's peace-building efforts in Cambodia been a success? It depends on whether the criterion of success emphasizes liberal democracy or political order, although the ideal outcome would be the achievement of both features. Cambodia today has political order but not liberal democracy, but then it did not have such features in the past. For a very poor and war-torn Southeast Asian country without any firm tradition of democracy, it would be indeed naive to expect rapid democratic consolidation in Cambodia. But at least, there has been political stability and rapid economic progress in Cambodia since 1993, despite some mishaps along the way. These are excellent achievements, when compared to the totally destroyed country under the KR, and the poor and isolated Cambodia under the Heng Samrin regime.

10

CAMBODIA-JAPAN RELATIONS

Pou Sothirak and Yukio Imagawa

INTRODUCTION: HISTORICAL RELATIONS BETWEEN JAPAN AND CAMBODIA

On 17 May 2010, His Majesty the Emperor of Japan remarked at a state banquet in honour of His Majesty the King of Cambodia that the relationship between the Kingdom of Cambodia and Japan had begun in 1569 when a Cambodian merchant ship arrived on the shores of Kyushu looking to establish contact with Japan. Further, from the Japanese side, there were 44 Japanese merchant ships which sailed to Cambodia with travel certificates issued by the government between 1604 and 1645.[1]

More recently, Cambodia and Japan have enjoyed over 50 years of a long-standing relationship during the reign of the King Father, His Majesty Norodom Sihanouk. Samdech Sihanouk has been an eminent leader of Cambodia, who has paved the way for a strengthened friendship which enables the people of both countries to develop the tradition of mutual respect and support over a wide range of areas, including politics, economy, culture, social affairs, and religion.

The following is a brief historical chronology of the relationship between Cambodia and Japan in recent times:

- 4 September, 1951 Cambodia participated in the San Francisco Peace Treaty Conference, and on 8 September 1951, it signed the Peace Treaty with Japan.
- From 9 February to 13 May 1953, King Norodom Sihanouk visited France, Montreal, New York, Washington D.C., San Francisco, Honolulu, and Tokyo in an effort to claim independence from France.
- 9 November 1953, King Norodom Sihanouk achieved full independence for Cambodia from France.
- 19 March 1954, Cambodia established a diplomatic legation in Japan.
- 4 May 1954, Japan established a diplomatic legation in Cambodia.
- 27 November, 1954, the Cambodian government informed its official position to the Japanese legation in Cambodia that it would not claim war damages from Japan.
- 2 December 1954, Japan informed Cambodia of her readiness to assist the Cambodian people through economic and technical cooperation.
- 21 February 1955, full diplomatic relations were established between Cambodia and Japan.
- 4 December, 1955, King Norodom Sihanouk visited Japan and met with His Majesty the Emperor Showa of Japan. During his stay in Japan, on 6 December, 1955, the House of Representative of Japan passed a resolution to express gratitude to Cambodia for its decision to abandon any claims of war damages from Japan.
- 9 December, 1955, King Norodom Sihanouk signed with H.E. Mr Shigemitsu, Foreign Minister of Japan, the "Friendship Treaty between Cambodia and Japan" to promote eternal friendship, independence, and peace.

The first diplomatic envoy to Japan was HRH Prince Norodom Kantol who arrived in Tokyo on 19 May 1954. Relations remained in place until April 1975, when Cambodia's Embassy in Tokyo was closed, following the Khmer Rouge takeover of power in Phnom Penh. Similarly, the Embassy of Japan in Phnom Penh ceased operations at the same time. In 1992, Japan re-opened its embassy in Phnom Penh and in 1994 Cambodia re-opened its Embassy in Tokyo.

Since the re-opening of its embassy in Tokyo, the Kingdom of Cambodia has established four Honorary Consuls in four Japanese prefectures: Osaka, Nagoya, Hokkaido, and Kyushu. This undertaking is in line with the Royal Government of Cambodia's strategy to further strengthen the existing cordial and productive diplomatic relations between Cambodia and Japan, thereby strengthening the strategic partnership and enhancing the promotion of small and medium enterprise investments, encouraging people-to-people exchanges as well as attracting tourists from Japan to Cambodia, which can contribute significantly toward Cambodia's national development.

Cambodian and Japanese leaders have regularly visited each other's countries to develop many shared interests and relevant concerns, as well as engaging in sincere discussions on the broader aspects of regional cooperation based on mutual interests, and learning from each others' experiences to further improve what has already been achieved in peace, stability, security and prosperity in the region.

From the Japanese side, there have been official visits by prominent leaders such as Vice Prime Minister and Minister for Foreign Affairs Tsutomu Hata in September of 1993, Vice Prime Minister and Minister for Foreign Affairs Yohei Kono in January 2000, Prime Minister Keizo Obuchi in January 2001, Their Imperial Highnesses Prince and Princess Akishino in June 2001, Prime Minister Junichiro Koizumi in November 2002, Minister for International Trade and Economy Takeo Hiranuma in September 2003, Foreign Minister Nobutaka Machimura in June 2005, Vice President of the House of Representatives Takahiro Yokomichi in August 2006, Foreign Minister Hirofumi Nakasone in January 2009, and Foreign Minister Katsuya Okada in October 2009.[2]

Cambodian dignitaries have also visited Japan regularly, including First Prime Minister Norodom Ranariddh in July 1996, President of the Senate Chea Sim in May 1999, President of the National Assembly Norodom Ranariddh in March 2002, Minister of Foreign Affairs and International Cooperation Hor Namhong in August 2002, in February 2003, and in February 2007, Deputy Prime Minister and Minister in charge of the Council of Minister Sok An in March 2005, Deputy Prime Minister and Minister of Interior Sak Kheng in May 2006, President of National Assembly Samdech Heng Samrin in October 2010, and Deputy Prime Minister and Minister of National Defence Tea Banh in March 2008.[3]

Prime Minister Hun Sen has visited Japan several times: in February 1999, June 2001, December 2003, and in May 2005. In June 2007, Prime Minister Hun Sen visited Japan as an official guest of the Japanese government. He met Prime Minister Shinzo Abe and many distinguished Japanese politicians and business leaders. During the summit meeting, the two prime ministers signed the Joint Statement reaffirming the strong ties and mutual trust that have been nurtured through the history of cooperation in peace building and national reconstruction. They also signed an Agreement for the Liberalization, Promotion and Protection of Investment to promote investment and strengthen economic relations between Cambodia and Japan. These two documents reaffirmed the important partnership between Cambodia and Japan, which has entered a new phase of strong ties and mutual conviction, and stressed that both countries will endeavour to further strengthen the bilateral relationship and address regional and global challenges together. In November 2009, Prime Minister Hun Sen visited Japan again.

The highest dignitary from Cambodia to visit Japan on an official state visit was His Majesty King Norodom Sihamoni in May 2010.

THE ESSENCE OF JAPANESE ASSISTANCE TO CAMBODIA

Through its contribution to the peace process in Cambodia, Japan has played a vital role in efforts to bring peace and progress to Cambodia. Japan's open-handed aid program has brought considerable benefit to Cambodia and its people over the past two decades. In July 1989, Japan played a prominent role in the preliminary negotiations that led to the Paris International Conference on Cambodia and in October 1991, co-chaired this with France, concluding successfully with the signing of the Paris Peace Agreements on Cambodia.

The deep bonds of friendship and cordial collaboration between the two countries have expanded and strengthened every year since 1991 in all the fields of Cambodia's national reconstruction and rehabilitation, which are strongly supported by Japan. Tokyo has provided substantial financial and technical assistances to Cambodia especially for repairs and rehabilitation of the infrastructure of the country. Since 1993, Japan has helped to build and rehabilitate schools, hospitals, roads, ports, bridges, electrical systems, and water treatment facilities across the country. These projects are durable, quality construction that promotes further development of the country.

Japan has been the biggest donor to Cambodia for the reconstruction process. The Japanese government, through the good offices of Japan International Cooperation Agency (JICA), has been extending Official Development Assistance (ODA) to Cambodia actively since peace and stability returned in the early 1990s. The Japanese Government has provided financial assistance (1992–2010) amounting to 189.36 billion Yen (approximately US$1.76 billion) under Japan's ODA bilateral grant aid for the peace process and the rehabilitation and development of Cambodia.[4]

The Japanese ODA comprises loan aid, grant aid, and technical assistance. Japanese ODA disbursements by Japan to Cambodia from 2005 to 2009 are listed below (net disbursements, in US$ million) in Table 10.1.

These ODA funds have been provided in line with Japan's aid policy and in conformity with the Country Assistance Program for Cambodia, and are

TABLE 10.1
Japanese Official Development Assistance (ODA) to Cambodia from 2005 to 2009
(US$ millions)

Year	Loan Aid	Grant Aid	Technical Assistance	Total
2005	4.07	53.10	43.45	100.62
2006	9.50	56.93	39.83	106.25
2007	11.36	62.35	39.84	113.56
2008	4.82	70.21	39.73	114.77
2009	19.94	59.40	48.14	127.49
TOTAL	73.87	1,062.53	549.60	1,686.03

Source: Japan's ODA Disbursement to Cambodia <http://www.mofa.go.jp/policy/oda/data/pdfs/cambodia.pdf> (accessed 23 June 2011)

intended to secure Cambodia's regional status within ASEAN and the Mekong Basin. Accordingly, Japanese assistance has been focused in four areas:

1. To strengthen government organizations as bases for future development, particularly reforms of the administrative and fiscal systems and consolidation of the legal system, as well as the reinforcement of the human resources undertaking these tasks.
2. To help Cambodia integrate in the regional economy, after it had joined ASEAN and the World Trade Organization, by creating an environment conducive to economic growth.
3. To rebuild the infrastructure destroyed by over 20 years of conflict, in order to improve the country's socioeconomic growth, leading to balanced development, and the forging of links between the urban and the rural areas, where there are large numbers of poor.
4. To assist in finding solutions to the unexploded anti-personnel mines and bombs, which are holding back Cambodia's development and to assist the many people who are physically or mentally disabled.

Furthermore, the priority areas for Japanese assistance cover: (1) good governance, (2) creation of an environment conducive to economic growth, (3) consolidation of the economic and social infrastructure, (4) strengthening of the health and medical care framework, (5) strengthening of the education system, (6) agriculture and rural development, (7) clearing of anti-personnel mines and aid for the disabled, and (8) management of environmental resources.[5]

Japanese assistance to Cambodia has been formulated based on policy dialogue with the government by providing grant aid and technical assistance to help develop the social and economic infrastructure, improve basic public service such as health care, promote agriculture and rural development and develop human resource. In addition, since 1999 Japan has been active in providing meaningful contribution in the area of administrative and fiscal reforms, demobilization of armed forces, and forest preservation. Subsequently, Japan has helped Cambodia with social services improvement and good governance.[6]

Capitalizing on the country's stability and wanting to help the Cambodian government to rebuild the economy, Japan focuses on rehabilitating major infrastructure projects in Cambodia. For instance, in 1999, Japan decided to extend to Cambodia a loan of up to 4 billion yen for the rehabilitation of the dilapidated Sihanoukville port.[7] More recently in June 2011, the Japanese government agreed to provide funding support of $131 million to build a second 2-km long Mekong bridge at Neak Loeung town with construction scheduled to start in late 2011 and expected completion in 2015.[8] The Cambodian government acknowledges with gratitude the Japan's valuable support and assistance in the process of national restoration and development. As such, on 17 August 2011 during the inauguration of a 9.10 km section of the 56 km National Road No 1, the Cambodian Prime Minister Samdech Akka Moha Sena Padei Techo Hun Sen said that "*The Royal Government and people of Cambodia would like to extend the most profound and grateful thanks to the government and people of Japan as one of the most important development partners with Cambodia*".[9]

Japan has also been very active in the area of Cambodian cultural heritage preservation and has supported many international conferences and activities on the preservation of the Angkor monuments. Under the framework of the UNESCO-Japan Trust Fund, the Japanese Government Team for Safeguarding Angkor (JSA) has assisted the Cambodian authorities to develop the International Program for Safeguarding Angkor, and has also begun to undertake the conservation and restoration of the whole Bayon Temple and Angkor Temple complexes.

Japan has been the most generous and single largest donor to support a tribunal set up to put on trial the Khmer Rouge leaders. The Government of Japan has provided financial assistance of about US$67 million or about 49 per cent of the total Pledges and Contributions to the Extraordinary Chambers in the Court of Cambodia (ECCC).[10] Japan considers the years

2011 as crucial for the operation of ECCC to carry on its mandate and had given Cambodia US$11,705,975 which represents 25 per cent of the annual operational costs.[11] On 26 July 2010, when a verdict was delivered against Kaig Guek Eav (alias "Duch"), who was sentenced to 35 years in prison by the ECCC, Japanese Foreign Minister Katsuya Okada issued a statement welcoming the progress made by the ECCC in its judicial process. He said "Japan regards the Khmer Rouge Trials as a crucial step towards the conclusion of the entire peace process in Cambodia, and believes that it will contribute to delivering justice and will strengthen the rule of law in the country…"[12]

Furthermore, numerous Japanese NGOs have been generously involved in helping Cambodians to restore their livelihood. Their activities cover the fields of education, health care and other related sectors. These projects have been implemented in line with the Government's policies focused on poverty reduction, and are highly appreciated and really beneficial to the Cambodian people.

CHANGES IN JAPAN'S DIPLOMATIC POSTURE IN ASIA

After its defeat in the Second World War, and even after the restoration of independent diplomacy by the entry into effect of the San Francisco Peace Treaty in 1952, Japan hesitated to take positive actions to solve local conflicts in Asia, particularly in the politico-military field. It was Cambodia's peace process which changed Japan's characteristically passive diplomatic posture to a more positive and creative one.

In December 1989, after nearly two decades of warfare between Cambodians, Prince Norodom Sihanouk, then head of three anti-Vietnam factions united in the coalition CGDK and Prime Minister Hun Sen, then head of the Vietnam-supported Phnom-Penh Government met at Ferre en Tardenois in France, some 120 kilometres east-northeast of Paris. It was the first attempt to have a direct face-to-face dialogue between Cambodians, working toward their reconciliation. Considering the Sihanouk-Hun Sen talks to be a clue to the peace process in Cambodia, Japan commenced to watch the situation closely and endeavoured to find out what Japan would be able to contribute to peace in Cambodia.

From the end of July to the end of August 1989, the year of the declaration of the end of the Cold War by US President Bush and Soviet President Gorbachev at Malta, France hosted the Paris International Conference on Cambodia (PICC) to try to solve the intractable conflict in Cambodia. Japan was, for the first time since the end of the Second World War, not only invited to participate in the conference but also requested to co-chair with

Australia the Third Committee which was to deal with the problems of refugees and reconstruction of Cambodia. Japan did so willingly.

Mr Merrilees from Australia and Ambassador Imagawa from Japan were chosen as Co-Chairmen of the Third Committee. After a month of very tough discussions, only the Third Committee co-chaired by Japan and Australia succeeded in the adoption of two official documents by consensus. It was a huge success for Japanese (and also Australian) diplomacy. As both the First Committee which dealt with military matters and the Second Committee which dealt with matters of international assurance were unable to achieve any conclusion, PICC was adjourned on 30 August 1989.

After the adjournment of the PICC, and particularly after January 1990, the five permanent member countries of the UN Security Council (P5) began a series of high-level meetings and negotiations in Paris and in New York. At the same time, talks among the Cambodians were revived and took place in Jakarta, Bangkok, Tokyo and other places. It was in Tokyo in June 1990, thatthe principle of equal presence of both CGDK and the Phnom Penh Government in the Supreme National Council (SNC) of Cambodia was agreed upon by Prince Sihanouk and Hun Sen.

The Paris International Conference on Cambodia (PICC) was reconvened on 21 October 1991 and the agreements for the comprehensive settlement of the Cambodian conflict (Paris Peace Agreements) were signed on 23 October 1991 by all the Cambodian delegates and representatives of 18 countries.

NORMALISATION OF JAPAN-CAMBODIA DIPLOMATIC RELATIONS AND THE OPENING OF THE NEW JAPANESE EMBASSY IN CAMBODIA

On 10 November 1991, 18 days after the signing of Paris Agreements on Cambodia, by order of the Government, Ambassador Imagawa flew to Phnom Penh to assume the post of Ambassador, and Head of the Japanese Delegation to the Supreme National Council of Cambodia. On the day of his arrival, the Office of Japanese Delegation was opened in Hotel Cambodiana in Phnom Penh.

On 14 November 1991, Prince Norodom Sihanouk, President of SNC, returned to Phnom Penh from Beijing, accompanied by SOC (State of Cambodia) Prime Minister Hun Sen.

On 15 March 1992, Mr Yasushi Akashi, Special Representative of the Secretary General of the United Nations arrived at Phnom Penh to lead the United Nations Transitional Authority in Cambodia (UNTAC), with Australian Lt. General John Sanderson, as Commander in Chief of the Military Contingent of UNTAC. Thus the structure of Cambodia for its peace process according to the Paris Agreements, comprised the SNC presided over by Prince Sihanouk, UNTAC lead by Mr Akashi and the actual administration headed by Hun Sen. On 25 March 1992, the Government of Japan nominated Imagawa Yukio as Ambassador Extraordinary and Plenipotentiary of Japan to Cambodia. At the same time, the Office of Japanese Delegation to the SNC was changed to the Embassy of Japan in Cambodia. Thus the Japanese Embassy in Cambodia, which had been closed in April 1975 when the last Ambassador Otori Kurino accredited to the Lon Nol Government had withdrawn from Cambodia some days before the Khmer Rouge's entry into Phnom Penh, was reopened and the diplomatic relations between Japan and Cambodia were normalized. On 14 April 1992, Ambassador Imagawa was solemnly received by Prince Sihanouk, President of SNC and presented to him the credentials signed by H.M. Emperor Akihito of Japan.

JAPAN'S PARTICIPATION IN UNTAC

On the date of Mr Akashi's arrival, the peace-keeping operations (PKO) by UNTAC were implemented throughout Cambodia. Japan was strongly requested to participate in the PKO by UNTAC and Cambodia.

Concerning the request from Cambodia to Japan, Ambassador Imagawa was deeply moved especially by the enthusiastic urging of Mr Hun Sen. On 21 March 1992, he returned to Japan for a short stay to receive His Majesty the Emperor's credentials and attestation as to him being Ambassador Extraordinary and Plenipotentiary, of which ceremony took place on 25 March. Coincidentally on the same day of his return to Japan, Mr Hun Sen also arrived in Tokyo for the purpose of requesting and persuadingJapan to participate in the PKO in Cambodia. As Ambassador Imagawa accompanied him and attended all his meetings during his stay in Tokyo, he witnessed how eager Mr Hun Sen was to strongly urge Japan's participation in the PKO in Cambodia.

On 22 March, a day after his arrival, he visited Minister of Foreign Affairs Michio Watanabe, and discussed matters for almost two hours. Hun Sen strongly requested that Japan should participate in the PKO in Cambodia. Also at the dinner hosted by the Minister of Foreign Affairs, Hun Sen reiterated that the success of the PKO would depend on Japan's participation. It was really surprising how with extraordinary vigour, Hun Sen went around trying to convince everyone he met to support Japan's participation in the PKO in Cambodia. From morning to early evening, he met with Liberal Democratic Party Secretary General Koichi Kato, Prime Minister Kiichi Miyazawa, Chairman of Komeito Party Koushiro Ishida, Finance Minister Tsutomu Hata, Chairman of the Japan Socialist Party Makoto Tanabe and other important parliamentary members. After having met with these persons in Japan's political circle, Hun Sen left Tokyo, in the late evening of the same day, for Washington, New York and Paris.

The question whether to participate or not in the PKO had caused political turmoil in Japan. After a long dispute in political circles, Japan finally decided, for the first time in its history, to send Self Defence Force officers and soldiers abroad and it dispatched 16 officers as military observers, 1,200 officers and soldiers from engineer battalion, 75 civilian police and some 50 election observers to Cambodia. It was indeed a significant breakthrough in Japan's national and international policy to respond positively to local conflicts in Asia and in other areas.

Throughout the transitional period in Cambodia, Japanese diplomats did their best to support UNTAC led by Mr Akashi. For the purpose of supporting and cooperating with UNTAC, at Imagawa's initiative as Japanese Ambassador, a unique consulting and coordinating body of ambassadors called the Expanded P5 (EP5) or core group was formed by Ambassadors in Cambodia of P 5 countries plus Indonesia, Japan, Australia and Thailand. EP5 usually met once or twice a week but sometimes, when the situation in Cambodia seemed critical, even three times a day to discuss measures to assist UNTAC and to cope with the situation. Mr Akashi or his assistant Sadri was also present at EP5 meetings.

SUCCESS OF THE PEACE PROCESS IN CAMBODIA

UNTAC eventually overcame all difficulties, especially those caused by the Khmer Rouge, and succeeded in organizing and executing a free and fair general election of Constituent Assembly members all over Cambodia in May 1993.

The Constituent Assembly whose 120 members were elected democratically through the UN-organized election established a new Constitution of the Kingdom of Cambodia on 21 September 1993, which made Cambodia a constitutional monarchy again. The Constituent Assembly transformed itself into a Legislative Assembly. On 24 September 1993, under the rules of the new Constitution, Prince Norodom Sihanouk, at the request of the Crown Council, resumed the throne as King of Cambodia. H.M. the King Norodom Sihanouk nominated Norodom Ranariddh of FUNCINPEC party as First Prime Minister and Hun Sen of the CPP as Second Prime Minister. Thus a new two-headed Royal Cambodian Government was formed. With the promulgation of the new constitution of the Kingdom of Cambodia, the transformation of the Constituent Assembly to a Legislative Assembly, the re-enthronement of H.M. King Norodom Sihanouk and the formation of the new Royal Government, UNTAC completed its mandate and Mr Akashi left Cambodia on the 26 September 1993. Thus, the peace process to resolve the Cambodian conflict was successfully completed.

JAPAN'S CONTRIBUTION TO THE RECONSTRUCTION OF CAMBODIA

Japan is not only the top donor to Cambodia, but also plays a leading role in the reconstruction of Cambodia. In June 1992, Japan, as co-chair with UNDP, organized a Ministerial Conference on the Rehabilitation and Reconstruction of Cambodia, in Tokyo, where 33 countries including Cambodia and 13 international organizations including UNTAC participated. About US$80 billion in pledges was gained. Japan also co-chaired with France three meetings of the International Committee for the Reconstruction of Cambodia (ICORC) — which had been formed at the proposal of Japan in the Third Committee of PICC — in September 1993 in Paris, in March 1994 in Tokyo and in July 1996 in Paris. Since 1996, ICORC changed to CG-type meetings and these have taken place annually in Tokyo and in Paris in turn. In these international conferences and meetings, a huge amount of foreign aid for the reconstruction and development of Cambodia has been pledged by various donor countries and international organizations.

THE ROLE PLAYED BY JAPAN IN SOLVING POLITICAL CONFLICTS AFTER 1997

The relationship between the First Prime Minister and the Second Prime Minister in Cambodia was more or less cooperative for about two years. But the relationship between the two prime ministers turned sour as the next general election slated for 1998 drew near.

On the night of 17 June 1997, minor gunfights between the security guards of First Prime Minister and those of the Second Prime Minister occurred in Phnom Penh. A shell also landed in the garden of the American ambassador's residence. The incident drew wide attention in the international media. At the G8 Summit Meeting which took place rightafter the incident, from the 20 to 22 June in Denver USA, Japan's Prime Minister Hashimoto announced his concern over the tense situation in Cambodia and proposed that he send a special envoy to Cambodia. Hashimoto's proposal was endorsed by French President Chirac, who said that he would also send his special envoy to Cambodia. With the consensus of G8, Ambassador Imagawa was appointed as special envoy of Japanese Prime Minister and Claude Martin, Assistant Undersecretary at Quai d'Orsay was appointed as special envoy of the French President. Mr Claude Martin and Ambassador Imagawa went to Phnom Penh, met and had long talks with Second Prime Minister Hun Sen and First Prime Minister Ranariddh on 26 June, in their respective residences. They delivered letters from their heads of state or our government to both prime ministers. These letters expressed the wish that the Cambodian co-Prime Ministers should not disrupt the peace. They requested that the two Prime Ministers and two ruling parties, FUNCINPEC and the Cambodian People's Party (CPP), cooperate with each other to ensure that the general elections scheduled for the following year should be carried out freely and fairly. They also requested that the two prime ministers confirm a specific date for holding the election. Both Hun Sen and Ranariddh, though far from being reconciled themselves, stated that they would establish closer contacts aimed at overcoming the differences in their views and promote their coordination to organize the coming election. They then had contact with each other and later informed the ambassadors, before their departure from Phnom Penh, that the election would be held on 23 May (later delayed to 26 July for technical and financial reasons) of the following year.

However, on 5–6 July, only ten days after the two Denver Summit special envoys visited Cambodia, a fierce military clash broke out in Phnom Penh and its surrounding suburbs between government troops supporting Hun Sen and one of Ranariddh's military units. Ranariddh's military units and private army were virtually decimated. Hun Sen declared that he took military action as a duty to save the nation. He also claimed that Ranariddh had brought more than 100 Khmer Rouge fighters to his camp outside Phnom Penh city. Ambassador Imagawa noted that he was not in a position to judge which side was right or wrong and he could only say that the position of Japan at that time was neutral. Japan sincerely hoped not to re-internationalize the Cambodian problems but wished that the Cambodians themselves could resolve the conflict.

After the above-mentioned July incident, Claude Martin and Ambassador Imagawa were received in audience separately by H.M. King Norodom Sihanouk at Beijing on 15 and 16 July. H.M. the King and Ambassador Imagawa talked very frankly and privately for more than three hours. In their conversation, His Majesty the King confirmed to me that what Hun Sen had done against Ranariddh was not a coup d'état, but a "coup de force" in French, which meant political change realized by military power, because Hun Sen had not changed Cambodia's Constitution, the monarchy, the government system with First and Second Prime Ministers or any other political system. Ambassador Imagawa was deeply moved by the passionate and dignified manner of H.M. King Sihanouk who had very fair, just, unselfish and patriotic ideas for the peace and stability of Cambodia.

Cambodia finally succeeded in carrying out the general election on 26 July 1998. In this way, neither Hun Sen nor Ranariddh, who had been in voluntary exile in France opposing Hun Sen's politics, never reneged on their international promise to hold a free and fair election. Therefore, both Hun Sen and Ranariddh honoured their international commitment to the two special envoys and through them to G8 member countries and the world.

After the elections in 1998, two parties, FUNCINPEC and the Sam Rainsy Party, who could not overcome the power of the Cambodian People's Party, had refused to recognize the result of the election for more than four months. There was a danger that a new political instability would emerge in Cambodia. Nevertheless this time, by the very clever good offices of H.M. the King Sihanouk, a compromise was made and a new Government, led by a single Prime Minister Hun Sen of CPP, and comprising a coalition between the CPP and FUNCINPEC, was created on 30 November 1998. Prince Ranariddh of FUNCINPEC was nominated as the President of the National Assembly.

On 26 July 2003, the third election after the signing of the Paris Agreements was held. To observe the election situation, Ambassador Imagawa was sent to Cambodia as the head of the Japanese Government observers' team, composed of 26 members. The official Japanese team's conclusion was that as far as we observed in several localities in Cambodia, the general election was held more or less free and fair and neither violent disturbances nor unjust actions were recognized. However, in this time also, FUNCINPEC and the Sam Rainsy Party, which had lost the election to the CPP, did not recognize the result of the election, and again political instability continued for about one year. To solve this difficult political situation, Hun Sen did his utmost using his ability to the full, and finally did achieve the renormalization of the political situation in Cambodia. On 15 July 2004, a new CPP-FUNCINPEC coalition Government headed by Hun Sen was formed.

On 6 October 2004, while staying in Beijing, H.M. the King Norodom Sihanouk suddenly expressed his intention to abdicate from the throne, as his health had been failing due to his 83 years of age. The Cambodian Government had urged H.M. the King to reconsider his intention but had been rejected. On 18–20 October, the enthronement ceremony of H.M. King Norodom Sihamoni, H.M. Sihanouk's youngest son, who had been elected unanimously by the Throne Council, was celebrated at the Royal Palace in Phnom Penh.

REALISATION OF PEACE AND STABILITY IN CAMBODIA AND RELATIONS WITH JAPAN

Under the reign of H.M. King Sihamoni, the mutual coordination and close relations between the new King and Prime Minister Hun Sen were smoothly advanced.

The year 2008 saw the 55th anniversary of Japan-Cambodia diplomatic relations. Both Cambodia and Japan celebrated "Cambodia-Japan Friendship Year." In this year, the two countries, on both the governmental and private levels, made efforts to further promote political, economical and cultural cooperation. In June 2008, Prime Minister Hun Sen visited Japan, as an official guest of the Japanese Government.

On 27 July 2008, the 4th general election after the Paris Agreement took place in Cambodia. The CPP gained 90 seats out of the total 123 seats of the National Assembly. It was the first time since the signing of the Paris Agreements that there occurred no political disorder after the election, and thereafter, the peace and stability in Cambodia has become really solid.

From 16 to 20 May 2010, H.M. the King Norodom Sihamoni visited Japan as a state guest. The King was warmly received by H.M. Emperor Akihito and talked cordially between them. The King was also respectfully welcomed at a meeting with Prime Minister Hatoyama and other top leaders of Japan's political and business circles. The state visit by H.M. the King Sihamoni contributed much to improved Cambodia-Japan relations.

CONCLUSION

The Royal Government of Cambodia has worked hard to restore peace and stability, and maintains security for the nation and people with help from the international community, especially Japan.

Cambodia is a land of opportunity for the travellers and businessman alike. Between the eastern hills of Mondulkiri and the beaches and islands of the western coast, Cambodia offers a broad palette of landscapes and exciting opportunities for enterprise. The infrastructure, so long a barrier to travel and commerce, is now improving in leaps and bounds. New all-weather roads, many funded by Japan, open the countryside to all who wishes to come and visit. The country is blessed with a great combination of historical and cultural charm, with fine-looking surroundings; Cambodia abounds with the greenery of a beautiful environment: a fine coastline, unspoiled mountains, rivers, lakes, hill tribes, and abundant wildlife and rain forests.

If we look at Cambodia today, we see how the generosity of Japan has lightened the burdens and empowered so many citizens of Cambodia. From smooth roads to new schools, from the restoration of Angkor temples to new business opportunities, Japan has touched many lives in some way. The Japanese do not forget that it was King Norodom Sihanouk who did not claim war damages from Japan, and Cambodians do not forget that it was a citizen of Japan, Yasushi Akashi, head of the 1992–93 UN Mission in

Cambodia, who helped guide Cambodia out of the mire of civil war towards an era of democracy, peace, and development. Because of this excellent bond that has existed over a great period of time, the bilateral relations between Cambodia and Japan will continue to improve in the years ahead both for mutual benefit as well as for the greater good of the world at large.

Notes

1. Remarks by His Majesty the Emperor of Japan at the State Banquet in Honour of His Majesty Preah Bat Samdech Preah Boromneat Norodom Sihamoni, King of Cambodia, 17 May 2010 <http://www.kunaicho.go.jp/e-okotoba/01/address/okotoba-h22e.html#0517> (accessed 1 November 2011).
2. Ministry for Foreign Affairs of Japan: Japan-Cambodia Relations <http://www.mofa.go.jp/region/asia-paci/cambodia/index.html> (accessed 24 October 2011).
3. Ibid.
4. For more details on Japanese's assistance to Cambodian see Japan's ODA to the Kingdom of Cambodia <http://www.kh.emb-japan.go.jp/economic/oda/odalist_march2011-e.pdf> (accessed 24 October 2011).
5. For more details on Japanese Country Assistance Program for Cambodia, see JICA Cooperation to Cambodia, 2006 <http://www.jica.go.jp/cambodia/english/activities/pdf/basic.pdf> (accessed 24 October 2011).
6. For more details see Japan's Assistance Policy for Cambodia <http://www.kh.emb-japan.go.jp/economic/cooperation/japc/japc.htm> (accessed 1 November 2011).
7. Ibid.
8. The Cambodia Daily, "Japan to Fund $131 Million Bride Across the Mekong River", dated 24 June 2010.
9. Agence Kampuchea Press, "PM Grateful to Japan's Development Assistance to Cambodia", 1 November 2011 <http://www.akp.gov.kh/?p=9300> (Accessed 1 November 2011).
10. As reported by Associated Press "Japan, biggest donor to Cambodia's genocide tribunal, contributed another $11.7million", 28 January 2011.
11. Press Release by the Japanese Embassy in Cambodia: "Japanese Assistance for the Extraordinary Chambers in the Courts of Cambodia (ECCC), 28 January 2011.
12. Statement by Mr Katsuya Okada, Minister for Foreign Affairs of Japan, 26 July 2011 <http://www.mofa.go.jp/announce/announce/2010/7/0726_01.html> (accessed 2 November 2011).

11

CAMBODIA'S RELATIONS WITH FRANCE SINCE THE PARIS AGREEMENTS OF 1991

Julio A. Jeldres

Cambodia and France have had a close relationship since France intervened in 1863 and colonized the country, whilst helping Cambodia to fend off the territorial ambitions of Thailand on the East and Vietnam on the West. For France, Cambodia, together with Laos, constituted an "island of French culture in the Far East".[1] This is not to say that their relationship has not suffered periods of stress. A former French diplomat wrote astutely in his memoirs that the relationship between France and its former colony Cambodia was "an amalgamation of amorous heartache, mutual irritation, and nose-dives".[2] A close look at the relationship between the two countries since the signature of the Paris Agreements on Cambodia in October 1991 may explain the reasons behind the ups and downs of this special rapport.

At the outset, it should be pointed out that the relationship between the two countries had been shaped, as in the case of Cambodia's relations with China, by the close bonds existing between King Norodom Sihanouk, a francophone and Francophile, and leading French personalities, in particular General Charles de Gaulle. The French disapproved of the overthrow of

Samdech Norodom Sihanouk as they felt that it had complicated the situation in the whole of Indochina. "Sihanouk, whatever his failings, had kept his country out of the war. General de Gaulle had chosen Phnom Penh as the locality in which to deliver his key speech on Indo-China, precisely because Cambodia could pre-figure a neutral Indo-China. The problem was no longer a purely Vietnamese problem but a global problem of Indochina".[3]

Relations between Cambodia and France nose-dived from being excellent to almost reaching a breaking point during 1970-75, as France refused to grant accreditation to a new Cambodian Ambassador, in the weeks after the overthrow of Norodom Sihanouk on 18 March 1970. After the proclamation of the Khmer Republic, France withdrew its Ambassador from Cambodia in July 1971 while maintaining increasingly close contacts with the exiled former monarch through France's Ambassador in Peking.

Cambodia's new leaders in Phnom Penh were profoundly disappointed with France's attitude, but they saw use in maintaining relations with the former colonial power as there were strong personal and cultural ties. They hoped, by maintaining an Embassy in Paris that the French would come to see the truth about the situation in Cambodia, as they regarded France as an essential political factor in any future settlement, which the Cambodians wanted to be on the basis of the Geneva Agreements of which France was a signatory. It seems that the ambivalence of French attitudes towards the new regime in Phnom Penh did not reflect so much its appreciation of the situation in Cambodia, but rather what France regarded at the time as the requirements of its policies for the whole of Indochina.[4] The French basically wanted Cambodia to maintain its neutrality granted by the Geneva Agreements of 1954, the respect for the sovereignty and territorial integrity of each country in Indochina, the cessation of foreign intervention and a negotiated settlement of the conflict in Vietnam, which was dangerously expanding to the other two countries of the peninsula.[5]

Following the Khmer Rouge victory in April 1975, France ceased to be represented in Phnom Penh as the new Cambodian regime did not allow the French Embassy, then led by a Vice-Consul, to continue operating in the Cambodian capital, and ordered all Cambodian citizens who had taken refuge at the Embassy to leave. They expelled under military escort all the remaining French diplomats, experts and citizens (as well as other Westerners who had taken refuge in the French Embassy) to the Thai border.

Even though France had allowed a semi-diplomatic mission of the National Liberation Front of Kampuchea (FUNK) and the Royal Government of National Union of Cambodia (GRUNC) to operate in Paris since late 1970, it did not recognize GRUNC until 12 April 1975, just five days before the fall of Phnom Penh. From 1975 to 1989, France was not represented in Cambodia because the Khmer Rouge regime had not allowed the French Embassy to re-open in Phnom Penh, in spite of many requests by French ministers to the new "Democratic Kampuchean" authorities who had replaced the GRUNC.[6] The following countries only were allowed to open diplomatic missions in Phnom Penh: Albania, Cuba, China, Egypt, Laos, North Korea, North Vietnam, Romania and Yugoslavia.

Frustrated by the lack of response from the new Cambodian regime, France withdrew recognition from the Democratic Kampuchea mission in Paris which lost its semi-diplomatic status on 12 July 1976.[7] They no longer had diplomatic identity cards, diplomatic automobile plates and if they tried to fly the Democratic Kampuchea flag, the police would take it down. France also let it be known that recognition of the new Cambodian government was rescinded and would only be reinstated when the Cambodians made a proposal to the French Government to establish relations, which would need to be studied before a decision could be made.[8] The French government had reportedly been "rather vexed" by the priority given by the new regime in Phnom Penh to other countries which had no particular ties or association with Cambodia, as far as allowing the establishment of diplomatic missions in Phnom Penh was concerned.[9]

Diplomatic relations were not restored between the two countries until 1991, and the relationship between the former colonial protector and its former protégé was based purely on informal contacts between the People's Republic of Kampuchea (PRK), which had followed the Democratic Kampuchea regime, and the long-standing friendship between French leaders and the former monarch Norodom Sihanouk, who spent several months every year in France from his exile base in Beijing. In 1979, Sihanouk had requested political asylum for himself and his wife in France, but was informed by the French Ambassador to the United Nations, in New York, that asylum was granted but Sihanouk "would have to abstain from any political activity while in France and would not be allowed to grant press, radio or television interviews on political matters".[10]

Prior to the Paris Agreements on Cambodia of October 1991, French policy towards Cambodia had been consistent with overall French policy in Indochina, which was based on long term considerations. As far as the political relationship was concerned, France's historical ties had been with the Cambodian monarchy. In the 1980s, France was a strong supporter of former King Norodom Sihanouk's activities to obtain the withdrawal of Vietnamese forces from Cambodia, while at the same time France was reluctant to allow Sihanouk to use French territory for his nationalist activities, which may upset any influence France may have had with Vietnam. This was why French officials always hastened to make it clear that Sihanouk visited France "on a private capacity as a long-standing friend of France", which did not imply "political recognition".[11]

During a visit to China in October 1980, President Giscard D'Estaing had a two-hour meeting with Sihanouk, during which the former monarch asked the French leader "to use his influence so that a UN Force of Blue Helmets or another International Army could be sent to protect Cambodia".[12] This was a request that Sihanouk would repeatedly make to successive French leaders.

It was not until 1981, that Socialist party leader and presidential candidate, Francois Mitterrand, during a secret visit to North Korea on 14–15 February that year, met Sihanouk and was convinced by the former monarch's arguments which called for the urgent convening of an international conference, preferably hosted by France, to discuss the Cambodia conflict and how to settle it under UN supervision. Within the French Socialist Party, there was no unanimity on this approach and Claude Cheysson, who would later become Mitterrand's first Foreign Minister, was more inclined to agree with Hanoi's arguments which presented its invasion of Cambodia in January 1979 as a humanitarian act to save the Cambodian people from the horrors of Pol Pot.[13] The election of Mitterrand as President also caused a reassessment of French policies towards Cambodia, and France began to provide facilities and some financial assistance for Sihanouk's activities. In 1988, during a visit to the United Nations, Mitterrand told the UN General Assembly that he intended to call an international conference in Paris to discuss the Cambodian conflict and find a way to peaceful settle it.[14]

In July 1989, France finally took up the request of Sihanouk and organised the first session of the Paris International Conference on Cambodia (PICC) which would eventually lead to the sending of the United Nations Transitional Authority in Cambodia (UNTAC), a multilateral force to keep the peace in Cambodia, prior to general elections for a Constituent Assembly. However, this session of PICC failed to achieve agreement on a settlement but was successful in keeping the warring Cambodian factions meeting in different capitals around the world. During the conference, France appeared as supporting a Hanoi-instigated initiative which would see a Sihanouk-Hun Sen bilateral government established in Cambodia, which would regain a strong francophone influence. This deal was opposed by China, ASEAN, Australia and the US.

That year France also began, unofficially, a process of restoring its relations with Cambodia through the opening of an Alliance Francaise, at that point the largest in Asia, to teach the French language, but also offering specialised local training to civil servants and a one month's training course in Paris for senior officials, including vice-ministers of the new regime. Staffed by diplomats on secondment from the Ministry of Foreign Affairs, the guidelines of the new Cultural French Centre were simple: to re-establish French influence in Cambodia. By November 1991, the Alliance Francaise had 7,500 students enrolled, charging each of them a token fee of about US$2.00 per semester.[15]

On 15 November 1991, a day after the return to Phnom Penh of Norodom Sihanouk, the new French envoy to the SNC,[16] Ambassador Philippe Coste, presented his credentials to Sihanouk at a colourful ceremony in the Royal Palace. Contrary to the understanding reached by the SNC, foreign envoys would be accredited to the SNC as Permanent Representatives, with or without the personal rank of Ambassador, because at the time Sihanouk was not considered to be the Head of State of Cambodia, as no election had been held in the country. All these arrangements had been firmed up to avoid countries having to recognize the State of Cambodia (SOC) regime, which was the successor to the pro-Vietnam People's Republic of Kampuchea. The letter of accreditation was to be signed by the accrediting country's foreign minister.

However, Ambassador Coste was accredited as Ambassador Extraordinary and Plenipotentiary to the SNC and his credentials were signed by French President Francois Mitterrand, which caused the Cambodian royal protocol to expect that all future accreditation letters should be signed by the accrediting country's Head of State. This French action was the beginning of a series of machinations to reassert French ascendancy over the other countries-signatories of the Paris agreements on Cambodia, causing many misunderstandings and some costly delays. In the days that followed, Ambassador Coste called on all the senior leaders of the State of Cambodia, themselves not members of the SNC, thus granting a kind of recognition by France of the SOC, something that the Paris Agreements specifically had avoided, as the SOC was considered to be part of the problem caused by Vietnam's invasion of Cambodia.[17]

Following the presentation of his credentials, Coste told journalists that France's "wish was to return to Cambodia and we are ready to re-establish the links. We have decided to reconstruct Cambodia".[18] France's ambitious plans for their former colony soon created problems for the implementation of the Paris Agreements, which had formulated as an interim measure the immediate dispatch to Cambodia of a UN advance mission or UNAMIC, which was under the command, because of France's leading role in the peace process, of a French parachute officer, General Michel Loridon.

The General's first demand was that French would be the "lingua franca" of his mission, even though he spoke impeccable English. Loridon's demand caused unnecessary delays in UNAMIC's arrival in Cambodia, and he only changed his mind after the other members of his team, mostly Australians and New Zealanders, insisted that they could only communicate in English.[19]

But France did not give up easily. A report commissioned for President Francois Mitterrand and authored by the former French Ambassador to Angola, Jean-Jacques Galabru,[20] proposed several important measures to establish a permanent French influence in Cambodia, by targeting the rehabilitation of Cambodia, in particular concerning the training of public servants. It pointed to the Technological Institute of Phnom Penh and the Economic and Commercial Sciences Institute (formerly known as Lycee Descartes) as two of the education centres that needed to be "rescued" from what Galabru considered was an "Anglo-Saxon, American-led campaign to regain influence in Cambodia, managed by the United Nations and financed by the Japanese".[21] From what followed, the French logic as far as helping Cambodia rehabilitate was, in the words of a French diplomat in Phnom Penh "We renovate the buildings, provide the teachers, pay for everything on condition that the courses are taught in the French language, we are not paying for everything in order for them to be taught in English".[22]

Thus, by the time President Mitterrand arrived in Cambodia on 11 February 1993, on the first visit to Cambodia by a French Head of State since 1966, the French push for greater influence in Cambodia was in full swing, raising criticism that the French stance showed disregard for the terms of the Paris Agreements.[23] The arrival of the French President in Cambodia just before the UN-supervised elections was timed to show France's full support for Norodom Sihanouk and the peace process. However, France also supported a crucial adjustment of the peace process which was opposed by the "Anglo-Saxons", Australia, Britain and the United States. This was the holding of a presidential election concurrently with the legislative elections, a Sihanouk initiative which received the blessing also of UN Secretary General Boutros Boutros-Ghali.[24]

Sihanouk felt, at the time that upon the withdrawal of the United Nations from Cambodia, after the elections without one leader unambiguously in charge would reduce Cambodia to lawlessness, something which Sihanouk wanted to avoid at all costs, as it could rekindle the civil strife of the recent past.[25] However, the above-mentioned countries were concerned that any election of Sihanouk as Head of State would confer on him all the powers which the existing Supreme National Council (the 12-member body representing Cambodia's sovereignty during the transitional period and which Sihanouk headed) would give the former monarch an open-ended mandate, thus disregarding the Paris Agreements which called for a multiparty system of government.[26] Immediately after Mitterrand's visit, Sihanouk issued a communiqué announcing that he had decided not to run for president.[27]

As it turned out, Cambodia newly-elected National Assembly, taking the lead from a French drafted text, decided to make Cambodia again a monarchy, installing Sihanouk as a reigning but not ruling King on 23 September 1993.

But the visit of the French leader coincided also with French urgings for the three countries of Indochina to join ASEAN as a counterweight against China's, and to a certain extent Japan's, aspirations to play an influential post-conflict role in the region and in Cambodia, in particular. At the same time, France urged Cambodia to re-join the Association of French-speaking countries or "Francophonie", something which caused considerable debate within the new Cambodian government, after the elections, as it was not supported by some of the ASEAN countries, in particular Singapore.[28] In spite of a promise made by Prince Ranariddh to Lee Kuan Yew, Cambodia duly joined and remains a member of the Association of French-speaking countries. At about this time, French influence in Cambodia began to lessen as Cambodia actively pursued membership of ASEAN.

But there were also instances when Cambodia took an independent stand and did not agree to requests from its former colonial power. During the visit of the French Finance Minister, Edmond Alphandery, to Cambodia in July 1994, Alphandery requested the two Co-Premiers, Prince Ranariddh and Samdech Hun Sen, to pay compensation to the French companies which had lost property in Cambodia. He argued that this "would be a significant gesture encouraging the French companies as well as other prospective investors to come and invest in Cambodia".[29]

The French Minister was particularly disappointed by Prince Ranariddh who had been a colleague of his at the University of Marseille, because the French were prepared to offer a US$60 million grant to Cambodia on condition that 10 per cent of that grant be given back by Cambodia to the owners of rubber plantations in Kompong Cham province. Because of Ranariddh's refusal, the grant was put on hold and the French were merely prepared to go ahead with another aid package amounting to US$15.8 million, which had been previously offered by France to Cambodia.[30]

In 1994, Cambodia and France signed a Memorandum of Understanding (MOU) by which the French company which had previously owned, up to 1975, the three main rubber plantations at Mimot, Chup and Snuol in Kompong Cham province, would return to Cambodia to repair and rehabilitate them to international standards, and then get one of the plantations back in return for the investment and would forego any further compensation from the Cambodian government for the other properties. However, in 1996–97, the deal was not being fulfilled by the Second Co-Premier, Hun Sen and his brother, the Governor of Kompong Cham, after the plantations had been rehabilitated and were producing rubber of high quality which was being sold in the international markets, prompting the French Foreign Minister to warn his Cambodian counterpart, during a visit to France in early 1997, that France would be forced to review its program of assistance to Cambodia.[31]

In the event, the plantations became state companies, and in 2009 they were sold to private interests linked to the Cambodian People's Party. France has provided some assistance in the form of bilateral aid through the French Development Agency for private pilot projects on rubber cultivation by families of farmers, which have developed rapidly around the whole country. Because of the technical assistance provided by France, these smaller family-run plantations have performed better than the larger ones.[32]

France also aspired to train the new Cambodian army, which was to be established following the elections and the formation of a government. Thus, two months after the elections, in July 1993, the French Minister for Defence, Francois Leotard, arrived in Phnom Penh for an official visit during which he signed with his Cambodian counterparts (there were two Co-Ministers of defence at the time in the new Cambodian government) a bilateral agreement of military cooperation, by which the establishment of a French military mission in Cambodia to finance and train elements of the new Cambodian army was authorised by the Royal Government of Cambodia.[33]

The first trainees were those of the "Royal Gendarmerie", a kind of paramilitary force in charge of public safety, with police duties among the civilian population which, as it is the case in France, should work together with the National Police but in the case of Cambodia, often found itself in conflict with elements of the National Police, because of the policemen's often unruly behaviour. French military instructors also took part in the training of regiment 911 of the new Royal Cambodian Armed Forces (RCAF). This regiment, initially trained by Suharto's Special Forces in Indonesia, became an elite force "having the competences of Special Forces", announced General Ke Kim Yan, Chief of the Joint Staff at a ceremony marking the completion of the training by the French instructors and in the presence of Gildas Le Lidec, the French Ambassador to Cambodia.[34] Both the Royal Gendarmerie and Regiment 911 would cause severe embarrassment to France as some units were detached from their headquarters and transferred to the bodyguard corps of Second Prime Minister Hun Sen. During the coup of July 1997, they took part in the torturing and extrajudicial killings of FUNCINPEC party members at the military base of Kambol, about 12 kilometres from Phnom Penh airport, according to a report issued by the

Cambodian Office of the UN High Commissioner for Human Rights on 5 September 1997.[35]

The issue of the use of the French language continued to create tensions in the relationship between Cambodia and France because of the latter insistence in the teaching of French at higher education institutions in Cambodia which France funded, even though the numbers of students voluntarily learning French in Cambodia had declined rapidly from almost 8,000 to less than 5,000 in 1995.[36] In May 1995, students at the Institute of Technology of Cambodia began demonstrations which disrupted classes for three weeks; the students burned tyres in the Institute's courtyard and torched effigies labelled simply "French". The students did not advocate the use of Khmer language but rather the use of English. Some of the students felt that by being compelled to learn French and with Cambodia getting ready to join ASEAN, they argued that Cambodians would not be able to participate in ASEAN conferences or training courses or simply to communicate with their ASEAN counterparts.[37]

For the Cambodian Minister of Education, the late Tol Lah, the situation was particularly distressing, as at the time France was the second largest donor to Cambodia, after Japan, providing about US$7 million per year for education purposes, a large amount that supplemented the scarce resources allocated by the Royal Government to the education portfolio. "If Cambodia loses the aid from France, where would we get that amount of money for our education services", he would say with an air of resignation.[38]

When King Norodom Sihanouk paid a state visit to France in April 1996, his good friend and supporter Francois Mitterrand had passed away and there was a new man at the Elysee. Jacques Chirac, the former Mayor of Paris, had established a rapport with Sihanouk by providing vehicles for the cleaning of Phnom Penh city. But regarding foreign affairs, he had a different approach than Mitterrand, which was not based on personalities but rather on France's interests. Thus, Sihanouk was visibly disappointed during his visit because of France's support for Cambodia's bid to join ASEAN. Sihanouk felt that by joining ASEAN, Cambodia would be abandoning its neutrality, which is inscribed in the 1993 Constitution and also in the Final Declaration of the Paris International Conference on Cambodia of October 1991.[39] "Instead during the State Visit to France, our President and Prime Minister encouraged him to support the Royal Government's effort to win ASEAN membership, the King was not pleased".[40]

Sihanouk would make his displeasure known during an interview with Marie-Ange Lescure of Radio France-Inter in which he stated "*Since France is present, and more and more present in Cambodia, it is a guarantee of independence for my country. Anglo-Saxon influence and ASEAN influences are neutralized. I am not a supporter of joining ASEAN. I have never particularly liked ASEAN. I prefer to be neutral, but, nevertheless, neutral with the support of France*".[41]

The real test of the strength of the Cambodia-France relationship came in July 1997 when Second Co-Premier, Hun Sen, launched a coup against the First Co-Premier, Prince Norodom Ranariddh, while a meeting of international donors was being hosted by the French government in Paris. While France initially condemned Hun Sen's coup, it also conveyed a message which basically suggested that as long as Hun Sen took appropriate measures to give a "constitutional appearance" to his recent "coup de force", then things would be forgiven, including the killings, summary executions and disappearances that took place during and after the coup.[42]

On 15 July 1997, the deputy Secretary General of the French Foreign Ministry, Ambassador Claude Martin, called on King Norodom Sihanouk in Beijing, and suggested that the Cambodian monarch "helps the parties present in Phnom Penh to organise the return to normalcy and to the peace process in Cambodia".[43] France did not clarify what it considered as "the parties present in Phnom Penh" but it was clear to fair-minded observers that Phnom Penh, and for that matter the whole of Cambodia, was under the tight control of the military apparatus of the Cambodian People's Party, and what was left of the royalist party, FUNCINPEC, was almost completely destroyed with the exception of a small group of senior and middle rank officials under Ung Huot, who were ready to work for Hun Sen under the facade of the "FUNCINPEC Party", thus giving some kind of normalcy to the political scene in Phnom Penh, just as France, Japan and other countries wanted.

Since 1994, the French Ambassador's relationship with Prince Ranariddh had been marked by misunderstandings on both sides over the increasing lawlessness existing in Phnom Penh and in the countryside. When Khmer Rouge soldiers with the help of some government officials kidnapped three foreign tourists, an Australian, a British and a Frenchman and subsequently murdered them, the relationship turned sour as the French Embassy lodged protest after protest with the Cambodian Foreign Ministry over serious incidents of robbery and assault against French citizens in Phnom Penh. The Embassy's complaints were legitimate, because at the time there was an increasing wave of street attacks against foreigners and, particularly against French citizens.[44] In one of the most serious cases, a young French woman, who had just arrived from France to spend her holidays helping Cambodia, was raped by a police officer. The assault against her happened the day after

King Sihanouk had issued a warning to foreigners to be extra careful in Phnom Penh's streets.[45]

Ambassador Le Lidec, had sent copies of the letters to King Sihanouk and the monarch, who was horrified by the attacks against foreigners, something that was until then unknown in Cambodia, had made them public in his Monthly Information Bulletin known as "BMD", belittling the royal government's assurances to the public that it was clamping down on street anarchy. This had infuriated Prince Ranariddh, while Hun Sen simply ignored the whole affair.[46] Prince Ranariddh was unable to grasp the seriousness of the incidents or to accept this attitude of the French mission, which he considered as tantamount to interference in Cambodia's internal affairs.

Soon afterwards, Le Lidec began to have difficulties getting access to Ranariddh, and also had a number of unpleasant exchanges with the Prince's French adviser and the Prince's chief of protocol, a French-educated Cambodian. This, it seems, influenced the Ambassador's subsequent negative behaviour towards the Prince and the royalist party.

Just before the coup, Le Lidec officially complained to the Cambodian Foreign Minister that next door to his residence, at the headquarters of FUNCINPEC, there were "illegal Khmer Rouge forces". According to UN investigators, the charge was false and only served to increase the tension between the coalition partners, CPP and FUNCINPEC, leading to the coup. Later on, CPP officials would use Le Lidec's complaint to justify both the coup and the extra judicial killings that ensued.[47]

In all fairness, it should be said that the French Ambassador in Bangkok, Gerard Coste, despite not being responsible for Cambodian affairs, apart from those which touched Thai-French relations, had a better informed view of events in Cambodia and tried hard both to establish a dialogue with Cambodian leaders, including Prince Ranariddh and SRP party president, Sam Rainsy, who had exiled themselves in Bangkok after the coup and to convey his understanding of developments to the French Foreign Ministry in Paris, while remaining impartial in the dispute between France and the Cambodian opposition. The way the French Embassy in Bangkok assessed the situation seemed completely different to the way the French Embassy in Phnom Penh did and at times, it became quite ridiculous with the French Embassy in Bangkok addressing Prince Ranariddh by his official title of "First Prime Minister of the Kingdom of Cambodia" while the French Embassy in Phnom Penh would only address him as "President of the FUNCINPEC Party".[48]

But it was clear to any fair-minded observer that in the developing contest between the French Ambassadors in Bangkok and Phnom Penh, the latter had the upper hand. Following a briefing by Prince Ranariddh to the Ambassadors representing the so-called "Friends of Cambodia" countries in Bangkok on 21 November 1997, Ambassador Coste asked to see the prince alone and passed on the following message from Paris: "The French government wishes to avoid any misunderstandings between the Cambodian exiles and France. France strongly condemns the events of July but France must be pragmatic. As far as Ambassador Gildas Le Lidec is concerned, he retains the trust of the French government".[49]

What neither the French Foreign Ministry in Paris nor the French Ambassador in Phnom Penh seemed able to appreciate was that the longer France adopted such a negative attitude towards the return of Prince Ranariddh to Cambodia, the more difficult it was for Ranariddh's staff, to get him to do the right thing for Cambodia and its people. Ranariddh, who had spent much of his life in France, truly loves that country and everything that comes from France, but when he saw that France was the principal obstacle to the diplomatic proposals put forward by different countries, he felt betrayed and his attitude began to change for the worse.[50] He rapidly lost interest in the diplomatic initiatives and was critical, at different times, of the different countries involved in trying to find a way out of the impasse in Cambodia.

It also became very difficult for those advising Prince Ranariddh to follow the nuances of France's position. Was the Ambassador in Phnom Penh taking personal initiatives or was the French envoy following the instructions received from the Quai d'Orsay?[51] Le Lidec often shocked even his colleagues in the diplomatic corps by his abrasive defence of the coup authorities. At a meeting of the Ambassador's group on the Cambodian Elections on 7 July 1998, he opposed a démarche to the Cambodian government expressing concern over human rights' violations.

When the Thai Ambassador and the Special Representative of the UN Secretary General, Lakhan Mehrotra, supported by the Indian and British Ambassadors, pointed out that this was an area of continuing concern and thus advocated an intervention by the Ambassadors particularly regarding reports of intimidation, Le Lidec pressed his viewpoint and the demarche was abandoned.[52]

However, even though he did not speak out on human rights issues, Le Lidec is credited to have convinced Prime Minister Hun Sen, who speaks no French, not to abolish the monarchy, after his coup as Hun Sen had planned to do, explaining to the Cambodian leader that he needed the monarchy if he wanted social and political stability in the country.[53]

In the years after the 1997 coup, France pushed hard for the admission of Cambodia to ASEAN, the preservation of the constitutional monarchy and the retention of France's cultural and linguistic influence in Cambodia. As a pamphlet published by the French Embassy in Phnom Penh stated in its introduction "The French language in Cambodia occupies an eminent place and history. It is both a language of culture and language of access to knowledge, language of modernity and language of aperture to the world. It reflects the choice made by Cambodia to commit to adhering to cultural diversity in institutions of la Francophonie, of which His Highness the King Father Norodom Sihanouk, was one of the founding figures".[54]

France which had initially been the leading investor in Cambodia ceded its place to China in the early 2000s, with direct French investments reaching US$43.4 million for the period 2007 to mid 2009 and budgeted aid of 59.34 million of Euros for the period 2009–2011.[55] Most of France's direct investments in Cambodia are geared towards maintaining its monopolistic position in the international airports' concessions through the VINCI conglomerate or the activities of other large French companies such as Total (Oil exploration); Accor (Property and Hotel Management); Victoria Hotels (Hotel Management); ALCATEL (Mobile telephone equipment) and others. France and Cambodia signed a bilateral Agreement of Protection of Investments in 2001.[56]

However, the number of students of the French language has diminished considerably, together with the number of investment proposals put forward by French companies which, according to French officials "were subject to frustration and uncertainty, with agreements often failing to materialize at the last minute" in favour of "the strong presence of Chinese, Vietnamese or other powers that harm the clarity of business".[57] Since 1991, France has contributed 21 million Euros (US$30 million) to help restore the Angkorian patrimony of Cambodia, thus remaining the leading contributor in the cultural field to the reconstruction and restoration of the country's cultural heritage.[58]

France has also recently stated through its Prime Minister, during a visit to Cambodia in early July 2011, that it was ready to help resolve the Cambodian-Thai border dispute by providing maps it had made at the start of the last century, when it ruled Indochina and by helping to find "a peaceful solution for the Cambodian and Thai conflict".[59]

While France has lost in today's Cambodia its former predominant influence to China, because of the historic links existing between Cambodia and France, the latter is still recognized by many Cambodians as their principal bridge with Europe, the one country they can turn to represent Cambodia's aims and aspirations to the remainder of Europe. Some Cambodians have a second house in France, they have French nationality as well as Cambodian, they send their children to be educated in France and when things become politically incorrect in Cambodia, they exile themselves to Paris or Aix-En-Provence.

Notes

1. Spokesman of French Council of Ministers on 19 March 1970 as reported in Australian Embassy Paris to External Affairs Canberra, Telegram No. 1698, 20/3/1970 NAA Series A1838 Control Symbol 25/1/4/37 Part 1.
2. Froment-Meurice Henri, "*Journal d'Asie: Chine-Inde-Indochine-Japon 1969–1975*". Paris, L"Harmattan, 2005, p. 374.
3. French Secretary of State, Jean de Lipkowsky, during a visit to Australia, Canberra, 22 January 1971, NAA Series A1838 Control Symbol 25/1/4/37 Part I.
4. Record of conversation between the Australian Ambassador in Phnom Penh and the Director of Asia-Oceania of the French Foreign Ministry, Henri Froment-Meurice, Phnom Penh, 29 January 1971, NAA Series A1818 Control Symbol 3107/40/112 Part 1.
5. Statement of the French Government, Paris, 1 April 1970.
6. See for instance "*Le Monde*", 15 May 1975 and 18 September 1975.
7. Agence France Presse, 29 July 1976 and US Embassy Paris to State, Telegram No. 21593, 23 July 1976.
8. US Embassy Paris, telegram No. 21593, op. cit.
9. Australian Ambassador Paris to Foreign Affairs Canberra, Memo No. 835, Paris 20 August 1976 NAA Series A1838 Control Symbol 25/1/4/37 Part 2.
10. Norodom Sihanouk, "*Prisoner of the Angkar- Political Asylum*", chapter 23, unpublished memoir, 1980.
11. See for instance "*Sihanouk*". Paris, AFP French Press Agency, 13 December 1980.
12. Paris Domestic Service in French, 18 October 1980.
13. Interview of Jean-Marie Cambaceres, Asian affairs officer, French Socialist Party, "*La Lettre de L'Institut Francois Mitterrand*", Paris, No. 21, September 2007.
14. See Speech by the President of the Republic to the UN General Assembly, Permanent Mission of France to the UN, New York, September 1988.
15. See "*France Keen on Renewing its influence in Cambodia*". *The Bangkok Post*, 18 November 1991, p. 4.
16. Supreme National Council of Cambodia, a largely ceremonial body established in 1991 gathering together the warring Cambodian factions, which was the legitimate representative of Cambodia's sovereignty during the transitional period.
17. See "*French Ambassador Meets high-level officials*". Kampuchea Radio Network in Cambodian, 14 December 1991. FBIS, Daily Report, Asia & Pacific, 18 December 1991.
18. *The Bangkok Post*, op. cit.
19. The Observer, London, 16 February 1992, pp. A34 & A35.

20. Ambassador Galabru, had been posted in Phnom Penh in the late 1960s and married a Cambodian lady, whose father was President of the High Council of the Throne. In the early 1980s, he had met Hun Sen while posted as Ambassador to Angola and had become the intermediary between him and former monarch Norodom Sihanouk. His intervention, authorized by President Mitterrand, led to the first meeting between Sihanouk and the Prime Minister of SOC at Fere-En-Tardenois, outside Paris in December 1987. Interview with Ambassador Galabru, Paris 14 June 1995.
21. Copy of the unpublished report to President Mitterrand entitled "*Training of Men, the Promotion of the Francophonie: A Crucial Role for France*" by Ambassador Jean Jacques Galabru, given to the author by Ambassador Galabru.
22. See Thayer, Nate; "*The Grand Illusion*". Hong Kong, *Far Eastern Economic Review*, 25 February 1993, p. 12.
23. Author discussion with a senior Asian diplomat in Phnom Penh, 25 February 1993.
24. Author discussion with King Norodom Sihanouk, Beijing, 16 November 1996.
25. Ibid.
26. Author discussion with Nick Warner, Deputy Permanent Representative of Australia to the SNC, Phnom Penh, 10 March 1993.
27. Statement of Norodom Sihanouk, President of the SNC, Royal Palace, Phnom Penh, 13 February 1993.
28. Prince Ranariddh had been questioned about this matter during his first official visit to Singapore as First Prime Minister in August 1993 by Prime Minister Lee Kuan Yew. Author's discussion with a senior Minister of the Royal Government, Phnom Penh, 29 August 1993.
29. As related to me by Samura Tioulong, Governor of the Cambodian Central Bank, who had attended the meetings of the visiting French Minister. Phnom Penh, 4 August 1994.
30. Ibid.
31. Author's discussion with the Cambodian Under Secretary for Foreign Affairs, Pok Marina, Phnom Penh 8 February 1997.
32. "*Le Cautchouc au Cambodge*". Mission Economique, Ambassade de France, Phnom Penh, 14 November 2006.
33. *The Phnom Penh Post*, Issue 2/15, 16–29 July 1993.
34. See for instance "Cette Soldatesque formee par la France" (This Soldiery formed by France). Paris, L'Evenement du Jeudi, 18-24 September 1997.
35. Memorandum to the Royal Government of Cambodia, "*Evidence of Summary Executions, Torture and Missing persons since 2–7 July 1997*". Cambodia Office of the UN High Commissioner for Human Rights, Phnom Penh, 21 August 1997.
36. Clayton, Thomas "*Language Choice in a nation Under Transition: English Language Spread In Cambodia*". New York, Springer, 2006, pp. 215–23.
37. Author's discussions with students from the ITC. Phnom Penh, 10 May 1995, at a forum hosted by the Khmer Institute of Democracy (KID).

38. Author's conversation with the late Tol Lah, Minister of Education. Phnom Penh, May 1995.
39. Author's discussion with the French Ambassador to Cambodia, Gildas Le Lidec. Phnom Penh, 6 August 1996.
40. Ibid.
41. FBIS, East Asia Report 22 April 1996, p. 79.
42. Author's discussion with a senior French diplomat, who disagreed with his country's policy. Paris February 1998.
43. Le Monde, 17 July 1997, p. 3.
44. Ambassador Le Lidec clearly did not enjoy his posting to Cambodia and he particularly resented late night telephone calls from the First Co-Premier or members of the Royal Family, all of them holding French citizenship. Author's discussion with Ambassador Le Lidec op. cit.
45. See Message from H.M. King Norodom Sihanouk, 17 July 1996
46. See Bulletin Mensuel de Documentation du Secretariat Privée de S.M. Norodom Sihanouk, Roi du Cambodge, June–July 1996 issues.
47. The Secretary of State at the Ministry of Tourism, Thong Khon, told French journalists that the French Ambassador had been very helpful and provided them with tapes of film of FUNCINPEC's headquarters taken by the security cameras of the French Embassy. Notes of conversation with French Journalists Francois Danchaud et M Jaslet. Bangkok 27 January 1998.
48. Letters from the French Embassy Bangkok to Prince Ranariddh's office, No. 64 IAE, 19 November 1997 and letter from French Ambassador in Phnom Penh to Prince Ranariddh, No. 553 of 6 July 1998.
49. Record of conversation prepared by H.E. Xavier d'Abzac, Adviser to Prince Ranariddh, copy in the author's possession.
50. The author served as Special Adviser to Prince Ranariddh from August 1997 to May 1999.
51. Quai d'Orsay = French Foreign Ministry.
52. Report from Ambassador Lakhan Mehrotra to Sir Kieran Prendergast, UN Under Secretary General, 8 July 1998, copy in the author's possession.
53. Author's discussion with a senior member of the Royal Family of Cambodia, 20 December 1997.
54. "Francophonie Cambodge", French Embassy and Agency Universitaire de la Francophonie. Phnom Penh, 2005, 35 pages.
55. French Economic Presence in Cambodia, French Embassy. Phnom Penh, 13 August 2009.
56. Direct Foreign Investments in Cambodia, French Embassy. Phnom Penh, 15 November 2010.
57. Marks, Simon, "*French Premier Signals Investor Frustrations*". *The Cambodia Daily*, 4 July 2011.
58. Cambodge Nouveau, No. 299, July 2011.
59. Xinhua-New China News Agency, Phnom Penh, 3 July 2011.

PEACE AND RECONCILIATION IN CAMBODIA

12

AN ASSESSMENT OF THE UNITED NATIONS TRANSITIONAL AUTHORITY IN CAMBODIA (UNTAC)

Yasushi Akashi

There are divergent appraisals on the outcome of the United Nations Peace-keeping Operation in Cambodia, which took place for 18 months from March 1992 to September 1993. In my view, such divergence of views is inevitable; it arises from degrees of prior expectations, varied estimates regarding the capacity of the United Nations to deploy and implement a complex peace-keeping mandate, as well as the degree to which a UN intervention could make a serious impact upon the socioeconomic and political structure of a country within a limited time span.

Michael W. Doyle, for example, argues that, while the peace-keeping operation in Cambodia produced positive results, the subsequent peace-building phase was not entirely satisfactory, since the war against the Khmer Rouge was inconclusive and some opportunities to reform the Cambodian state were missed. Samol Ney, Deputy Director General for the Association of Southeast Asian Nations (ASEAN) in the Ministry of Foreign Affairs of Cambodia, said in a Tokyo workshop of the ASEAN Regional Forum (ARF) that the UN peace-keeping in his country had achieved a great success and that the general elections in 1993 were a turning point in Cambodian history. But he added that the task of UNTAC under the Paris Peace Agreements was too ambitious and, therefore, was an impossible one to implement as the cease-fire was not honoured and demilitarization was not achieved. In his view, UNTAC was too passive vis-à-vis the Khmer Rouge resistance. He argued that the most serious UNTAC failure was its inability to "bring about the disarmament and demobilization of the Khmer Rouge".

Despite these critical appraisals, it cannot be denied that during its 18-month mandate, UNTAC achieved many of its ambitious tasks, particularly its core objective, namely the conduct of free and fair general elections, which led to the creation of a new government of Cambodia with considerable success, although as will be noted later in this paper, there were shortcomings and defects in the operation, more particularly due to the fact that there had been little time to prepare logistically for the commencement of a huge peace-keeping operation and, most of all, UNTAC met a totally unanticipated armed resistance from the Party of Democratic Kampuchea (PDK, also known as the Khmer Rouge).

In short, UNTAC played an indispensable role in bringing to birth a new Cambodian polity, based on the unity it had carefully cultivated among the major factions with the exception of the Khmer Rouge. It organized from scratch a complex nation-wide voter registration and the general elections, in which 90 per cent of the electorate participated with clear enthusiasm. However, it was beyond the capacity of UNTAC to put an end to the bitter political bickering among the factions, nor was it within its reach to lift Cambodia from its endemic poverty or serious urban-rural disparity within a year and a half of its mandate. The new government of Cambodia, which came into being on the basis of a Constitution hammered out by the Constituent Assembly in 1993, had to struggle with remnants of the Khmer Rouge for several years, even though the strength of the Khmer Rouge (or PDK) was considerably weakened by its dogged boycott of the democratic elections organized by UNTAC. One has to pay tribute to Mr Hun Sen, the Prime Minister, for having achieved the final demise of the Khmer Rouge.

FACTORS BEHIND THE SUCCESS

It is undeniable that a deep and pervasive aspiration of the Cambodian people for peace and democracy after more than 20 years of the incessant strife and suffering was a vital under-pinning which enabled UNTAC to achieve its fundamental objectives, namely, the conduct of free and fair general elections in a neutral political environment, in spite of numerous obstacles along the way.

Secondly, the consistent support given by the relevant UN Member States, including the five Permanent Members of the Security Council, major Asian countries, including Indonesia, Japan and Australia and other signatories of the Paris Peace Agreements, signed on 23 October 1991, was undoubtedly an essential element which enabled UNTAC to overcome several crises of implementation. In the heady optimism of the immediate post-Cold War era, the UN Security Council showed a remarkable unity of outlook and consistency among its members in its unusual show of unity on the question of Cambodia.

Thirdly, I also wish to mention the strong personal commitment by UNTAC personnel to their tasks, their extraordinary flexibility to cope with challenges and their dexterity to find a pragmatic solution. These fine qualities are not always found in a motley international grouping, hastily assembled. Aware of the serious risks they faced, UNTAC gambled on carrying out the free elections as scheduled, defying repeated Khmer Rouge threats and acts of sabotage and violent attacks, as well as the wavering of other parties in conflict. In the end, its gamble paid off well. UNTAC had anticipated Khmer Rouge challenges — political, physical as well as psychological — to its plans, and carried out contingency plans of action during the thirteen months of Khmer Rouge opposition, starting from May 1992 to the holding of elections in May 1993. Contrary to widely-held apprehensions, the final disruption of the balloting process by the Khmer Rouge did not materialize, due probably to the inability of the Khmer Rouge to do so even if they would have wanted to.

Fourth, the Paris Agreements, which had been carefully prepared and negotiated over several years and signed on 23 October 1991, provided a sound political framework for the challenging work by UNTAC. These Agreements had the merit that they were subscribed to by all players — the four Cambodian factions and the Member States who could have affected the outcome. However, there had to be pragmatic, patient and imaginative interpretation and application of the Agreements so as to resolve unforeseen problems which arose later. In the process, a rather rigid and legalistic attitude shown by UN headquarters in New York had to be overcome. For example, in the course of the Supreme National Council (SNC) deliberations of a draft electoral law which lasted for four months, UNTAC decided on two significant departures from the texts of the Paris Agreements regarding general elections, which New York accepted only grudgingly. These departures dealt with tightening the voter qualifications and amending the venues for registration and balloting, which the three factions wanted strongly. Furthermore, as the Special Representative of the Secretary-General (SRSG), I was keenly aware of the vital need to keep good relations with Prince Sihanouk, the hereditary monarch and the President of the SNC, and for that reason wished to avoid overriding him on the basis of a literal interpretation of the Paris Agreements. Even during the stormy days when Prince Sihanouk severed his personal ties with UNTAC, a cordial relationship was maintained between the monarch and SRSG. This cordiality helped immensely in resolving a number of crises.

Fifth, UNTAC's "supervision and control" of the State of Cambodia (SOC) administration (Article 6 of the Paris Agreement on a Comprehensive Political Settlement of the Cambodia Conflict), was hampered by the serious shortage of experienced supervisory personnel in the UN Secretariat and in Member States. Nevertheless, UNTAC strongly endeavoured to create a "neutral political environment" considered essential for holding free general elections. The creation of the post of Special Prosecutor within UNTAC was controversial due to the lack of any specific reference to it in the Paris Agreements, but it was one example of UNTAC improvisation in response to felt political needs. At the same time, I felt that it was not necessary to engage in an endless dispute with the SOC by arresting many junior officials for their infractions of UNTAC decrees and regulations. Nevertheless, Hun Sen and the SOC leadership were made fully aware of UNTAC's firm intention to protect freedom of political action, and UNTAC placed distinct limits upon their acts of harassment of other parties in the elections.

Sixth, FUNCINPEC, headed by Prince Norodom Ranariddh, was at one time tempted to boycott the elections owing to SOC's acts of harassment. However, UNTAC encouraged them to stay in the race and gave all legitimate assistance such as (a) encouraging political rallies which were numerous and well attended, (b) providing helicopters to carry opposition leaders to remote areas for campaigning, (c) having SRSG visit their headquarters with the diplomatic corps, etc.

Seventh, in a country with a weak tradition in human rights, democratic governance and the rule of law, democracy could be installed in the society only through persistent and incremental process of grass-root education, supplemented by steps such as punishing blatantly offending officials by example and through face-to-face talks with SOC leaders. Despite dissent which emerged within UNTAC in which younger, idealistic officials wanted more radical and forceful action to be taken, I favoured a dual approach with regard to realizing human rights through popular education and support for non-governmental organizations on the one hand, and action from the top, namely, myself talking to Prime Minister Hun Sen. The SNC also was frequently requested to accede to UN human rights covenants and treaties. At one time, Hun Sen complained to me that UNTAC's approach on human rights was so harsh as to be reminiscent of Khmer Rouge tactics! We also gave a strong encouragement to the growth of indigenous NGOs in the human rights field, knowing well that UNTAC's stay in Cambodia was of limited duration. Hundreds of NGOs emerged, and many of them still persist. Free media activities were also encouraged, and the freedom of the press remained after the departure of UNTAC in September 1993.

Eighth, as SRSG, I frequently consulted with the "core" group (or "expanded permanent five" group) of ten key ambassadors, consisting of the United States, China, Russia, the United Kingdom, France, Indonesia, Japan, Australia, Thailand and Germany. This group served as my sounding board and a crucial mechanism for an informal exchange of views and ideas. I told the ambassadors about the challenges faced by UNTAC and in turn they gave me their frank analysis of the Cambodian situation based on their experience and perspectives. Our discussions were lively, and their views often differed from more legalistic or institutional advice given to me by UNTAC directors. The discussions I held with the ambassadors in Phnom Penh were communicated by them to their capitals, which in turn kept their permanent representatives in New York updated with the situation on the ground, balancing and correcting sensational media reports published outside the country. It was through such diplomatic communication that the US ambassador Charles Twining was able to persuade Washington to reverse its opposition to Prince Sihanouk's proposal to create two Prime Ministers. In the same manner, I persuaded UN headquarters in New York not to object to the revised Sihanouk proposal after the general elections. I also stayed in close touch with the Chinese government in Beijing and its ambassador in Phnom Penh to gain its understanding of UNTAC's difficulties with the Khmer Rouge.

NON-USE OF CHAPTER 7 OF THE UN CHARTER

It was remarkable that the Security Council resolutions concerning Cambodia never made an explicit reference to Chapter VII of the UN Charter concerning enforcement action. It was a conscious attempt by those of us concerned to avoid a frontal confrontation with Cambodian parties and save the face of the parties, including the Khmer Rouge and their Chinese supporters. In the late spring of 1992, Force Commander John Sanderson and myself resisted calls by Deputy Force Commander Jean-Michel Loridon of France and some civilian "young Turks" around me who advocated the use of force to invade Khmer Rouge controlled areas when the latter began boycotting cooperation with UNTAC. Khmer Rouge refusal on entering Phase II of the Paris Agreements concerning re-groupment, cantonment, disarming and demobilization of forces in June 1992 compelled UNTAC to revise its original plan to enter the next phase.

My basic thinking was expressed in my confidential letter to the Secretary-General dated 27 July 1992, from which I quote a few paragraphs. "I am thus forced to the conclusion that DK (Democratic Kampuchea, the so-called Khmer Rouge) is trying to gain what it could not get either in the battlefield or in the Paris negotiations, that is, to improve its political and military power to such an extent that the other parties will be placed at a distinctive disadvantage when UNTAC leaves. So long as we stand firm on the strict implementation of the Paris Accord, there is not too much we can do to satisfy DK, except to make our control of civil administration more effective, ameliorate the protocol and a few other matters. We are doing all of these and will continue doing so. While professing its fidelity to the Paris Accord, DK in reality defies it openly and consistently by ignoring the cease-fire, by refusing cantonment and free access to their areas and by boycotting the Mixed Military Working Group, a statutory body. .... My basic approach is to combine patient persuasion with sustained pressure. We will continue to work with the SNC, where we can count on the consistent support of Prince Sihanouk as well as the three factions. At the same time, we will do our best not to alienate DK as the permanent disgruntled minority. We will adhere to an impartial stand, while criticizing any acts in violation of the Paris Agreement. .... In the likely event that DK's non-cooperation with UNTAC continues unabated, you may wish to consider presenting another report to the Security Council in about a month's time. At that time, we would need a stronger resolution with particular emphasis on economic pressures against DK. This should not however involve any spectacular action, but rather a steady strengthening of our border checkpoints adjacent to the DK zones, in order to control the inflow of arms and petroleum and the outflow of gems and logs, a major source of DK's income. Thailand has promised to cooperate in the establishment and functioning of our checkpoints, several of which can only be supplied from the Thai side. Our military people are working on the details of these checkpoints with expanded terms of reference. Thailand will certainly have to do more than it has done in the past. So far it has not even signed a Status Agreement with us. Gen. Sanderson will visit Bangkok soon to follow up on my talks there on 17 July. Through such steady external pressures and through a combination of UNTAC's even-handed approach and the solid common front of three factions, DK may well change their tune in two months or so and agree to our entry into their zones and start cantoning its troops. .... I am well aware of the financial implications of any delay in adhering to our timetable set out in your February plan of implementation. At the same time, we must be free from any accusations that we are going through the "motion" of democratic elections in a superficial manner, allowing DK or other anti-democratic elements to surface soon after the elections and UNTAC's departure." (Quoted from *The United Nations and Cambodia 1991–1995*, published by the United Nations Department of Public Information 1995).

A carefully orchestrated mixture of graduated pressures and diplomatic persuasion vis-à-vis the Khmer Rouge was devised on the basis of informal consultations between Phnom Penh and New York. These consultations involved myself, some key Security Council members and others. It included Jean-David Levitte, a French diplomat of great distinction, who later became his country's ambassador to the United Nations, to Washington and then the diplomatic adviser to the French President. We agreed on a two-stage strategy, in which Thailand and Japan would be asked to start talks with the Khmer Rouge to ascertain if there was any room for compromise. These quiet talks, if unsuccessful, were to be followed by the second stage, in which the Security Council would step in with more explicit external pressure, which however would be adopted in the form of a recommendation by the SNC in Cambodia and not as an action taken by the UN Security Council.

The progression of these steps may be perceived by comparing Security Council resolution 766 of 21 July 1992 with subsequent resolutions 783, 792 and 810. When subtle, carefully calibrated steps aimed at concrete effects contained in resolution 766 did not produce hoped-for results, they were to trigger a stronger consensus against the Khmer Rouge, to which countries friendly to the Khmer Rouge like China would find it difficult to object. These Security Council actions regarding Cambodia were taken over a period, with full endorsement of myself as SRSG. They were in sharp contrast to the fruitless Security Council action in the case of the former Yugoslavia during 1993 to 1995, where there was much "sound and fury" with little practical outcome. (See resolution 783 of 13 October 1992, resolution 792 of 30 November 1992 and resolution 810 of 8 March 1993 on Cambodia).

THE SUPREME NATIONAL COUNCIL

Maximum effort was made to utilize the SNC even though its deliberations were often sterile and led only to deadlocks. Moreover, in the absence of SNC President, Prince Sihanouk, from Cambodia, I chaired the working group of the SNC with his consent to continue debate among the four parties. This was intended to create a sense of ownership among the Cambodian parties on their budding democracy and get representatives to become accustomed to a new habit of resolving their differences through discussion and negotiation rather than by the use of force. These debates, however, became so embittered and polemical at times that they often left a bitter after taste.

PRINCE SIHANOUK

Prince Sihanouk was a brilliant, shrewd but somewhat moody SNC President. However, conscious of his unparalleled prestige throughout the country, I showed highest respect towards the Prince at all times. Secretary-General Boutros-Ghali was once tempted to criticize the Prince for his frequent absence from the country. But I dissuaded him from doing so. The Prince in turn responded by being extremely cordial and cooperative with me, even when he formally broke relations with UNTAC.

ADMINISTRATIVE ACHIEVEMENTS

The generally high calibre and high morale of the UNTAC directorate, with only a few disappointments, was a remarkable asset for me. They worked extremely hard, despite difficult living conditions. This was made possible by Secretary-General Boutros-Ghali who gave me "carte blanche" in the selection of directors. I chose the best persons available for each post among many internal and external candidates, making use of my wide network of acquaintances at the UN Secretariat.

More than in any previous peacekeeping operations, UNTAC gave a very high priority to information and educational activities. With good advice from the head of the information component, who was recruited from the White House in Washington and a Cambodian expert, I pressed repeatedly for the establishment of a UN radio station in the country, with three boosters in the rural areas, which enabled a full coverage of the country. After being rebuffed a few times by New York for budgetary reasons, the proposal was finally approved. With generous assistance of funds and transistor radios from Japanese non-governmental sources, Radio UNTAC proved to be a most potent and reliable means of appeal to the hearts and minds of average Cambodians regarding their human rights and UNTAC's role in giving birth to democracy, at a time when 70 per cent of Cambodian people were still illiterate. Closer to the general elections, the UN Radio disseminated rich information and an effective message of total electoral freedom at balloting boxes for 15 hours a day, in the popular, everyday language of simple peasants.

As SRSG, I was able to create a small analysis unit, where top experts on Cambodian history and society with linguistic skill were assembled and gave an in-depth evaluation of the mood of the people in the country. UNTAC probably employed one half of the world's expertise available on Cambodia. They were very helpful in providing a penetrating insight into the complex working of Cambodian culture and society.

BUDGETARY AND PERSONNEL MATTERS

UNTAC was at that time in keen competition regarding budgetary resources with another gigantic peace-keeping operation, namely, the United Nations Protection Force for the former Yugoslavia (UNPROFOR), which was being mounted at the same time. (It was ironic that I had to head UNPROFOR in December 1993 after my mission in Cambodia was completed!) UNTAC was fortunate to receive generous financial resources from the United Nations on a timely basis. The prompt endorsement by the Advisory Committee on Administrative and Budgetary Questions (ACABQ) of $200 million as an advance authorization by the UN General Assembly towards the adoption of the UNTAC budget was exceptional, to say the least. I admit that this was facilitated by my experience of budget procedures as a former member of ACABQ in the 1970s. In addition, major contributors such as Japan, the United States and France offered handsome voluntary contributions beyond their regular budget assessment to enable commencement of a large-scale rehabilitation and reconstruction projects in Cambodia. At the Tokyo Ministerial Conference on the Rehabilitation and Reconstruction of Cambodia, held in June 1992, 33 countries pledged a total of $880 million, which was substantially in excess of $599 million called for by the UN Secretary-General. This was a rare occurrence in UN history. I remember Prince Sihanouk was visibly moved by this generous manifestation of the international community's good will. He told his colleagues to stop bickering and make use of the magnanimity shown by other countries.

An effective coordination was achieved under UNTAC leadership among diverse UN programs and agencies as well as with the World Bank, the Asian Development Bank and others. This made it possible to avoid the legendary bureaucratic bickering among myriad international bodies. The head of the refugee repatriation component of UNTAC was Sergio Vieira de Mello, who simultaneously served as the special envoy of the United Nations High Commissioner for Refugees (UNHCR). UNTAC was also blessed by an able economic adviser, David Laurence, seconded by the United Nations Conference on Trade and Development (UNCTAD). Laurence was the first and last representative of Cambodia at the World Bank, who was white and 6 and a half feet tall! The fact of the matter was that UNTAC was in competition with UNPROFOR in the former Yugoslavia not only regarding its budget, but also for a scarce pool of able international civil servants willing to serve in challenging working conditions. I was relieved to find that those who joined me in Phnom Penh from New York, Geneva and other comfortable cities never once complained about their work and life in Cambodia and remained always cheerful. They showed personal dedication, high morale and a wonderful sense of humour. I particularly value a good sense of humour as an indispensable spice of life in a challenging multi-national mission of peace.

PROBLEMS AND CHALLENGES

There were obviously many problems and challenges in the UNTAC operation. Many of them arose from the fact that it was the first large-scale and multi-dimensional peace-keeping operation in the post-Cold War period, with an ambitious and comprehensive mandate. UNTAC consisted of about 1,200 international civilian staff, 3,600 civilian police, 15,900 military personnel, and 400 UN volunteers. This was augmented by over 10,000 local staff, which was supplemented by an additional 10,000 prior to the general elections. The total UNTAC budget was estimated to exceed $1.8 billion — larger than the UN regular budget. This diverse group of personnel was assembled in Cambodia from all over the world within a period of a few months. Their equipment had to be decided, ordered and delivered in an even shorter period. This was an almost impossible task. And yet it had to be done, even if it was somewhat untidy and disorganized. Among the most serious problem areas were:

1. Civilian police, who numbered 3,600, the largest number in UN history, were of uneven quality. Many of the policemen recruited were excellent, but some lacked the necessary qualifications, possessing a minimum or even no training in human rights. Some civilian policemen could not even drive a car; and they had to be sent home. I have to admit that a serious discrepancy existed between the original mandate given to civilian police (supervision and training of local police) and the reality on the ground, which called for actual police work by UN civilian police in order to supplement weak local police. I recall tense discussion we had in Phnom Penh whether to arm or not to arm our civilian police in an increasingly insecure environment. Our final conclusion was that it was safer not to arm our policemen.
2. Detrimental to UNTAC credibility was the late recruitment of administrators, who were supposed to "ensure a neutral political

environment conducive to free and fair general elections". These administrators were to place "under direct UN supervision or control" "administrative agencies, bodies and offices which could directly influence the outcome of elections". In this respect, special attention was to be given "to the five ministries of foreign affairs, national defence, finance, public security and information". However, it was only towards the end of 1992, after ten months of UNTAC deployment, that the requisite number of administrators was finally assembled in Phnom Penh and deployed elsewhere in the country. Since the UN Secretariat possessed only several qualified candidates, the Organization had to turn to Member Governments to come up with good candidates for administrators, an extremely time-consuming process. In this matter, the Khmer Rouge had some legitimate reasons to complain. It must be said that the Paris Agreements were not realistic to expect more than a selective "supervision" or "control" of SOC administration by international personnel who did not possess either linguistic or cultural skills required. This is, however, not to agree with the criticism by Michael W. Doyle who seems to assume a virtual take-over by UNTAC of key ministries and agencies of the SOC under the Paris Agreements.

3. The UNTAC military leadership did not initially have a clear understanding of the degree to which the use of force was permitted under the rules of engagement (ROE) for its personnel. Upon inquiry from the field, UN headquarters clarified ROE for UNTAC to include resistance by force to an attempted seizure of arms and vehicles and other blatant moves to obstruct the fulfilment of the mission. UNTAC resistance to the Khmer Rouge attacks and seizures became more vigorous as a result.
4. Communication with UN headquarters in New York left much to be desired. Despite frequent cable traffic, UN headquarters did not always appreciate the precise scope or implications of the challenges faced by UNTAC in the field; as a result, there were instances of "micro-managing" UNTAC or second-guessing its policies and action. However, New York granted considerable delegation of authority without its prior consent to UNTAC with regard to expenditures incurred, due to the fact that both myself and my Deputy SRSG Behrooz Sadry possessed long experience in UN financial management.
5. I am of the view that the peacekeeping operation in Cambodia was subjected to tendentious and inaccurate mass media reports which often dramatized UNTAC's difficulties and perceived incompetence, particularly UNTAC's inability to cope with threats from the Khmer Rouge. The so-

called "bamboo curtain" incident of 30 May 1992, in which SRSG and Force Commander were prevented from moving within the Khmer Rouge controlled area adjacent to the Thai border, by the order of a few sentry personnel, was depicted by the media as a spineless humiliation suffered by UNTAC. I am tempted to ask if the media would have preferred dramatic, if bloody, fighting by us rather than patient diplomacy.

Some media characterized this setback by General John Sanderson and myself as an appeasement of evil, comparable to Neville Chamberlain and Édouard Daladier who had meekly surrendered to the Nazis' bully tactics in 1938. I am convinced, however, that UNTAC was neither authorized nor capable of fighting its way into the Khmer Rouge area and winning a messy guerrilla war. It is likely that public opinion in troop-contributing countries would have reacted badly to hundreds of casualties which could have resulted from UNTAC engaging in such messy warfare. The end result would then have been a total disintegration of UNTAC, in the wake of hasty withdrawals of national contingents.

Furthermore, world media, with a notable exception of the London Economist, largely assumed the worst case scenario in the outcome of the elections, which took place in May 1993. Most media felt that the Khmer Rouge was somehow formidable and UNTAC was just a paper tiger. On his second visit to Cambodia in April 1993, Secretary-General Boutros-Ghali told me that he was amazed to find a considerable difference between pessimistic news reports which he had read in New York and the reality on the ground, in which UNTAC personnel were working hard as professionals in its second and third lines of defence against possible Khmer Rouge disruptions of the elections.

POST-UNTAC ACTIVITIES

In hindsight, planning for the post-UNTAC presence should probably have started earlier. However, the timing of UNTAC's departure in September 1993 was not sudden or abrupt. It had been firmly fixed in Security Council resolutions, and UNTAC's departure had been foreordained. There simply was no other possibility than to adhere to the deadline set by the Security Council, due largely to the very heavy financial burden the United Nations had to bear and the diverse world-wide mandates it had to implement. I also felt that a large UN presence in Cambodia was inflationary, distorted its modest economy and tended to produce an unhealthy habit of dependence on foreigners. Having said this, a more graduated reduction of UNTAC's strength might have been called for. In actual fact, responding to the wishes of the new government of Cambodia, UN presence in Cambodia after the withdrawal of UNTAC continued, on a modest but significant scale, in overall coordination, in mine clearance, in human rights and in developmental activities. In each area the United Nations played a significant role in bridging the essential transition from complex peace-keeping to peace-building. By resolution 880 of 4 November 1993, the Security Council agreed to the Secretary-General's proposal to appoint a "person to coordinate the UN presence" in several different areas in Cambodia; agreed to the continuation of assistance in mine-clearance; and decided to establish a team of 20 military liaison officers for a six-month period. The General Assembly, by resolution 48/154 on 20 December 1993, welcomed the establishment in Cambodia of an operational presence of the Centre for Human Rights as well as the appointment by the Secretary-General of a Special Representative to "undertake the tasks suggested by the Commission on Human Rights." The Human Rights Special Representative's relationship with the government of Cambodia has, however, generally been tense and stormy.

UNTAC was fortunate to operate in Cambodia during 1992 to 1993, a period of heady optimism in the post-Cold War era and generous voluntary contributions by donor countries to major UN activities. These same countries later became plagued by growing aid fatigue. In so far as the development of a more comprehensive UN approach to post-conflict peace-building was concerned, it had to wait for the publication of the seminal Brahimi Report issued in August 2000, and its subsequent consideration by the Security Council and the General Assembly, which resulted in the official adoption of several of the important recommendations contained in the report.

13

THE 1991 PARIS PEACE AGREEMENT
A KPNLF Perspective

Son Soubert

I cannot speak on behalf of the other Khmer component parties to the Paris Peace Agreements, whose objectives and interests might be different from the democratic ideals and hope for change which the Cambodian people pursued through UN intervention, just after the Kuwait war and the UN exercises in Yugoslavia.

The Khmer People's National Liberation Front (KPNLF), since its official inception on 9 October 1979, was not meant to fight the Vietnamese occupying forces, but to bring about peace negotiations, which would involve not only the regional powers, but also the global powers, especially the five Permanent Members of the UN Security Council. Aligned with the People's Republic of China and the USA, we were conscious of our limited capacity to move toward peace, because of the involved powers. Our mechanisms for the liberation of Cambodia were double: political-diplomatic; and limited guerrilla action against the formidable fire power of the North Vietnamese, supported by the COMECON and the Soviet bloc.

Since the Khmer Rouge had lost legitimacy as the representatives of the Cambodian People, the USA, some European countries and the People's Republic of China, allied since 1973 with the USA against the Soviet Union and its bloc in the new phase of the Cold War, were looking for a viable democratic force to be the voice of the Cambodian people. Before the June 1982 formation of the Coalition Government of Democratic Kampuchea, presided over by H.R.H. Samdech Norodom Sihanouk, the KPNLF was invited to participate in the 1981 International Conference on Kampuchea, which served as a UN framework for negotiations for a peace solution. Unfortunately, the Vietnamese and the Soviet bloc refused to join in.

We were left with no other choice, except to fight for the liberation of Cambodia with the help of the People's Republic of China, which provided a limited amount of a few thousand new weapons to the KPNLF soldiers, at the end of 1979. The KPNLF refused to have any joint action with the Khmer Rouge; we operated separately in the field. It was a cycle of guerrilla warfare in the rainy seasons, when the resistance movement would have the upper hand; and the dry season offensives, during the long months of the dry season from November to June, when the conventional warfare waged by the Vietnamese had the advantage, with their armoured vehicles, tanks and big artillery. Every year also, since 1982, the leaders of the Coalition Government of Democratic Kampuchea would attend the UN General Assembly Session to make the statement on Kampuchea and get the maximum votes from the UN members to support the Cambodian seat and the liberation struggle of the Cambodian people. Thanks to the active participation of the diplomats of the six ASEAN member-states, especially those from Singapore, the votes increased regularly, year after year until the 1991 Paris Peace Agreements.

THE INITIAL PUSH FOR TALKS

While the initiative for the formation of the Coalition Government of Democratic Kampuchea came from the ASEAN 6 countries, with Singapore hosting the preliminary agreement in September 1981 and Malaysia witnessing the formal implementation a year later in June 1982, the initiative for the contact came from an informal meeting between the KPNLF members and the Vietnamese-backed Phnom Penh regime officials, in 1985.

The year 1985 was the turning point, when during the dry season offensives the Vietnamese troops destroyed all the KPNLF and FUNCINPEC villages inside Cambodia, along the Thai border. Coupled with this dramatic loss of our KPNLF villages, there were tremendous pressure from some ASEAN countries and the USA for a change of leadership, with the aim of handing power to General Sak Sutsakhan, the more flexible military commander of the KPNLF who would be favourable towards the merger between the KPNLAF (Khmer People's National Liberation Armed Forces) and ANKI (Armée Nationale du Kampuchea Indépendant) of the FUNCINPEC. The aim was to have a unified military leadership, with General Sak Sutsakhan as President and General Teap Ben of FUNCINPEC as Vice-President, working under the combined ASEAN and American Working Group, situated at Soi Sasin (Bangkok). A split was promoted to demote the President of the KPNLF, H.E. Son Sann, who was not allowed to visit his people in the border camps or make any press statements to answer attacks waged against him, under various pretexts. Without Prince Sihanouk's intervention in favour of H.E. Son Sann, there would have been a leadership change.

To counter this pressure, the KPNLF made efforts to show that talks could be possible with the other side, which until then seemed psychologically impossible, and that we could change alliances, if pressure continued against our own policy. This was facilitated by the opportunity offered by friends from Europe and America, who had invited some Phnom Penh representatives, namely Dr My Samedi (Secretary General of the Phnom Penh Red Cross) and Mr Uch Kim An from the Phnom Penh Foreign Ministry, to their International Conference Centre in Caux (Switzerland), while they were visiting the International Committee of the Red Cross in Geneva. It was somehow a psychological breakthrough, and the Phnom Penh Prime Minister, Mr Hun Sen, thereafter wished to have a more formal meeting, instead of the informal one. Although this contact was kept confidential, somehow Thailand got to know about it. The meeting in Caux took place in August 1985. On the KPNLF side, there were the late General Thach Reng, myself as President of the KPNLF Red Cross and some other members.

THE FRENCH INITIATIVES

After this psychological breakthrough, the French authorities, especially under Foreign Ministers Claude Cheysson and Roland Dumas started to make approaches, favouring bilateral negotiations between the Khmer factions, mainly Prince Sihanouk (and eventually Prime Minister Son Sann) and the Phnom Penh Vietnamese-backed regime, which would have helped Hanoi to escape the responsibilities of the invasion and occupation of Cambodia, and turned the whole affair into a civil war. This move was started in 1986 and resulted in the Ferre-en-Tardenois (France) meeting, followed by that of Saint-Germain-en-Laye. The solution would have been out of the framework of the internationally-sponsored negotiation, i.e. the UN framework established since 1981. The KPNLF refused this bilateral framework for a solution without any international guarantees.

THE INDONESIAN INITIATIVES

With the French solution failing, Indonesia on behalf of the 6 ASEAN and viewed by Hanoi as a more neutral member of ASEAN because of its rather anti-Chinese past, initiated a formula involving Jakarta Informal Meetings (JIM) followed by the Working Group. The first meeting, not in Jakarta, but in Bogor, involved the two Prime Ministers, namely Mr Hun Sen and Mr Son Sann meeting in the morning. This went well, but was without concrete results. Mr Hun Sen was in fact interested in meeting Prince Sihanouk, the President, and negotiating directly with him. The meeting was followed by a luncheon organized by the Indonesian hosts, placing Vice-President Khieu Samphan at the same table as Mr Hun Sen who very diplomatically started to give news to Mr Khieu Samphan about the latter's brother, but met a very stern and silent interlocutor: the whole luncheon became embarrassing, with Mr Hun Sen leaving the table before the end of the meal, under the pretext of some stomach trouble. At the evening reception, the Vietnamese Foreign Minister, Mr Nguyen Co Thach, the UN observer and Secretary of the ICK (International Conference on Kampuchea) Mr Rafee-udin Ahmed and other observers from the ASEAN 6 were also present.

His Excellency Foreign Minister Ali Alatas and his colleagues from the Indonesian Foreign Ministry were very efficient. The Working Group Session of JIM I took place in Jakarta the next day and lasted the whole day and the whole night, until 6 o'clock in the morning. The meeting was held at the level of experts and ambassadors. The whole exercise involved an explanation and the purpose of JIM I and the statements of intention from the parties involved — ASEAN and the Vietnamese, as well as the four Cambodian factions. The FUNCINPEC party remained uncommitted and silent during the whole meeting. Following one of Mr Hor Nam Hong interventions relating to the formation of the Phnom Penh government, which he placed before Phnom Penh City was taken over by the Vietnamese troops, I intervened by inserting the historical fact at its right chronological place, noting that the Phnom Penh government was set up after the invasion of foreign troops, that is, after the 7 January 1979 takeover of Phnom-Penh. Finally, there was no real breakthrough at this meeting either.

OTHER INITIATIVES AND JIM II

In the wake of the end of the Cold War, with President Ronald Reagan and Mikhail Gorbachev — with his Glasnost policy — speaking to each other in tête-à-tête at Reykjavik Summit (Iceland), concrete results could not be reached without the agreement among the Five Permanent Members of the UN Security Council. The 5 Perm offered a UN framework resolution of the problem and seem to have agreed on a plan devised by the Australian Foreign Minister Gareth Evans and his Deputy, Mr Costello, a plan which was also presented to the Cambodian factions and served as a basis for the Paris Agreement. The Socialist Republic of Vietnam, following the Soviet Union withdrawal from Afghanistan and a lack of funding from the COMECON, was obliged to withdraw its troops from Cambodia, which it did on 30 September 1989, easing the way for further negotiations.

With this further development, Indonesia was ready to host a Second Jakarta Meeting or JIM II. But the Khmer Rouge Democratic Kampuchea party was not ready and advocated further military actions; Prince Sihanouk from Beijing had also exchanged acrimonious statements with Mr Hun Sen. Obviously, the hosting of JIM II did not start well. The KPNLF party decided nevertheless to respond to the invitation of H.E. Mr Ali Alatas, the Indonesian Foreign Minister, and went to attend JIM II on its own initiative. Because of this move, the other three Cambodian parties finally joined in. Unexpectedly, an important breakthrough was achieved, with the Cambodian parties agreeing to form the Supreme National Council. At a morning session, under the chairmanship of H.E. Ali Alatas, it was decided on the composition of the Supreme National Council: for the KPNLF, they were Samdech Son Sann and Mr Ieng Mouly (Secretary General of the KPNLF); for FUNCINPEC, H.R.H. Samdech Sihanouk and Prince Norodom Ranariddh; for the Democratic Kampuchea Mr Khieu Samphan and Mr Son Sen; and for the State of Cambodia Mr Hun Sen and five other Members.

To iron out the differences, there was a meeting in Bangkok to find a compromise as to where would devolve the Presidency of the Supreme national Council — either to the CGDK which became the Coalition Government of Cambodia (no longer Democratic Kampuchea) or the Phnom Penh Government which became the State of Cambodia (no longer the People's Republic of Kampuchea). Conditions were established that Prince Sihanouk would stay neutral and distance himself also from the royalist party, that the National Flag of Cambodia would not be used by any political party, and neither would the image of Prince Sihanouk be used by any political party etc.

There was also the Pattaya meeting, where Prince Sihanouk made an eloquent indictment against the American involvement in his ouster, to which the American Assistant Secretary of State, Richard Salomon, replied by stating that that was due to the Cold War. The aim of the Pattaya meeting was also to find out what electoral system the Cambodian parties wished to opt for. Prince Sihanouk advocated the constituency system, while the KPNLF would prefer the proportional system, which would allow the other small parties to win the elections in the process of national reconciliation; finally the proportional system was adopted.

Finally the Tokyo meeting was arranged, mostly for Prince Sihanouk and the Hun Sen party to meet. The topics discussed may have included the involvement of Japan in the reconstruction of Cambodia and the UN Transitional Authority in Cambodia.

THE PARIS PEACE AGREEMENT OF 23 OCTOBER 1991

To reach the final stage of the meeting at the international conference centre on Avenue Kléber (Paris), first, there was the Rambouillet Chateau meeting in France among Cambodians and many discussions at the Conference Centre itself, mostly co-chaired by Roland Dumas and Ali Alatas.

At the Paris Conference, the KPNLF party raised the question of the Vietnamese troops to be demobilized on the spot, which H.E. Son Sann estimated to be between one and one-half million, according to calculations based on 1970 statistics and the declaration of Mr Hun Sen to Professor Peter Shier from Hamburg University, who estimated that 25 per cent of Cambodia's population were foreigners. In response to H.E. Son Sann, Mr Hun Sen declared that there were only 40,000 foreigners, a figure which the Ambassador of Russia corrected to a figure in excess of 100,000. Another point of discussion concerned the term "Cambodian Conflict", which the KPNLF corrected to "Cambodia Conflict", because it did not involve the Cambodian parties at the start, but foreign intervention.

With most of the main problems being resolved beforehand, the Paris conference created three Working Committees chaired by Laos, the Philippines and France respectively, to sort out details in the implementation.

After the conclusion of the Paris Peace Agreement, all the Cambodian parties went to the UN General Assembly and later to Shanghai and Beijing at the invitation of the People's Republic of China. It was at the Diaoyutai State Guest House that Samdech Sihanouk announced through his envoy, Madame Khek Sisoda, to Samdech Son Sann, H.E. Khieu Samphan and Prince Ranariddh, that he had ceased to be in alliance with them and would join the Phnom Penh party. The Shanghai meeting, before Beijing, was just a visit to view the modern realization of China and to promote familiarization between the Cambodian parties.

CONCLUSIONS

The stipulations of the Paris Peace Agreement dealt with all the aspects of the implementation of a UN Transitional Authority in Cambodia. But these stipulations were not respected by the UNTAC, as regards the main and vital stipulations of the cantonment, disarmament and the demobilization of the four Khmer factions' armed forces. Since the UN Peace Keeping forces could not intervene in the Khmer Rouge's Pailin zone, Samdech Son Sann had suggested to Mr Yasushi Akashi and General Sanderson that they should utilize the FUNCINPEC and the KPNLF Armies to force the opening of the Pailin zone for the UN. French General Loridon had rightly suggested that, if the State of Cambodia would join, it would help to create a National Army in that transitional period, but he was removed from his post. The 5–6 July 1997 fighting between the Royalist FUNCIPEC and the CPP (Cambodian People's Party) was a grave consequence of this failure to deal with and dissolve the four factions' armed forces, as well as a failure of achieving national reconciliation through a democratic process instead of a military process.

Another important issue was the repatriation of the Cambodian border refugees which was supposed to be done in time for them to participate in the elections, from the voter registration period to the electoral campaign and the voting, but at least 10,000 of them could not be repatriated in time and could not participate in the elections. Furthermore, according to the Paris Conference discussions, the UN should have checked who were Cambodians and who were not at the registration process, but this could not be done properly for lack of a serious information process.

In 2001, for the 10th Anniversary of the Paris Peace Agreement, the KPNLF party organized a one-day Conference, where all the participant countries to the Paris Accord were invited. A diplomat from Vietnamese Embassy attended as did the US Deputy Chief of Mission (Mr Mark Storella) and the Japanese Ambassador, who agreed on the continued validity of this Agreement. Today, the Cambodian government can still refer to this framework in the conflict where Cambodia is opposing Thailand.

14

THE ROLE AND PERFORMANCE OF UNTAC
An Australian Perspective

Ken Berry

The UN intervention in Cambodia was an important, if flawed success. Many people these days, with the benefit of hindsight, tend to see the mistakes made by UNTAC (the UN Transitional Authority in Cambodia) during the operation, and the subsequent somewhat slow pace of consolidation of democracy in Cambodia, as indicating that the UN intervention was a failure. In doing so, however, they are confusing what was intended by the international community in the 1991 Paris Agreements with a 'wish list' of popular expectations which could never have been realistically met. It was never, for example, the expectation of those directly involved that a full-fledged, Western-style democracy could be created in the less than two years that the whole UN operation lasted. Similarly, it was simply never realistic to contemplate that 15,000 widely-scattered international troops could, if the need arose, defeat the Khmer Rouge militarily, when 200,000 battle-hardened Vietnamese troops had not achieved that after ten years in Cambodia; nor that the 10 million mines strewn across Cambodia's countryside could be removed during the operation. Neither was it possible that the Cambodian economy and infrastructure — weak even in its heyday — could be rebuilt in so short a time.

Rather, the ultimate aim of those countries involved in negotiating the Paris Agreements had always been the simple proposition of creating conditions whereby the Cambodian people could for virtually the first time in their existence have a direct say in their own governance and future, and to that extent the whole exercise should be judged a success.

And let there be no doubt about it: UNTAC certainly succeeded in achieving many of the major objectives set down for it:

- It succeeded in the then relatively new function for the UN of organising and conducting free and fair elections despite the far from ideal conditions.
- It also made a genuine, and hopefully lasting, improvement in the human rights situation in Cambodia.
- UNTAC also achieved the logistically daunting task of repatriating more than 365,000 displaced Cambodians from camps on the Thai border, thus removing a situation which had of itself become a source of regional tension.

More generally, the Paris Agreements — and UNTAC — also succeeded in removing the Cambodian conflict as a source of regional tension. The Khmer Rouge insurgency ended and Cambodia has as a consequence reassumed its place in the community of nations.

A FLAWED SUCCESS

The fact remains, however, that UNTAC was a flawed success, and it exposed a number of aspects of the UN system which either did not work or were simply no longer suited to either the conditions in the post-Cold War world or the types of new and complex operations the UN is now called upon to undertake.

Many of the problems which occurred in UNTAC, moreover, had already surfaced in previous UN operations — which underlines the lack of an effective system to maintain corporate memory.[1] The early intention of the Secretariat to produce at least two reports critically assessing UNTAC's performance was never followed through. On the other hand, no number of reports and reviews will achieve much unless the governments that make up the UN show the necessary political will to undertake the reforms necessary to avoid repetition of the mistakes. Needless to say, gathering that political will is far from guaranteed.

LESSONS FOR THE UN MEMBERSHIP

UNTAC was one of the United Nations' most complex operations, though it is no longer its largest. Its mandate was also possibly the broadest, going far beyond traditional peacekeeping to include comprehensive efforts towards institution-building and social reconstruction as integral parts of a peace-building package designed to secure a lasting end to armed conflict and a genuine transition to democracy. To this end, UNTAC was endowed with significant electoral, civil administration, police, human rights, and repatriation, rehabilitation and reconstruction functions. The authority devolved on it to carry out some of these functions, particularly in the civil administration of a UN member state, was, moreover, amongst the most intrusive conferred on a UN operation.[2]

Perhaps the most obvious lessons to be drawn from UNTAC relate to the basic conditions which need to be satisfied for a peacekeeping operation to be considered effective. At least five suggest themselves from the UNTAC experience:

1. There should be a conceptually sound and appropriately detailed peace plan;
2. There must be clear and achievable goals;
3. There should be early deployment of adequate resources as soon as possible after the parties to the conflict have reached agreement;
4. The parties to the conflict must genuinely support the settlement; and
5. There needs to be an appropriate kind of external support for the operation.

A CONCEPTUALLY SOUND AND APPROPRIATELY DETAILED PEACE PLAN

Turning to the first of these conditions — a conceptually sound and appropriately detailed peace plan — many of the ideas reflected in the Paris Agreements can be traced to the original Australian 'Red Book' which contained a comprehensive plan for resolving the Cambodian conflict. One of its primary objectives had not been to try to dictate how the final settlement should look, but more to convince both the sceptics and the waverers that it was even possible to reduce the wide variety of complex problems involved in the Cambodia conflict to a single, detailed, comprehensive plan.

The Paris Agreements themselves represent a re-working and adaptation of the Australian plan. In retrospect, however, and in view of the process of compromise inherent in such protracted negotiations, it was perhaps inevitable that there could be no agreement on more detailed provisions to cover certain central issues. There was, for example, no guidance on what should happen in the event of non-compliance by one or more of the parties. Although some of the plan's central assumptions, especially about military demobilisation, were in the event undermined by non-compliance by the Khmer Rouge, it nevertheless proved, for the most part, sufficiently detailed and robust in practice to give effective guidance and support to UNTAC and the international community throughout the operation.

CLEAR AND ACHIEVABLE GOALS

The logical corollary of this is the second condition for a successful PKO, namely the establishment of clear and achievable goals, not least to avoid unrealistic or ill-founded expectations of the UN's role as peace keeper. It has been pointed out that a PKO mandate — and indeed any international agreement on which it is based — will never be perfect because of a number of inherent contradictions and tensions in the international system.[3]

Others might argue tangentially that the best can sometimes be the enemy of the good: that the time taken and angst generated as negotiators search for a perfect phrase, let alone a perfect solution, can often result in the political will to find a speedy, yet practicable, solution slipping away and the opportunity consequently lost.

The primary objective of the Paris Agreements was the holding of free and fair elections — a realistic and practical enough goal, even given the lack of infrastructure in Cambodia and the tight timetable imposed. There were nevertheless serious weaknesses in the implementation of what was in many ways the most innovative single element of the Paris Accords — the civil administration function, whereby the UN was meant to exercise effective control over the civil administrations existing in Cambodia until the elections could be held, to ensure they were held in as free and fair an atmosphere as possible. These weaknesses were largely due to the UN mandate being overly ambitious and in some respects clearly not achievable, given the United Nations' stretched resources and the years of armed struggle in Cambodia which had entrenched confrontation between the various factions. The concept of less than 200 UNTAC civilian administrators effectively overseeing the operations of even five central Ministries — let alone controlling them as they were supposed to do under the Paris Agreements — seems, in retrospect, implausible.

Whatever the case, UNTAC's failure to take rapid and, in some cases, adequate control of the key areas of the civil administrations of the factions

— particularly that of the State of Cambodia (SOC) which controlled Phnom Penh and much of the country, since this was the largest and really the only effective one — and to initiate corrective action when necessary (or even only in the most glaring cases), meant that UNTAC was unable to deal effectively with corruption and with the continuing intimidation of political figures from other parties during the election period.

This failure by UNTAC also served up on a silver platter spurious justification by the Khmer Rouge for not complying with key provisions of the Paris Agreements, including the process of cantoning, disarming and demobilising their military forces. This in turn meant that the elections could not be held in a strictly neutral political environment. While there can be endless, and probably fruitless, debate over whether the Khmer Rouge would ever have complied with the Paris Agreements, it must be acknowledged that it should not have been the UN which gave them such a tailor-made excuse in the first place.

EARLY DEPLOYMENT OF ADEQUATE RESOURCES

This third condition for a successful PKO needs to occur as soon as possible after the parties to the conflict have reached agreement, not only to enable the effective implementation of the PKO's mandate, but also to build and maintain the confidence of the parties and, just as importantly, the confidence of the local population as well. The UN operation in Cambodia unfortunately highlighted significant weaknesses in UN structures. The first UNTAC elements arrived in Cambodia in mid-April 1992 — six months after the Paris Agreements were signed. This proved in the event to be a dangerous delay — yet it took a further five to six months for UNTAC to become fully operational, particularly in the all-important civil administration component. By that time, the situation on the ground for the UN had almost become untenable — because of Khmer Rouge non-compliance, political violence and a severe undermining of popular confidence in the UN — with a change in the mandate becoming necessary as a consequence.

Forward planning: In part, the delays in UNTAC's deployment were due to, or aggravated by, inadequate planning and preparation caused by deficiencies in the work of the UN's Advance Mission in Cambodia, UNAMIC. However, it must also be acknowledged that UNAMIC cannot wholly be blamed, being in itself the victim of insufficient preparedness — most of it budget-related — to react to the pace of developments on the part of UNHQ in New York. The reality was that no single office had the organisational capability to run planning and operations of the magnitude confronting the UN. Such a situation had the potential for significant duplication of effort, and hence waste and potential confusion.

Other obstacles to advance planning proved to be staff-related, and included not only insufficient numbers of headquarters personnel trained in different fields of relevant expertise, but also a mind-set in some parts of the UN Secretariat which resisted input from 'outsiders'. There were also considerable delays in deployment caused by the inevitable concerns, endemic to all PKOs and not just UNTAC, from the UN's Field Operations Division that all necessary support and infrastructure needs of a PKO be assured almost to the last detail before a single soldier left base.

An effort to get around the usual labyrinthine UN procedures was made in Cambodia where national units of the UNTAC military component were tasked to arrive in country with enough stores to allow for 60 days self-sufficiency. Some units, however, arrived with equipment which was either old (with no spare parts) or totally inappropriate (e.g. electrical equipment running on 110 volts and not UNTAC's 240 volts, thus necessitating the purchase of extra generators). While this may sound picayune in comparison to the scale of the task facing UNTAC, cumulatively, such factors caused further pressures to be placed on an already overburdened central UNTAC administration. They also added to the expense of the operation, since UNTAC had to maintain large, diverse stocks of equipment and spares to cover the diversity of national contributions.[4]

There were also complaints about engineering support arriving too late in-country (often with inappropriate equipment), and delays in the creation of an efficient logistics chain. One possible way of minimising such delays in future operations might be the use, as far as possible, of regionally-sourced engineering and logistics units. The selection and rapid deployment of Australian personnel to provide communications in both UNAMIC and UNTAC was a useful model in this regard and this certainly seems to have been borne out in later operations in East Timor, as well as in a number of UN-backed actions in Africa.

In the event, it is no exaggeration to suggest that deficiencies in the UN system with regard to multi-dimensional peacekeeping contributed significantly to the creation of the UN Department of Peacekeeping Operations (DPKO) in 1992 — coincidental with the deployment of UNTAC,[5] though probably not soon enough to improve UNTAC's performance. While the DPKO was a welcome development which continues to be refined, that is not to say that it is immune to other deficiencies inherent in the UN system.

Budget aspects: The slow and labyrinthine process followed in the UN for budget approvals, even for the most clearly essential items, remained a serious problem for the duration of the UNTAC operation, and highlighted the need for reforms both in the UN's Advisory Committee on Administrative and Budgetary Questions (ACABQ) and the General Assembly's Fifth (Financial) Committee processes, as well as in UNHQ procedures. These reforms have still not occurred, and this only emphasises the need for the Secretary-General to urgently consider further structural changes in the Secretariat to meet the increasing demands being put on it and as a means of improving the administration of peacekeeping operations.

Staffing aspects: Another essential part of adequate preparation is the early designation of senior staff — again both civilian and military — and their rapid involvement in the planning of the operation. In the case of UNTAC, the Special Representative of the Secretary-General was only appointed in January 1992 — three months after the Paris Agreements had been signed; the Force Commander in December 1991; the Police Commissioner and Human Rights Director in March 1992; and the all-important Civil Administration Director in April 1992 — in other words, a full six months after the Paris Agreements came into effect. UNTAC subsequently suffered from a lack of both continuity and institutional memory due largely to the even later appointment of many of the lower level staff and the ensuing rapid — and often arbitrarily timed — rotation out of many of them.

The final judgment must be that these cumulative delays were critical in that they cut into the tight (and equally tightly-funded) timetable outlined in the Paris Agreements, and affected UNTAC's credibility in the eyes of the Cambodian people (not to mention the critical eyes of some donor and other countries).

Various bodies have looked at options for facilitating identification and deployment of military units for UN operations, including the creation of a standing UN force capacity or stand-by arrangements, but the going has been slow. In the meantime, the onus is really on UN member states to at least ensure that they provide the best qualified, professional and well-disciplined personnel in order to maintain the credibility of an operation. There should be an obligation on the part of the contributing countries to meet the criteria set by the United Nations for personnel, and a right for the UN to reject unsuitable or unqualified personnel at the donor's expense.

UNTAC's 21,000 personnel ranged from highly-qualified professionals to those who were incompetent and, in some cases, a menace to their colleagues and the Cambodian population. Unfortunately, there were far too many instances of these sorts of personnel not being rejected, possibly for fear of offending contributing countries or simply because there were no alternative personnel available. Worse for morale within UNTAC was the appointment (or even 'promotion') of such personnel to more comfortable jobs back in Phnom Penh, simply to get rid of them from sensitive areas. Moreover, the unacceptable behaviour of some military personnel caused resentment and alienated Cambodians. As a result of such behaviour in this and other operations, UN military personnel have since 1998 been provided with pocket cards containing a "Code of Personal Conduct for Blue Helmets."

SUPPORT OF THE PARTIES TO THE CONFLICT

The fourth condition essential for a successful PKO — support of the parties to the conflict — is self-evident, but worth repeating. The signature of the Paris Agreements by all four warring Cambodian factions provided at least prima facie evidence of their support for the UN operation — despite the suspicions others may have harboured as to the ulterior motives of individual factions in doing so. We shall probably never know definitively Khmer Rouge motives for not complying with their undertakings, but on balance it would appear that the Khmer Rouge had never really intended to cooperate fully with the UN or otherwise would have intended to undermine the situation once the UN had left Cambodia. Whatever the case, their overt non-compliance with Phase 1 of the military arrangements (regrouping and cantonment of the factional forces), not to mention the less than full compliance by the SOC with aspects of the civil administration and electoral provisions of the Paris Agreements, subsequently affected every aspect of the UNTAC operation.

One of the questions which have often been asked is whether the UN was right to proceed, as it did, without Khmer Rouge cooperation. The options open to the United Nations in these conditions were largely those which have since confronted the UN in Somalia, Bosnia and even more recently in East Timor and Sierra Leone: first, to use force against the Khmer Rouge or other defaulting party, going beyond mere self-defence, and thus in effect changing the peacekeeping mandate to one of peace enforcement; secondly, to persevere in the peacekeeping role (though perhaps with a modified mandate), re-emphasising the peace-making functions, at the risk of both physical danger to the peacekeeping force and of the peace process becoming bogged down indefinitely; or thirdly, to withdraw, which would have meant abandoning the advances that were being made in returning Cambodia to the community of nations.

There were, of course, some advocates, including from within the UNTAC military component, of the use of force to ensure Khmer Rouge compliance.

To be generous, some of these people may have been confusing the controlled use of force by UN troops in the exercise of self-defence with the central objectives of UNTAC as a peacekeeping operation. However, even self-defence has its problems. As General Sanderson, the Australian commander of UNTAC military forces put it:

> The problem is that any use of force can create its own dynamic of escalating violence ... Anyone who thinks they can bluff their way through these things with a mandate and troops designed for peacekeeping has little understanding of the nature of conflict and the consequences of the use of force.[6]

As far as the possibility of actually converting the UNTAC mandate to one of peace enforcement, a mid-stream change of this kind was unlikely to appeal to many of the troop-contributing countries, and would almost inevitably have led to the withdrawal of some units from Cambodia. Equally, the increased costs implicit in an enforcement operation of the requisite size was unlikely to be approved by the wider UN membership. And despite the number of troops already deployed, it had to be recognised that an enforcement operation, even in the unlikely event of a massive injection of further military units, probably also faced an uncertain outcome. After all, 200,000 well-trained Vietnamese troops had not succeeded, during their ten years in Cambodia, in eradicating the Khmer Rouge.

A corollary of all this is that if the international community knows when it should get involved in a conflict, it must also be capable of taking a rational decision as to when to get out of the conflict. However, in the Cambodian situation, simply walking away from Cambodia seemed to be unacceptable to the majority of countries involved in UNTAC. Perseverance was thus the only alternative and, as things turned out it was the right choice. Although a central element of the Paris Agreements, namely cantonment and demobilisation of the factional armed forces, was not in place, the Secretary-General correctly decided to continue on to the elections even though this risked the operation failing altogether, as had already happened in Angola. An adjustment in the mandate, however, diverted some of the UNTAC military forces to greater protection of the voter registration and polling processes.

APPROPRIATE EXTERNAL SUPPORT FOR THE OPERATION

Stepping back to the origins of the Cambodia peace process, we would do well to remember that although there was a distinct and tragic Cambodian dimension to the problem, the main issues really had little to do with the country itself. They were, rather, geopolitical and reflected the broader divisions which existed at that time between the permanent members of the Security Council. It was only with developments such as an initiative by Mikhail Gorbachev in 1986 to get some of the major parties, notably China, to talk about this and other global issues, that individual members of the P5 began to see Cambodia no longer as justification for keeping apart, but as a good reason to get together, on the wider issues. Real movement forward on Cambodia then became possible.

Consensus amongst the P5 was thus a central factor in the whole peace process — although it was a regional initiative which provided the framework in which that consensus could be manifested. Such consensus will obviously also have to be a central factor in future UN operations. Nevertheless, as UNTAC proceeded, the P5 representatives in Phnom Penh were unable to generate or maintain consensus on a number of issues — the central one being how to handle Khmer Rouge non-cooperation, but also included issues such as presidential elections (which were not included in the Paris Agreements since it was felt this should be left to the new Cambodian constitution to be drafted by the Cambodians themselves once the elections were held). This led at times to a lack of direction on UNTAC's part. And even when UNTAC itself was prepared to act, for instance by setting up the Office of the UN Special Prosecutor, the lack of P5 consensus on how far the UN should go in backing the Special Prosecutor not only placed UNTAC in a difficult position, but also further eroded the confidence the Cambodian people had in UNTAC.

Thus while the P5 had a central role to play; it was not necessarily an exclusive role. The bottom line is that other countries, though not in the Security Council, can and should continue to play an active role in building and maintaining consensus in UN operations. In Cambodia the evolution of what became known as the 'expanded P5' or 'Core Group', which included Australia, Canada, Germany and others, provided the requisite mechanism through which to focus and maintain pressure and persuasion on the Cambodian factions. One reason for the success of holding the elections in Cambodia was that the external backers of the various factions — who were not limited to the P5 — pressed their client factions not to return to violence, while at the same time reducing the factions' ability to do so by withholding (and convincing others to withhold) arms, supplies and other material support. The same group also bolstered the confidence of the factions by showing that the international community had a continuing commitment to Cambodia's future. The success of this expanded P5 mechanism in the implementation of UNTAC suggests that it is worth considering in other such situations.

OTHER SPECIFIC QUESTIONS

All of this raises a number of questions relevant to future operations. Perhaps the most important question relates to situations where the observance of human rights is critical to the comprehensive settlement of a conflict — and this is arguably so in most operations. Other questions relate to whether there is a need to include budget support for new governments as part of the overall funding calculations for an operation, and for a more coordinated approach to public relations, in order to maintain public confidence in the UN. In the 'food for thought' category is the question of future defence cooperation with countries in which the UN becomes involved.

HUMAN RIGHTS

Given Cambodia's long history of some of the most brutal violations of human rights in a century known for its brutality, it may have seemed logical that this would be one of the more sensitive areas of the UN operation. And in fact, the provisions built into the Paris Agreements relating to international monitoring of the ongoing human rights situation in Cambodia were arguably amongst the most intrusive ever included in such a document. The international community followed up after the elections with the appointment of a Special Representative for Human Rights in Cambodia and the establishment of a Centre for Human Rights in Phnom Penh.

The Red Book[7] recognised that there was a potential problem in the judicial area, and sought to deal with it in a manner which need not have been labour-intensive, but that view did not prevail. UNTAC also planned a mechanism to review judgments handed down by the Courts, but this never became a reality, although UNTAC civil administrators occasionally succeeded in preventing the execution of minor decrees they considered unjust. UNTAC had even drafted quite long, detailed and impartial guidelines for a new judiciary and penal system during the transitional period which was, however, never implemented.

The problem in practice during the UNTAC operation was that only 10 people were initially assigned to the Human Rights Component of UNTAC — the assumption by the UN planners having apparently been that the rest of UNTAC would monitor human rights observance as a subset of their other responsibilities. The obvious weakness in this approach was that the other components had their hands full with their primary tasks, and in any case few of the UN officials in those components had any real training in human rights.

UNTAC appointed a Special Prosecutor in January 1993, but when it came to the crunch of actually bringing human rights offenders to justice, UNTAC found itself hamstrung by the unwillingness of the SOC authorities in Phnom Penh to prosecute suspects. There was also an impasse over what to do with offenders. UNTAC granted itself the power of arrest, but initially there was nowhere to hold detainees. (This was subsequently corrected by the establishment of the UN's first "detention facility".) There is more than a little irony in the fact that the UN's first two prisoners in Cambodia were held without habeas corpus or trial.

The question is whether the Paris Agreements should have included specific measures for, initially, providing a temporary substitute for, and subsequently building, a functioning criminal justice system as part of the transitional period and post-conflict peace-building exercise. In the wake of UNTAC, for instance, the former Special Prosecutor and others raised the idea of including 'justice packages' as part of future operations. These would have the dual objectives of dealing with law and order during a UN operation, and also training existing or new legal personnel on the ground. The latter is particularly important if the UN is to promote a wider commitment to impartial justice and human rights. Fortunately, this is one idea which has been taken up by the UN, with a policy finally developed in 2009.[8]

WAR CRIMES TRIBUNAL

A related issue over the years has been the question of bringing the remaining Khmer Rouge leaders to justice. It was impossible to include provisions on this in the Paris Agreements since of course neither the Khmer Rouge nor China would have supported any peace settlement which included them. After some years, however, remaining Khmer Rouge leaders are finally facing justice in an international tribunal in Phnom Penh. The Hague Tribunals on former Yugoslavia had already set a precedent for this sort of trial; not to mention the Ad Hoc tribunals for crimes against humanity in Rwanda and Liberia; and the International Criminal Court in The Hague will deal with such crimes in future.

BUDGET SUPPORT

Similar to the question of the possible inclusion of 'justice packages' in future operations is that of whether provision for the payment of the wages of the armed forces, police and civil service out of the UN budget during the course of the operation, should also be included. This had proved to be a lacuna in the Paris Agreements which was serious at the time (as the SOC had spent its Treasury on its election campaign).

The immediate problem was resolved by an arrangement for budget support based initially on the remnants of the 1991 trust fund set up by Australia and a handful of other countries. But it is a situation which should have been foreseen. Given the overall costs of an operation such as UNTAC, the extra amount required for this purpose was relatively small, yet could have done much to wean away many Cambodian police, soldiers and civil servants from their factional allegiances.

PUBLIC RELATIONS

Given the intense international media interest in every step of the Cambodia peace process, and others which have followed, it may be surprising to learn that there was no coordinated approach within the UN or UNTAC to the public relations aspects of the operation. Although UNTAC had an information division, it was mainly occupied with educating the Cambodian people for the electoral process. Subsequent UN operations tend to indicate that this lesson has still not been fully learned, at least within the UN — though the intensive media briefings and arrangements which accompanied US-led coalition operations in Iraq and Afghanistan, and the NATO bombing of Serbia in 1999 and Libya in 2011, show that at least some countries grasp the importance of planning actively to deal with the CNN factor. The importance of properly-planned public relations as an integral part of an operation is also underlined by the fact that more often than not, bad news is what the international media is after.

CONCLUSION

The UN, it has to be acknowledged, has taken some steps to reform its structures, with the establishment of mechanisms such as the Electoral Assistance Unit, the Situation Centre and, importantly, a Planning Division. Efforts have also been made to improve coordination among relevant Secretariat Departments involved in PKOs, and the Secretariat, with the active support of some Members, is also pursuing initiatives to create more effective stand-by arrangements and civilian personnel rosters. In tandem with this activity, a number of international non-governmental bodies are examining the feasibility of creating a UN standing force.

At the same time, however, many fundamental problems remain, most of them budget- and resources-driven. While some of these might be susceptible of structural solutions (such as further reform of the UN budgetary processes), in reality they all turn on whether the UN membership can collectively generate the political will necessary not only to undertake such reforms, but also to make them work by putting the needed financial and human resources at the UN's disposal.

In addition, if there is one fundamental lesson which Cambodia, Bosnia, Somalia, Rwanda, Kosovo and Timor can teach us all, it can be summed up in the paradoxically mundane expression that prevention is better than cure. In terms of resource outlay, preventive diplomacy could be significantly more cost-effective than either peacekeeping or peace enforcement. In terms of preventing human suffering, however, the savings would be immeasurable.

Notes

1. One of the few UN bodies to involve itself in an exercise of this nature has been UNITAR which co-hosted, with the Singapore Institute of Policy Studies, an International conference on UNTAC: Debriefing and Lessons in Singapore, 2–4 August 1994. A collection of the Conference Papers was produced by UNITAR in Geneva in December 1994: *The United Nations Transitional Authority in Cambodia (UNTAC): Debriefing and Lessons* (Kluwer Law International, London, 1994).
2. "The creation of laws and procedures regarding elections was a critical function granted to UNTAC. The authority to draft legislation was not provided to UNTAC in other areas of civil administration and signified an innovative and intrusive role for the UN in the internal affairs of a member state." Michael Doyle, *UN Peacekeeping in Cambodia: UNTAC's Civil Mandate*. International Peace Academy, Occasional Paper Series, Lynne Rienner, Boulder CO, 1995, p. 28.
3. Doyle op. cit., p. 82.
4. The UNTAC operation cost US$4.5 billion, and this does not include reconstruction costs.
5. For a summary of the 1994 reorganization of the DPKO, see Pamela Reed, J. Matthew Vaccaro, and William Durch, *Handbook on United Nations Peace Operations*. Stimson Centre Handbook 3 (Washington DC: Henry L. Stimson Centre, 1995), pp. 7–9.
6. Lt Gen John Sanderson, *Peacekeeping or Peace Enforcement: Global Flux and the Dilemmas of United Nations Intervention*. Paper presented at the Conference on "The United Nations: Between Sovereignty and Global Governance". La Trobe University, Melbourne, 26 July 1995.

7. See pp. 1718, 3536.
8. "Justice Components in UN Peace Operations", UN Dept of Peacekeeping Operations, Dept of Field Support, Ref. 2009.30, 1 December 2009, <http://www.unrol.org/files/Justice%20Components%20in%20United%20Nations%20Peace%20Operations.pdf>.

15

JUSTICE AND RECONCILIATION IN CAMBODIA

Jean-Marc Lavergne

INTRODUCTION

Countless challenges have arisen in the efforts to create a court with jurisdiction to try "senior Khmer Rouge leaders and those who were most responsible" for the crimes committed during their regime within Cambodia. These efforts were met with scepticism by those who considered judicial intervention either impossible or meaningless in a country such as Cambodia. Despite all this, the long-awaited time for justice in Cambodia has finally arrived. It is not, however, an easy task. As it is a work in progress, results cannot yet be finally assessed.

The Khmer Rouge Tribunal, officially named the Extraordinary Chambers in the Courts of Cambodia (ECCC), faces many challenges. However, the issuing of its first judgment in July 2010 and the start of a second trial in 2011 are unquestionably important and concrete steps in "moving forward through justice" and give hope for reconciliation. Before focusing on the ECCC, it is necessary to put the Cambodian experience into a broader context. The development of International Criminal Law and transitional justice is relatively new. The path from impunity to accountability for the perpetrators of the most serious crimes has seen the emergence of international norms and now offers an increasingly effective response to post-conflict situations.

FROM IMPUNITY TO ACCOUNTABILITY OR THE EMERGENCE OF NORMS TO PROVIDE JUSTICE TO VICTIMS OF THE MOST SERIOUS CRIMES AND ITS DEVELOPMENT

The 20th century had witnessed systematic violations of fundamental rights in different regions of the world. The responses to those crimes were different: retaliation, amnesty, regular trials, Truth and Reconciliation Commissions, international tribunals or simply, oblivion. Since awareness grew for the need to prosecute and to sentence perpetrators for the most serious atrocities that touched the universal conscience, the path to an effective international criminal justice has been long. It is generally recognised that it is the duty of the international community to ensure that victims of genocide, crimes against humanity and war crimes receive justice. But it would be wrong to believe that the implementation of this principle has resulted in a smooth process, with regular advances. The development of international criminal justice comprises both backward and forward steps while the balance between ethical imperatives and political constraints is always a complex and perilous exercise. On the one hand, this depends on specific political circumstances, tragic events, or the conscience of the international community when it has failed to prevent foreseeable atrocities or to maintain peace. On the other hand, political, financial or economic considerations also come into play when relationships between States are aimed at protecting national or strategic interests.

At the end of the 19th century, when adopting the Convention on Laws and Customs of War, State representatives noted that "populations and belligerents remain under the protection and empire of the principles of international law."[1] They recognized that these principles resulted from "the usages established between civilized nations, from the laws of humanity and the requirements of the public conscience."[2] This clause marked a real starting point for the evolution of humanitarian law, but no mechanism was developed to enforce these principles. In particular, no international court was established to provide justice to victims.

Despite plans to try those considered as perpetrators of the crime of aggression and those deemed responsible for World War I,[3] no trials were conducted in its aftermath. Efforts to give more effect to humanitarian law continued in vain until the end of World War II. In the 1920s, the Council of the League of Nations mandated a committee to examine the feasibility of creating a permanent international criminal tribunal. However, this plan was considered premature and was rejected by several countries on the basis of the principle of non-interference in domestic affairs.[4]

It was only in the aftermath of World War II that international criminal justice was born to try those individually accountable for the horrors committed under the rule of fascist States. The International Military Tribunal of Nuremberg and the International Military Tribunal for the Far East were however criticized as "Tribunals of the victors" and for applying criminal law retroactively. Nonetheless they contributed by providing the foundation for modern international criminal law, in particular by defining crimes against peace, war crimes and crimes against humanity, but also by developing principles of international law. In 1950, the International Law Commission of the United Nations adopted a list of the principles contained in the Charter of the Nuremberg Tribunal and in the Judgment of the said Tribunal.[5] These principles remain crucial and are as follows:

> Principle I: Any person who commits an act which constitutes a crime under international law is responsible therefore and liable to punishment.
> Principle II: The fact that internal (domestic) law does not impose a penalty for an act which constitutes a crime under international law does not relieve the person who committed the act from responsibility under international law.
> Principle III: The fact that a person who committed an act which constitutes a crime under international law acted as Head of State or responsible Government official does not relieve him from responsibility under international law.
> Principle IV: The fact that a person acted pursuant to an order of his Government or of a superior does not relieve him from responsibility under international law provided a moral choice was in fact possible to him.
> Principle V: Any person charged with a crime under international law has the right to a fair trial on the facts and law.

CONVENTION ON GENOCIDE AND GENEVA CONVENTIONS

At the same time and in response to the atrocities committed during World War II, the Convention on Genocide was adopted in 1948 by the United Nations.[6] Moreover, the Geneva Conventions and their Additional Protocols, which constitute the core of international humanitarian law, were adopted in 1949 and 1977 respectively.[7] In the Convention on Genocide, the State Parties recognized that "genocide is an international crime, which entails the national and international responsibility of individual persons and states."[8] This Convention, which provides a precise definition of the crime of genocide, in particular in terms of the required intent and the prohibited acts, has since then been widely accepted by the international community and ratified by the overwhelming majority of States. The Geneva Conventions constitute the body of international law that regulates the conduct of armed conflicts and seeks to limit their effects. They specifically protect people who are not taking part in the hostilities or who are no longer participating in the hostilities.

International law was further developed with the adoption of these international instruments, which were complemented by domestic legislation in many countries. However, concomitant attempts to establish a permanent international criminal tribunal failed at this time. In fact the prevailing consensus disappeared and the UN General Assembly did not adopt the International Law Commission's 1954 submission of a Draft Statute for an International Criminal Court and a revised draft code of offenses.[9] Political tensions associated with the Cold War largely obstructed progress of the war crimes agenda, particularly with regard to the sensitive issue of defining the crime of aggression.

INTERNATIONAL CRIMINAL TRIBUNAL FOR THE FORMER YUGOSLAVIA

The interest in international criminal justice changed with the end of the Cold War. The war in the Balkans made western countries realize that mass crimes and atrocities could also directly affect Europe. It is in this context that the International Criminal Tribunal for the Former Yugoslavia was established in 1993.[10] This Tribunal undoubtedly changed, for all time, the landscape of international humanitarian law. It has demonstrated that fair and independent justice is possible and has provided victims with an opportunity to describe the horrors they witnessed and experienced.

The dramatic events that occurred all around the globe during the 1990s in Rwanda, East Timor, Sierra Leone and Liberia reinforced the development of international criminal justice. These events have shown that those suspected of bearing the greatest responsibility for atrocities can be called to account in an effective and transparent manner, and that leaders suspected of mass crimes may well have to face justice.

INTERNATIONAL CRIMINAL COURT

The creation of *ad hoc* Tribunals (the ICTY in 1993 and the ICTR in 1994)[11] initiated an exceptional decade that culminated in a historic milestone on 17 July 1998 when 120 States adopted the Rome Statute establishing the International Criminal Court (ICC).[12] The ICC is an independent, permanent court that tries persons accused of the most serious crimes of international concern, namely genocide, crimes against humanity and war crimes.[13] The ICC is a court of last resort that will not act if a case is investigated or prosecuted by a national judicial system unless national proceedings are not possible or are not genuine, for example if formal proceedings were undertaken solely to shield a person from criminal responsibility.[14] In addition, the ICC tries only those accused of the gravest crimes.[15]

Around the time the *Rome Statute* entered into force on 1 July 2002, a new generation of internationalised or hybrid courts appeared. In 2000, the Special Panels for Serious Crimes were created in East Timor and in 2002 an agreement between the United Nations and the Government of Sierra Leone established the Special Court for Sierra Leone.[16]

At the domestic level, political changes and specific events such as the arrest in London in 1998 of General Augusto Pinochet contributed to increasing pressure from civil society to end impunity, to reveal the truth about atrocities committed during military dictatorships in South America and to deliver justice to victims by providing them with a legal remedy in the form of accountability for these crimes. The domestic judicial systems of Chile, Argentina and several other South American countries reopened or initiated previously barred prosecutions and trials of persons suspected of crimes against humanity. For example, in March 1998, the National Congress of Argentina repealed the Full Stop and Due Obedience Laws.[17] In 2005, the Argentinean Supreme Court declared these amnesty laws concerning crimes against humanity to be unconstitutional.[18]

During the same period, domestic legislation in several countries gave to their domestic courts universal jurisdiction to prosecute perpetrators of the most serious crimes and in particular, crimes against humanity.

TRUTH AND RECONCILIATION COMMISSIONS

The response to post-conflict situations or periods where the most serious crimes were committed has not necessarily or exclusively been judicial. In the 1980s and 1990s, more than 16 countries established truth and reconciliation commissions, of which the South African Truth and Reconciliation

Commission is the most famous example.[19] Despite criticism of the lack of real accountability of some important perpetrators of crimes committed during the apartheid regime, it has helped turn the page following a tragic period and has facilitated development and transition to democracy.

Transitional justice can therefore bring about a wide range of responses. Cambodia and the international community have chosen the judicial path by attempting to provide justice for the Cambodian people through the prosecution of those charged with being the most responsible for serious crimes committed during the Khmer Rouge regime.

THE LONG-AWAITED TIME FOR JUSTICE IN CAMBODIA: THE CHALLENGES OF THE ECCC AND THE HOPE FOR RECONCILIATION

Factual background[20]

On 17 April 1975, the army of the Communist Party of Kampuchea (CPK), the Kampuchea People's National Liberation Armed Forces (KPNLAF) entered Phnom Penh and seized national power. With the end of the civil war against Lon Nol's Khmer Republic and during the three years, eight months and twenty days that followed, the CPK exercised effective authority over Democratic Kampuchea (DK). It pursued a policy aimed at completely disintegrating the economic and political structures of the Khmer Republic and creating a new, revolutionary state power.

Historians and observers agree that this program was implemented through a number of means including the forced transfer of residents of Phnom Penh and other former Khmer Republic strongholds to the countryside; the creation of Party-controlled agricultural production cooperatives where people were made to work under extremely difficult conditions to increase food production; and the elimination of officials and supporters of the previous regime.[21]

Many of these CPK policies required the transformation of "new people" into peasants. New people were made up broadly of evacuated city-dwellers and peasants living under Lon Nol control until April 1975; they were distinct from "old" or "base" people who were essentially peasants from areas already under the authority of the CPK during the Khmer Republic period. Politically motivated extra-judicial executions were committed from the outset by military units. They continued thereafter in security centres throughout the country.[22]

According to the demographic survey produced during the investigation, these actions resulted in millions of victims, including an estimated 1.7 to 2.2 million deaths, of which approximately 800,000 were violent.[23]

CREATION OF THE ECCC

In its preamble, the Agreement between the United Nations and the Royal Government of Cambodia, dated 6 June 2003, concerning the prosecution of crimes committed during the period of Democratic Kampuchea, refers to the legitimate concern of the Government and the people of Cambodia in the pursuit of justice and national reconciliation, stability, peace and security.

Justice, national reconciliation, peace and security are therefore key words that have accompanied the establishment of the Extraordinary Chambers in the Courts of Cambodia. It is clear that peace, or at least security, must be achieved before justice can be delivered and that justice is frequently considered as a prerequisite for reconciliation. However, these notions encompass purposes that are not exactly similar and that may even diverge. In post-conflict situations, stability and peace are reasons frequently put forward to explain that the time for justice has to be delayed as the search of individual accountability might create chaos or contribute to the continuation or re-opening of hostilities. There are obviously different approaches to such notions. Due to the specific Cambodian context and because priorities defined at the state level, the international level and the individual level differ, victims in Cambodia have long awaited the time for justice for what are frequently described as some of the most awful atrocities of the 20th century.

The first explanation for this long waiting period is the complete destruction of the state institutions by the Khmer Rouge. During the Khmer Rouge regime, the judicial system of Cambodia disappeared entirely. No laws or enforcement mechanisms, including courts that might conduct trials, were ever established. There was no functioning judicial system to provide procedural safeguards for detainees. It is also undisputed that in the aftermath of the Democratic Kampuchea regime the Cambodian judicial system was severely weakened and compromised due to the impact of, inter alia, the destruction of public institutions and qualified personnel during this period, and of ongoing civil war.

In 1979, several leaders of the Khmer Rouge regime were tried, convicted and sentenced to death in absentia.[24] The judicial value of this trial is disputed. Many consider that it did not meet international standards, and numerous commentators perceived it as tainted by political considerations.[25]

After the 1979 trials, political agreements among the various Cambodian factions, and in particular the 1991 Paris Agreements, excluded any direct reference to the mass crimes committed during the Khmer Rouge era.[26] At this time, the prosecution of perpetrators and official acknowledgement of the existence of crimes suffered by countless victims were not considered by the international community as a mandatory precondition for a transition to peace. Moreover, until 1993 the official delegation representing Cambodia at the UN was led by the Khmer Rouge. The Cambodian approach of rallying former Khmer Rouge to the side of the governmental authorities favoured obliteration of the past and mercy. Nonetheless the royal pardon granted in 1996 to Ieng Sary, the former Minister of Foreign Affairs of the Democratic Kampuchea, caused quite a stir and voices demanded an end to what was denounced as a culture of impunity.

In 1997, the Co-Prime Ministers Norodom Ranariddh and Hun Sen sent a letter to the UN Secretary-General asking the UN to assist Cambodia in establishing a tribunal to prosecute the senior leaders of the Khmer Rouge.[27] Seven years elapsed before the Extraordinary Chambers in the Courts of Cambodia for the Prosecution of Crimes Committed during the Period of Democratic Kampuchea or "ECCC" were established.

During these years, negotiations were difficult as the UN suggested a UN-run tribunal in the same form as the *ad hoc* tribunals, ICTY and ICTR, relying mainly on international staff. The Government of Cambodia considered however, that for the sake of the Cambodian people, the trial must be held in Cambodia using Cambodian staff and with Cambodian judges presiding, assisted by foreign personnel. Acknowledging the weakness of the Cambodian legal system, the international nature of the crimes, and to help in meeting international standards of justice, Cambodia invited international participation. But following recommendations made by a group of experts, mistrust between the two negotiating teams and intense pressure from human rights advocates, the United Nations put an end to the negotiations with the Cambodian government in early 2002.

At the insistence of several Member States of the United Nations, negotiations were resumed in 2003. An agreement was ultimately reached in June 2003, detailing how the international community would assist and participate in the Extraordinary Chambers.[28] It took another four years to make the ECCC effectively operational. During these years a new Cambodian law on the establishment of the ECCC was promulgated in 2004, and the ECCC Judges adopted internal rules[29] in June 2007.

The result of this long process was the establishment of a hybrid or internationalized tribunal with unique features, comprising a Cambodian court supplemented by international participation and assistance.

The Office of the Co-Prosecutors, comprising two Co-Prosecutors, one Cambodian and one international, conducts preliminary investigations. If they have reason to believe that crimes within the jurisdiction of the ECCC have been committed, they send an Introductory Submission to the Co-

Investigating Judges. This triggers the opening of a judicial investigation, which must be conducted impartially by two Co-Investigating Judges, one Cambodian and one international. It is then for the Co-Investigating Judges to decide whether the acts in question amount to crimes within the jurisdiction of the ECCC. They also assess whether the evidence gathered is sufficient, either to indict the charged persons and send them to trial, or to dismiss the case. Their decisions are subject to appeal before the Pre-Trial Chamber.

Once the Trial Chamber is seized of an Indictment, it has jurisdiction to try the accused. A decision of the Trial Chamber requires the affirmative vote of at least four of the five judges. Judgments and decisions of the Trial Chamber are subject to appeal before the Supreme Court Chamber, comprising seven judges, four Cambodians and three international.

The Supreme Court Chamber has jurisdiction to decide an appeal against a judgment or a decision of the Trial Chamber. A decision of the Supreme Court Chamber requires the affirmative vote of at least five of the seven judges.

This dual structure has the advantage of combining the skills of the Cambodian Judges who unquestionably have legitimacy to try crimes perpetrated in Cambodia, by Cambodians and mainly against Cambodian victims with those of international Judges. The two components of this Court have the duty to ensure that the trials will meet the international standards and in particular that the ECCC proceedings are fair, adversarial and preserve a balance between the rights of the parties.[30]

STATE OF PROCEEDINGS

Case 1

The first case at the ECCC was against a man with the revolutionary name "Duch," a former mathematics teacher who served as Deputy and then Chairman of S-21, a security centre tasked with interrogating and executing perceived opponents of the Khmer Rouge regime from 1975 to 1979. As Chairman of S-21, his role consisted of overseeing the entire S-21 operation including annotating confessions and ordering executions. S-21 was a very important security centre. It reported to the very highest levels of the Khmer Rouge leadership, carrying out nation-wide operations and receiving high-level cadres and prominent detainees. The majority of the detainees were systematically tortured. Victims who were not executed died as a result of the detention conditions, which led to widespread disease, malnourishment and physical and psychological pain, as well as extreme fear. More than 12,000 individuals were detained and executed at S-21. The actual number of detainees is likely however, to have been considerably greater, given the incompleteness of the records. The Trial Chamber issued a judgment on 26 July 2010 finding Duch guilty of crimes against humanity, including extermination and torture, and of grave breaches of the Geneva Conventions of 1949.[31] He was sentenced to 35 years of imprisonment, of which he has already served 11. Following the appeals filed by the Defence, Prosecution and Civil Parties, this case is currently before the Supreme Court Chamber.

Case 2

In a second case, the Co-Investigating Judges issued a Closing Order indicting four people.[32]

The Closing Order was appealed and has now been confirmed by the Pre-Trial Chamber.[33] The four Accused have now been sent for trial before the ECCC Trial Chamber on charges of crimes against humanity, grave breaches of the Geneva Conventions of 12 August 1949, and genocide of the Cham and of the Vietnamese people, together with Offences under the Cambodian Criminal Code 1956 (murder, torture and religious persecution).[34]

Given the magnitude of the crimes allegedly committed under the Democratic Kampuchea regime, the Co-Prosecutors seized the Co-Investigating Judges only with a specific selection of sites and criminal activities. The judicial investigation thus focused in particular on the following issues:

- The displacement of the population from urban to rural areas, and later between rural areas;
- The establishment and operation of cooperatives and worksites;
- The re-education of "bad elements" and the elimination of "enemies" in security centres and execution sites;
- Crimes against specific groups, including the Cham, the Vietnamese and Buddhists; and
- The regulation of marriage.

Initial hearings in this trial started in June 2011.

ADDITIONAL CASES

Following a disagreement between the Co-Prosecutors on the decision to prosecute additional suspects, an appeal to the Pre-Trial Chamber was filed, but the supermajority vote needed to resolve the dispute was not achieved.[35] In such a situation, the default position is that the decision taken by one

Co-Prosecutor to prosecute shall stand. The international Co-Prosecutor then filed two new introductory submissions with the Co-Investigating Judges, thus opening judicial investigations against additional suspects (Cases 3 and 4).[36]

The International Co-Prosecutor has stated that prosecution of Cases 3 and 4 would lead to a more comprehensive accounting of the crimes that were committed under the DK regime, but has also indicated that he has no plans to conduct any further preliminary investigations into additional suspects at the ECCC.[37]

The fate of these additional judicial investigations has sparked controversy, in particular the allegation that the judicial process may damage the process of reconciliation. The Secretary-General of the United Nations during his visit to the ECCC in October 2010 stressed however that: "*it is only natural that [the] parallel structures [of the ECCC, the Cambodian and the international] lead at times to differences of opinion and approach. This is why the Agreement between the Royal Government of Cambodia and the United Nations lays down procedures for dealing with such problems. The ability of the Court to resolve them through an independent judicial process, free from political influence is one of its greatest assets*".[38] The independence of the Judges is a cornerstone on which depends the credibility of the Court. Currently the Co-Investigating Judges are investigating these two additional cases, and the judicial process continues in accordance with the Agreement between the Cambodian Government and the UN, the ECCC Law, and the procedural rules.

VICTIM PARTICIPATION

In the Duch trial, the Trial Chamber heard the statements of survivors who witnessed the atrocities endured by detainees at S-21. The extent of the tremendous suffering endured by the Cambodian people whose dignity and humanity were denied during the Khmer Rouge regime is hard to conceive. Among Cambodians, there are very few who did not lose a family member or who were not seriously traumatized during this period, including those who were associated with the revolutionary movement. In this context, the issue of the victims' participation at trial and their right to seek compensation has a particular significance.

A specific feature of the ECCC is that Cambodian criminal procedure, which applies at this Court, stems from the Civil Law system. This distinguishes the ECCC from the international *ad hoc* tribunals, where victims of international crimes have neither a voice beyond that of a witness nor the right to demand reparations for what happened to them or to their loved ones. One of the main characteristics of the Civil Law system is the importance of the role of the victims in criminal proceedings. This can however be problematic in cases of mass crimes where thousands of people may seek to exercise their individual rights, creating an obstacle to expeditious proceedings. The purpose of Civil Party action before the ECCC is to participate in criminal proceedings by supporting the prosecution of those responsible for crimes within the jurisdiction of the ECCC, and to seek collective and moral reparation.

In order to participate, Civil Parties have to prove that they have personally suffered an injury as a result of the direct action of the Accused. Due to the time that has elapsed since the crimes, the absence or the incompleteness of official records, the loss of documentary evidence or the disappearance of witnesses, many Civil Party applicants in the first trial were unable to prove their relationship with S-21. As a result, their applications were rejected. Many applicants considered that the burden and the standard of proof imposed on the Civil Parties were an unbearable experience and re-traumatizing.

Many were also disappointed by the fact that the Tribunal did not provide them with financial and individual reparation. The Internal Rules limit reparation to collective and moral.[39] Due to the large number of victims, it would in practice, have been very difficult to assess the harm suffered by each victim and then to rule on each claim individually. In addition, one of the key features of Civil Party participation is that awards are directed against and borne exclusively by the accused. It would have been unrealistic to order significant financial compensation against an Accused already considered by the Court as indigent.

As a result, the lessons learned from the first trial forced the ECCC Judges to adopt a new system of victim participation at their seventh and eighth plenary sessions.

The new scheme maintains individual participation of Civil Parties at the pre-trial stage. At the trial stage and beyond, the rights of the Civil Parties are exercised through a single, consolidated group whose interests are represented by two Civil Party Lead Co-Lawyers, one Cambodian and one international. The Civil Party Lead Co-Lawyers bear the ultimate responsibility for the overall advocacy, strategy and in-court presentation of the interests of the group. They are in charge of presenting a single claim for collective and moral reparation on behalf of the entire Civil Party group.

In order to provide more effective forms of redress, the Judges created an additional avenue that may enable external resources or third party funding to support claims for reparations.

The adaptation of the Civil Party scheme for victim participation in ECCC proceedings is aimed at safeguarding the ECCC's ability to reach a more timely verdict in future trials, which have many other challenges, such as the advanced age of the Accused.

CONCLUSION: HOW TO DELIVER JUSTICE IN THE FACE OF CRITICISM AND CHALLENGES?

When the ECCC started its operations, many people were sceptical and did not believe that such a tribunal had the capacity to bring effective and fair justice to Cambodian people. On the one hand there was much criticism that justice came too late, that the suspects are too old, that their victims are dead, and that the evidence has disappeared. Others claimed that such justice would be too expensive and that the money could be better used. Others considered that the scope of the Tribunal's temporary jurisdiction was too narrow as it did not provide for prosecution for the massive bombing of Cambodia before 1975 or for acts committed after 1979. On the other hand there were doubts concerning the capacity of the Cambodian judiciary to act competently and independently. But above all, many Cambodians were not even aware of the existence of the Court.

The credibility of the Court and public interest started to grow with the arrest and detention of the first five suspects. Then the broadcasting on TV channels of the public hearings of the first case allowed a huge audience to watch the Duch trial. This was seen as an attempt by the ECCC to act transparently. The first trial was also supported by an important outreach campaign, both by the ECCC Public Affairs Section and by NGOs. Among the latter is the Documentation Centre of Cambodia (DC-Cam), which has gathered an extraordinary quantity of material on Democratic Kampuchea. A tangible sign of public interest in the ECCC's activities was the high attendance at hearings. A total of more than 30,000 people attended the first trial, with the 500-seat public gallery full on most days. Such interest is the result of the fact that the Court is on Cambodian soil and in the capital, Phnom Penh. The Court is also accessible to the Cambodian people because justice is delivered with the full participation of the Cambodian judiciary. Things would undoubtedly have been different if the trial had occurred in the Netherlands or in any other foreign country.

However, this proximity does not necessarily assist the public in understanding the legal issues faced by the Court. Some of these issues are particularly complex and require the review of customary international law, treaties and case law.

Sometimes misunderstandings may also arise when the Judges refer to a specific word that has a precise legal definition deviating from the common popular meaning. The use of the word "genocide" is a typical illustration of such difficulties. A reference to the Cambodian "genocide" does not have the same meaning for the public, historians and lawyers.

The ECCC has been given the task of providing accountability for perpetrators, acknowledging the existence of atrocities, officially recognising the status of victims, and imposing a sentence that does not constitute revenge, but rather a balance between aggravating and mitigating circumstances. These factors pre-suppose the conduct of a fair trial and an impartial assessment of evidence in order to decide on the guilt or innocence of the Accused.

The Judges are not historians, but the judicial findings contained in the Judgment contribute to creating a historical record of the crimes committed during the era of Democratic Kampuchea. The result counteracts denial and revisionism, and will facilitate the task of educating Cambodia's youth about the darkest chapter in the country's recent history. Obviously, true reconciliation can only be achieved once the reality of the crimes and the suffering endured has been officially acknowledged.

This is the judicial process currently underway, in which I have the honour of participating.

I hope that the ECCC will demonstrate its capacity to achieve its duty. This duty includes strengthening the rule of law in Cambodia by showing a model of fair and transparent trials conducted in conformity with international standards. The Cambodian people and the international community have already expressed the hope that the trials will be a powerful signal that atrocities cannot stay concealed and unpunished.

Finally, I believe strongly that justice can work together with Buddhism to facilitate what is Buddhism's greatest strength — compassion. I am convinced that compassion is a lever that can increase reconciliation. I have been impressed by the following words of Maha Ghosananda, who is a patriarch of the Buddhist church in Cambodia and which I would like to share with you:

The suffering of Cambodia has been great

This suffering gives rise to a great compassion
A great compassion creates a generous heart
From a generous heart is born an honourable person
An honourable person builds a united family
A united family generates a gentle community
A gentle community creates a peaceful nation.[40]

My wish is that Cambodia will forever be a peaceful nation.

Notes

1. Preamble to the Convention (II) with Respect to the Laws and Customs of War on Land and its annex: Regulations concerning the Laws and Customs of War on Land. The Hague, 29 July 1899.
2. Ibid.
3. See Article 227 of the Treaty of Peace between the Allied and Associated Powers and Germany (Treaty of Versailles), 28 June 1919 (which provided for the creation of a special tribunal for the trial of Wilhelm II, the German Emperor).
4. Third Committee of the Assembly of the League of Nations.
5. Principles of International Law Recognized in the Charter of the Nuremberg Tribunal and in the Judgment of the Tribunal, 1950.
6. Convention on the Prevention and Punishment of the Crime of Genocide, 9 December 1948, 78 UNTS 277.
7. Geneva Convention I for the Amelioration of the Condition of the Wounded and Sick in Armed Forces in the Field of 12 August 1949, 75 UNTS 31 ("Geneva Convention I"); Geneva Convention II for the Amelioration of the Condition of Wounded, Sick and Shipwrecked Members of the Armed Forces at Sea of 12 August 1949, 75 UNTS 85 ("Geneva Convention II"); Geneva Convention III Relative to the Treatment of Prisoners of War of 12 August 1949, 75 UNTS 135 ("Geneva Convention III"); Geneva Convention IV Relative to the Protection of Civilian Persons in Time of War of 12 August 1949, 75 UNTS 287 ("Geneva Convention IV", and collectively "Geneva Conventions").
8. See Article 1 ("Genocide [...] is a crime under international law"); Article 4 ("Persons committing genocide [...] shall be punished, whether they are constitutionally responsible rulers, public officials or private individuals"); and Article 6 ("Persons charged with genocide [...] shall be tried by a competent tribunal of the State in the territory of which the act was committed, or by such international penal tribunal as may have jurisdiction with respect to those Contracting Parties which shall have accepted its jurisdiction").
9. Revised Draft Statute for an International Criminal Court (Annex to the Report of the 1953 Committee on International Criminal Jurisdiction on its Session held from 27 July to August 1953 (G.A., 9th Sess., Supp. No. 12, A/2645, 1954); Draft Code of Offences against the Peace and Security of Mankind, International Law Commission, 1954 ILC Report (A/CN.4/88 (E)).
10. International Tribunal for the Prosecution of Persons Responsible for Serious Violations of International Humanitarian Law Committed in the Territory of the Former Yugoslavia since 1991, established by Resolution 827 of the United Nations Security Council, 25 May 1993.
11. The International Tribunal for the Prosecution of Persons Responsible for Serious Violations of International Humanitarian Law Committed in the Territory of the Former Yugoslavia since 1991, and the International Criminal Tribunal for Rwanda.

12. Rome Statute of the International Criminal Court, 17 July 1998 (entered into force 1 July 2002), 2187UNTS90.
13. Article 5.1 of the Rome Statute.
14. Article 17.2.a of the Rome Statute.
15. Article 17.1.d of the Rome Statute.
16. Special Panels for Serious Crimes in East Timor established by the UN Transitional Authority in East Timor Regulation 2000/15; Report of the Secretary-General on the establishment of a Special Court for Sierra Leone S/2000/915, 4 October 2000.
17. Ley 25.779 — Declaranse insanablemente nulas las Leyes Nros. 23.492 y 23.521, promulgated 2September2003.
18. Corte Suprema de Justicia de la Nación, S. 1767. XXXVIII, PrivaciÛn Ilegitima de la Libertad Etc. — Causa n∞17.768, 14 June 2005.
19. South African Truth and Reconciliation Commission based on the final clause of the Interim Constitution of 1993 and passed in Parliament as the Promotion of National Unity and Reconciliation Act, No. 34 of 1995.
20. This presentation reflects the facts alleged in the indictment against the Accused in case 002 (ECCC, Case 002/19-09-2007-ECCC-OCIJ, Closing Order, 15 September 2010, doc n. D427). It should not be considered as the expression of my personal opinion nor of any judges of the Trial Chamber of the ECCC.
21. See for example "Brother Number One: A Political Biography of Pol Pot", David P. Chandler, 1999, pp. 104 & 117 and "Pol Pot: The History of a Nightmare", Philip Short, 2005, pp. 277 & 345.
22. See ECCC, Case 002/19-09-2007-ECCC-OCIJ, Closing Order, 15 September 2010, D427, pp. 51–59.
23. ECCC, Case 002/19-09-2007-ECCC-OCIJ, Demographic Expert Report, Khmer Rouge Victims in Cambodia, April 1975 – January 1979. A Critical Assessment of Major Estimates, 30 September 2009, D140/1/1 p. 19.
24. UN Document A/34/491 Judgment of the People's Revolutionary Court in Phnom Penh, 19 August 1979.
25. See e.g. "Genocide in Cambodia, Documents from the Trial of Pol Pot and Ieng Sary" edited by Howard J. de Nike, John Quigley and Kenneth J. Robinson, pp. 7–18.
26. Paris Peace Agreement signed in Paris, 23 October 1991.
27. Letter from Norodom Ranariddh, Cambodian First Prime Minister, and Hun Sen, Cambodian Second Prime Minister, to Secretary General Kofi Annan (21 June 1997).
28. Draft Agreement between the United Nations and the Royal Government of Cambodia concerning the Prosecution of Crimes Committed during the Period of Democratic Kampuchea, U.N. GAOR 3D Comm., 57th Sess., Annex, Agenda Item 109(b), U.N. Doc. A/57/806 (2003).
29. The role of the Internal Rules is to adapt applicable Cambodian procedure for proceedings before the ECCC and to adopt additional rules where these existing

procedures do not deal with a particular matter, or if there is uncertainty regarding their interpretation or application, or if there is a question regarding their consistency with international standards.

30. Nonetheless such specificity leads to some very complex issues which were not experimented by other internationalized tribunals. For example it was necessary to find a solution in case of disagreement between the two Co-Prosecutors or two Co-investigating judges. The Agreement and the Internal Rules provide for a procedural solution which is certainly innovative, as it is for the Pre-Trial Chamber to settle such dispute.
The default decision of this Chamber will be that the action or decision of one Co-Prosecutor, or one Co-Investigating Judge will stand.
The fate of the decision in case of impossibility to reach a supermajority vote by the Pre-Trial or Trial Chamber judges is also one of the examples of the complexity of such situation. For example, if the majority of the Trial Chamber is not attained for a judgment on the merits, the Accused will be acquitted.
The complexity of the functioning of the Court is also reinforced by the fact that there are three official working languages, Khmer, English and French, which creates a whole set of challenges related to translation.
31. ECCC, Case 001/18-07-2007/ECCC/TC, Judgment, 26 July 2010, E188.
32. ECCC, Case 002/19-09-2007-ECCC-OCIJ, Closing Order, 15 September 2010, D427 ("Closing Order").
33. ECCC, PTC Decision on Khieu Samphan's appeal against the closing order, D427/4/14, 13 January 2011; Decision on Ieng Sary's appeal against the Closing Order, D427/1/26, 13 January 2011; Decision on Ieng Thirith and Nuon Chea's appeal against the Closing Order, D427/2/12, 13 January 2011.
34. See the Closing Order, Para 1613.
35. Disagreement No. 001/18-11-2008-ECCC/PTC; Press Release, 2 September 2009 (available at <http://www.eccc.gov.kh/english/cabinet/press/127/ECCC_Press_Release_2_Sep_2009_Eng.pdf>).
36. Statement of the Acting International Co-prosecutor, Submission of Two New Introductory Submissions, 8September 2009 (available at http://www.eccc.gov.kh/english/cabinet/press/130/ECCC_Act_Int_Co_Prosecutor_8_Sep_2009_(Eng).pdf>).
37. Statement of the Co-Prosecutors, 5 January 2009 (available at <http://www.eccc.gov.kh/english/cabinet/press/84/Statement_OCP_05-01-09_EN.pdf).
38. UN Secretary General Ban Ki-moon's Speech at ECCC, 27 October 2010
39. Extraordinary Chambers in the Courts of Cambodia, Internal Rules (rev. 7), Rule 23 quinquies. Civil Party Claim.
40. "Step by Step: Meditations on Wisdom and Compassion". Maha Ghosananda.

16

HOW HAS CAMBODIA ACHIEVED POLITICAL RECONCILIATION?

Phoak Kung*

INTRODUCTION

After achieving independence from France in 1953, Cambodian history has been characterized by deep conflicts, social fragmentation and political turmoil. The arrival of the Khmer Rouge regime began a genocidal period, from 1975–1979, in which the vast majority of Cambodian people faced unspeakable sufferings, and in less than three years, nearly 2 million people were killed (Chandler 1991, Kiernan 1993). Despite the collapse of the Khmer Rouge regime in early 1979, the fighting was still continuing between the People's Republic of Kampuchea (PRK), which was installed by the Vietnamese government in the aftermath of their invasion into Cambodia, and the resistance factions along the Cambodian-Thai border. The signing of the Paris Peace Agreements (PPAs) on 23 October 1991 concluded this long period of conflict, and helped all the parties in dispute to finally achieve peace, stability and democracy through political reconciliation. Like most post-conflict societies, Cambodia was overwhelmed with the task of ensuring a permanent ceasefire, disarming and demobilising the various armed forces and arranging a national election that would allow all parties to compete for power through a democratic and peaceful process.

The term 'political reconciliation' has been used loosely by the Cambodian leaders to simply mean a conclusion of disagreement and conflict through compromise and mutual benefits. Thus, the process happens mainly at the top level among the contentious factions, and the political reconciliation process has always been attached to the necessity to preserve peace and stability. However, this top level approach is just the beginning of a long road to fully achieve political reconciliation. It also requires more efforts from citizens and government officials to deal with the past memory of hatred, resentment and fragmentation. Without successfully resolving the underlying causes of conflict and violence, the top level approach may exacerbate the already divisive and contentious politics among parties in dispute, because the dominant party will attempt to weaken or eliminate their opponents rather than reconcile with them. Since there is no sincere political will among the leaders, the national reconciliation is no more than just a lip service.

Despite the shortcomings and challenges, the top level approach of political reconciliation establishes a necessary foundation for the citizens and government officials to go beyond political settlement among leaders of all the parties in dispute in order to achieve the society-wide national reconciliation. To realize this goal, the problems of the rule of law and economic inequality have to be properly addressed and resolved by the government, because they help to rebuild the political relations between citizens and government officials, in which shared norms and rules would be endorsed to enhance the political reconciliation process. This paper attempts to examine the efforts made by all parties in dispute to achieve national unity since the signing of the Paris Peace Agreements (PPAs), and discusses the challenges that remain a hindrance to the political reconciliation process.

To unpack these puzzles, this paper is organized as follows. The first section looks at the variety of political reconciliation, especially the Cambodian leaders' conceptualization, because their subsequent actions will reflect their understanding of the term 'reconciliation'. As mentioned earlier that the signing of the PPAs was a necessary step to end the conflict, the second section discusses the PPAs in a broader picture in terms of their role in the political reconciliation process. The third section provides a historical account of the efforts made by all parties in dispute to achieve political reconciliation after the 1993 election arranged by the UNTAC, and looks into divisions in Cambodian politics, and its implications on the reconciliation process following fierce competition between the major parties to consolidate power. The final section investigates the problems of the rule of law and economic inequality, especially their implications on the reconciliation process, and it also observes various efforts made by the government to strengthen the rule of law and reduce the inequality gap.

CONCEPTUALIZING POLITICAL RECONCILIATION

Political reconstruction in a post-conflict society has always been a complex and difficult process, and it may take decades for all parties involved in the violence to fully embrace a peaceful solution to resolve their differences and put an end to the conflict. As part of the peace-building process, political reconciliation has played a very important role not only to prevent conflicts and violence from happening again, but also allow a post-conflict society to successfully consolidate democracy (del Castillo 2008, Murphy 2010). Both scholars and practitioners of conflict resolution strongly emphasize the importance of political reconciliation. However, the controversy over its concept has never been completely settled. One of the most influential ways of understanding reconciliation is in terms of forgiveness, which requires the overcoming of negative emotions such as hatred and revenge as a response to wrongdoings, and policies should aim at changing citizens' attitudes to restore political relations (Richards 1988, Hughes 1997, Hieronymi 2001). This view also suffers severe criticisms that it is not realistic (Dwyer 1999), and it does not provide an enduring solution, because the underlying problem of reconciliation is not fully addressed, so the possibility of renewing conflict and violence is still prominent (Murphy 2010).

Another conception of reconciliation focuses on trust (Govier and Verwoerd 2002, Walker 2006). In a post-conflict society, widespread abuses of human rights, oppression and state-sponsored crimes significantly erode trust in political relationships, and prevent people from actively participating in politics and civil society. Therefore, the cultivation and maintenance of trust between citizens and government officials have to be appropriately addressed in the reconciliation process. However, Murphy (2010) argues that psychological attitudes like trust are inadequate to explain the breakdown of a shared system of rules that regulates the political relationship, and he stresses instead on a critical role of institutions 'in defining and maintaining the shared standards of behaviours and normative expectations constitutive of political relations' (p. 16). To overcome the limitations of reconciliation as forgiveness and trust, Moellendorf (2007) views reconciliation as a political value, where citizens recognize each other as equals, and come to endorse a set of rules and institutions that structure political relationships based on democratic equality and protections under the law. This conception of reconciliation provides a more specific and narrow definition, which is useful for politicians and international community to design institutions and policies to reconstruct post-conflict countries, but the main problem with this conception is that it ignores 'the important inter-personal, relational aspects of political interaction among citizens and officials' (Murphy 2010, pp. 18–19).

Looking from a different perspective, Schaab (2005) challenges a normative ideal of political relations imposed upon citizens without their endorsements, and he sees these processes as illiberal, oppressive and irrelevant to transitional contexts, because people may substantively disagree with these political relationships. In Schaab's (2005) words, 'there is a good reason to be suspicious of an ideal community as it is in the name of this ideal that oppression is legitimized' (p. 85). Therefore, the conception of reconciliation as a process of rebuilding or repairing the existing political relationships is irrelevant to particular transitional contexts, and the focus should be on the founding of political community, in which shared standards must be clearly defined and adopted by citizens. Moreover, Schaab (2005) also warns that the ideal view of political reconciliation can be manipulated by politicians to consolidate their power, so the fragility of politics in particular transitional contexts needs to be seriously considered. There are several important strengths in this conception of reconciliation, but several problems are still persistent due to its abstractness and complexity, and it does not address the immediate response to the fragility of peace in a post-conflict society, which may undermine the political reconciliation process in the future. Also, the overemphasis on the role of citizens in endorsing a new set of shared standards in the political relationships can be misleading and unrealistic, because politicians, who are also involved directly or indirectly in violence, are still in power, so an ideal of political relations, even with the endorsements from citizens, can be still manipulated in favour of the elites.

Lederach (1997) discusses the tension between justice and peace in the reconciliation process, and argues that the values of justice should not be achieved entirely at the expense of peace. Moreover, the primary goal of reconciliation 'is to seek innovative ways to create a time and a place, within various levels of the affected population, to address, integrate, and embrace the painful past and the necessary shared future as a means of dealing with the present' (Lederach 1997, p. 35). Kriesberg (2007) offers a more in-depth study of reconciliation by discussing its four major aspects such as 'the units engaged in reconciliation, the dimensions of reconciliation, the degree of reconciliation, and the symmetry of each aspect' (p. 2), and he argues that 'each aspect of reconciliation is fulfilled in various degrees for different parties, at any given time in a social relationship. They are combined into 'a variety of types of reconciliation, depending on the parties involved and their social context' (Kriesberg 2007, p. 8). Moreover, he also claims that:

> In some circumstances, people accord great importance to security. The past victims want safety and assurances that their ordeal is over; many prefer living peacefully with their former oppressors to continuing a destructive conflict. At the same time, victimizers also want assurances of safety and protection from retribution. Mutual security may be more important to many people than seeking retributive justice, which appears to threaten peace. This preference for safety often is particularly strong among the leaders of the antagonistic groups who feel themselves threatened by legal prosecution and punishment or by non-official revenge seekers. (Kriesberg 2007, p. 9)

Kriesberg's (2007) arguments substantially contribute to the understanding of the political reconciliation in Cambodia after nearly three decades of conflicts and violence. As pointed out by Lambourne (2001) that the use of the term 'national reconciliation' in Cambodian context is more pragmatic and highly politicized, where stability, security and peace are the primary concerns. Due to these factors, the reconciliation process was largely happening at the top level among parties in dispute, where an act of compromise such as amnesties, power-sharing and balance of interests plays the most crucial role. Even this practice allows the antagonists to come to terms with one another, and to prevent conflicts and violence from arising, but this type of settlement is very fragile and unsustainable, because the underlying causes of enmity are not completely addressed and resolved. Therefore, reconciliation in this sense does not necessarily lead to public endorsement of shared rules or standards for future political relations. Furthermore, most post-conflict societies including Cambodia are generally characterized by weak and undemocratic state institutions and high level of distrust among parties in dispute, which further exacerbate the already difficult and complicated political reconciliation process, because all parties involved in the dispute settlement do not have strong commitments towards national unity and cohabitation, and their ultimate goal is only to end the conflicts and to have their shares in the new government. Therefore, to what extent reconciliation can be achieved will largely depend on the political calculations of all parties in dispute, in which cases, the most powerful party will seek to weaken or undermine their opponents, and they only share power when they are left with no choice. Following this analysis, it is possible to argue that the political reconciliation is said to be completed when the dominant party can effectively remove major threats from their former enemies such as military, electoral and revolutionary threats that can cause severe damage to security, stability and peace in the country.

Despite all the problems mentioned above, Cambodia has succeeded in bringing all parties in dispute together to compete for power through a relatively free and fair election, and the current government has also performed very well in developing the economy and maintaining stability and peace, so it is reasonable to argue that at least, Cambodia has achieved a certain level of political reconciliation. However, this does not necessarily suggest that reconciliation process has been successfully completed, or citizens and government officials should not be concerned anymore, because the problems associated with reconciliation process in Cambodia such as resentment, social fragmentation and divisive politics are still persistent. As a result, there are still many things to do to bring about a genuine and long lasting peace. Kriesberg (2007) eloquently argued that 'there are many kinds and degrees of reconciliation, with different mixes of elements... that what cannot be accomplished at one time can be built later on the foundations previously laid' (p. 17). In this chapter, I strongly argue that Cambodia has to go beyond the top level approach, and to focus on the society-wide political reconciliation that is very crucial for successful consolidation of democracy and for peace-building processes. There are two important dimensions of political reconciliation such as the rule of law and economic equality that play a pivotal role in reconstructing political relations, and allow the Cambodian citizens and the government to fully realize a successful completion of political reconciliation.

PARIS PEACE AGREEMENTS AS A FIRST STEP TOWARDS POLITICAL RECONCILIATION

The collapse of the Khmer Rouge regime after the Vietnamese invasion on 25 December 1978 marked another period of civil war and entrenched violence between the People's Republic of Kampuchea (PRK), which was installed by the Vietnamese government, and the defeated Khmer Rouge soldiers, the Khmer People's National Liberation Front (KPNLF), and National United Front for an Independent, Neutral, Peaceful and Co-operative Cambodia (FUNCINPEC) along the Cambodian-Thai border. Under pressure from their international allies including the US, China and ASEAN, the three resistance factions agreed to form a coalition known as Coalition Government of Democratic Kampuchea (CGDK) on 22 June 1982, and they were able to keep their seat at the United Nations, while the PRK was considered as an illegitimate government under the Vietnamese control. Moreover, Cambodian conflicts were trapped in the middle of the international political divisions, with the CGDK receiving support from the US, ASEAN and China, while the PRK was backed by the USSR and Vietnam (Hughes 2003, p. 2). These international involvements made any peace agreements more difficult, because each party came with their own agenda on what should be included in the agreements. This prolonged the conflicts in Cambodia for more than a decade before the Paris Peace Agreements (PPAs) were signed by the PRK and the CGDK on 23 October 1991.

The signing of the Paris Peace Agreements was considered as a significant breakthrough that helped to conclude the Cambodian conflict; however there is no consensus among scholars on the very purposes of these agreements. Ott (1997) noted that many foreign participants in Paris were not really concerned about the Cambodian conflict itself, and the PPAs were seen as an exit for them 'from a nasty little problem' (p. 433). Similarly, Ashley argues that 'the interest of the international community was not primarily in the development and democratization of Cambodia, but rather in stopping a prolonged military conflict involving major external interests' (cited in Roberts 2001, p. 30). Another view was that the PRK and the CGDK were forced by their foreign backers to enter into the agreements, because they believed that it was time for all factions to end the conflict (Jeldres 1993, p. 107). Despite strong emphasis on the role of international players in influencing and shaping the agreements in their favour, the political reconciliation was seriously considered by all Cambodian factions and international participants, and it was also one of the primary goals of the Paris Peace Agreements (Peou 2000, p. 251, Heder and Ledgerwood 1996, p. 14). This point was clearly presented in the agreements such as the use of proportional representation for the electoral system, permanent ceasefire, demobilization of the military forces of all factions and the provision of economic and financial support from the international community for the rehabilitation and reconstruction of Cambodia.

Another important aspect of the Paris Peace Agreements was the establishment of the Supreme National Council (SNC) headed by King Norodom Sihanouk with six members from the PRK and two members respectively from the Khmer Rouge, KPNLF and FUNCINPEC. The SNC was 'the unique legitimate body and source of authority', and decisions within the SNC were made based on the agreements of its members to ensure support from all factions. Throughout the transition period, the SNC occupied the seat at the United Nations, and it also represented Cambodia at all international institutions and conferences. To implement the PPAs, the SNC had to delegate 'all powers necessary' to the United Nations Transitional Authority in Cambodia (UNTAC), and to offer advice in case there were problems in the implementation process. Therefore, forging an agreement among factions within the SNC is very important, as Ratner (1993) noted 'the extent to which [UNTAC's head] exercises his authority depend upon the SNC's success in achieving consensus'.

RECONCILIATION PROCESS AFTER THE 1993 ELECTION

With a mandate from the Paris Peace Agreements, the United Nations Transitional Authority in Cambodia (UNTAC) helped to arrange a national election on 23 May 1993 to allow all parties in dispute to compete for power through a peaceful and democratic process. The success of the election was not only seen as a major step to end a long drawn-out conflict, but also a positive progress towards political reconciliation between the State of Cambodia (SOC), formally known as the PRK, and the resistance factions. To establish itself as a viable option for the people to vote during the general election, the PRK was later renamed as the Cambodian People's Party (CPP), and it started to enlist millions of people into the party, regardless of their political backgrounds to ensure its victory over the resistance forces (Frieson 1996, Gottesman 2003). Despite political uncertainty and security concerns, there were 29 political parties registered to compete during the election, including the CPP, FUNCINPEC and BLDP (formerly known as KPNLF), except the Khmer Rouge that withdrew from the election and accused the UNTAC of not effectively enforcing the Paris Agreements by allowing the CPP to continue to control much of the state apparatus and armed forces.

UNTAC managed to hold the national election on 23 May 1993, as required by the PPAs, and most observers agreed that the Cambodian people were able to freely and fairly select their preferred political parties during the election (Roberts 2001). The electoral results came as a shock to the CPP as they lost to the royalist party, the FUNCINPEC. They strongly protested irregularities to UNTAC, and 'they would not accept the results of the electoral process unless new elections were held in four provinces' (Widyono 2008, p. 124). However, the UN electoral component rejected the validity of the accusations (Roberts 2001, p. 105). Since the CPP was determined to stay in power at all cost, and without an appropriate solution, the tension could have pushed Cambodia to the brink of conflict and violence. As noted by Roberts (2001) that 'the only option for any form of peace and stability was political inclusion of the CPP in the proportion they sought' (p. 107).

Realising the risk of the outbreak of civil war and under pressure from the CPP, Prince Norodom Sihanouk decided to intervene, and on 3 June 1993, there was an announcement that a 'Provisional National Government' would be formed with Prince Sihanouk acting as a head of state and Prime Minister; Hun Sen, deputy leader of the CPP, and Prince Ranariddh, the leader of FUNCIPEC, would be Deputy Prime Ministers and the power would be shared on a fifty-fifty basis between these two major parties (Jeldres 1993, Roberts 2001, Widyono 2008), but these initiatives were quickly denounced by the United States, the United Kingdom, China and Australia (Carney and Choo 1993). Moreover, the proposed establishment of this interim government was a surprise to Prince Ranariddh, and he responded by calling it an 'irresponsible arrangement' (Peou 2001, p. 219). Facing resistance, Prince Sihanouk had no choice but to abandon the plan, and he accused 'some Cambodian politicians, certain members of UNTAC, the United States and some other countries of having meanly attacked him over the plan' (cited in Roberts 2001, p. 107).

Another major event was the secessionist movement on 12 June 1993 led by Prince Chakrapong, deputy Prime Minister of the Phnom Penh Government, and General Sin Song, and they publicly declared an autonomous zone in the country's Eastern provinces; however this movement collapsed only a few days after Prince Sihanouk was appointed by the Constituent Assembly as the Head of State, and he was granted full and special powers to save the country (Lizée 2000, p. 126). Knowing that it would be impossible to establish a new government without the CPP, and also being persuaded by Prince Sihanouk and Yasushi Akashi, the head of UNTAC, Prince Ranariddh entered into an agreement with Hun Sen on 21 June 1993 to create a Joint Interim Administration, in which both of them would be 'co-chairmen and co-ministers of defence, interior and public security' (Widyono 2008, pp. 129–30). Following the ratification of a new Constitution of the Kingdom of Cambodia on 21 September 1993, the Constituent Assembly was transformed into the National Assembly, and Prince Sihanouk was crowned as King again on 24 September 1993, who reigned but did not rule, and he then appointed Prince Ranariddh first Prime Minister and Hun Sen second Prime Minister (Peou 2000, Widyono 2008). Besides the two largest parties (the CPP and FUNCINPEC), one of the resistance factions, the BLDP led by Son Sann won 10 seats, and Molinaka that obtained only one seat, also participated in the newly established coalition. The rationality of such a move was to increase the legitimacy and recognition of the new government from all major political factions, which was very crucial to secure peace and stability after a long period of divisive politics, especially to heal the past memory of hatred, resentment and distrust through political reconciliation.

Although the initiatives to broker a peace deal pioneered by Prince Sihanouk and supported by domestic politicians and several foreign countries, except the Khmer Rouge, helped prevent the bloodshed and the renewal of civil war, there were still several major problems that were not effectively addressed and resolved, and they seriously undermined and derailed any attempt at political reconciliation in the future. The problems of distrust among leaders of the coalition parties were so severe and deep (Lizée 2000, p. 156, Widyono 2008, p. 130), and they only worked together because of mutual interests and power-sharing, so the major task of all factions was to ensure and maintain this balance if they wanted to continue the coalition government. Furthermore, failing to achieve such a balance would result in more conflicts and violence, because each faction was ready to sink or swim with their opponents, if they were left with no choice. Another stumbling-block to the political reconciliation process was the Khmer Rouge that defied the Paris Peace Agreements and did not participate in the national election arranged by UNTAC. The armed struggles between the Khmer Rouge and the new coalition government were still persistent, and there were no signs of a permanent ceasefire, unless the Khmer Rouge cadres would receive significant power in the government, and they were given amnesties for all their crimes committed during their control over Cambodia in the 1970s.

Even previous efforts to bring the Khmer Rouge to the negotiating table and to persuade them to disarm and stop the fighting did not produce any fruitful results; however the talks were not immediately completely abandoned. A roundtable discussion was called by the King on 21 April 1994 after receiving a secret letter from Khieu Samphan requesting him to leave the country to avoid Khmer Rouge disturbances, and leaders of the coalition government also agreed to participate in the meeting, but once again, 'the Khmer Rouge pulled out of the negotiations' (Widyono 2008, p. 162). Responding to the failure of this roundtable discussion, second Prime Minister Hun Sen declared that the coalition government would pursue military action against the Khmer Rouge, and there were no more talks with the rebels. On 7 July 1994, the National Assembly passed a bill to outlaw the Khmer Rouge. The King warned from Beijing that he would not sign the law; however, on 15 July 1994, Chea Sim, the President of the National Assembly and acting Head of State, signed on his behalf (Peou 2000, p. 223).

Throughout this period, King Sihanouk was seen as a father of national reconciliation, and he received strong support from all political factions in Cambodian politics as well as international community. Prior to the national election, Prince Ranariddh of FUNCINPEC promised that he would give the necessary powers to the King to lead the national reconciliation process if the party won the election. Similarly, the Khmer Rouge also recognized the King as the only person who could bring unity to Cambodia (Peou 2000, pp. 219–21). Moreover, the CPP and its leaders always showed support for the King's initiatives in the political reconciliation process (Widyono 2008). The Association of Southeast Asian Nations (ASEAN) also believed that 'Prince Sihanouk would be able to play a pivotal role in bringing about national reconciliation among all Cambodians, which is essential if genuine and lasting peace in Cambodia is to be attained' (cited in Peou 2000, p. 263). The King was not only considered as an iconic figure in helping to achieve the political reconciliation, some scholars even suggest that 'it would be necessary to rely on the formation of some forms of national reconciliation government under Prince Sihanouk, if immediate risks to peace were to be avoided' (Lizée 2000, p. 127, Hughes, 2001). However, the unsuccessful attempts by King Sihanouk to establish a permanent ceasefire and integrate the Khmer Rouge into the coalition government made all political parties stop taking his ideas seriously, and by late 1994, 'the King saw his role diminished to the point of no return' (Peou 2000, p. 223).

In the aftermath of the 1993 election, the establishment of the coalition government did not happen easily and smoothly, it was a product of intensive bargaining between FUNCINPEC and the CPP under the leadership of King Sihanouk and international pressure, especially from those who were the signatories to the Paris Agreements. The new government was still weak and unstable, and coalition members viewed each other with deep suspicion, but soon they were able to develop a working relationship. This breakthrough was seen as an important step toward political reconciliation, where old enemies could stay and work together to bring peace and prosperity to the Kingdom. Even the political situations were gradually improving, but another major challenge emerged. Rather than accommodating and conciliating among coalition members, the CPP and FUNCINPEC encouraged the fragmentation of other parties, and offered various benefits to attract the defectors from those parties to join them in order to increase their political base (Roberts 2001, p. 124). This point was clearly illustrated with the split within the Buddhist Liberal Democratic Party (BLDP)/KPNLF, in which Ieng Mouley challenged Son Sann to become a new leader. Responding to this event, both FUNCINPEC and the CPP threw their supports behind Ieng Mouley in attempts to weaken and divide the BLDP, while at the same time; they were also competing to attract the BLDP's defectors to join their parties (Peou 2000, p. 218).

Starting from late 1995, the relationship between FUNCINPEC and the CPP was alarmingly deteriorating due to several factors. First, as pointed out earlier, the balance of power and interests between the two major parties was very important to ensure coalition unity. However, after working in the government for almost two and a half years, there was growing discontent among FUNCINPEC members, because the real power was effectively in the hand of the CPP (Doyle 1998, p. 82). Second, the CPP held a tight grip on local government, and they were unwilling to share power with FUNCINPEC, which put Prince Ranariddh under heavy pressure from his own party to take a tougher stance against the CPP. Third, perceiving that FUNCINPEC was militarily and organizationally weaker than the CPP, Prince Ranariddh then joined with his old enemies BLDP and Khmer Nation Party (KNP) established by Sam Rainsy after he was expelled from FUNCINPEC in 1995, and this alliance was called National United Front (NUF) (Peou 2000, pp. 191–92). Fourth, both the CPP and FUNCINPEC were fiercely competing to co-opt some elements of the Khmer Rouge by offering generous benefits such as amnesties to the crimes they committed in the past and senior positions in the government (Curtis 1998, Slye 2003). Hoping to increase tension, Khieu Samphan planned to form a Khmer National Solidarity Party, and he would join the NUF to fight against the CPP (Peou 1998, p. 70, Widyono 2008, p. 240). Probably the most serious problem that caused severe fractures to the coalition was that FUNCINPEC secretly imported weapons into the country by labelling them as spare parts, and this move was severely condemned by the CPP (Hughes 2003, pp. 121–22).

The war of words and several armed clashes in the provinces led to deadly fighting between the CPP and FUNCINPEC armed forces in the middle of Phnom Penh on 5–6 July 1997. There were mixed reactions among the international community, and most of them stopped short of using the term 'coup d'état' to characterize the events (Roberts 2001). These skirmishes dealt a severe blow to the efforts to achieve national reconciliation among Cambodian political factions, and put the process on hold indefinitely. Under enormous pressure from donor countries and the international organizations, the CPP agreed to arrange for a national election scheduled for late July 1998, and allow Prince Ranariddh and all members of opposition parties who were forced into exile to return to the country (Curtis 1998, p. 57).

After losing the election to FUNCINPEC in 1993, the CPP substantively strengthened their support base through complex and extensive patron-client networks in the rural areas. During the 1998 election, the CPP performed very well, and they won 64 seats, while FUNCINPEC and Sam Rainsy Party received 43 seats and 15 seats respectively. The losing parties rejected the results, and they accused the CPP of committing electoral fraud, and requested donor countries to suspend aid to the government (Hughes 2003, pp. 196–97). They also claimed that the National Election Committee (NEC) was created to rig the election for the CPP, and that it was not independent and impartial. Ironically, many international observers including the Joint International Observer Group (JIOG) issued a statement confirming that the election was 'relatively free and fair', and there were no systematic errors or any major irregularities (Peou 2000, p. 321). In protesting against the electoral results, the opposition parties organized a mass demonstration in front of the National Assembly, but the demonstration soon became violent. The government responded with force from the armed forces and police, and around 26 protestors were killed (Peou 2000, p. 319–20). Moreover, FUNCINPEC and Sam Rainsy Party also refused to work in a coalition government with the CPP, unless Hun Sen resigned from premiership. However, after many rounds of talks and with a strong push from King Sihanouk, the CPP and FUNCINPEC finally reached a power-sharing deal, and Prince Ranariddh was appointed as President of the National Assembly, which left Sam Rainsy Party as the only opposition party in the parliament (Peou 2000, p. 328, Kevin 2000). Again, this compromise was seen as another effort to achieve political reconciliation after a bloody fight between the CPP and FUNCINPEC.

In 1996, there were massive Khmer Rouge defections and several commanders laid down their guns and joined the CPP. These defections and internal divisions severely weakened the Khmer Rouge from posing any serious threats to the government. By late December, Khieu Samphan and Noun Chea surrendered to Hun Sen, and many other Khmer Rouge senior officers fled to Thailand (Peou 2000, pp. 357–59). In March 1999, Ta Mok, the Khmer Rouge/CPK military commander, was captured (Linton 2004, p. 52). The Royal Government of Cambodia (RGC) eventually declared that political reconciliation and peace were finally achieved, and it also praised Prime Minister Hun Sen's 'win-win policy' as the backbone of the great success to bring about national unity and stability.

After being defeated in the 1998 election, FUNCINPEC was much weaker than during the previous coalition government. Their armed forces were completely disarmed and integrated into the Royal Cambodian Armed Forces (RCAF) (Hughes 2009, p. 56), and they now lived at the mercy of the CPP. Moreover, the CPP markedly reconsolidated power, and more resources, especially from big businessmen and state institutions, were available for them to support their gigantic patronage networks. The broadcasting systems were also under their tight control (Albritton 2004, p. 102). Simultaneously, the SRP was facing severe resource constraints, because the private sectors were told by the government that financing the SRP would be an 'economic suicide' (Heder 2005, p. 118).

The 2003 election marked another major victory for the CPP, and they won 73 seats in the parliament, while FUNCINPEC and the SRP obtained 26 and 24 seats respectively. It was no surprise that both the FUNCINPEC and the SRP rejected the electoral results, and they accused the CPP of stealing the votes and using intimidation and violence against their supporters. The SRP was also actively lobbying the West to not recognize the CPP's victory; however the international observers still went ahead to declare that the election was 'relatively free and fair', and they accepted the electoral results (Un 2005, p. 208). Despite having a solid parliamentary majority, the CPP did not have a two-third majority as required by the Constitution to establish the new government, so they had to turn back to their old coalition partner. Just like the 1998 political deadlock, it took the CPP and FUNCINPEC almost a year before they eventually agreed on a power-sharing formula, in which FUNCINPEC was paid handsomely with patronage (McCargo 2005, p. 108).

The CPP became more hegemonic, and Prime Minister Hun Sen substantively consolidated power both in the government and the party after winning the 2003 election (Levitsky and Way 2010, p. 336). Furthermore, a number of SRP leaders were charged with defamation or libel, and even Sam Rainsy himself, leader of the SRP, was also forced into exile to avoid jail terms. In 2006, the National Assembly passed a constitutional amendment changing the requirement to form the government from the two-third majority to 50 per cent, which helped the CPP to overcome the political deadlocks that they always faced in previous elections. The SRP also supported the amendment, and this move was seen as revenge against Prince Ranariddh who broke his promises with the SRP, when they were allies to protest against Prime Minister Hun Sen. Moreover, Prince Ranariddh was also charged with adultery and corruption, and he fled the country to avoid imprisonment in 2006. After his departure, FUNCINPEC led by Nhek Bun Chhay voted to oust Prince Ranariddh as president, and blamed him for bringing the party to the brink of collapse. Those who were still loyal to the Prince left FUNCINPEC and formed another political party called Norodom Ranariddh Party (NRP). Hoping to join the opposition forces to compete with the CPP, the Human Rights Party (HRP) was founded in 2007 led by Kem Sokha, who has been a very vocal critic of Prime Minister Hun Sen. In the 2008 election, the CPP won a landslide victory, and they captured 90 seats in the National Assembly.

The SRP came second with 26 seats, and even though the party was just established, the HRP managed to get 3 seats, while FUNCINPEC and the NRP suffered big losses, and they received only two seats each.

After receiving a pardon from the King, Prince Ranariddh returned to Cambodia, and he suggested a merger between FUNCINPEC and NRP to strengthen their support base for the next election, and he made it clear that his intention was not to challenge the CPP, but to seek an alliance (Mengleng 2010, pp. 1–2). Keo Put Rasmey, president of FUNCINPEC, welcomed the plan, but the merger stopped short when Prime Minister Hun Sen publicly declared that the CPP would only work with FUNCINPEC led by Keo Put Rasmey and Nhek Bun Chhay, not Prince Ranariddh. Seeing the necessity of staying united and strengthening the opposition parties, there were also many talks between the SRP and the HRP on a merger plan, which had been first proposed more than two years earlier. However, their relationships became sour, and they started to blame each other for the delay of the merger (Seiff and Mengleng 2011, p. 23). The leak of a recorded conversation between Prime Minister Hun Sen and the leader of HRP, Mr Kem Sokha, brought the merger plan to a halt. Despite strong denial from the HRP of any secret deals with the CPP, the SRP was not convinced, and they believed that the proposed merger was another plot to ruin their party. Mr Kem Sokha also denounced the release, and he called the incident 'a CPP ploy meant to ignite tensions between opposition parties and confusion among voters' (Bopha and Seiff 2011, p. 25). The SRP also suffered the same problem when the Prime Minister claimed that his conversation with Sam Rainsy in the aftermath of the 2003 election was also recorded. Another major challenge facing the SRP was massive defections, which amounted to roughly 160,000 members according to a source from the CPP, but the SRP argued that the number was overstated by the CPP (Meas and Sebastian 2009). Prime Minister Hun Sen has never shied away from publicly declaring that he has always been the architect behind the splits within the opposition parties through his 'divide-and-conquer' strategy (Human Rights Watch 2008), as he once said that 'when I want the alliance to separate, they will be separated' (Xinhua News Agency 2009).

SOCIETY-WIDE POLITICAL RECONCILIATION: RULE OF LAW AND ECONOMIC INEQUALITY

The fierce competition between the CPP and FUNCINPEC after the 1993 election to divide smaller parties such as BLDP and take over the defectors seriously undermined the reconciliation efforts. Moreover, the power-sharing deal between the CPP and FUNCINPEC, which was supposed to bring about national unity and accommodation, further exacerbated the problems of distrust and resentment. In strengthening their support base, the CPP and FUNCINPEC have been establishing complex and extensive patron-client networks, which subsequently reinforce social fragmentation and inequality because they only provide private goods specifically targeted at their loyal supporters, while punishing and excluding those who vote for the opposition parties from enjoying the same benefits. Furthermore, corruption in the public bureaucracy is also a major obstacle to political reconciliation process, because it significantly undermined the legitimacy and credibility of the government, and the population only support the leaders out of fear and compliance rather than loyalty. The government institutions, particularly the judicial systems and the security apparatus, are still weak and less accountable. These problems of impunity and injustice worsen the past grievances and hatred, which are a potential threat to the political reconciliation process.

These problems can be overcome by strengthening the rule of law, because 'resentment builds when officials expect citizens to fulfil certain duties, like obedience to law, despite the failure of government officials to fulfil their reciprocal duties' (Murphy 2010, p. 44). Moreover, when the rule of law is not strongly enforced, members of the government tend to use arbitrary power to oppress citizens and opposition parties in order to cling on to power and amass wealth, and they are not punished for their wrongdoings. At the same time, the people are largely deprived from receiving justice and fair trial. This culture of impunity contributes to the growing distrust and discontent toward the government, and it also significantly erodes the government's legitimacy and credibility, which forbid citizens from actively participating in political activities to successfully achieve meaningful political reconciliation.

According to the World Justice Project rule of law index, Cambodia ranks last among 66 nations on several sub-factors such as limited government powers, absence of corruption, fundamental rights and access to civil justice (Agrast et al. 2011, p. 49). However the government strongly rejected the ranking, and they called it 'baseless' (Phorn and de Certo 2011, p. 25). The passage of the anti-corruption legislations in 2009 after more than a decade in a draft form is an attempt by the government to tackle the problems of corruption, and the laws were also welcomed by foreign donors and aid agencies, while Non-governmental Organizations (NGOs) and Global Witness believed that the anti-corruption unit will fail to deal with corruption at the top level of the government (Peter and Kuch 2010). Despite the criticisms, the anticorruption unit (ACU) has been trying to prove its credibility by making a high profile arrest on the charge of corruption of Lieutenant General Moek Dara, the Secretary-General of the National Authority for Combating Drugs, along with Lieutenant Colonel Chea Leng (Phann 2011, p. 13). The arrests showed a positive sign that the government is ready to take tougher measures on corruption cases, but the ACU is still facing legitimacy and credibility deficits, and it is the role of the government to ensure that the ACU can independently perform its functions in a more transparent manner.

More importantly, improving the rule of law will also require a strong and independent judicial system, in which criminals will be brought to justice, including elites involved in illegal activities. However, the judiciary in Cambodia is still facing several challenges, notably corruption and government interference, preventing this institution from effectively performing its functions (Un 2009, p. 90). Moreover, the judicial system also suffers from the legitimacy deficits, and according to the survey, 58% of the respondents believed that 'the judicial system does not deserve any trust' (World Bank 2000, p. 29). In 2005, Prime Minister Hun Sen vowed to fix the problems in the judiciary with his 'iron fist' strategy, and several judges were subjected to corruption charges, but progress was limited (Phnom Penh Post 2007). Another challenge to the reform process is that the judiciary is 'underfunded, overwhelmed and lacking both legal know-how and political independence', and in the 2011 budget plan, only 8.5 million US dollars has been allocated to the Ministry of Justice (Neou 2011, p. 25).

Another attempt to restore the rule of law was the negotiation between the RGC and the UN in early December 1999 about the possibility of forming a joint tribunal for the trials of the Khmer Rouge leaders, but it was not until 6 June 2003 that the formal agreement was signed, and the Extraordinary Chamber in the Courts of Cambodia (ECCC) was then established (Linton 2004, pp. 52–56). The reason for this delay was the disagreement between the UN and the Cambodian government on the structure and procedures of the ECCC, because the government's major objectives are: 'preserving a veto on the number of people who would be brought to trial, and maintaining political control over the outcome of cases by ensuring that Cambodian judges were in the majority' (McCargo 2011, p. 619). This point was clearly made when the government responded to the UN in late February 1999:

> We have never rejected the accountability of the Khmer Rouge leaders for the crimes of genocide in Cambodia. We just want, however, to caution that any decision to bring the Khmer Rouge leaders to justice must take into full account Cambodia's need for peace, national reconciliation, rehabilitation and economic development for poverty reduction. Therefore, if improperly

> and heedlessly conducted, the trials of Khmer Rouge leaders would panic other former Khmer Rouge officers and rank and file, who have already surrendered, into turning back to the jungle and renewing the guerrilla war in Cambodia. (Cited in Donovan 2003, p. 558)

As a result, the composition of the ECCC is a mixture of international and Cambodian staff at all levels of the proceedings such as co-prosecutors and co-investigating judges. In the Trial Chamber, there are 3 Cambodian judges and 2 international judges, and an affirmative vote of at least four out of five judges is required to make decisions in the chamber (ECCC 2011). This requirement helps the government to block any investigations or cases that they perceive as threats to stability and national reconciliation. For example, Prime Minister Hun Sen once made an apparent reference to the Pre-trial Chamber that before any new investigations can begin; they need to find a supporting force first, which means they need to have four votes (Vong 2009). During the visit of the UN secretary general to Cambodia, the Prime Minister told Ban Ki-moon that Case 002 was the last trial at ECCC, and he repeatedly said that 'we have to think about peace in Cambodia or the court will fail' (Cheang and James 2010).

Beyond the concern for stability and peace, some scholars have argued that the government has neither resources nor the will to pursue a meaningful political reconciliation, so they hope that the ECCC would deliver justice to the victims and satisfy their needs (Gellman 2008). Yet Chigas (2000) believed that the main purpose of Prime Minister Hun Sen in supporting the ECCC was to satisfy the donors and improve the government's international recognition. Despite the importance of the ECCC in bringing truth and justice to the victims, it would be unreasonable to think that only institutional responses to wrongdoings would achieve political reconciliation, because responding to the abuse of human rights through criminal trials 'will not be sufficient to enhance individuals' capabilities of participating in the social, political and economic life', which will play a pivotal role in the political reconciliation process (Murphy 2010, p. 193).

The use of economic oppression on opposition forces — such as job and wage discrimination and segregation in social benefits — by the government as a way to consolidate power and to strengthen the support base leads to high level of economic inequality. Another major factor is the 'trickle-down approach' used to develop the economy, in which the government pursues economic policies more favourable to the private sector elites than the vast majority, because they believe that when development reaches a certain level, then inequality will decline over time. Consequently, wealth and other resources are heavily concentrated in the hands of the private sector elites, while the poor are living at the subsistence level. The sense of injustice has increased due to the widening gap of inequality, and the population has begun to perceive economic inequality as a result of unfair treatment by the government that is supposed to ensure the welfare of its people. The inability of the government to appropriately address the problems of economic inequality aggravates resentment and distrust between citizens and the elites, which subsequently puts political reconciliation at risk of falling apart.

Following the Paris Peace Agreements, Cambodia has enjoyed strong economic growth, and poverty has been gradually reduced from 45–50 per cent in 1993 to 30.1 per cent in 2007 with a rate of poverty reduction between 1 and 1.6 percentage points per annum (World Bank 2009, p. 25). According to the Human Development Index, Cambodia has improved in ranking to 124 out of 169 countries with a life expectancy of 62.2 years and adult literacy rate of 78.3 per cent (UNDP 2010). Despite the steady decline of poverty rate in recent years, the inequality gap is gradually widening over time, for example, from 2004 to 2007 the Gini coefficient increased from 0.39 to 0.43 with 1 as perfect inequality (World Bank 2009, p. 29). The Cambodia Socio-Economic Survey 2009 conducted by the National Institute of Statistics also showed rising income inequality, where 'the bottom 20 per cent income group earning only 2 per cent of all household income in 2009, while the top 20 per cent earned 67 per cent of all income' (cited in Paul and Chhorn 2010, p. 26).

CONCLUSION

The evidence presented so far makes a fairly convincing claim that Cambodia has achieved a certain degree of political reconciliation, particularly at the top level among leaders of parties in dispute. Moreover, political compromise and coalition building have always played a pivotal role in ensuring peace, stability and security in the country since the signing of the PPAs in 1991 under the name of political reconciliation, but it has turned out that resentment and distrust among the contentious parties has worsened. Even if the 'divide-and-conquer' strategy of the CPP has allowed it to consolidate substantial power and to remove all the potential threats from the opposition parties to its rule, division in Cambodian politics is still a big challenge to the political reconciliation process. Responding to the lack of the rule of law, the government introduced several tough measures including the passage of the anti-corruption laws, judicial reforms and the establishment of the ECCC to try the Khmer Rouge leaders, but the progress was very limited, and the prospects of successful reforms are still in question. Despite strong economic growth in the last decade, the inequality gap has been widening over time, and there is no indication that it will decline in the near future. Since the lack of rule of law and economic inequality reinforce resentment, fragmentation and distrust; they remain a major stumbling-block to the political reconciliation process. My perspective is that the government and citizens must pursue a society-wide political reconciliation in order to attain prosperity and long lasting peace; therefore, the rule of law has to be protected through a strong and independent judicial system, and the government's policies need to aim at reducing poverty and inequality gap, not just pursuing economic growth. Furthermore, political will is extremely important, because before any rigorous reforms can be successfully implemented, the leaders have to perceive them as the long-term benefits for the country, not as a threat to the survival of the regime.

References

Agrast, M, Botero, J and Ponce, A. *World Justice Project: rule of law index 2011*. The World Justice Project, Washington D. C., USA, 2011.

Albritton, B. R. "Cambodia in 2003: on the road to democratic consolidation". *Asian Survey* 44, no. 1 (2004): 102–09.

Brady, B. "Cambodia's one-party future". *The Wall Street Journal Asia*, 18 February 2010.

Carney, T. and Choo, L. T. *Wither Cambodia: beyond the election*. Institute of Southeast Asian Studies, Singapore, 1993.

Chandler, D. *The tragedy of Cambodian history: politics, war and resolution since 1945*. Yale University Press, New Haven, USA, 1991.

Cheang, S. and James, O. "Hun Sen to Ban Ki-moon: Case 002 last trial at ECCC". *Phnom Penh Post*, 27 October 2010.

Curtis, G. *Cambodia reborn? the transition to democracy and development*. The Brooking Institute Press, Washington D. C., USA, 1998.

del Castillo. *Rebuilding war-torn states: the challenges of post-conflict economic reconstruction*. Oxford University Press, Oxford, United Kingdom, 2008.

Doyle, M. W. "Peace-building in Cambodia: the continuing quest for power and legitimacy". In *Cambodia and International community: the quest for peace, development and democracy*, edited by Brown, Z. F. and G. D. Timberman. The Asia Society, New York, USA, 1998.

Dwyer, S. "Reconciliation for realists". *Ethics and International Affairs* 13 (1999): 81–98.

Donovan, K. D. "Recent developments: joint UN-Cambodia efforts to establish a Khmer Rouge tribunal". *Harvard International Law Journal* 44, no. 2 (2003): 551–76.

ECCC. "Organs of ECCC". Viewed on 28 June 2011, <http://www.eccc.gov.kh/en/organs>.

Kiernan, B., ed. *Genocide and democracy in Cambodia*. Yale University Press, New Haven, USA, 1993.

Frieson, K. "The politics of getting the vote in Cambodia". In *Propaganda, politics and violence in Cambodia: democratic transition under United Nations peace-keeping*, edited by S. Heder and J. Ledgerwood. M. E. Sharp, New York, USA, 1996.

Gottesman, E. *Cambodia after the Khmer Rouge: inside the politics of nation-building*. Yale University Press, New Haven, USA, 2003.

Govier, T. and Verwoerd, W. "Trust and the problem of national reconciliation". *Philosophy of Social Sciences* 32, no. 2 (2002): 178–205.

Heder, S. and Ledgerwood, J. "Politics of violence: an introduction". In *Propaganda, politics and violence in Cambodia: democratic transition under United Nations peace-keeping*, edited by S. Heder and J. Ledgerwood. M. E. Sharp, New York, USA, 1996.

Heder, S. "Cambodia Hun Sen's consolidation: death or beginning of reform?" *Southeast Asian Affairs*, pp. 113–30, 2005.

Hieronymi, P. "Articulating an uncompromising forgiveness". *Philosophy and Phenomenological Research* 62, no. 3 (2001): 529–55.

Hughes, M. P. "What is involved in forgiving?" *Philosophia* 25 (1997): 33–49.

Hughes, C. *The political economy of Cambodia's transition, 1991–2001*. Routledge, London, UK, 2003.

Hughes, C. "Reconstructing legitimate political authority through elections?". In *Beyond democracy in Cambodia: political reconstruction in a post-conflict society*, edited by K. Ojendal and M. Lilja. Nordic Institute of Asian Institute Press, Copenhagen, Denmark, 2009.

Human Rights Watch. "Cambodia: opposition officials arrested to sway election". Viewed on 26 June 2011, <http://www.hrw.org/en/news/2008/03/22/cambodia-opposition-officials-arrested-sway-elections>, 2008.

Jeldres, J. A. "The UN and the Cambodian transition". *Journal of Democracy* 4, no. 4 (1997).

Kevin, T. "Cambodia's international rehabilitation, 1997–2000". *Contemporary Southeast Asian* 22, no. 3 (2000).

Kriesberg, L. "Reconciliation: aspects, growth and sequences". *International Journal of Peace Studies* 12, no. 1 (2007): 1–21.

Lambourne, W. "Justice and reconciliation: post-conflict peace-building in Cambodia and Rwanda". In *Reconciliation, justice and coexistence: theory and practice*, edited by M. Abu-Nimer. Lexington Books, New York, USA, 2001.

Levitsky, S. and Way, A. L. *Competitive authoritarianism: hybrid regimes after the cold war*. Cambridge University Press, Cambridge, UK, 2010.

Lederach, P. J. *Building peace: sustainable reconciliation in divided societies*. United States Institute of Peace Press, Washington DC, USA, 1997.

Ledgerwood, J. "Patterns of CPP political repression and violence during the UNTAC period". In *Propaganda, politics and violence in Cambodia: democratic transition under United Nations peace-keeping*, edited by S. Heder and J. Ledgerwood. M. E. Sharp, New York, USA, 1996.

Magaloni, B. *Voting for autocracy: hegemonic party survival and its demise in Mexico*. Cambridge University Press, Cambridge, UK, 2006.

McCargo, D. "Cambodia: getting away with authoritarianism". *Journal of Democracy* 16, vol. 4 (2005): 98–112.

McCargo, D. "Politics by other means' the virtual trials of the Khmer Rouge tribunal". *International Affairs* 87, no. 3 (2011): 613–27.

Meas, S and Sebastian, S. "SRP members defected, says ruling party". Phnom Penh Post, 30 November 2009.

Mengleng, E. "Ranariddh retakes helm of his former party". *The Cambodia Daily*, vol. 47, issue 36 (2010).

Moellendorf, D. "Reconciliation as a political value". *Journal of Social Philosophy* 38, no. 2 (2007): 205–21.

Murphy, C. *A moral theory of political reconciliation*. Cambridge University Press, Cambridge, United Kingdom, 2010.

Neou, V. "Small budget for justice, despite calls for reform". *The Cambodia Daily*, 28 October 2011.

Ott, M. C. "Cambodia: between hope and despair". *Current History: a Journal of Contemporary World Affairs*, 1997.

Paul, V and Chhorn, C. "Disparities continue despite drop in poverty". *The Cambodia Daily*, 21 October 2010.

Peou, S. "Cambodia in 1997: back to square one?" *Asian Survey* 38, no. 1 (1998): 69–74.

Phann, A. "Anticorruption unit reveals details of corruption investigation". *The Cambodia Daily*, 22–23 January 2011.

Phnom Penh Post. "Judicial reform 2007: an iron fist gone limp". 26 January 2007/

Phorn, B. and di Certo, B. "Cambodia ranks last in global rule of law index". *The Cambodia Daily*, 13 June 2011.

Richards, N. "Forgiveness". *Ethics* 99, no. 1 (1988): 77–97.

Schaab, A. *Political Reconciliation*. Routledge, New York, USA, 2005.

Seiff, A. and Bopha, P. "Opposition merger nixed after Hun Sen recording leaks". *The Cambodia Daily*, Monday, 30 May 2011.

Seiff, A and Mengleng, E. "SRP-HRP merger looks poised to implode". *The Cambodia Daily*, Friday, 22 April 2011.

Slye, C. R. "The Cambodian amnesties: beneficiaries and the temporal reach of amnesties for gross violation of human rights". *Wisconsin International Law Journal* 22, no. 1 (2003).

UNDP. "Human Development Index (HDI): 2010 rankings". Viewed on 27 June 2011, <http://hdr.undp.org/en/statistics/index.html#hdirank>, 2010.

Un, K. "Patronage politics and hybrid democracy: political change in Cambodia, 1993–2003". *Asian Perspective* 29, no. 2 (2005): 203–30.

Un, K. "The judicial system and democratization in post-conflict Cambodia". In *Beyond democracy in Cambodia: political reconstruction in a post-conflict society*, edited by J. Ojendal and M. Lilja. NIAS Press, Copenhagen, Denmark, 2009.

Vong, S. "Inquiries could sink ECCC: PM". *Phnom Penh Post*, 10 September 2009.

Walker, M. U. *Moral repair: reconstructing moral relations after wrongdoing*. Cambridge University Press, Cambridge, United Kingdom, 2006.

Widyono B. *Dancing in shadows: Sihanouk, the Khmer Rouge, and the United Nations in Cambodia*. Rowman & Littlefield Publishers, New York, USA, 2008.

World Bank. *Cambodia governance and corruption diagnostic: evidence from citizen, enterprise and public official surveys*. World Bank, Phnom Penh, Cambodia, 2000.

———. *Sustaining rapid growth in a challenging environment: Cambodia country economic memorandum*. The World Bank, Washington D. C., USA, 2009.

Xinhua News Agency. "Hun Sen predicts hasty demise of new opposition alliance". Viewed on 26 June 2011, <http://news.xinhuanet.com/english/2009-01/22/content_10 701136.htm>, 2009.

*This work is dedicated to my soul mate Yany for her unconditional love, support, patience and encouragement, without her it would not have been possible.

CAMBODIA
TODAY

17

THE CONTEMPORARY POLITICAL LANDSCAPE IN CAMBODIA

Wolfgang Sachsenröder

A FLEDGLING POLITICAL SYSTEM

The ill-fated modern history of Cambodia shows a country ravaged by a long series of national calamities, among them the attempt by France to re-establish colonial rule after World War II, the Vietnam War which spilled over into Cambodia, the genocidal Khmer Rouge regime, and ferocious factional competition under the so-called Coalition Government of Democratic Kampuchea, with the continuing influence of the Khmer Rouge as well as the interference of Chinese, Vietnamese and American interests throughout the 1980s. Cambodia slowly started to recover and consolidate only after the 1991 Paris Peace settlement and with the help of the United Nations Transitional Authority in Cambodia (UNTAC) and the UN-organised general elections in 1993.

With the immense loss of educated citizens and potential leaders during the Khmer Rouge and war period as well as through emigration, jump-starting the devastated country in terms of economic and political reconstruction was an incredible challenge. The political landscape being as ravaged as it was, experience, expertise, connections and the political survival instincts of a group around King Sihanouk and a group around ex-Khmer Rouge leader Hun Sen were the ones calling the shots. Though the Cambodian People's Party did not win the UNTAC-supported 1993 election, its leader Hun Sen managed to share the premiership with Prince Ranariddh, to increasingly consolidate the CPP and to entrench its grip on power until its quasi-monopoly today. This has created a somewhat uneasy semblance of stability, including the major flaws which the opposition tries to highlight for the benefit of neglected sectors of the Cambodian society, and its own survival under difficult conditions.

Economically, after all the previous destruction, the consolidation started from a very low level but the growth rates are constantly improving. With continuing severe shortcomings in infrastructure, education, industrial base and business experience, the country still relies very much on agriculture and tourism as domestic sources of growth. But the great potential in hydropower and hydrocarbons, as well as the growing integration into the regional markets and increasing foreign investment may speed up the economic recovery in the coming years. But Cambodia is still very reliant on foreign Official Development Assistance (ODA) and the help of foreign NGOs.

A decisive political watershed for the consolidation was the 1992–93 UN-intervention UNTAC, with its huge input of money (an estimated US$1.5 billion) and human resources (well over 20,000 soldiers, policemen, administrators and volunteers). The UNTAC mission failed to disarm the remaining Khmer Rouge, but successfully organized democratic elections in May 1993 with a voter turnout of about 90 per cent. The winner, with 45 per cent, was the royalist FUNCINPEC Party (a French acronym meaning "National United Front for an Independent, Neutral, Peaceful, and Cooperative Cambodia"), founded by King Sihanouk in Paris in 1981. Second and third were the Cambodian People's Party (CPP) and the Buddhist Liberal Democratic Party (BLDP). This result led to a coalition government of the three parties under Sihanouk's son, Prince Ranariddh, as first prime minister and CPP-leader Hun Sen as second prime minister. Wasting no time, the new parliament had adopted a new Constitution in September 1993, which reinstated the monarchy with former King Norodom Sihanouk as Head of State. But Sihanouk, seriously ill, abdicated in 2004 and was succeeded by his son, Norodom Sihamoni, who is the current king.

Under the 1993 Constitution, Cambodia is a constitutional monarchy governed by a bicameral, multi-party parliamentary system. The kingship is not automatically hereditary, with the king being selected from the royal family by a Throne Council, consisting of top political and religious leaders. The lower house or National Assembly has 123 seats and five year terms. Out of the 61 senators in the upper house, two are appointed by the king and two by the National Assembly, all for five-year terms as well. In the following general elections, 1998, 2003 and 2008, the once-leading FUNCINPEC Party has shrunk nearly to oblivion, whereas the Cambodian People's Party has cemented its grip on power and control of the state.

In the international comparison of democratic development by the Economist Intelligence Unit, Cambodia is ranked somewhat lower than the middle ground but higher than the lowest tercile among the approximately 190 nations covered. Freedom House rates the country as "not free" with 6 for political rights and 5 for civil liberties, 1 being the highest and 7 the lowest score. Among the regional neighbouring countries in Southeast Asia, Cambodia is ranked as follows in the latest 2011 survey by the Economist Intelligence Unit: (See Table 17.1)

The Economist Intelligence Unit's definition of 'hybrid regime' reads as follows:

> Elections have substantial irregularities that often prevent them from being both free and fair. Government pressure on opposition parties and candidates may be common. Serious weaknesses are more prevalent than in flawed democracies — in political culture, functioning of government and political participation. Corruption tends to be widespread and the rule of law is weak. Civil society is weak. Typically there is harassment of and pressure on journalists and the judiciary is not independent.[1]

Probably it is not unfair to state that all of these flaws are observable in Cambodia today. But the flaws are also creating discontent among the voters. It is noteworthy, therefore, that the practised multi-party system, introduced by and after UNTAC is still evolving despite the dominance of the CPP, and that opposition parties find leaders, members and funding to work, campaign and grow. While the royalist parties seem to have lost ground, the Sam Rainsy Party and the Human Rights Party garnered together between a quarter and a third of the votes in the last elections in 2008. (See Table 17.2)

The seat allocation as part of the electoral rules favours the big parties, so that the CPP obtained more seats than a proportional system would have allowed. With 90 seats out of 123, it commands a very comfortable absolute majority now.

THE MAIN POLITICAL PARTIES

Cambodian People's Party (CPP)

The dominant ruling Cambodian People's Party (CPP) is probably the most closed and secretive of the country's political parties. This does not come as a surprise, as the roots of the CPP are communist, revolutionary and anti-

TABLE 17.1
International Comparison of Democratic Development — Southeast Asia

	Rank*	Overall score	Electoral process/ pluralism	Functioning of government	Political participation	Political culture	Civil liberties	Regime type
Thailand	57	6.55	7.83	6.07	5.56	6.25	7.06	Flawed democracy
Indonesia	60	6.53	6.92	7.50	5.56	5.63	7.06	Flawed democracy
Malaysia	71	6.19	6.50	6.79	5.56	6.25	5.88	Flawed democracy
Philippines	74	6.12	8.33	5.00	5.00	3.13	9.12	Flawed democracy
Singapore	82	5.89	4.33	7.50	2.78	7.50	7.35	Hybrid regime
Cambodia	100	4.87	6.08	6.07	2.78	5.00	4.41	Hybrid regime
Vietnam	140	2.94	0.00	4.29	3.33	5.63	1.47	Authoritarian
Myanmar	163	1.77	0.00	1.79	0.56	5.63	0.88	Authoritarian

Source: Economist Intelligence Unit, March 2011
*out of 167 countries

TABLE 17.2
The Main Election Results since 1993

Cambodian General Elections	1993 %	1998 %	2003 %	2008 %
FUNCINPEC	45.47	31.7	20.8	5.6
Cambodian People's Party	38.23	41.4	47.3	58.1
Buddhist Liberal Democratic Party	3.81			
Sam Rainsy Party		14.3	21.9	21.9
Human Rights Party				6.6
Norodom Ranariddh Party				5.0

Source: Pan Sopheap and team, Phnom Penh, in an unpublished research paper on political parties in Cambodia

colonialist at the same time. Today's CPP developed out of the Kampuchean People's Revolutionary Party (KPRP), founded in 1951 during the struggle for national independence. It gained credibility with the Cambodian people by its resistance against the Khmer Rouge, finally toppled by the Vietnamese invasion in 1979, which also explains the CPP's close and complex relationship with the Vietnamese Communist Party.

In 1991, in tune with the collapse of the Soviet Union and the decline of Communism internationally and the economic necessities of reconstruction, the party abandoned its Marxist-Leninist ideology, which, according to some of the true-blue Communists in Europe, was not fully understood and sufficiently deep-rooted among the Cambodian clients anyway. In a discussion with the author of this paper, a former young East German diplomat who had been trained for his assignment to Cambodia for many years in Berlin and Moscow said that the Cambodian counterparts had not understood what Communism was all about. This may partially explain the easy adoption of market principles and other more liberal features in the new platform of the party. One feature, though, is prominent, and potentially detrimental to the country and the relations with its neighbours: the strong nationalist undertones. But they may be more understandable in a sparsely-populated country under reconstruction, sandwiched between the bigger and stronger neighbours, Vietnam and Thailand, and their historical propensity of meddling and interfering frequently in Cambodia.

In its policy platform for the five-year period 2008–13, the CPP makes quite a number of promises, from safeguarding national cohesion and the integrity of its territory, and strengthening multi-party liberal democracy and good governance, to developing the economy and creating jobs. The economic promises are especially interesting, because they emphasize the development of the private sector and the encouragement of foreign investment by improving infrastructure, education, human resources development and labour market regulations. Though all these intentions are laudable, the practice of government and administration and the results on the ground fall short of the expectations of the voters. Corruption and embezzlement are all too obvious for the common people, and seem to strengthen support for the opposition parties, despite their uphill battles against the powerful CPP and state machinery.

As the longest ruling party, the CPP has managed to penetrate the public sector to a rather high degree, subjecting public servants to membership and strict hierarchical control. The party has staff embedded all over the state administration and related organizations, which also gives it opportunities to generate sources of funding by blurring the line between state and party. This, of course, is not just a Cambodian feature but is found worldwide as a result of power being held for a long or over-long period. The party's monopoly on all sorts of administrative decisions and the distribution of enrichment and advancement opportunities explains the membership development of the CPP. If membership comes with privileges, and, in stark contrast, support of or membership in opposition parties may be followed by sanctions, the results are predictable. The CPP is a real catch-all party, which has been rather successful in bonding with the sectors of the society, whom it can provide with privileges and special attention.

The opposition has criticized the CPP for maintaining a special focus on the Vietnamese[2] minority in Cambodia, which has been granted access to voting rights, and consequently tends to vote for the ruling party. Historically, while accommodating a Chinese immigrant minority of traders and entrepreneurs, most of who are considered to be rich in comparison with the average Khmer Cambodians, the influx of more Vietnamese is a contentious issue already in its own right. It is aggravated by what many Cambodians regard as preferential treatment by government and the CPP, and by Hun Sen's special relationship with Hanoi. Many Vietnamese immigrants get identity cards rather easily and are entitled to vote, which they normally do for the CPP. Besides, they often outperform the local businesses, and this creates resentments against Vietnam and the CPP alike.

Sam Rainsy Party

The Sam Rainsy Party (SRP) was first established in November 1995 as the Khmer Nation Party by Sam Rainsy, a former FUNCINPEC member and ex-Economics and Finance minister in the coalition government after the 1993 election. After a no-confidence vote in 1994, he was expelled from FUNCINPEC. Dissatisfaction with growing corruption, poverty, human rights violations, and exploitation of national resources led Sam Rainsy and his followers to start a new party. The fact that the party is now named after its leader, somewhat strange for a party with liberal aspirations, reflects Sam Rainsy's rivalry and dissent with Prime Minister Hun Sen and the CPP's attacks on the Khmer Nation Party. For practical reasons of being registered as a political party and to enable it to contest the 1998 elections, the party had little choice than adopting the name of its leader. The SRP and Sam Rainsy himself are constantly kept under pressure by the ruling CPP and the Hun Sen government. From their viewpoint, both are too popular as a viable opposition and a threat to the comfortable majority of the CPP. Sam Rainsy, because of his popular appeal, had his share of attacks, being stripped of his parliamentary immunity, convicted of criminal defamation, and pardoned later, accused again, and is now living in exile in Australia, waiting for another court decision in connection with his activities at the Vietnamese border.

Because of the harassment, the SRP has problems recruiting enough qualified members in the country and to mobilise the necessary funding for its operational activities, though some moral and financial support comes from Cambodians abroad. But the leading opposition party seems to have become more popular among the younger generation, despite its organizational shortcomings and probably because it is perceived as being serious against the prevailing corruption. Sam Rainsy's wife, Tioulong Saumura, is a Member of Parliament and a sort of personal liaison officer for the leader in exile. But his physical absence has some advantages, too. By means of internet video conferences (much like Thaksin Shinawatra in Thailand), he can connect with many more constituencies in a single day than he could cover by travelling in the country. Also, on the other hand, he can keep up with the pulse of the voters and the daily developments in the country.

The political platform of the SRP party includes the following main objectives: 1. Fighting against violence in the society, 2. Protection of human rights, 3. Fighting against corruption, 4. Reform of the judicial system, 5. Reform of the administration, 6. Land reform in favour of the poor, 7. Territorial integrity, 8. Solution of the (illegal) immigration problem, 9. Stopping deforestation and protecting natural resources. 10. Review of illegal contracts between government and private companies. The numbers seven and eight point to the nationalistic and anti-Vietnamese stands of the party, as perceived by the public. Number ten refers to the privatisation drive under Hun Sen and the CPP government, castigated by Simon Springer as

"Cambodia's Neo-liberal Order."[3] One may have doubts about Springer's bias with Liberalism or Neo-liberalism, but the practice of privatisation has not been fair and open, and in many ways has created victims and concentrated the spoils in the hands of a privileged few, normally in or close to the CPP.

Human Rights Party

The Human Rights Party, founded in 2007, is the youngest party in Cambodia. Its founder and elected leader is Kem Sokha, a human rights advocate and activist with quite a long history in Cambodian politics. He served among other positions as deputy secretary general and senator of FUNCINPEC, and secretary-general of the former Buddhist Liberal Democratic Party. What made him popular was his leading role in building the human rights movement in the country. Most of the other leading personalities in the party have been politically active before in the Buddhist Liberal Democratic Party or its later splinter, the Son Sann Party, and follow their basic liberal orientation. But the human rights activities and practical interventions against the widespread violations make the party especially attractive to considerably large numbers of the affected vulnerable sectors in the urban and rural areas, where about 75 per cent of the population are subsistence farmers. The party's self-image is not really that of a normal political party competing for power as such. They see themselves more as an interest group for better human rights protection in a country pockmarked by political violence. They do not strive for a maximization of seats and influence but more for a role as conscience of the nation. This is why it considers a closer cooperation or eventually even a merger with the Sam Rainsy Party as natural and it tries to avoid three-corner-fights in elections, which can only be useful for the ruling CPP.

The Buddhist Liberal Democratic Party (BLDP), third force in the 1993 elections, dissolved itself after the disastrous 1998 election results, when it did not win a single seat. After the dissolution, most members joined FUNCINPEC or the SRP and later the HRP as well.

FUNCINPEC, the royalist party founded in 1981 by King Sihanouk and other exiles in Paris, is an appendix of the CPP government as a very junior coalition partner. It had a strong start in the 1993 UNTAC-supported election. It also enjoyed regional and international support as one possible vehicle of fighting the Vietnamese presence in Cambodia. But the party continually lost votes in the following elections, and was further weakened by a split before the 2008 elections, which led to the formation of the Norodom Ranariddh Party. Personality clashes and poor leadership, a weak organizational structure, but also a dose of corruption, have played their part in nearly destroying FUNCINPEC and wiping it off the political map of the country. Consequently, its image has suffered to a degree that many citizens see FUNCINPEC as no more than a puppet of the prime minister. But it also still has nine members in the 54-seat Senate, last elected in 2006 and due for re-election in early 2012. Because of the coalition arrangements with the CPP and the attached funding opportunities, the party is still considered rich. And since respect for the royalty is still alive, it is not yet dying, and may be of some tactical use for Hun Sen in his attempt to prevent further growth of the opposition.

The situation of the Norodom Ranariddh Party looks similar to that of FUNCINPEC. Prince Ranariddh, who had retired from politics two years ago, re-emerged at the end of 2010 and was re-elected as president of the party in December 2010. According to the declarations of this party congress, the intention is to unite the royalist camp and contribute to unification and reconciliation of the society. As in the FUNCINPEC case, financial considerations may have played a role in this resurrection, because the Prince has a certain reputation in this field.

Opposition

With the dominant role of the CPP and its tight control of power in the country, the question of sufficient space for the opposition seems to be futile. The reality, though, is a bit more complicated. Cambodia is a Southeast Asian country with a higher flexibility of characters, behaviour and political manoeuvres than the more open and blunt Western traditions. The switching of leading politicians between FUNCINPEC, BLDP, SRP, HRP and CPP demonstrates the more informal and hidden communication channels between competing parties. First of all, the UNTAC meant to install a pluralistic democratic regime in Cambodia. Despite the CPP's iron grip on power and level of control, the semblance of a multi-party system is an important part of the international image for Hun Sen and his government. Smashing or eradicating the opposition altogether could harm this image and the investment climate.

Hun Sen as well as some other authoritarian regimes in the region are more intelligent and sophisticated than to fall into such a trap. That means that the CPP tries to control the opposition parties as much as possible without hurting them too much. The indictment and conviction of Sam Rainsy may be more of a personality clash with Hun Sen and due to concern that the SRP could become too popular. The newest developments among the bigger opposition parties, therefore, are being carefully observed by the government. Since February 2011, the SRP and HRP have established a common commission to gauge the possibility of cooperation or merger, and the commission had met already four times by end of March 2011. If they manage to join forces in the different upcoming elections (the parliamentary one is due only in summer 2013), they could be a more realistic threat to the ruling party. This threat is not as improbable as it seems from earlier election results. Hun Sen must be aware enough of the internal weaknesses of his dominance of the party scene.

On the one hand, the election results in 2008 are due to rather massive manipulation of the voting and counting procedures. Many citizens have been prevented from voting if they were known by the local authorities to be pro-opposition. Many votes have been won for the CPP by bussing voters to certain polling stations. Votes have been bought by a number of tricks, like giving voters a marked ballot paper already outside the polling stations and buying back the empty ballot paper they brought from the polling station after casting the manipulated vote, etc. But the growing awareness of Cambodian voters and the possibility that manipulated ballot papers could disappear instead of ending up in the ballot box, gives no guarantee that the system will work in the future. Psychologically, and that is of course world-wide, every fraudulent activity in elections creates the fear that it may not work in the future.

Until the last election in 2008, anyway, the positive report cards of international observers, like the much-quoted "miracle on the Mekong", are not in line with the reality and the perception of a majority of Cambodian voters. As the opposition hopes, the dominance of the media by the ruling party and the government may be reduced or even shattered by the availability of mobile phones (95 per cent of the country is covered by providers) and the fast-growing internet and social media penetration.

The events in the Middle East in the beginning of 2011, perceived as a popular revolt against the iron grip of single or dominant parties, have created hope on the opposition's side and at least some concern on the side of the government. Comparing Arab countries and Cambodia may be difficult in many ways, but a number of features are similar. Cambodia has a very young population, the generation below thirty years of age constitutes half or even a bit more of the total 14 million Cambodians. For this young generation, there are far from enough jobs and the quality and cost of education is a difficult barrier for many among them. At the same time, access to information by TV and internet is widespread and creates more impatience and unhappiness with the prevailing conditions. Another possible reason for concern on the government's side is the reliability of the CPP membership. Since the penetration of the provinces, municipal and village structures with the party network is very much based on corruption and pressure to join, the number of real activists may be open to doubts. The higher levels of the corruption pyramid — which works much like a Ponzi scheme — may be the most reliable because they have much more to lose. The further one goes down to the grassroots, the lesser people have to lose when they are no longer loyal to the party or when the party can no longer deliver on their promised material incentives.

The CPP total membership, according to the perception of observers in the country, is being officially exaggerated (with claims of up to five million) and sometimes even the number of votes for the CPP does not match with these membership figures. All in all, despite the efforts of the ruling party and its government to contain the opposition as much as possible, the limited space is surviving and will possibly widen in the future. The dream of many Cambodians to enjoy more freedom and political choices is still there and opposition parties like SRP and HRP are trying their best to keep these hopes alive.

PRIME MINISTER HUN SEN AND HIS GRIP ON POWER

Hun Sen has been the dominant political figure in Cambodia for the last three decades and is one of the longest-serving leaders in the region. Born in 1951, he has gone through all the turmoil and violence that his country has suffered. His iron grip, therefore, has also deep roots in the historical use of force for political purposes within Cambodia. A politician like Hun Sen is not likely to take risks either. In May 2010, "The Cambodian People's Party has begun to identify supporters and dissenters of the party nation-wide; categorizing them by the amount of support they give in apparent preparation for the next national elections, according to documents and officials. The CPP has ordered government officials to identify constituents by three levels of support: white, grey and black. Those who are most supportive of the party in different communes are labelled 'white', the least are labelled 'black.' "[4]

Money politics, as a widespread regional phenomenon in Southeast Asia, is also rampant in Cambodia. With the privatization drive during the opening-up vis-à-vis economic regionalization and globalization, most of the spoils have gone to members and cronies of the CPP. The legal void left by the Khmer Rouge and internal conflicts has made it easy to profit from concessions for the lucrative logging industry and issuing of land titles to the detriment of supposedly "squatting" folks in the countryside. The lack of the rule of law is one of the Achilles heels of Cambodia's reconstruction drive and a historical burden: "In Cambodia's history (...) power has rarely been constrained by law. Instead, law has been an instrument to be used arbitrarily by the holders of power to suit their ends."[5]

PM Hun Sen is said to have enriched himself in a big way, but the assumption that he pays for schools and hospitals out of his own pocket[6] is probably untrue. When he turns to people in his entourage beside and even behind the rostrum in public speeches, a rare gesture among politicians facing a TV camera, the open secret is that he is urging one of the rich local cronies to foot the bill in return for the enrichment opportunities provided by the party. On 1April 2011 — but not an April fool's joke — Hun Sen declared his monthly income at 4.6 million riels (approx. US$1,150, the assets remaining unrevealed) to the new anti-corruption unit. He also urged all officials to follow him in the bid to tackle rampant graft in the country.[7] Following a common development in some other Southeast Asian countries, when corruption is becoming too visible and dangerously unpopular, the leaders start to officially fight it and implement anti-corruption watchdogs. This may indicate the shrewd flexibility and political skills of the prime minister, even conceded by the opposition.

Hun Sen is said to be extremely well-informed and able to listen, endowed with a remarkable memory. This may indicate that Hun Sen's era and political dominance is not yet over, but that the iron grip may withdraw gradually and hide in a velvet glove, be it only for tactical reasons. The special relations between PM Hun Sen and Vietnam are noteworthy as well. From early on in his career, his personal qualities have impressed the external friends. He is noted for his intelligence, being a quick learner, being ambitious and highly motivated, and gifted with the verbal skills needed in politics and diplomacy. His selection and grooming proved to be one of their most astute decisions. Hun Sen has shown his affinity for bureaucratic patronage, and he has nurtured an extensive patronage system within the central bureaucracy. Described as realistic and clear-headed, Hun Sen has cleverly kept within the broad parameters of Vietnam's policies. His ouster of Co-Prime Minister Prince Ranariddh in the July 1997 crisis was a very clear example of his tough political style. Evan Gottesman, in his book entitled "Cambodia after the Fall of the Khmer Rouge" (Yale University Press, 2003) has described Hun Sen's rise to power and his links to Vietnam in more detail. In return for their support, Gottesman writes, Hun Sen showed his loyalty by supporting them on various issues, such as the border demarcation.

On the other hand, the close relationship with Vietnam may turn out to be a trump card vis-à-vis the growing influence and investments of China. Being surrounded by bigger and stronger neighbours often leads weaker countries to play them off against each other.

Finally, how secure is Hun Sen's position as supreme leader? There are reports about a possible factional struggle with Chea Sim, the senate president. But details are sketchy, and hence we can only observe from a distance whether a power struggle may reveal the outline of a future political leadership succession.

POLITICAL VIOLENCE IN CAMBODIA

During the last few years, politically-motivated violence has been gradually receding. Unfortunately, though, it has by no means vanished completely. Springer (2010:135) quotes Human Rights Watch[8] as follows:

> Human Rights Watch reported that while overt political violence was not as evident, more sophisticated forms of intimidation and coerced party membership replaced it. Village and commune chiefs, most of whom are members of the ruling CPP, threatened opposition party supporters with violence, expulsion from their villages, and denial of access to community resources such as rice distributions.

On the local level, especially in the rural areas, where everybody knows everybody, not many citizens are willing to differ and risk repercussions of the sort described by Human Rights Watch. Conformity with the mainstream may also match better with rural traditions of tolerance and conflict avoidance. Cambodians are said to prefer to let the boat go with the current instead of forcing it upstream. But anybody you ask in 2011 will tell you a number of examples of this type of coercion, including violent ones. There are more and more cases being brought to the pliable courts, when oppositionists are being sued and silenced by legal means. The underpaid and mostly corrupt judges and prosecutors have little choice than following the political directions they get from above. The stripping of Sam Rainsy's parliamentary immunity and the law suit which eventually forced him into exile is certainly a case in point.

THE BIGGER ISSUES AND DEBATES IN 2011

This can only be a sketchy and short selection of domestic issues under discussion in the first half of 2011, without ranking. But they are on the minds of Cambodians and have to be addressed by the government and the opposition parties.

- The Preah Vihear Temple and the border dispute with Thailand, one of several territorial disputes in the region undermining the Treaty of Amity and Cooperation in Southeast Asia. In 1962, the International Court of

Justice decided that the temple belongs to Cambodia, but Thailand is disputing a part of the adjacent area. So far, five military clashes have been registered, regularly fanning nationalistic feelings and movements on both sides, which in turn are exploited politically.

- The corruption, very obvious especially in Phnom Penh by increasing numbers of flashy cars and conspicuous villas, is leaving the overwhelming majority in poverty. Since the general perception is pointing at CPP and government as the source of this growing social imbalance, it dominates much of the public debate and supports opposition efforts to tackle it. But PM Hun Sen has already reacted and passed an anti-graft law in 2010, which requires asset declarations by more than 100,000 state officials.
- Economic activities from regional and international players are all too often not perceived as profitable or useful for the country. Cambodians are weary of business people who only come for the famous fast bucks and disappear soon after. This is especially so of the last big tropical timber reserves in Southeast Asia, which have been plundered by local and foreign profiteers.
- After the Khmer Rouge destroyed practically the whole legal system of the country and decimated the population, a regular administration of land titles was made nearly impossible. Insecurity about property rights is therefore common and opens the doors for land-grabbing practices at the expense of the poor and powerless. At the same time, land speculation is one of the biggest sources of fast profits and obviously favours the members and cronies of the CPP. Normally, the courts are of little or no help to the evicted.
- On a larger scale, land titles are leased to foreign companies, in big way to Vietnamese companies along the common border. Since many of the lease contracts for rubber and palm oil plantations for huge areas are being signed for 99 years, and the contracting companies bring their own workers from Vietnam, local Cambodians have to be resettled. This, of course, creates a lot of concern in a difficult neighbourhood, split already in traditional distrust of Vietnam in the population and Hun Sen's and the CPP's special relationship with Hanoi.
- The growing Vietnamese minority and Chinese immigration as well, are emotional concerns for many Cambodians. Doing business, and very often rather successfully so, without enough efforts to assimilate with the Khmer majority, these immigrant communities may develop into a domestic time bomb if not handled with care on both sides.

CONCLUSION

As mentioned earlier, the iron grip of the CPP government has created a semblance of stability with a number of rather uneasy undertones. The challenges are many and strong, and it is easy to blame internal and external culprits. Many blame UNTAC for the failure to create a "neutral political environment" as was its mandate. Given the extremely messy domestic situation before the UNTAC intervention, this expectation was certainly unrealistic. The legacy of the pre-UNTAC era remains an enormous burden until today, ranging from the unresolved landmine problem through the difficult reconstruction of a viable legal system to education problems, economic recovery and social reconciliation and bringing Khmer Rouge culprits to justice. As usual, there are different ways of seeing the water level in the glass. Compared to the situation 20 years ago, there is progress in the direction of reconciliation, reconstruction and stability. In terms of good governance and democratic consolidation, there is much to be desired. ASEAN membership and the growing economic integration may help to further consolidate and stabilize the country without being able to heal its vulnerability. But stability and consolidation are what the Cambodians deserve after all their sufferings. May the political system allow a soft landing.

Notes

1. Economist Intelligence Unit, *Democracy Index 2010*, p. 31.
2. Official sources on the Internet claim that 90 per cent of the population is Khmer. Wikipedia, "Ethnic Groups in Cambodia", though, states that only 55 per cent are Khmer, 6 per cent Chinese and 33 per cent Vietnamese!
3. Simon Springer. *Cambodia's Neoliberal Order: Violence, authoritarianism, and the contestation of public space*. London and New York, 2010.
4. <http://detailsaresketchy.wordpress.com/2010/05/21/the-cpp-and-black-label-politics/>.
5. Gallup, Jeffrey C. "Cambodia: A Shaky Start for Democracy". In *How Asia Votes*, edited by John Fuh-Sheng Hsieh and David Newman. New York, Seven Bridges Press, 2002, p. 183.
6. Simon Springer provides a lot of practical information, but seems to be wrong here.
7. *The Straits Times*, Singapore, 2.4.2011
8. HRW, The Run Up to Cambodia's National Assembly Election: Political Expression and Freedom of Assembly under Assault. Briefing Paper (June 2003) www.hrw.org/legacy/backgrounder/asoa/cambodia.

18

THE CAMBODIAN ECONOMY
Charting the Course of a Brighter Future

Hang Chuon Naron

INTRODUCTION

Since 1993, the Cambodian economy has undergone a dramatic and rapid transformation. The traditional economy, based on agriculture, is now driven increasingly by the industrial and the tertiary sectors. With the return of peace in the early 1990s, a sense of confidence and pride pervades the country. All Cambodians now share a common vision of sustained economic growth with employment and a secure future for all. The government strategy is to help realize this vision by reinforcing Cambodia's comparative advantages both regionally and internationally. In the era of globalization the fortunes of all countries in the world are intertwined; autarky is not an option for sustained high economic growth for a small sized economy as Cambodia. Hence Cambodia's continued economic success will depend on the availability of full market access for its products and the cooperation of its development partners.

Cambodia had to virtually start from the scratch to rebuild the country after the defeat of the Khmer Rouge regime. At the very outset, the country had to face the harmful consequences of the economic embargo imposed in

1979. The annual rate of economic growth did not exceed 3.4 per cent during 1988–91, even though average annual growth in the manufacturing sector reached 6.3 per cent. Growth has been particularly strong since the early 1990s, with the implementation of macroeconomic reforms and normalization of economic and trade relations with the countries of the region. An annual average rate of growth of 6.3% was achieved during 1994–98, despite the upheaval caused by the Asian financial crisis of 1997–98.

It was only after the successful implementation of the "win-win" policy put forward by Samdech Hun Sen in 1998 that the RGC was able to finally dismantle the politico-military organization of the Khmer Rouge, thus re-establishing peace throughout the Kingdom, and achieving the physical and political unification of the country. The government could then take steps to strengthen the spirit of national reconciliation. The elections of 1998 created the conditions for political stability in the country and allowed the government to focus on macroeconomic management.

Following the July 1998 elections, the RGC adopted the Triangular Strategy with the objective of promoting sustainable development in Cambodia. The strategy aimed at restoration of peace and stability, as well as maintenance of security for the country and its people. The strategy was by and large successfully implemented and the process of robust economic recovery initiated.

At the opening meeting of the Council of Ministers on 16 July 2004, Prime Minister Hun Sen launched the "Rectangular Strategy *for Growth, Employment, Fairness and Effectiveness in Cambodia*." The core of the strategy is good governance. The successful implementation of the strategy depends on establishing a conducive environment in four critical areas: (i) peace, political stability, and social order; (ii) partnership for development, particularly partnership with the private sector, donor community, and civil society; (iii) economic and financial stability; and (iv) integration of Cambodia in the region and in the world. The strategy was reviewed and reinforced after the elections of 2009 and is currently under implementation.

During the 1990s, the Cambodian economy was transformed from a centrally planned to a market economy. Reforms and policies intended to encourage development of the private sector were adopted in 1989–90. RGC liberalized the economy by dismantling price controls and encouraged private sector development including foreign investment. During this period, growth was achieved mainly from the production and service sectors. Agricultural production, on average, remained lower than population growth.

Since 1999, Cambodia has been working towards accelerating development based on market principles and private sector development. Growth was

11.9 per cent in 1999 and recorded annual average rate of 8.8 per cent during 1999–2003. Growth performance was consolidated further during 2004–2008. In the decade ending 2010 Cambodia's GDP rose at an average annual rate of 9.3 per cent. Growth in the last decade was based on the strong performance of garments and tourism. From the policy side, sound macroeconomic management, in particular a prudent fiscal policy and tight monetary management supported by structural reforms contributed to this performance.

In 2005 questions arose on the capacity of Cambodia to sustain high growth due to loss of competitiveness. The Multi-Fibre Agreement (MFA) expired in December 2004, which allowed WTO member countries, primarily China, to export clothing on a worldwide basis with no quotas imposed. It was anticipated that while the larger and more efficient textile manufacturers in Cambodia would be able to survive the global competition, the smaller ones would perish as they would be unable to compete. The recent Global Economic Crisis had a crushing impact on Cambodia and growth slowed down sharply in 2009. The country has to rethink and reformulate its development strategy.

Moreover, the economic success of recent years has been accompanied by rural and agricultural stagnation, growing inequality between urban and rural sectors, social problems of landless farmers, and the growing pressure of finding productive employment for the youth who are swelling the labour force day by day. Cambodia, with an annual per capita GDP of US$700, remains a least developed country (LDC). Cambodia's economic future depends on how effectively it will be able to address the following challenges:

First, political stability, governance and respect for law and order must be strengthened and law enforcement must be guaranteed. Cambodia has adopted systems of governance appropriate for its culture and history. Elections are organized regularly, transparently and with fairness. Individual and collective freedoms are assured. Political parties, labour unions, and the press function freely in this young democracy. Cambodia has also signed and ratified most of the international agreements on human rights protection. Education of citizens about their rights and responsibilities is an important area of government responsibility. However, the pursuit of political liberties should not derail political and social stability achieved after decades of turmoil and bloodshed by overstretching the capacity of the fragile political, social, and governance institutions of the nascent democracy. Also, the fruits of development must be shared equitably between the rich and the poor for preserving social stability.

Second, much remains to be done to correct social injustices. The press, including the foreign press enjoys great freedom in Cambodia and several non-government organizations both national and foreign are working in the country in diverse areas of social development. Though their activities have helped to increase awareness of social ills prevailing in the community, social equity remains a distant goal. In particular, human trafficking in women and children and the deprivation of landless farmers are serious concerns.

Third, the capacity to implement policy must be improved. Several institutional and policy reforms were undertaken during 1993–2008. Much more effort is needed to ensure that institutions function effectively, and concrete actions follow approved strategies and policies. The top priorities are the implementation of an employment oriented and market responsive education policy along with provision of technical and vocational training, improving access to good quality health care and swiftly propagating the latest advances in information and communications technology to the public to serve the cause of progress.

Fourth, protecting and developing natural resources will be crucial for sustaining development. Fair and equitable access to resources must be ensured to sustain social stability. Government policies and actions in technical, financial, cultural and academic sectors as well as in institutional coordination must reflect the political will to protect the environment. A transparent mechanism must be put in place to implement the sub-decree on social concessions to address the problem of landless farmers.

Fifth, in the area of capital accumulation, emphasis should be put on domestic resource mobilization and in the selection of efficient investment projects. For augmenting human capital, human resource development at all levels should be encouraged. Skilled entrepreneurs and administrators and technical knowledge are key factors of production no less important than physical capital. The business class of Cambodia needs to improve its institutional and technical capacity. Investments for raising labour productivity and introduction of improved technology should be given priority. Cambodia has seen a middle class emerge in recent years; this is a welcome development which will contribute to social stability. The middle class should strengthen its capacity to benefit fully from the opportunities of development.

Sixth, Cambodia needs to attract private investment and mobilize broad based international support for its development effort. In particular international cooperation must be enhanced in: (i) official development assistance; (ii) direct foreign investment; and (iii) foreign trade. The activities and outcomes of the Cambodian Development Forum (CDF), advice of the IMF, World Bank, Asian Development Bank, and other donors of bilateral funds, along with deliberations in ASEAN, ASEAN plus Three, and the World Trade Organization (WTO) will provide important policy inputs to the government. Cambodia is committed to cooperate with these agencies.

This article is a survey of Cambodia's achievements in the last two decades and the problems that the country must address in the future. The rest of the article is organized as follows: the next section presents an overview of Cambodia's geography and demographics; section III presents an review of macroeconomic performance; section IV reviews public finance and fiscal policy; section V monetary and financial sector developments; section VI describes the balance of payments; section VII deals with sector assessments including agriculture and rural development, industry and private sector development, services and utilities, education and health; and Section VIII with international economic relations and regional cooperation. The paper concludes with a discussion of the governance aspects of the Rectangular Strategy which is the government's socioeconomic agenda for policy and institutional reform, the crucial challenge facing Cambodia.

GEOGRAPHY AND POPULATION

Cambodia is located in Southeast Asia. It lies between the 10th and 15th degrees north latitude, and between the 102nd and 108th degrees east longitude. It has a tropical climate and receives monsoon rains. Its climate is generally hot and humid, but the temperature and humidity vary according to regions and seasons. Cambodia's climate is characterized by two major seasons: wet and dry. With an area of 81,035 square kilometres, Cambodia is polygonal in shape, with the centre located near Kampong Thom Province.

Cambodia possesses abundant natural resources including forests, coastal and inland fisheries, a rich biodiversity, and a great variety of soils suitable for a broad spectrum of crops and animal husbandry. The vast alluvial basin of the Tonle Sap Lake with an area which can double during the rainy season shapes the country's ecology and economy. The Mekong and the Tonle Sap Lake are important resources for irrigation and fisheries.

The geological mapping of Cambodia in the 1960s confirmed mineral occurrences at 145 sites. Additional geological surveys and exploration conducted during the 1970s and 1980s identified more than 10 sites of gold deposits. Based on a survey carried out from 1966 to 1970, the government reprinted the mineral maps in the 1980s in which twenty-five kinds of mineral resources were identified. While Cambodia's mineral resources remain largely unexplored, several important minerals have already been discovered including bauxite, copper, zinc, gold, iron ore, nickel, granite, gemstones and tungsten. Minerals currently extracted include gemstones, gold — mostly mined by small-scale operators, marble, granite, sand, limestone and salt.

At present some 20 Korean, Vietnamese (Vinacomin), Chinese and other foreign companies have received in all 42 mineral exploration licenses extending over half of the surface area of eastern Cambodia. The important mining activities underway are described in Box 1.

BOX 1: Natural Resources

Gold: The gold bearing belt of the Chatree gold mine in Thailand extends south-eastward into the northern part of Cambodia. This area has recently become the focus of exploration by licensees.

Iron: Four Chinese steelmakers have established a joint venture to explore and develop iron ore mines in Cambodia. Some early estimates show that the Preah Vihear region may have 2.5 billion tons of iron ore reserves.

Oil and gas: Oil and gas exploration has been conducted in Cambodia's off-shore blocks. Chevron Texaco announced in December 2004 the discovery of three wells, with a reserve of 400 million barrels of oil and five billion cubic meters of natural gas, located 90 miles off the coast of Sihanoukville. Drilling began in 2007. Oil and gas discovery in the off-shore Block A has attracted some international companies to invest in oil and gas exploration in Cambodia.

War, social breakdown, and genocide have exacted a heavy toll on the people of Cambodia. A source has estimated the total population at 6.9 million in 1970, and 7.9 million in 1975. The 1979 population was estimated at 6.3 million. Based on these estimates more than a million Cambodians perished during the Khmer Rouge period. The total population of Cambodia was 11.4 million according to the 1999 census and 13.3 million according to the 2008 census i.e. the population rose by 1.95 million between the two censuses. See Table 18.1.

Ninety per cent of Cambodians are Khmer, a people belonging to the Austro-Asiatic group that settled in Southeast Asia in the prehistoric period. There are also Chinese-Khmer, Thai-Khmer, and Vietnamese-Khmer, progeny of mixed marriages. Following the 1860 Treaty with China to establish the protectorate regime in Cambodia a fresh wave of Chinese immigrants arrived in Cambodia. The number of Chinese in Cambodia in the 1970s was estimated at 150,000. The Chinese are engaged mostly in trade and wield considerable economic power. Vietnamese and Cham minorities also live in Cambodia.

TABLE 8.1
Population of Cambodia

Year	Population			Remarks
	Total	Male	Female	
1920	2,600,000			
1962	5,728,771	2,862,939	2,865,832	Population census
1970	6,800,000			
1975	7,900,000			
1980	6,589,954	3,049,450	3,540,504	General Demographic Survey
1993–94	9,870,000	4,714,000	5,156,000	Socio-Economic Survey
1996	10,702,329	5,119,587	5,582,742	Demographic Survey
1998	11,437,656	5,119,587	5,582,742	Population census
2004	12,824,000	6,197,000	6,627,000	Demographic Survey
2008	13,388,910	6,495,512	6,893,398	Population census

Source: Migozzi, Mysliwiec, *Cambodia Soir*, November 5–7, 2004.

MACROECONOMIC PERFORMANCE

The economic development in Cambodia can be divided into three distinct phases:

- The rehabilitation phase, 1989–1998;
- The reconstruction phase, 1999–2003;
- The economic take-off phase, 2004 onwards.

The rehabilitation phase, 1989–1998: The rudiments of a market economy were established in this period. However the progress in market reforms was undermined by emergence of macroeconomic imbalances due to the following reasons:[1]

- Revenue mobilization suffered following introduction of economic liberalization measures since 1989. Privatization of State-Owned Enterprises (SOEs) and enterprise reform together with price and trade liberalization slashed economic rents which had accrued to public sector monopolies. The introduction of new taxes on the other hand made only a small contribution to the exchequer in view of the small tax base and the unfamiliarity of the tax payers and the revenue authorities with the new tax system. Non-tax revenue declined from 5.5 per cent of budget expenditure in 1989 to less than 1 per cent in 1991. However, elimination

of customs duty exemptions increased the contribution of customs revenue from 8.5 per cent of public expenditure in 1989 to 37 per cent in 1991;
- On the expenditure side, the removal of price controls considerably increased the unit cost of the goods and services procured for public consumption and investment. The budget came under severe stress as government's policy to protect wages and defence expenditures crowded out public investments and operations and maintenance. Their share in the budget declined from 41 per cent in 1989 to 16 per cent in 1991;

The Reconstruction Phase, 1999–2003: The emphasis during this period was on establishing macroeconomic stability, consolidating the peace and order situation and integrating Cambodia with the rest of the world. Cambodia joined the ASEAN in April 1999. To help the process of global and regional integration Cambodia supported by the donor community embarked on a program of reconstructing the transport infrastructure destroyed during the Khmer Rouge regime. GDP growth averaged 8.8 per cent during 1999–2003 despite natural disasters such as repeated floods and droughts exceeding the targeted economic growth of 6–7 per cent envisaged in the Triangular Strategy which guided the second mandate of the government.

The economic take-off phase, 2004–08: In this phase RGC implemented a range of second generation reforms as envisaged in the Rectangular Strategy including the first phase of the Public Financial Management (PFM) reform program and continued to investment heavily in provincial and rural roads. Economic growth during 2004–08 averaged 10.3 per cent per annum. Investment was financed mainly by the rapidly growing banking sector and FDI inflows. The high performing sectors were rice and cash crops (average annual growth of 9.7 per cent), mining (18.2 per cent), textiles (16.1 per cent), utilities (16.7 per cent), construction (15.5 per cent), tourism (17.4 per cent), telecom and transportation (8.3 per cent), finance (21.6 per cent) and real estate (12.4 per cent).

Overall, sustained economic growth in the last decade has raised living standards and reduced the national poverty headcount. However, poverty reduction is not keeping pace with growth, a sign that Cambodia is increasingly less egalitarian.

A World Bank study concluded that Cambodia was among the 15 fastest-growing economies in the world during 1998–2007, positioning slightly ahead of China and exceeding the Asia-Pacific average of 8.4 per cent. Two key features of economic performance in recent years are the increasing diversity of the sectors contributing to economic growth and the robust contribution of the agriculture sector to growth. Garment manufacturing has emerged as a major contributor to growth in the last decade though its prospects are uncertain. Its poor performance during the Global Economic Crisis was a key reason for the economic downturn of 2009. Apart from garment manufacture and agriculture, tourism and construction have also provided impetus to growth in the last decade. Overall recent economic performance has been characterized by diversified contributions to growth from agriculture, manufacturing, construction and services.

During 1993–2008, domestically financed investment accounted for 53 per cent of total investment, while externally financed investment made up the rest. FDI inflows have been on the increase, especially during the period preceding the Global Economic Crisis. Broadly, Cambodia's sources of investment financing on a yearly basis are: (i) US$600 million in ODA for building social and physical infrastructure (ii) US$700–800 million in FDI for expanding productive capacity of the economy; (iii) US$1.2 billion in government budget for both current expenditure and capital investments to improve public service delivery, and (iv) US$2.5 billion in bank loans to finance private sector projects. (See Figure 18.1)

The Global Economic Crisis had only an indirect impact on the Cambodian economy. Cambodia's commercial banks do not have direct exposure to the subprime loans. However the Crisis impacted on the real sectors, particularly export of garments severely. Cambodia's GDP growth fell from 10.2 per cent in 2007 to 6.7 per cent in 2008 and was projected at 2.1 per cent in 2009 and 5.5 per cent in 2010. The Cambodian economy is expected to grow at about 8–9 per cent per annum over the next several years, but growth will likely accelerate after oil production commences on a commercial scale, expected in 2011. The high growth seen in the last decade was partly a post-conflict 'catch up' phenomenon. As Cambodia confronts stiffer competition from globalization (e.g., Vietnam's entry into WTO), the high cost of doing business — characterized principally by high energy and transport costs — could also become a binding constraint. As a result growth could become less buoyant. In the near term, the economy will likely continue to be led by tourism, garment industry, and construction, with agriculture providing periodic but volatile spurts of growth depending on weather conditions.

FISCAL POLICY AND PUBLIC FINANCE

The long run objectives of fiscal policy are (i) to ensure a level of public spending consistent with macroeconomic stability and (ii) to maintain a sustainable fiscal balance with gradual increase in budget allocation for social and economic sectors through rationalizing public expenditure and broadening tax base, and preventing revenue leakages by strengthening customs and tax

FIGURE 18.1
Economic Growth in Cambodia

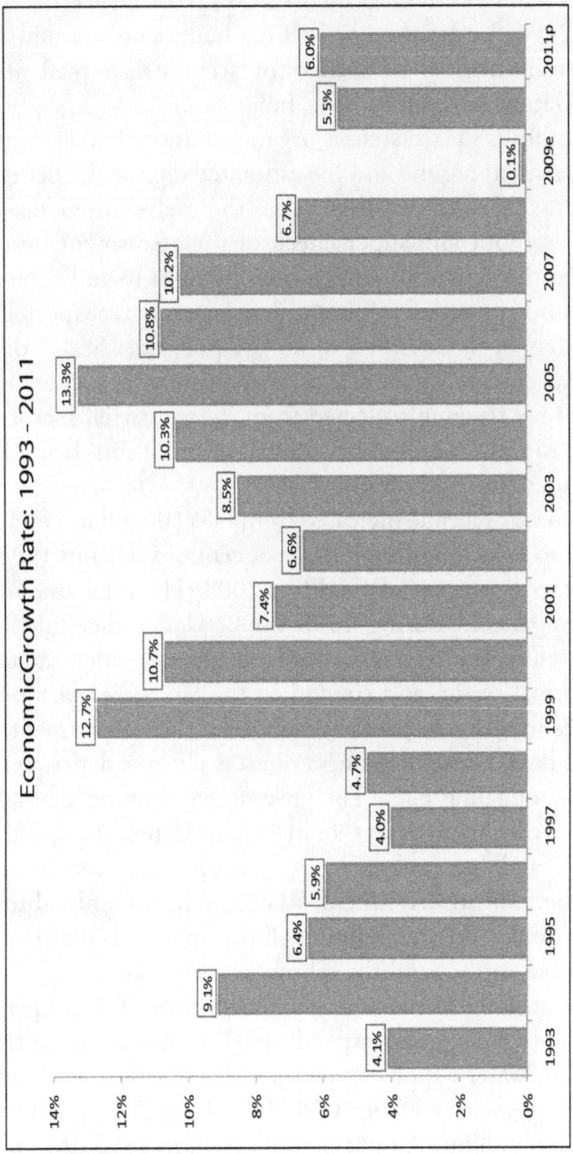

administration. Over the medium-term, the fiscal policy objectives are to enhance revenue performance and re-orient expenditures to pro-poor activities. In order to address these objectives, RGC adopted the Public Financial Management Reform Program (PFMRP), a comprehensive multi-year initiative in late 2004. Under the PFMRP the budget process and management have been streamlined, a new chart of accounts adopted and a new budget nomenclature introduced. (See Table 18.2)

Cambodia's tax system is organized under two assessment systems: the self-assessment regime and the estimated regime. Under the self-assessment regime taxable persons determine themselves their tax liability and pay the tax without any super check of the assessment by the tax authority. However the tax authority reserves the right to audit the return submitted on random basis or if any fraudulent practice is suspected. Self-assessment regime has been extended to all the provinces and 7 districts in Phnom Penh. Revenue from the self-assessment regime accounts for 90 percent of the total tax revenue collected from the industrial sector. In the estimated regime the tax authority obtains information from the assessed and determines the tax liability.

Domestic revenue increased from US$106 million (4.3 per cent of GDP) in 1993 to US$249 million (8.0 per cent of GDP) in 1998 and to US$1.37 billion (13.3 per cent of GDP) in 2008. The total amount of tax collected increased fivefold during 1998–2008. Under the PFMRP measures have been taken to enforce the Law on Taxation, broaden the tax base to include the informal sector, and strengthen the tax audit machinery. Other reform measures include reorganizing the general tax department, modernizing the customs department, creating a non-tax revenue department, and upgrading the anti-smuggling plan. The government requires that all tax collected by revenue receiving agencies should be immediately deposited into the National Treasury, and has prohibited tax exemptions exceeding the limit allowed under the Law on Investment. RGC is fully committed to zero tolerance of tax evasion. Further tax reform will continue with the view to strengthen tax compliance and expand the self-assessment regime.

The steadily improving revenue performance is opening up the fiscal space for higher public expenditures in all sectors, particularly in health, education, water supply, agriculture, irrigation, roads, and energy. Current expenditure increased from US$136 million (5.5 per cent of GDP) in 1993 to US$246 million (7.9 per cent of GDP) in 1998, then to US$930 million (9 per cent of GDP) in 2008. During the last decade, current expenditure more than tripled; it more than doubled after the introduction of the PFMRP during 2004–08.

TABLE 18.2
Cambodia: Fiscal Sector Indicators, 2001–2008 (as a percentage of GDP)

	1994	1999	2001	02	03	04	05	06	07	08
Fiscal sector										
Total revenue	8.3	9.9	10.0	10.6	9.8	10.4	10.6	11.4	12.1	13.3
Tax revenue	5.1	7.2	7.2	7.6	6.8	7.7	7.7	8.0	10.2	11.2
Domestic tax	1.2	4.0	4.8	5.0	4.7	5.3	5.5	5.9	7.3	8.4
Tax on foreign trade	4.0	3.2	2.4	2.5	2.1	2.4	2.2	2.2	2.9	2.8
Non-tax revenue	3.2	2.6	2.7	3.0	2.8	2.5	2.2	2.1	1.8	1.9
Capital revenue	0.0	0.1	0.1	0.1	0.2	0.1	0.6	1.3	0.0	0.2
Total expenditure	14.0	13.6	16.4	18.0	16.2	14.2	13.2	14.1	14.7	15.7
Current expenditure	9.3	8.2	9.3	9.7	9.7	8.5	8.0	8.3	8.6	9.0
Wages and salaries	4.1	3.9	3.3	3.5	3.3	3.0	2.8	2.8	3.0	3.4
Civil administration	4.9	4.5	6.2	6.8	7.1	5.9	5.7	6.0	6.2	6.9
Military and security	4.4	3.5	2.7	2.4	2.2	2.0	1.8	1.7	1.8	1.9
Interest payments	0.01	0.17	0.14	0.16	0.18	0.23	0.21	0.17	0.20	0.19
Internal debt	0.01	0.17	0.14	0.16	0.18	0.23	0.21	0.17	0.20	0.19
Capital expenditure	4.7	5.4	7.0	8.3	6.4	5.7	5.2	5.7	6.1	6.3
Primary balance (incl. grants)	–1.0	1.8	1.1	1.1	1.0	1.9	2.0	1.4	3.4	3.7
Aggregate deficit	–1.0	1.6	1.0	1.0	0.8	1.7	1.8	1.2	3.2	3.5
Aggregate deficit (incl. grants)	5.9	–3.8	–6.0	–7.2	–5.4	–3.8	–2.7	–3.3	–2.8	–2.7
Domestic financing	–0.2	–0.3	0.1	–1.0	0.5	–0.5	–1.5	–1.6	–2.2	–3.3
External financing	6.1	3.9	5.7	7.4	4.9	4.3	4.4	4.8	5.2	5.8

Payroll of civil servants and military and security personnel fell from 6.7 per cent of GDP (72 per cent of current expenditure) in 1994 to 3.6 per cent of GDP (44 per cent of current expenditure) in 2007, but rose to 4.6 per cent of GDP (51 per cent of current expenditure) in 2008. The sharp increase in payroll expenditure in 2008 was due to the 20 per cent salary increase granted to civil servants and military/security personnel and the implementation of civil service reform under the Merit-Based Pay Initiative (MBPI) and Priority Mission Group (PMG) schemes. The increased payroll expenditure is considered crucial for institutional capacity building and should have a positive impact on governance in the medium term.

INFLATION, MONETARY POLICY AND FINANCIAL SECTOR DEVELOPMENTS

Monetary policy is aimed at maintaining price stability. The National Bank of Cambodia (NBC) envisages inflation at less than 5 per cent in the near-term and at about 3.5 per cent over the medium-term. Cambodia is a small, open, dollarized economy. The shallow foreign exchange market and near total dependence on imports for most consumer goods and petroleum products make Cambodia vulnerable to external shocks. Under the current monetary regime, fluctuations of the exchange rate and prices in the world market immediately pass through to the domestic economy. (See Table 18.3)

Cambodia has adopted a managed floating exchange rate regime favouring a gradual accumulation of international reserves by the central bank. Within the context of a dollarized economy, the NBC uses interventions in the foreign exchange market as an indirect instrument of monetary policy. Through interventions in the foreign currency market, the NBC manages the stability of the exchange rate. The tight monetary policy pursued by the NBC and strict fiscal discipline adhered to by the RGC has resulted in a low inflation environment. (See Figure 18.2)

Cambodia witnessed a period of high inflation during 1995–98. Inflation accelerated to 14.7 per cent in 1998 as a result of monetary financing of the budget deficit. The implementation of the fiscal discipline by rationalizing expenditure, mobilizing revenue and stopping the practice of bank financing of the budget deficit, helped Cambodia keep inflation at a low level during 1999–2004. The strong growth of the money supply in circulation, the high prices of oil, and the rise in the cost of food products, especially rice, contributed to a moderate increase in inflation during the past few years. (See Figure 18.3)

TABLE 18.3
Cambodia: Monetary Sector Indicators, 2001–2008

Monetary sector	1994	1999	2001	02	03	04	05	06	07	08
Inflation (last quarter; % growth)	17.8	0.0	–0.5	3.0	0.5	5.8	6.9	3.4	9.7	15.8
Inflation (average; % change)	–0.7	4.0	–0.9	–0.1	1.2	3.9	5.8	4.7	5.9	19.7
GDP deflator (% change)	–4.4	2.0	2.6	0.7	1.8	4.8	6.1	4.6	6.5	12.3
Exchange rate	2,570	3,814	3,924	3,921	3,975	4,016	4,092	4,103	4,068	4,060
Liquidity (growth as a %)	35.1	17.2	22.3	28.9	15.3	30.4	16.1	38.2	62.9	4.8
Velocity (GDP/M2)	15.7	9.2	7.0	5.8	5.6	5.0	5.1	4.3	3.1	3.5
Credit to the private sector (% of M2)	52.6	52.9	41.7	36.7	40.2	42.0	43.9	52.3	56.4	83.4

FIGURE 18.2
Inflation and Exchange Rates

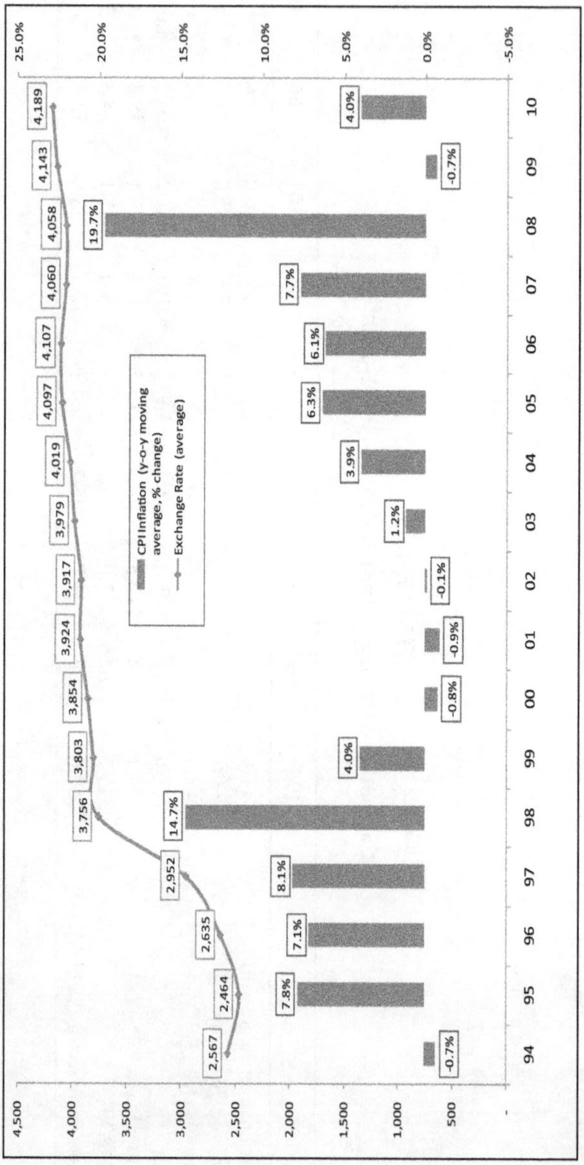

FIGURE 18.3
CPI % Contribution YoY Change

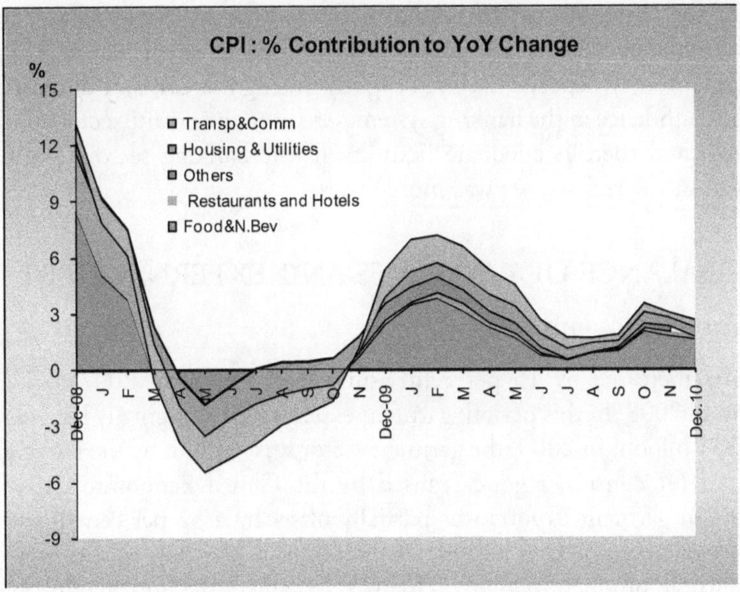

Interest rates for loans in US dollars (mainly in the urban and commercial sectors) and riel denominated loans have declined. The micro-finance loan interest rate has decreased to 36 per cent per annum recently as competition in the sector has increased. The key indicators for private sector credit and loans have shown strong growth in terms of both the number of loans and the total amount lent by commercial banks including microfinance institutions.

Cambodia's financial sector is vibrant, competitive and rapidly expanding. Value added by the financial sector expanded at an average annual rate of 24.7 per cent during past decades, reflecting the rapid financial deepening and the increase in financial intermediation. The rapid increase in the deposits and loans of the commercial banks reflects the growing public confidence in the banking sector. The lending by banks has diversified across the economic sectors and sub-sectors. There was a remarkable increase in the use of banking services by the public during 2006–08, following the entry of new banks in the system, the gradual modernization of the payment services by the major commercial banks, and the initiatives of the government to promote the use of the banking services under the PFMRP. Transparency of financial sector policies and the level playing field for investors have contributed to financial sector development. However Cambodia's financial sector is still evolving and lacks many features of a well developed financial market infrastructure.

In the aftermath of the Global Economic Crisis, Cambodia's banking sector remains resilient; the impact was limited to small banks. Although foreign currency deposits declined slightly during the Crisis, it did not affect public confidence in the banking system. Credit to the private sector continues to grow and there is adequate liquidity in the banking sector. The Crisis' impact on the real sectors was more severe.

BALANCE OF PAYMENTS AND EXTERNAL DEBT

(i) Current Account

Exports increased by 15 per cent from US$4 billion in 2007 to US$4.7 billion in 2008. In this period, garment exports grew marginally by 2 per cent to US$3 billion. In 2009, the garment sector was hard hit by the fall in global demand for consumer goods caused by the Global Economic Crisis. The decline in garment exports was partially offset by a 52 per cent increase in non-garment exports, as a result of the boom in the rice, rubber and other agricultural product markets. The US remained the top export market, accounting for 70 per cent of Cambodia's total exports, followed by the European Union (21 per cent) and Canada (4 per cent). (See Figure 18.4)

Imports increased by 19% from US$5.5 billion in 2007 to US$6.5 billion in 2008. In this period, retained imports increased by 19 per cent to US$6.3 billion. This growth was attributable to a 43 per cent increase in petroleum imports, 16 per cent growth in the imports of other consumer goods, and 31 per cent increase in imports for re-exports. Cambodia's trade deficit increased by 32 per cent from US$1.3 billion in 2007 to US$1.8 billion in 2008, mainly due to the increase in the US$ value of imported petroleum products. (See Table 18.4)

Services receipts increased by 6 per cent from US$1.5 billion in 2007 to US$1.6 billion in 2008. Net services posted a surplus of US$587 million, a decline of 4 per cent. Transportation and travel services grew by 14 per cent and 8 per cent respectively. The number of tourist arrivals increased by 5 per cent and reached 2.1 million in 2008. Tourism receipts were estimated at US$1.5 billion in 2008. The surplus in the capital and financial account increased by 41 per cent from US$1,184.2 million (13.5 per cent of GDP) in 2007 to US$1,670.2 million (16.2 per cent of GDP) in 2008. There was an overall balance of payment surplus of US$395.2 million (3.4 per cent of GDP) in 2008.

FIGURE 18.4
Trade Balance

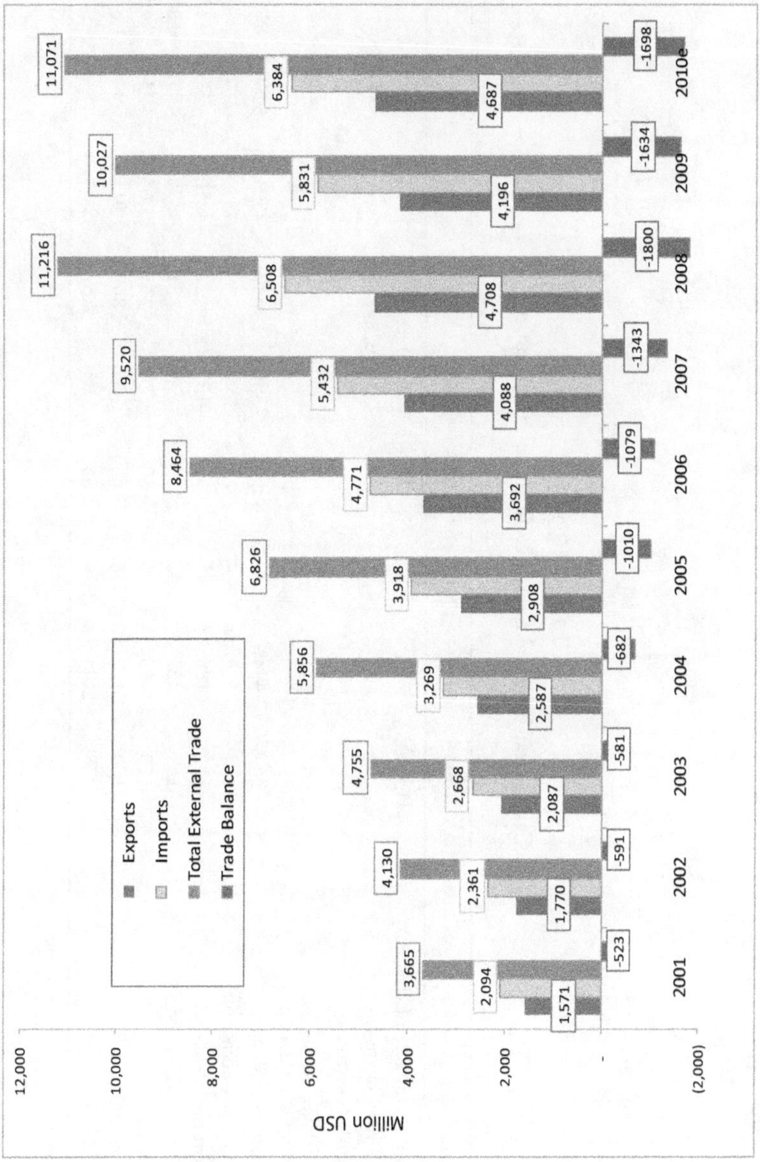

TABLE 18.4
Cambodia: External Sector Indicators, 2001–2008

External sector	1994	1999	2001	02	03	04	05	06	07	08
Domestic exports (as a % of change)	1315	47	15	13	16	29	13	28	11	9
Imports (as a % of change)	55	37	8	11	10	28	20	21	14	23
Imports (garments excluded, as a % of change)	55	28	6	8	8	29	27	21	16	32
Balance of current transactions (Excl. transfers) US$ Mns	−347	−444	−349	−359	−450	−440	−591	−526	−730	−1,705
Balance of current transactions (incl. transfers), US$ Mns	−112	−188	−45	−47	−137	−122	−256	−77	−332	−1,205
Direct investments (US$, Mns)	162	221	142	139	74	121	375	483	866	785
Aggregate balance	−113	−49	45	60	33	31	65	193	426	511
Gross reserves (US$, Mns)	100	422	548	663	737	809	915	1,097	1,616	2,104
(As months of imports)	1.78	2.84	2.79	3.05	3.08	2.67	2.55	2.54	3.29	3.51

(ii) Capital Account

External financing, especially Official Development Assistance (ODA), has played a crucial role in laying the foundation for Cambodia's economic growth. ODA, including grants, loans and technical assistance has grown from US$500 million in 1993 to US$700 million in 2008. During this period, on average, bilateral and multilateral partners pledged ODA of $450 million per year. Between 1993 and 2007, ODA disbursements amounted to $7.6 billion or $507 million a year on average.[2] As a borrowing strategy RGC gives priority to grants over concessionary loans. The RGC has generally avoided commercial borrowing. This strategy has helped maintain Cambodia's debt at a sustainable level. (See Figure 18.5)

FDI is playing an increasingly important role in Cambodia's economic development; FDI approvals amounted to US$867 million in 2007. During 1994–July 2008, the Council for the Development of Cambodia (CDC) approved FDI totalling US$21.2 billion. However, only US$4.2 billion of Foreign Direct Investment (FDI) has been disbursed. Both FDI and portfolio investment increased during 2003–08 reflecting the steady improvement in the investment climate and the dominant role played by the private sector in promoting social and economic development in Cambodia.

(iii) Gross International Reserves

In a dollarized economy such as Cambodia, gross international reserves (GIR) play a crucial role in instilling public confidence in the banking system. Cambodia's GIR doubled from US$1 billion in mid-2006 to US$2 billion in mid-2008. These reserves are held in various instruments, including overnight investments, short and medium term deposits, medium term notes and investment grade securities issued by highly rated non-resident institutions. By end 2008, investments (excluding gold and SDRs) amounted to US$2.25 billion, up 27.5 per cent from the level recorded at end 2007. The rapid increase in GIR reflects continued good export performance, increase in FDI and acceleration of capital inflows. This level of international reserves is sufficient to cover 3.9 months of imports of goods. (See Figure 18.6)

(iv) External Debt

As of December 31, 2006, Cambodia's external debt, including outstanding interest arrears, totalled US$3.2 billion (43.3 per cent of GDP). Cambodia's two main creditors are Russia and the United States. After rescheduling

FIGURE 18.5
Balance of Payments

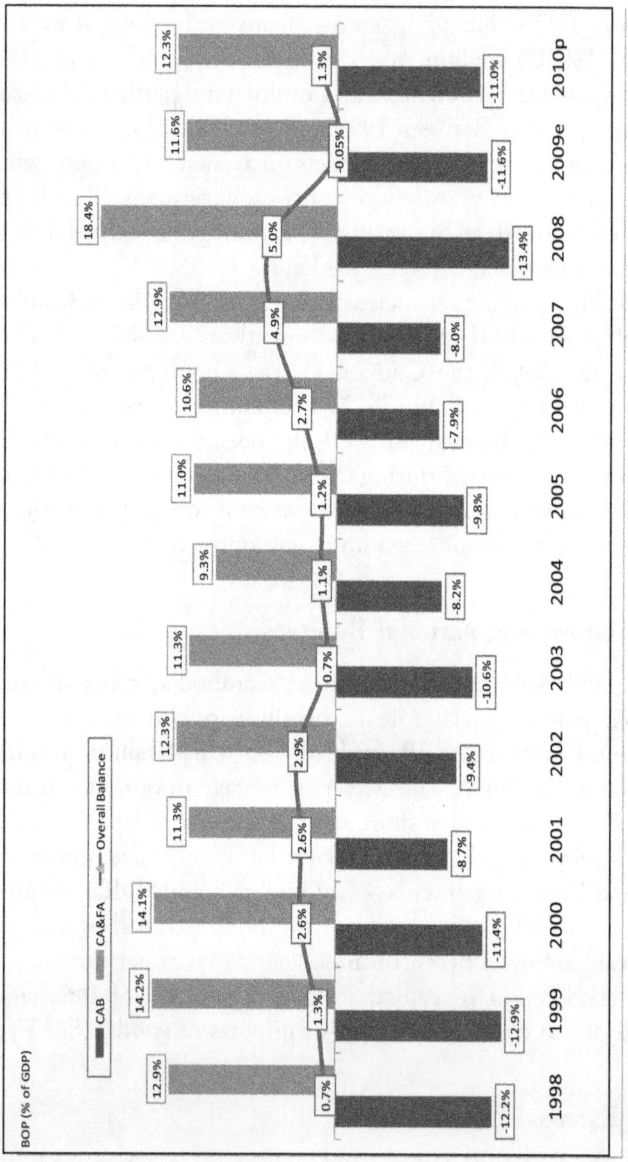

FIGURE 18.6
International Reserves

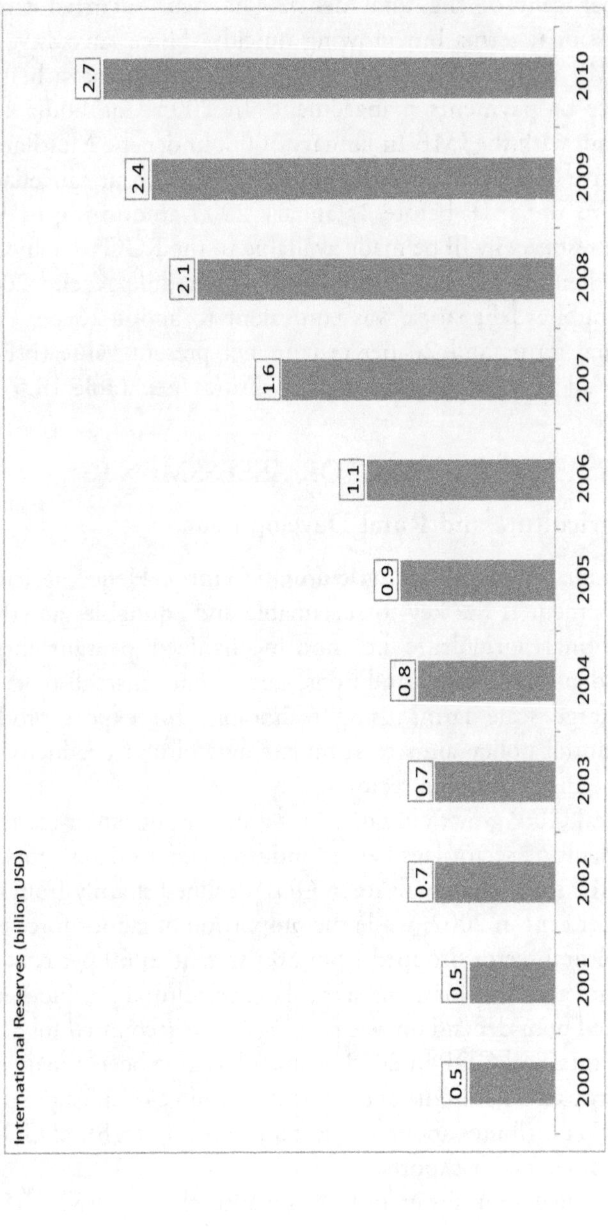

debt with both creditors, the total debt for Cambodia amounted to US$2.1 billion (29 per cent of GDP). The debt owed to multilateral creditors (WB, ADB, IFAD and OPEC) amounted to US$1.1 billion at the end of 2006 (52 per cent of the total debt). The debt incurred since 1993 is on concessional terms but growing quickly. Three successive programs with the IMF in a total amount of US$103 million have helped Cambodia's balance of payments management. In 2003 Cambodia exited the third program with the IMF. In January 2006, under the Multilateral Debt Relief Initiative (MDRI), the IMF granted a 100 per cent cancellation of the debt owed to the IMF before 1 January 2005 amounting to US$82 million. These resources will be made available to the RGC to help Cambodia reach the Millennium Development Goals on schedule. At end-2008, Cambodia's total public debt stock was equivalent to about 26 per cent of GDP in nominal terms and 20 per cent in net present value (NPV) terms, with nearly all of it owed to external creditors. (See Table 18.5)

SECTOR ASSESSMENTS

(i) Agriculture and Rural Development

Cambodia is largely an agricultural country. Hence agriculture and rural development is the key to sustainable and equitable growth in Cambodia. Traditional agriculture i.e. non-mechanized peasant farming, strongly dependent on climate conditions, carried out on small plots of land coexists with large scale farms using technology for export production. RGC's agricultural policy aims to stimulate agricultural productivity and increase income in the farming sector.

Real GDP growth has increased annually, but inter-sectorally the growth in agriculture sector lags behind industry and service sectors. During 1989–2007 the share of agriculture in GDP declined sharply from 45.8 per cent to 29.7 per cent in 2007, while the proportion of labour force employed in the agricultural sector dropped from 80 per cent to 60 per cent.

Rice accounts for about a third of agricultural production. 80 per cent of the rural poor depend on rice farming.[3] Rice accounted for about 10 per cent of the total real GDP in 2008. Rubber has long been a mainstay of industrial cash crops in Cambodia and a potential source of substantial export income. Fishery contributes about 10 per cent to the agricultural GDP. Fish is one of Cambodia's major exports.

The key input for increasing agricultural productivity is irrigation. Good quality seed and chemical fertilizer, skilful management of farms, use of

TABLE 18.5
Key Indicators of the Financial Sector

	2000	2001	2002	2003	2004	2005	2006	2007
Real GDP Growth (%)	8.8	8.1	6.6	8.5	10.3	13.3	10.8	10.2
Agriculture	35.9	34.3	31.1	32.0	29.4	30.7	30.1	29.7
Industry	21.9	22.3	24.3	25.0	25.6	25.0	26.2	24.9
Service	37.1	38.4	39.3	38.2	39.3	39.1	38.7	38.5
Inflation (yearly average)	(0.8)	(0.9)	(0.1)	1.2	3.9	5.8	4.7	5.8
Interest rate (dollar)								
– on savings deposits	2.3	1.6	1.5	1.3	0.9	0.9	1.0	1.0
– on time deposits	3.7	2.7	18.6	18.2	17.3	17.3	16.2	16.0
– on loans	17.4	15.0	2.8	2.6	2.4	2.4	3.3	4.9
Broad money (%)								
M2	26.9	20.4	31.1	15.3	30.0	16.1	38.2	62.9
Velocity	7.9	7.7	6.4	6.0	5.4	5.4	4.8	3.1
(PIB/M2)	12.6	13.0	15.6	16.5	18.6	18.7	20.8	32.3
Credit to the private sector and deposits								
Loans	6.4	6.0	6.3	7.3	8.6	9.4	12.3	18.3
Deposits	9.5	10.4	12.7	13.3	15.2	14.8	18.2	26.8
Ratio loans/ deposits	67.3	57.6	49.9	55.2	56.5	64.0	67.9	63.9
Ratio loans/ assets					42.9	45.6	46.1	
Commercial banks								
Number of loans	86,757	105,347	123,937	145,161	164,931	197,337		
Value of loans (in millions dollars)	269.3	360.7	482.7	598.4	882.3	2,480.0		
NPL	8.0	15.00	14.00	10.00	8.00	9.80	3.4	
Microfinance								
Number of loans	409,963	328,295	265,044	322,056	366,962	471,009	624,089	
Value of loans (in millions dollars)	35.9	51.3	32.6	40.8	49.2	92.2	160.4	

BOX 2: Tobacco and Nurseries

The main activity of British and American Tobacco (BAT) in Cambodia is the integrated production of cigarettes, from the tobacco plantations to marketing. It employs a regular staff of 485, plus 1,300 seasonal workers on its plantations, as well as at its Kampong Cham work centre, drying facility in Takhmau, and factory and headquarters in Phnom Penh. The company has made a corporate investment of $25 million.

BAT currently accounts for 50 per cent of the market, or 3 billion cigarettes per year. Cultivated areas: 800 hectares out of a total of 1,500 hectares in Cambodia. Its yields went from 750 to 1,950 kg/hectare and the quantity produced is 2,000 tons per year on average. BAT buys tobacco from the 747 farmers who work under contract with the company. BAT has agreed to buy the tobacco produced, thus ensuring the farmers a 40 per cent return on their investment. Currently, the tobacco produced is of average quality. Imports, which accounted for 55 per cent of tobacco used, are down to 20 per cent. Exports total 500 tons per year.

modern equipment and good soil fertility cannot contribute to high yields of rice if proper water management is lacking. Rice yields have varied considerably in recent years and correlate closely with climatic conditions. In 2008, the average rice yield in Cambodia reached a historic record of 2.7 tons per ha, mainly due to good climatic conditions and the irrigation systems put in place by the government.

In 2006, irrigated rice accounted for 29 per cent of the total rice-growing area, compared with annual average of 20 per cent during the five preceding years.[4] The Government has been emphasizing irrigation development as a strategy to tackle rural backwardness. Investment by the government in irrigation projects increased by an annual average of 2 per cent during 2003–06 and reached $10 million in 2006.

The lack of infrastructure, especially roads, constitutes a major obstacle to the development of rural areas. Without an adequate rural road infrastructure delays would occur in accessing markets resulting in loss of agricultural supply to the market and product quality at delivery. Consequently, it is necessary to invest in rural infrastructure through both public and private initiatives.

For infrastructure to yield the intended benefits, it is necessary to adopt the integrated rural development approach. Integrated rural development comprises provision of healthcare, roads, other infrastructure, extension services, credit, inputs, and marketing as a total package. Strengthening rural banks and micro-finance institutions is also crucial for implementing the integrated rural development strategy. The RGC's main institutional mechanism for channelling credit to rural sector is the Rural Development Bank funded by the State budget. However as part of the implementation of the Financial Sector Strategy, the government is encouraging private sector financial institutions, particularly the microfinance institutions to expand their activities in rural areas.

INDUSTRY, PRIVATE SECTOR DEVELOPMENT AND EMPLOYMENT

Cambodia's industrialization followed the pattern of many developing countries, starting with the development of light industry (e.g. textiles, garments) and processing of agricultural products (e.g. rice milling) and gradually moving to heavier industries (e.g. mining, oil and gas exploration and production and construction). A number of motor vehicle manufacturers have established assembly facilities for motorcycles in the country. In the medium term Cambodia is likely to diversify to IT, and assembly and production of electric and electronic equipment.

International mining firms see Cambodia as a new frontier in mining. The mining industry grew by almost 15 per cent per annum on average during 1994–2008. The main contributions came from oil exploration in the Gulf of Thailand and mineral exploration. This includes exploration of iron ore in Preah Vihear, and bauxite, copper and gold in the northeast. During the last decade, mining accounted for 0.2–0.4 per cent of GDP. This share is expected to increase as more and more companies move from exploration to development and production.

After achieving independence in 1953, Cambodia pursued a mixed economy model in which both State property and private property were recognized and allowed to coexist. Agriculture, light industry, and commercial services were left to the private sector, while heavy industry and finance were controlled by the public sector. Large SOEs were created in the 1960s. At that time, Cambodia pursued an import substitution policy in light industry and agricultural processing industries under an umbrella of strong protection and government subsidies. These industries were often allowed to function as monopolies.

In early 1989 with the introduction of the policy of economic liberalization almost 90 per cent of privately owned medium and large-size industrial enterprises which became dormant during the Khmer Rouge regime were revived. However, SOEs still formed the core of the Cambodian industrial structure.[5]

Cambodia's remarkable achievements in economic development during the last decade were driven by the vibrant private sector, with the public sector providing necessary support. The number of private firms registering with the government is increasing every year; the number rose from 720 in 2003 to 2,890 in 2007. Modernization of private sector firms is ongoing and is seen in the increasing proportion of firms using email and websites; and rapid growth in technology-based activities such as telecoms and banking. Some capital intensive industries, such as aluminium can manufacture are also emerging. The Cambodian private sector exudes optimism but lacks diversification and is burdened by an unorganized and large informal sector operating mostly as family businesses and lacking commercial orientation. The informal sector seldom pays taxes and has limited recourse to the banking system.

Cambodia suffers from poor infrastructure and high cost of utilities. Labour costs are rising steadily without a matching increase in productivity. Electricity prices, transportation and port handling costs in Cambodia, are high when compared to other countries in Asia. While the still cheap labour is an advantage, this alone will not be sufficient to attract foreign investors as large-scale producers such as India or China also enjoy a similar advantage.

Industrial development can commence straightaway in regions with adequate infrastructure and supportive facilities. On this basis, the RGC has formulated a plan for the promotion of three poles of development: Phnom Penh, Siem Reap and Sihanoukville. The government has launched the concept of growth corridors aimed at developing the areas along the road networks linking the different parts of the country and turn them into agricultural, industrial, and trade development zones. The growth corridors will get priority in the allocation of resources for physical infrastructure, such as telecommunications, water supply and electricity, as well as in the development of other ancillary facilities including social, banking and legal infrastructure.

Thailand and Viet Nam, have improved their competitiveness by concentrating infrastructure development in industrial estates. Cambodia has made far less progress in the development of Special Economic Zones (SEZs) and has few incentives to offer to potential investors to encourage them to locate their production facilities in the country. Utility costs are high, particularly electricity. Transport costs are substantially higher than most of the neighbouring nations, particularly in Phnom Penh. Realizing that the SEZs will be crucial to economic diversification, in December 2005 RGC adopted a sub-decree on the Establishment and Management of Special Economic Zones. The sub decree covered the development of export processing zones and free trade zones. RGC has since approved a total of 21 SEZs. These SEZs are located along the border with Thailand and Viet Nam (Koh Kong, Poipet, Savet, Phnom Den), and at Sihanoukville and Phnom Penh. Of the 21, six have commenced operations.

RGC's employment policy centres on (i) measures for enhancing the capacities and opportunities of the poor for employment; (ii) improvement of work force management practices and worker employability; (iii) strengthening the effectiveness and transparency of the employment market; and (iv) promotion of self-employment in both rural and urban communities. These measures will be accompanied by the promotion of labour-intensive activities (LIA) in construction, restoration, and upkeep of social and economic infrastructure. The LIA approach is expected to be intensively applied in works programs of the government and the local authorities.

The resumption of high industrial growth in the post Crisis period requires more concerted action aimed at strengthening competitiveness and improving business climate to diversify the production base. The effort toward full WTO compliance and lowering the cost of doing business is ongoing. However, the number of required new laws, amendments to existing laws and regulations is extensive. The implementation of post-clearance audits and simplified valuation and cargo processing procedures has reduced the time required for customs clearance. Further reforms should aim at improving basic logistics infrastructure and enhancing labour skills, as well as expanding market access through trade agreements and reducing the cost of doing business, particularly through streamlining investment approvals and customs procedures.

SERVICES AND UTILITIES

The service sector's value added grew at an average rate of 8.6 per cent during 1994–2007. This high growth was attributable to the expansion of tourism, transport and communications, banking and real estate. The share of the services sector has declined slightly from 39.4 per cent of GDP in 1994 to 38.5 per cent in 2008. The expansion of tourism and hotel industry continues, with a growth rate of 14.3 per cent in 2008. RGC is emphasizing stronger links between tourism and development of the rural economy, in order to enable the poor to benefit from tourism expansion. For example, the government intends to transform the Siem Reap region into a green belt for agricultural production so that strong backward linkages of tourism with local agriculture could be established.

Transportation and communications grew at the average annual rate of 8.5 per cent during 1994–2007. During the last 15 years, the RGC completed the reconstruction and rehabilitation of the national highway network and embarked on the improvement of provincial and rural infrastructure to facilitate more effective participation of rural communities in the growth process through better connectivity with urban markets.

In the last decade, the telecom sector has seen major structural changes including liberalization of markets and introduction of new technology, particularly the use of mobile phones. The ongoing development of networks and telecommunication services is of crucial importance for the modernization of Cambodia's economy and its integration with the rest of the world. At the macroeconomic level, the telecommunications has become an essential engine of economic growth. The value added of the telecommunications sector has more than quadrupled, rising from US$15.6 million or 0.56 per cent of the GDP in 1994 to US$65.5 million or 0.9 per cent of the GDP in 2006.

The energy potential of Cambodia is still not fully known. A thorough exploration and mapping of the geographical distribution of all available sources of energy is needed for preparing a plan for the systematic development of the energy sector. The availability of reasonably priced power is a key ingredient of rural development, particularly in such activities as irrigation, processing of agricultural products, and SME development. The high cost of rural electricity is an important reason for the slow development of the Cambodian rural economy. (See Table 18.6)

EDUCATION

Cambodia's educational system was totally revamped in 1979 with the establishment of the Ministry of National Education. The first primary

TABLE 18.6
GDP and Sector Growth (%)

(at constant 2000 prices, in percentage)	Share of GDP		Growth			
	2009	2010	2002–2007	2008	2009	2010e
Agriculture	28.0	27.4	5.6	5.7	5.4	4.0
of which crops	14.9	14.7	8.9	6.6	5.8	5.7
Industry	26.7	26.6	14.2	4.0	–9.5	13.5
of which textile	13.8	15.5	17.1	2.2	–9.0	18.5
of which construction	6.8	4.9	16.7	5.8	5.0	–25.5
Services	40.8	39.0	10.0	9.0	2.3	3.1
of which trade	8.9	9.0	6.2	9.4	4.2	7.1
of which hotels and restaurant	4.6	4.9	11.9	9.8	1.8	11.2
of which transport & communication	6.7	6.5	7.1	7.1	3.9	8.0
of which real estate	7.2	5.8	13.7	5.0	–2.5	–15.8
Net taxes	—	—	—	—	—	—
GDP	100	100	10.7	6.7	0.1	5.9

school was reopened in Phnom Penh in September 1979, followed by the reopening of the Sisowath High School. In the area of higher education, the Faculty of Medicine was the first to be reopened to respond to a multitude of health issues neglected during the Khmer Rouge period. In 1981, the Institute of Technology staffed with Soviet faculty was re-opened to respond to the need for Cambodia's reconstruction. However, by the late 1990's the national education service lacked policy and institutional coherence. The services delivered were not always equitable and did not always provide full national coverage. (See Figure 18.7)

Cambodia's education reform began in 1999. The first steps comprised the formulation of an education policy and a strategic framework that established the overarching priorities of the sector, goals for the sub-sectors, and a framework for allocating expenditures over the medium term. The Education Strategic Plan (ESP) prepared in 2001 was reviewed periodically to fine tune the programs so that they complied with the strategic priorities. Following an evaluation of the ESP, a more detailed education system support program (ESSP) was prepared with a view to implementing a joint action plan prepared in consultation with all the stakeholders, mainly RGC, donors, and NGOs. The reform focused on primary and secondary education.

HEALTH

The health sector in Cambodia is characterized by underdeveloped infrastructure and low quality service provision. Healthcare staffing is in short supply, and of increasingly unequal distribution due to disinclination of staff to work in the rural and remote areas of the country. The results of the perceptions survey of communities on access to healthcare services and the quality of care confirm this assessment. The RGC has given high priority to the provision of health services in the Rectangular Strategy since lack of access of the poor to health services worsens the sense of deprivation caused by income poverty. Key health parameters are rightly recognized as Millennium Development Goals by the UN. (See Table 18.7)

INTERNATIONAL ECONOMIC RELATIONS AND REGIONAL COOPERATION

The principal goal of Cambodia's foreign economic policy is to expand and strengthen economic ties and international cooperation through the integration of the Cambodian economy into the regional and world economy. This goal is designed to utilize the advantages of international division of labour to

FIGURE 18.7
Net and Gross Enrolment Rates at Primary School Level

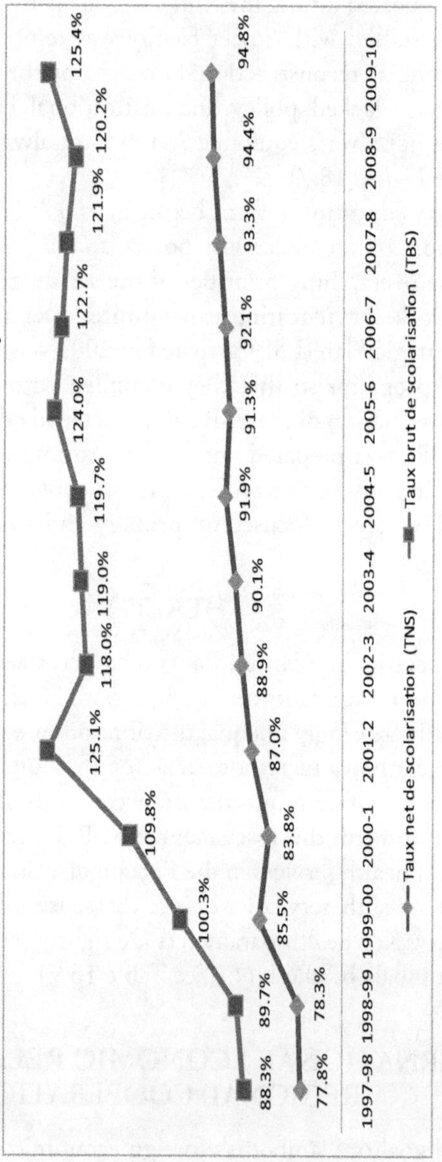

TABLE 18.7
Health Indicators

Life	CDHS 2000	CDHS 2005
Live expectancy (years)		
Female	58	64
Male	54	58
Mortality rates (per 1,000 live births)		
Infant mortality	95	66
Child mortality	33	19
Under 5 mortality	124	83
Maternal Mortality		
(per 100,000 live births)	437	472

Source: *Cambodia Demographic and Health Survey* 2005; NIS.

promote economic development and improve the welfare of the population. Since the late 1980s and especially the early 1990s, Cambodia has embarked on trade liberalization and regional integration. Trading companies were established in the private sector allowing foreign participation up to 49 per cent. Since 1993, licensing requirement has been dispensed with for the import of most goods undertaken by registered companies. A pragmatic trade policy is crucial for Cambodia's integration into the world economy.

Cambodia was admitted as the 10th member of the Association of Southeast Asian Nations (ASEAN) in April 1999. The RGC has strengthened its efforts to meet the demands of ASEAN membership. Domestic laws are being changed to conform to ASEAN standards in trade, finance, commerce and investment. Under the ASEAN Free Trade Agreement (AFTA), Cambodia is firmly committed to reduce the tariff to no more than 5 per cent on the majority of its tariff lines by 2010 and on the remaining tariff lines (which are mostly sensitive agricultural products) by 2017, within the framework of the Common Effective Preferential Tariff Agreement (CEPT). Cambodia will need rapid and comprehensive integration into AFTA/CEPT framework to bring it on par with its neighbours for improving the prospects for attracting ASEAN oriented investment originating in the region. This suggests the need for accelerating the tariff reduction program. A speedy implementation of CEPT tariff rates will also improve the predictability of Cambodia's trade policies.

Cambodia applied for accession to the World Trade Organization (WTO) in December 1994 under Article XII of the Marrakech Agreement establishing the WTO. On 22 July 2003 Cambodia submitted its acceptance of the terms and conditions of membership set out in the Accession Protocol, which was approved by the WTO Ministerial Conference in Cancun on 11 September 2003 subject to ratification by Cambodia. Cambodia ratified the agreement on 13 October 2004 and became the 148th member of the WTO. Cambodia and Nepal are the earliest LDCs to have acceded to the WTO, since WTO's transformation from the GATT in 1995.

Foreign trade has helped Cambodia to expand its markets and reap the benefits of economies of scale through export. In particular exporting enables the productive use of land and labour resources hitherto left unused due to the limited domestic market. Imports have allowed the Cambodian consumer to purchase high quality goods at lower prices thereby adding to economic welfare.

The RGC recognizes that Cambodia's successful integration with the region and the world will help create an appropriate environment for sustained growth. In the push for the closer integration of Cambodia into the region the top priority is narrowing the development gap between the member countries of ASEAN. To speed up the process, Cambodia will build its institutional capacity to implement joint initiatives with its neighbours, such as the "Four countries-One economy" initiative, the development of economic growth triangles and the creation of trans-border free trade zones.

RECTANGULAR STRATEGY FOR GROWTH, EMPLOYMENT, EQUITY AND EFFICIENCY

RGC's agenda is not limited to fighting poverty. Its vision of development is one of social cohesion, with a state-of-the-art education system and abundant cultural wealth. Its objective is to encourage economic growth, generate employment for the Cambodian work force, guarantee equity and social justice, and improve the efficiency of the public sector through implementation of the Governance Action Plan for in-depth, coordinated, and consistent reforms at all levels and in all sectors. The positive results obtained in implementing the Rectangular Strategy have strengthened the overall confidence in a bright future for Cambodia. Solid foundation has been laid for the development of the private sector, trade, investment, and tourism sectors, all generators of employment and income for Cambodians.

The Rectangular Strategy is an integrated structure of interlocking rectangles, as seen in the figure below. (See Figure 18.8)

Public sector reform and good governance are at the heart of the Rectangular Strategy. Cambodia has begun the implementation of a strategy to remodel the structure and size of the civil service and improve the quality

FIGURE 18.8
The Rectangular Strategy

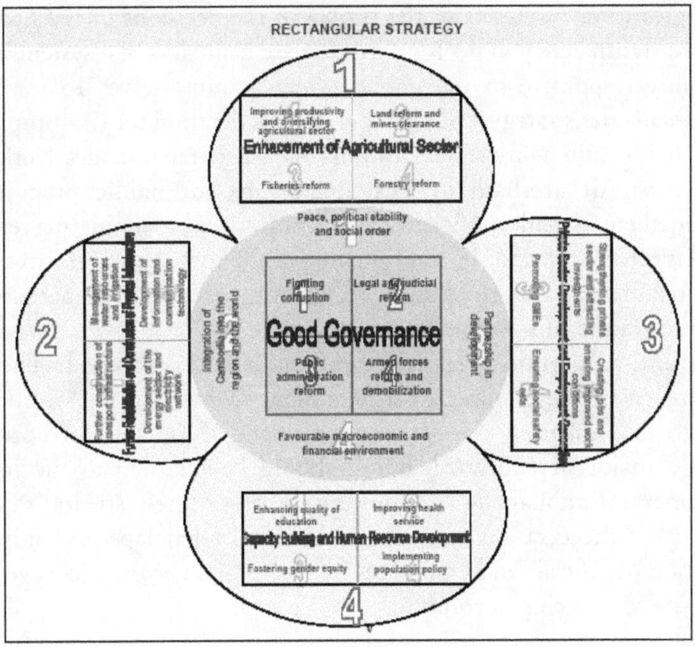

of public services. The building of institutional capacity and technical expertise within the administration is essential for success of the reforms. Cambodia is expanding e-government by encouraging increased use of electronic media and methods in public administration. E-government helps to improve administrative efficiency and flexibility to respond and adapt to rapid changes in the regional and international environment and the demands of an increasingly dynamic private sector.

The government is reforming civil service salary policy using two fundamental approaches: first, any changes in salary scales must respect the principle of relativity between the different categories of employees (political, civil service, military, and security officers). Second, these changes must be financially viable over the long term, in keeping with the fiscal framework. As a result, salary increases remain subject to availability of public revenue. RGC pledges a salary increase of 10 per cent to 15 per cent per year. Available funds will be allocated to priority areas by means of instruments such as the PMG programme, and through a system of compensation for complementing the basic salary.

An anti-corruption strategy must be accompanied by efforts to improve the quality of public services with full accountability of public officials for timely delivery of services. A specific program to promote justice and social equity, greater involvement of the people in the decisions of the State, and increased transparency in decision making are hallmarks of a system of good governance responsive to the public, which it must serve. To meet these requirements the strategy will give special consideration to: (i) improvement of the living and working conditions of magistrates, court clerks, and prosecutors; (ii) overhaul of legal documents for public procurement; (iii) strengthening market efficiency and performance by eliminating repressive control mechanisms; and (iv) continuation of the civil service reform through professionalization and emphasis on improving efficiency accompanied by better motivation of government employees.

An anti-corruption legal framework is being established. The RGC recognizes, as its development partners suggest, the need for an integrated approach to combating corruption. Enactment of the anti-corruption law will be a major step forward, but it should be followed up by its strict enforcement. Rationalizing administrative procedures, streamlining and modernizing the taxation system, elimination of red tape and improving motivation of officials and employees by means of an economic wage can all contribute to reducing corruption.

Notes

1. World Bank, 1992.
2. Total ODA during 1993–2008 was distributed as follows: 45% for technical assistance; 40% for investment projects; 8% for budget support; and 7% for food aid and emergency relief. UN agencies provided US$642 million (8.4%) of the development assistance; ADB — US$745 million (9.8%); WB — US$541 million (7.1%); IMF — US$241 million (3.2%); members of the European Union — US$1.8 billion (23.8%); other bilateral donors — US$2.9 billion (38.3%); and NGOs — US$652 million (8.6%).
3. 90% of the poor live in the countryside.
4. Source: Ministry of Water Resources and Meteorology,
5. In Cambodia, a state-owned company is a company whose capital is held solely by the State.

19

CHANGING THE COURSE OF CAMBODIA THROUGH THE BUSINESS OF EMPOWERING PEOPLE[1]

Ing Kantha Phavi and Winta Ghebreab

INTRODUCTION

Human resource development is globally considered a key business process to enhance performance. Women's empowerment is not always a crosscutting element of human resource development and this is a missed opportunity for government and business. Research shows that closing the gender gap in education and unleashing women's economic potential, may well be the highest return investment available in the rich and developing world.[2] As Cambodia is introducing new economic policies to boost sustainable growth, vast investment opportunities are becoming available to businesses. With an eye on both economic progress and development, this article discusses ways of doing business that are not only profitable but also bring equality and equity.

POST- CONFLICT CAMBODIA

Cambodia experienced almost three decades of conflict and instability between 1970 and 1998. During this period, Cambodia's physical, human and social capital was devastated. Its infrastructure, including roads, electricity and irrigation systems, was destroyed. Cambodians suffered from poor health due to malnutrition and lack of health services, especially during the Khmer Rouge regime. The country's intellectual class and educated people were either killed or forced to flee, while young Cambodians were unable to benefit from education. Gender inequality and gender based violence were prevalent in pre-war Cambodia; but the three decades of civil war seem to have increased violence.[3]

Cambodia has come a long way since the 1991 Paris Peace Agreement. The country has become politically stable and has initiated political, social and economic transformation. Since 1992 it has held four national and local multi-party elections. It is currently implementing its third five-year National Strategic Development Plan (NSDP). The NSDP is aligned with the United Nations Millennium Development Goals (MDGs) and the principles of good governance, pro-poor poverty reduction and gender equality. The government has initiated major reforms in order to deliver on these commitments, including public administration reforms, financial reforms, and a decentralisation and de-concentration process to enhance service delivery structures at all levels.

Furthermore, the government introduced a free market economy and has integrated Cambodia into the world economy. For more than a decade, the government has generated high economic growth sustained over an extended period of time. Moreover, the income per capita has more than doubled over the period of 1997 to 2007, while low inflation and a stable exchange rate have been maintained.[4] Key to economic growth has been foreign investment. Cambodia continues its successes in attracting investment for business as well as in mobilizing resources for development assistance. New investments coming from emerging markets and donors, such as Kuwait, China and South Korea, demonstrate this.[5] The drivers of the economic growth have been construction; the export-oriented garment industry as well as the tourism industry. These sectors were seriously hit by the economic crises but have shown recovery since late 2009. The agricultural sector was more resilient to the crises and has shown steady increase in output.

Years of high economic growth, development assistance and the Royal Government of Cambodia's (RGC) commitment to improvement have combined to yield success. There is a significant reduction in overall poverty levels from 47 per cent in 1993, 30 per cent in 2007 and 26 per cent in 2010, showing a poverty reduction of 1 per cent per annum. Life expectancy rates for women and men[6] have increased substantially and major improvements in health and education indicators have taken place.[7] Positive changes are also visible in gender equality. There is greater awareness of women's rights and the concept of gender equality. Since the early 1990s, the Ministry of Women's Affairs has promoted gender mainstreaming of government policies and programs which have contributed to a wider awareness among the public and the incorporation of gender equality commitments in the government's development plans and policies. Positive results are seen throughout Cambodian society, an example of which is the changing perceptions about violence against women. Compared to a 2005 baseline study, fewer respondents perceived violent acts as acceptable in 2009.[8] Also, women's economic status has improved substantially through increased labour and entrepreneurship opportunities for women; Cambodia enjoys high rates of female labor force participation and a high level of female entrepreneurship.

Despite strong progress, yearly poverty profiles in Cambodia show that the benefits of growth have not been equally distributed. Income inequality has increased between 2004 and 2007.[9] A fourth of the population still lives below the poverty line and approximately twelve per cent of the Cambodian population face hunger and food insecurity. The economic crises in combination with the increased prices of food and petrol have caused reversals of some of the gains in poverty reduction. These price shocks cannot be shielded by Cambodia's nascent social safety net.[10] Basic health care, education, employment and other social services are simply not sufficiently available to the predominantly rural population and this is limiting their economic potential.

Cambodia's socio-economic strategy (the Rectangular Strategy Phase II, 2008–2013) is designed to build upon the advances made to alleviate poverty and to address the continuing concerns listed above. The Rectangular Strategy focuses on four priority areas.

The first priority is to enhance the agriculture sector which is of high importance to sustainable economic growth, employment generation and food security. The agricultural sector accounted for over one-third of the nation's gross domestic product (GDP) and a livelihood to almost two-thirds of Cambodia's mainly rural workforce.[11] Women constitute over half of the workforce in agriculture.[12] Statistics show that three-quarters of all rural workers only have a primary education or less and no skills training other than by way of family tradition in agriculture.[13]

The second priority area is rehabilitation and construction of physical infrastructure. This will facilitate business development and access to services. Improving infrastructure is a necessity to address the third priority, which is the private sector development and employment generation.

The garment industry will play a large role in meeting the third priority. It accounts for sixteen per cent of Cambodia's GDP and ninety-five per cent of Cambodia's exports.[14] The garment industry is reliant on female workers, with over eighty per cent of the labour engaged in the industry being women. Given that one-third of the female labour force is employed in the garment industry, one can easily understand its substantial contribution to women's labour force participation and poverty reduction in Cambodia. The monthly flow of remittances from the garment workers to the countryside has an important and substantial anti-poverty effect and contributes directly to sustaining over one million people. Many of the workers are young uneducated women from rural areas, working under harsh conditions. Only nine-per cent of women in the labour force have more than a primary school education. Over seventy-per cent of women workers are either illiterate or have less than a complete primary school education.[15]

The other significant industries, such as tourism, transportation and communications often require human resources that possess a higher level of education and foreign-language skills, leaving the predominantly less educated labour force at a disadvantage. Therefore, paid employment opportunities for women outside of the garment industry are limited and few women also occupy professional and decision-making positions at national and sub-national level.[16]

The majority of enterprises in Cambodia are micro-enterprise sized and mostly in the informal sector of the economy.[17] Despite their size, they contribute to approximately sixty-two-per cent of the GDP. Entrepreneurs in Cambodia face significant difficulties in expanding their business. Among the obstacles are low skill levels of the workforce, poor infrastructure, insecure land rights, and limited access to credit, poor regulatory framework and unpredictable informal fees.[18] Women face particular challenges. These include socio-cultural, health, educational/capacity, logistical, representational, and legal constraints. For instance, education is still considered less important for girls than for boys. There are limited skills training services tailored to the needs of women, and as a result, women have lower levels of literacy, education and skills. Also, domestic work and child care are overwhelmingly the responsibility of women. Domestic work and child care are invisible, unpaid and undervalued in the Cambodian economy. They serve as a barrier to women and girls' workforce participation in the 'visible' sectors of the economy where women do get paid for their work.[19]

Recognizing that the current weakness of the Cambodian economy is the lack of skilled labour, the fourth priority area of the Rectangular Strategy is centered upon capacity building and human resource development. With limited opportunities for education or work in rural areas many, primarily young people, are migrating from rural to urban areas to look for work. Half the population is under 20 years of age and over 200,000 youths are entering the workforce every year.[20] Providing such a large and dynamic group, who possess changing values and aspirations but little work skills, with decent livelihood options is an enormous challenge.

TOWARDS HUMAN DEVELOPMENT

Many developing countries correctly stress economic growth in national development strategies, but due to various factors such as poor implementation, they do not generate sufficient and decent employment opportunities for all — especially youths and women. They also spend less on public services that are critical for building human capital. Low-skilled workers are hit first and hardest in economic downturns, leading to a continued increase of poverty and inequality.[21] The 2008–09 global economic crises as well as the ongoing so-called "Arab Spring" focused attention to these and other weaknesses in macroeconomic policies. Consequently, there is growing recognition in the world of the need to foster "high-quality" economic growth that is equitable and sustainable. A better term to use would be "human development." Human development is about promoting choices and opportunities for people, including political, economic and social opportunities. To achieve human development, people must have the capabilities to make choices and benefit from opportunities. Human resources development is about unleashing these capabilities. The need to foster human development becomes particularly obvious when looking at Cambodia's fast growing workforce, of which 52 per cent is female.

There is a global consensus on the importance of economic growth for development and (gender) equality. However, there seems to be less consensus about the importance of equality for economic growth and development. Gender equality, apart from a development outcome on its own, is also a strategic means to achieve economic growth and human development. "Governments should embrace the potential of women: they are the world's most under-utilized resource. Getting more of them into work is part of the solution to many economic woes, including shrinking populations and poverty."[22] This is evinced by the fact that, the main driving force of growth in the past couple of decades has been the increase in female employment in the rich world. "Women have contributed more to global GDP growth than has either new technology or the new giants, China and India".[23]

Studies have shown that education, particularly girls' education, may well be the highest return investment available in the developing world and generate significant social and economic returns. This impact is highest in low-income countries, as enrollment rates in these countries tend to be low and the scope for improvements high.[24] Mark Parker, President and CEO of Nike describe this impact as the "girl effect". Hence, (gender) equality should not be undervalued in macro-economic measures, and particularly in human resource development policies -and education more broadly. It is through education coupled with targeted macro-economic measures that the economic potential of women and youths can be unleashed.

DIVERSIFYING THE CAMBODIAN ECONOMY WITH THE COMMITMENTS TOWARDS POVERTY REDUCTION AND GENDER EQUALITY

In response to the recent economic crises, the Royal Government of Cambodia (RGC) has taken quick and pro-active measures. This includes a fiscal expansion policy focused on increasing public investment in physical infrastructure to improve agricultural output. Another key measure was the provision of a social safety net through capacity building and training of Cambodian workers. Another action is to enlarge the capacity of handicrafts and small industries that have the potential to grow and feed into domestic and foreign markets. The raw foundation of these industries is in place, but many of these enterprises are small, fragmented and in the informal sector of the economy. The focus is now on upgrading these businesses and building their competitiveness. Cambodia will also cultivate new industries. Emerging industries include labour-intensive manufacturing industries for toys, shoes, electronics, furniture; information and communication technology; extractive industries; food processing and assembly industries.[25]

The RGC is confident that Cambodia's comparative advantages will enable the development of these industries. It's first and foremost advantage is the large and inexpensive workforce, which is young, eager to learn and work and usefully mobile and flexible. This makes Cambodia, coupled with the rise in wages and production costs in neighboring countries, more attractive for investment. Cambodia also maintains high agricultural potential and is endowed with natural resources. Potential for tourism is another advantage, as evinced by the steady increase of tourist arrivals. The RGC is especially keen on broadening tourism attractions from cultural sites to the untapped potential of eco and community tourism. Finally, one of Cambodia key strengths is also its excellent geo-strategic location at the center of ASEAN, allowing Cambodia to benefit from its proximity to industrial clusters and emerging markets.[26] In bringing about this industrial transformation, the RGC strives to align industrial development policies with the commitments towards poverty reduction and gender equality.

Careful considerations will be needed as to which measures will benefit the youths and women most.

There exist a number of labour factors which should be considered as Cambodia implements its programs to diversify the economy. Firstly, demand for labour will enlarge the already sizable rural-urban migration of young people, stressing the infrastructure, services, social linkages and the labour market. Secondly, education and skills are factors to consider for improving productivity in the industries. A shortage of well trained labour impacts business efficiency and affects businesses' ability to retain staff. Career promotion and financial well-being is also dependent upon education. Therefore, an investment in formal and vocational education is needed which will ensure an increase in productivity. Parallel concern should be directed to the fact that employers face risks and challenges in retaining the employees that they have trained. An improvement in working conditions will also improve productivity and employee retention. Finally, given the positive impact the female workforce provides, care is needed to ensure that training opportunities tailored to the needs of women are available so that women's capacity is increased simultaneously as business develops.

In developing emerging industries, weight should be given to the fact that the majority of enterprises in Cambodia are micro-enterprise sized, which primarily operate in the informal sector of the economy. Micro-enterprises owned by women are mostly active in the retail and service industries, but they are becoming increasingly present in manufacturing, construction industries, and food-processing. The majority of these businesses is also home-based which enable women to work from home, but also implies that workers are unpaid. Therefore, special attention has to be paid to the particular challenges women entrepreneurs face. Developments that will help women entrepreneurs start up and scale up include improving access to finance, providing child care services and improving road and electricity services, "Supporting women's economic empowerment is good business and good practice for the private sector. Unlocking the economic potential of half the world's population is nothing short of sound strategy".[27]

CONCLUSIONS

In the last two decades, Cambodia has undergone a major transformation. The RGC has achieved high economic growth, brought political stability and taken firm ownership of its macro-economic and development strategy. In doing so, it recognized the importance of human capital for economic growth and equitable development, including gender equality. This has resulted in a reduced overall poverty level with a reduction of 1 per cent per annum and improvements in education, health and other sectors.

Cambodia is reforming its macro-economic policies and looking at how to build a diversified economy that can sustain recent growth, which is resilient to crises and can provide broad employment opportunities to its predominantly young rural workforce. In doing so, it is putting special emphasis on human resource development, while maintaining a pro-business environment. The refocused development strategy coupled with comparative advantages centered upon flexible and inexpensive labour, a conducive environment for doing business and abundant natural resources will broaden investment opportunities. Furthermore, Cambodia has a strategic location in the region and is an entry point for doing business in Asia, particularly the ASEAN countries.

The increasing foreign investments in Cambodia offer increasing opportunities for the government to discuss with private sector the benefits of investing in Cambodia's human capital for their business, as well as for the country. As large employers, multinationals have a broad understanding of human development issues and are well poised to interact with host governments in various aspects of social development especially that related to education. Multinational corporations, in particular, can import best practices related to standards of business responsibilities. Responsible practices of most multinational corporations include strong policies related to equality in employment opportunities. Furthermore, transfers of technology and infrastructure knowhow foster knowledge creation and accessibility. Jobs created by these companies can offer opportunities to workers to improve their lives and skills.

Investments in girls and women speed up development and growth. Studies across the world have demonstrated the powerful multiplier effects of girls' education and women's economic empowerment on all aspects of development as well as on economic growth. This realization makes education generally, and investing in girls and women particularly, not only a matter of human development, but also smart economics. This has to be reflected accordingly in human resource development policies of government and private sector, and more broadly in macro-economic and national development policies. Economically empowered women are good for business: they are potential customers, potential employees, they bring in diversity which is good for leadership, and can enhance a company's reputation and performance. Businesses claim themselves that economically empowering women is a sound business strategy and reduces their vulnerability vis-a-vis social issues in society.

Notes

1. Her Majesty Queen Rania Al-Abdullah of Jordan said "When you can get girls into schools and keep them there, you can change the course of a nation."
2. Lawrence Summers in his former capacity as World Bank Chief Economist said in 1992 already that investment in girl's education may well be the highest return investment available in the developing world.
3. Ministry of Women's Affairs. *A Fair Share for Women: Cambodia Gender Assessment.* Phnom Penh: Ministry of Women's Affairs, Royal Government of Cambodia, 2008.
4. Growth was 6 per cent from 1993 to 2003; 11% between 2004 and 2007; 0.1 per cent in 2009 due primarily to the global crisis and 5.5 per cent in 2010. The income per capita has increased from $285 to $593. See *Phase 2 Evaluation of the Paris Declaration: Technical Volume, Cambodia Country Study Report.* Phnom Penh: Cambodian Rehabilitation and Development Board of the Council for the Development of Cambodia, Royal Government of Cambodia, 2010. Growth is expected to be more than 6 per cent in 2011 according to the Prime Minister of the Kingdom of Cambodia, Samdech Akka Moha Sena Padei Techno Hun Sen, as announced at the opening speech "Cambodian Economy in Post-Crises Environment: Industrial Policy-Options Toward a Sustainable Development" of the 4th Cambodia Economic Forum, 16 February 2011.
5. The total Official Development Assistance (ODA) disbursements in 2009 were US$989.5 million which represented 9 per cent of GDP. ODA from China represented US$114.7 million in 2009 or 9 per cent of GDP. See 7.
6. The life expectancy rates have increased from 58 for women and 54 for men in 2000 to 64 and 58 respectively in 2005, see: National Institute of Public Health (NIPH) and National Institute of Statistics (NIS). *Cambodia Demographic and Health Survey 2005.* Phnom Penh/ Maryland: USAID/ADB/DFID/UNFPA/UNICEF/CDC, 2005
7. The Cambodian MDG target is to reduce overall poverty levels to 19.5 per cent by 2015. See Ministry of Planning. *Cambodian Millennium Development Goals Report.* Phnom Penh: Royal Government of Cambodia, 2003.
8. Ministry of Women's Affairs. *Violence Against Women: 2009 Follow-Up Survey, Final Study Report.* Phnom Penh: Ministry of Women's Affairs, Royal Government of Cambodia, 2009.
9. The overall Gini coefficient for Cambodia increased from 0.39 to 0.43. The Gini coefficient is the most commonly-used summary measure of income inequality. It ranges in value from zero, corresponding to complete equality in the distribution of income, to one, which would signify complete inequality. For further information, see World Bank. *Poverty Profile and Trends in Cambodia, 2007 — Findings from the Cambodia Socio-Economic Survey (CSES).* Washington: The World Bank, 2009.
10. UN Cambodia. *Common Country Assessment 2009.* Phnom Penh: UN Cambodia, 2009.

11. World Bank. *Sustaining Rapid Growth in a Challenging Economy — Cambodia Country Economic Memorandum*. Phnom Penh: The World Bank, 2009
12. 51% of the workforce in subsistence agriculture and 57% of the workforce in market-oriented agriculture is female. See ibid., p. 6.
13. See ibid., p. 6.
14. See ibid., p. 15.
15. See ibid., p. 6.
16. See ibid., p. 6.
17. See ibid p. 6. For a full definition of the informal sector, see ILO. Decent work and the informal economy, report VI. Geneva: ILO, 2002
18. See World Bank. *Sustaining Rapid Growth in a Challenging Economy*, p. 7.
19. See ibid., p. 6.
20. See ibid., p. 14.
21. The analysis was reported in: UNIFEM. *Financing Gender Equality is Financing Development*. New York: UNIFEM (Discussion Paper), 2008.
22. The Economist. "Women in the workforce: the importance of sex" 2006. Accessed on 31 March 2011 at <http://www.economist.com/node/6800723>.
23. See World Bank. *Sustaining Rapid Growth in a Challenging Economy*, p. 26. These findings are confirmed by many other reports, such as Daly, Kevin. *Gender Inequality, Growth and Global Ageing*. Global Economics Paper No. 154, New York: Goldman Sachs, 2007. This report concludes that closing the gender gap could boost GDP by as much as 9 per cent in the United States of America, up to 13 per cent in the European Union and up to 16 per cent in Japan.
24. These studies have been conducted by governments, influential public institutions such as the World Economic Forum, the World Bank and United Nations agencies, as well as corporations across the world. Lawrence Summers in his former capacity as World Bank Chief Economist said in 1992 already that investment in girl's education may well be the highest return investment available in the developing world.
25. See World Bank. *Sustaining Rapid Growth in a Challenging Economy*, p. 8.
26. See ibid., p. 8.
27. Quote by McKinsey & Company, see ibid., p. 30.

References

CDRI, "Returning to a High Growth Economy — Indicators, Prospects and Policy Priorities". *Cambodia Outlook Brief*, 2010 Nr.01.

CDRI, "Strengthening Key Sectors for Cambodia's Return to Growth, Sustainable Development and Poverty Reduction: Emerging Industries". *Cambodia Outlook Brief*, 2010 Nr.03.

Daly, Kevin. *Gender Inequality, Growth and Global Ageing*. Global Economics Paper No. 154, New York: Goldman Sachs, 2007.

Filmor, Dean and Norbert Schady. "Getting girls into school: evidence from a scholarship program in Cambodia". *Human Development Sector Reports, East Asia and the Pacific Region*. Washington: The World Bank, 2006.

ILO and World Bank. *Women and Work in the Garment Industry*. Phnom Penh: ILO and World Bank, 2006.

ILO. *Decent Work and the Informal Economy, Report VI*. Geneva: ILO, 2002.

McKinsey & Company. *Women Matter: Gender Diversity, a Corporate Performance Driver*. London: McKinsey & Company, Social Sector Office, 2007.

———. *Women Matter 2: Female Leadership, a Competitive Edge for the Future*. London: McKinsey & Company, Social Sector Office, 2008.

———. *The Business of Empowering Women*. London: McKinsey & Company, Social Sector Office, 2010.

Ministry of Planning. *Cambodian Millennium Development Goals Report*. Phnom Penh: Royal Government of Cambodia, 2003.

Ministry of Women's Affairs. *A Fair Share for Women: Cambodia Gender Assessment*. Phnom Penh: Ministry of Women's Affairs, Royal Government of Cambodia, 2008.

———. *Violence against Women: 2009 Follow-Up Survey, Final Study Report*. Phnom Penh: Ministry of Women's Affairs, Royal Government of Cambodia, 2009.

Murphy, Shannon, Wivinia Belmonte and Jane Nelson. *Investing in Girl's Education. An Opportunity for Corporate Leadership*. Boston: Harvard Kennedy School, 2009.

National Institute of Public Health (NIPH) and National Institute of Statistics (NIS). *Cambodia Demographic and Health Survey 2005*. Phnom Penh/ Maryland: USAID/ADB/DFID/UNFPA/UNICEF/CDC, 2005.

Phase 2 Evaluation of the Paris Declaration: Technical Volume, Cambodia Country Study Report. Phnom Penh: Cambodian Rehabilitation and Development Board of the Council for the Development of Cambodia, Royal Government of Cambodia, 2010.

Samdech Akka Moha Sena Padei Techno Hun Sen, Prime Minister of the Kingdom of Cambodia. *Cambodian Economy in Post-Crises Environment: Industrial Policy-Options Toward a Sustainable Development*. Opening speech at the 4th Cambodia Economic Forum, 2011.

The Economist. "Women in the workforce: the importance of sex", 2006. Accessed on 31 March 2011 at <http://www.economist.com/node/6800723>.

UN Cambodia. *Common Country Assessment 2009*. Phnom Penh: UN Cambodia, 2009.

UNIFEM. *Financing Gender Equality is Financing Development*. New York: UNIFEM (Discussion Paper), 2008.

World Bank. *Poverty Profile and Trends in Cambodia, 2007 — Findings from the Cambodia Socio-Economic Survey (CSES)*. Washington: The World Bank, 2009.

——— *Sustaining Rapid Growth in a Challenging Economy — Cambodia Country Economic Memorandum*. Phnom Penh: The World Bank, 2009.

20

PROGRESS AND CHALLENGES OF EDUCATION IN CAMBODIA TODAY

Pou Sovachana

Our progress as a nation can be no swifter than our progress in education.
— John F. Kennedy, 35th President of the United States

Nations will march towards their greatness in the direction given by its education. Nations will soar if its education soars; will regress if it regresses. Nations will fall and sink in darkness if education is corrupted or completely abandoned.
— Simón Bolívar (1783–1830, a Bolivian Liberator)

Our prime purpose in this life is to help others. And if you can't help them, at least don't hurt them.
— Dalai Lama

If Cambodia is to achieve the lofty goals quoted in the statements above, it is imperative that the country establishes a high-quality and sustainable education system with equal access to learning for all citizens. Choosing and implementing the proper strategy of the developmental path to produce graduates[1] with the virtue, knowledge, skills and qualifications needed in today's market and technology-driven environment will be the key to this noble endeavour.

INTRODUCTION

The education sector in Cambodia has come a long way and achieved a number of impressive accomplishments, following years of civil conflicts, internal strife, political instability and backwardness. It is noteworthy that the Royal Government of Cambodia (RGC) together with international partners and non-governmental organizations (NGOs) has done a remarkable job in rehabilitating a dysfunctional education system and rebuilding a shattered economy. The transformation of the basic education system, which includes solid growth in the number of schools and universities, and great strides towards universal primary education and gender parity, should be commended. The need to develop human capital has been crucial to the Royal Government's strategy to promote new and sustainable sources of economic growth as well as improved living standards.

Still, more fundamental challenges remain. These include ensuring equitable access to education, and improving the quality of education and efficiency at all levels. Moreover, the recent global economic slowdown since 2008 has prevented many disadvantaged children from starting school and more to drop out of the system before completing primary education. Failure to reach the marginalized has denied many people, especially in the rural and remote areas, their right to education.[2] There is an immediate need to better educate more people in order to promote more efficient and superior cadres to build up a stronger nation with economic self-sustainability. An education that supports the development of morality and critical thinking skills will be increasingly important for all Cambodian students to restore the identity of the Khmer people from one of victimhood to one of capacity, pride and honour, and also to enable us to compete regionally and globally.

This paper begins by identifying the near eradication of education in Cambodia during the Khmer Rouge epoch and will highlight the progress up to the present day. Figure 20.1 comprises a chronological chart showing the influence of the political events on the education sector. The paper will then examine the challenges of the educational reforms in which both the beneficial and the adverse effects will be presented. As this paper will show, the national strategy to promote sustainable sources of economic growth as well as to improve living standards is based on developing human resources and building human capacity, thus improving the overall quality of education.[3] Additional transformations in the educational sector are necessary for Cambodia to tackle the challenges of the 21st century, including those of globalization and the achievement the Millennium Development Goals. (See Figure 20.1)

FIGURE 20.1
Chronological Map of Key Governance and Sector Events

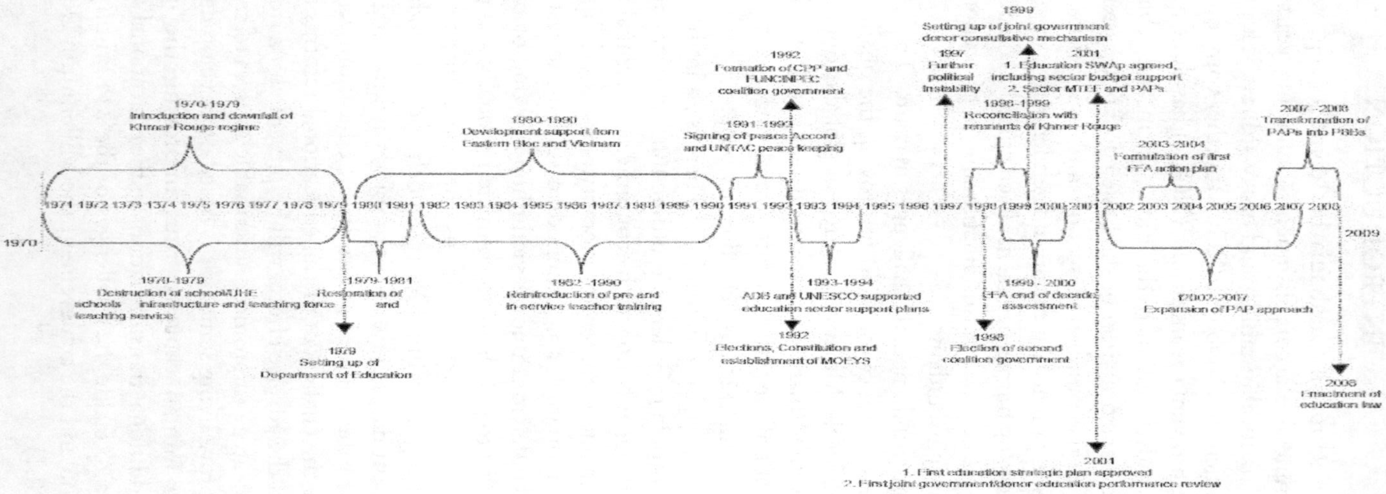

Source: Study on Governance Challenges for Education in Fragile Situations by European Union, Synthesis Report, December 2009, Euro Trends.

THE NEAR ERADICATION OF EDUCATION IN CAMBODIA

For nearly four years (17 April 1975 – 7 January 1979), the Khmer Rouge completely isolated Cambodia from the world, decimated the education system, and created severe disruption. With the goals of creating a utopian agrarian socialist state, the regime obliterated everything that promoted capitalism and class oppression. The Khmer Rouge leaders eliminated currency, abolished education, and destroyed key social-cultural institutions including family structure, Buddhism, and economic activities. Hospitals, factories, schools, and universities were closed, books were burned, libraries were destroyed, and a majority of Cambodia's brightest, talented, and most educated individuals were either eliminated or fled the country. (Chandler, 2000) Anyone suspected of being an "intellectual" was tortured and most often executed. Even wearing glasses was considered enough to warrant such treatment.[4] Hinton explains in his article "Truth, Representation and The Politics of Memory after Genocide," that the Khmer Rouge believed that the former education system corrupted the minds of the young and that the best education was political indoctrination and learning through 'struggle' on the economic 'front lines.' Like their Maoist counterparts in China, manual labouur and political viability were seen as better than knowledge. They affirmed that 'the spade is your pen, the rice field your paper' and 'if you want to pass your baccalaureate exam, you must build dams and canals.' (Hinton, 2005) As a result of brutality and an attempt to build this new type of utopia, almost two million Cambodian people died, either by torture and execution or by malnutrition and disease.[5] Cambodia was left in ruins and experienced a tragedy in term of human resources. It is estimated that 75 per cent of all teachers, 96 per cent of university students and 67 per cent of all primary pupils were killed. (Clayton, 1998) Although the atrocious regime is officially over, the effects are still prevalent in the mind of the people.

The legacy of the Khmer Rouge left a deep scar and long-term effects that resulted in a generation of illiterate children.[6] The entire education system needed to be reconstructed and rebuilt from the ashes to prepare and produce citizens to fit into a knowledge-based and technology-driven economy. No doubt there were many daunting challenges, but there were also long-term opportunities for Cambodia to move forward and to rebuild the future of its people. This development can be best characterized in gradual phases, from the post-conflict early recovery to the reconstruction and development period.

EARLY RECOVERY AND RESTORATION PERIOD 1979–1989

From 1979 to 1989, education in Cambodia saw a slow comeback. After coming to power and following the destruction of the Democratic Kampuchea regime, the People's Republic of Kampuchea (PRK) faced enormous reconstruction problems. With the help of the Vietnamese and its allies in the Eastern bloc countries, the PRK regime embarked on a massive task to redevelop, restore and expand the education sector by opening schools throughout Cambodia. This was then followed by a number of universities, notably, the Faculty of Medicine and Pharmacy, the Faculty of Agriculture, followed by the Technical Institute, the Institute of Languages, the Institute of Commerce, the Centre for Pedagogical Education and the School of Fine Arts. In education, the Eastern bloc countries provided assistance to the government in terms of professors, books, teaching materials, equipment, and thousand of scholarships for advanced study at universities.[7] Clayton reported that 2,650 Cambodians completed degree programs between 1983 and 1989 from the Soviet Union, East Germany, Vietnam, Bulgaria, Czechoslovakia, Hungary, and Cuba. He also noted that, by 1990, Cambodia's institutes of higher education had graduated 977 doctors, dentists, or pharmacists, 2,196 senior secondary teachers, 1,481 foreign language specialists, 474 technical engineers, 400 economists, and 184 agricultural engineers. The Vietnamese and Eastern-bloc assistance in producing this first generation of tertiary graduates was instrumental in the early development of human resources. A Euro Trends study on governance challenges for education in Cambodia's fragile situation in 2009 stated that by that time pupil enrolment had risen from zero to 1.6 million, a nationwide system of schools had been created, and the teaching service had been restored, including voluntary service and an extensive programme of accelerated learning.[8]

Under the PRK regime, the basic education system was developed closely following the Vietnamese model. The structures and procedures were highly centralized using the top-down approach to teaching and learning. (Ledgerwood, 1996) According to Martin in 1986, the original Cambodian terms for primary and secondary education have been changed into direct translations of the Vietnamese terms.[9] The primary cycle had four instead of six years, the first level of secondary education had three instead of four years, and the second level of secondary education had three years. Studying Vietnamese language was made compulsory from the beginning of the secondary cycle.[10] Another example, according to Clayton in 1999, the tertiary students were required to complete the five courses on the "objectives of socialism" taught mostly by Cambodians trained in Vietnam.[11]

During this period, the lack of human and educational resources compounded with budget constraints hindered the progress of educational redevelopment. The government attempted to enroll as many students as possible at schools using "those who know more teach those who know less." (Ledgerwood, 1996) A notable effort was made by the PRK government to identify and recruit former intellectuals, professors, teachers, and bureaucrats to enter the field of education. Everyone was encouraged to participate in this challenging endeavour to help rebuild the country. Potential teachers received minimal training before being assigned to teaching jobs. To fill the void, the Vietnamese provided aid and sent thousands of development personnel, a significant number of whom worked in education. (Clayton, 1999) In terms of education infrastructure, because 90 per cent of school buildings were destroyed during the Khmer Rouge regime, classes were often taught in huts, thatched buildings and sometimes under the trees.[12]

During that time, while the system of education involved enrolling as many students as possible, the government set a limit on the number of students that could enter into upper secondary schools and universities. Such practices generated favoritism, nepotism and widespread corruption in the education system as wealthy and influential parents either paid bribes or used their political power to secure places for their children at the universities. (Ledgerwood, 1996) The lack of school resources and little government funding affected the quality of education. There was no educational freedom, autonomy or social protection for higher education students and faculty. Without the assistance from the West, the students "pragmatically accepted socialist ideology as a necessary condition to the receipt of educational resources from Vietnam and other Eastern-bloc countries." (Clayton, 1999) With state revenue being spent mainly on security and defense to fight the civil war with the Khmer Rouge as well as two non-communist movements,[13] the education sector was never a top priority for the PRK government. However, from an empty-handed position as described above, the PRK regime struggled and succeeded initially to overcome the legacy of the Khmer Rouge and was able to restore a semblance of educational normality in Cambodia. (Ledgerwood, 1996) The school system was built rapidly and education represented one of the greatest achievements of the PRK regime. (Hinton, 2008) The progress, though impressive, still faced many problems.

THE RECONSTRUCTION STAGE IN THE 1990s

It is important to note that after Vietnam withdrew from Cambodia in late 1989 as a result of the heavy pressure of the West and the diminishing support of the Soviet Union, the functioning government chose a multiparty political system and shifted from a command and control economy toward a free market orientation. And to maintain viability, the Ministry of Education at that time initiated reforms congruent with post-occupation ways of thinking. Most significantly, between 1989 and 1991, it eliminated the system of political education in place during the occupation and cancelled courses in Marxism-Leninism. (Clayton, 1999)

After the 1991 Paris Peace Accords and the United Nations sponsored election in 1993, the education sector (with the support of the United States, UN agencies and other countries) moved into a new era where "schools should operate in the best interests of the child. Educational environments must be safe, healthy and protective, endowed with trained teachers, adequate resources and appropriate physical, emotional and social conditions for learning. Together, we can help ensure that every child — regardless of whether he or she attends school in a building, a tent or under a tree — receives a rights-based, quality education."[14] The foundation of this modern education system and practices replaced the Vietnamese and Eastern Bloc socialist system. Moreover, in response to the severe problems in Cambodia, the international community also began to support Cambodia. International and developmental aid started to flow. Donor countries have provided an estimated $500 million or more since the early 1990s.[15] Today, Cambodia is still dependent on international aid, which comprise approximately one third to almost one half of the national budget.

The newly-elected coalition government set education as a priority and emphasized human resources development as the key to poverty alleviation and national socio-economic development. Everyone was given the same education opportunities as safeguarded by the Cambodian Constitution. Adopted on 21 September 1993, the Constitution guaranteed the universal right to quality education as stated in Article 65.[16] Furthermore, to invest in Cambodia's future, the government is fully committed to providing free compulsory education for nine years by the year 2015.[17] This is an ambitious task. The right to quality education imposed an obligation upon the Cambodian government and all stakeholders to ensure that all children and people had opportunities to meet their basic learning needs.[18] The newly-elected coalition government started constructing many new school buildings as part of their election campaign pledge. The education sector was further strengthened by the support of the international organizations and NGOs. However, public expenditures were limited and many under-served provinces received limited backing from external programs, largely due to continued security concerns and instability from remnants of the Khmer Rouge. Despite these factors, around 2.5 million children were enrolled in schools during that period, state paid teaching was established, and public examinations were re-introduced. Increasing and standardizing compulsory schooling to 12 years, up from 11 in 1996, was another key policy contributing to this improvement (Euro Trends, 2009). (See Figure 20.2)

THE DEVELOPMENT TRANSITION PERIOD OVER 2000/2010

After the political integration of the remnants of the Khmer Rouge in 1998, Cambodia saw notable progress in the normalization of life that resulted in a steady improvement in economic growth and social development. The average economic growth rate during 2003–08 was around 10 per cent per year, with the record high annual rate of growth of 13.3 per cent in 2005.[19] Peace and political stability also allowed Cambodian citizens to go about their normal lives. Now, ordinary people have better access to key goods and services. More and more children are now going to schools.

The last decade has also been marked by the extensive restructuring of education reforms that include a rising share of government expenditure and improved donor, NGOs, and government accountability processes. With the abolition of enrolment fees in 2001, the establishment of special incentives to the poor, girls and ethnic minority students to attend schools (scholarships, dormitories) and the introduction of school block grant, schools' enrolment rates have been growing at all levels, including an expanded private higher education sector.[20]

NATIONAL STRATEGIES FOR EDUCATION

The Royal Government is now committed to the development of its human resources and capacity building through the leadership of the Ministry of Education Youth and Sports (MoEYS). This political platform is defined by the Rectangular Strategy, first formulated in 2003–08, while the legislature for 2008–13 has placed capacity-building and human resources development — including strengthening quality education, improvement of health services, fostering gender equality, and implementing population policy — as one of the four pillars to support good governance. The Rectangular Strategy is operated under the National Strategic Development Plan (NSDP), which includes poverty reduction strategies, national growth, and inclusive education. In 2004, Samdech Hun Sen, Prime Minister of the Royal Government of Cambodia, spelled out his commitment to implementing the Rectangular

FIGURE 20.2
School Enrolment Patterns 1980–2009, Cambodia

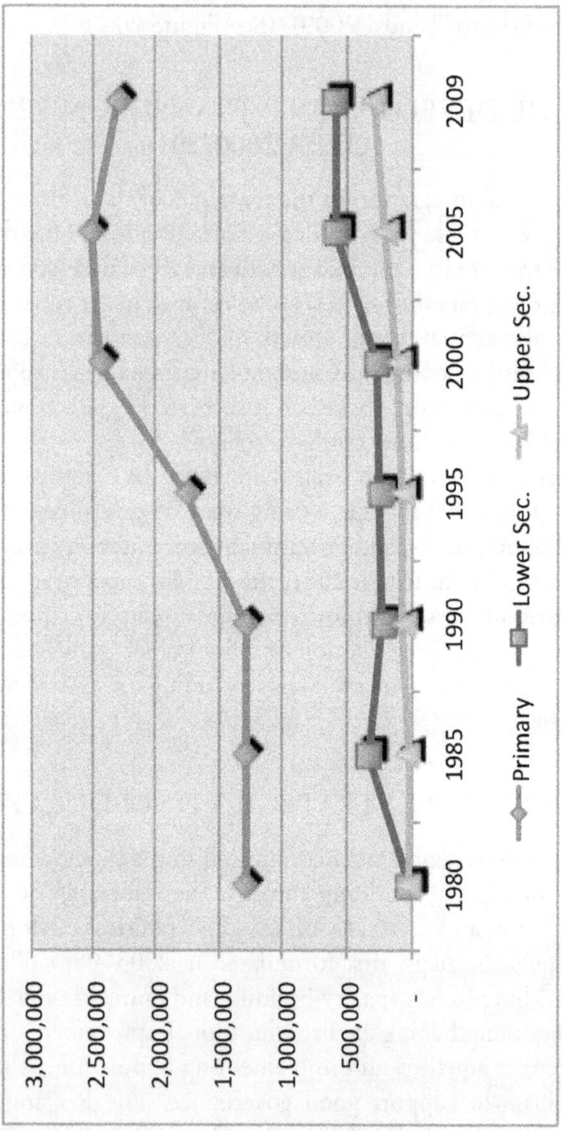

Source: Study on Governance Challenges for Education in Fragile Situation, Euro Trends, 2009.

Strategy: "The Royal Government will promote sustainable and equitable development, and strengthen Cambodia's social fabric to ensure that the Cambodian people are well-educated, culturally advanced, engaged in dignified livelihood and living in harmony in their family and the society."[21] (See Figure 20.3)

MOBILISING THE RESOURCES: BUDGET AND FINANCIAL MANAGEMENT

With the political commitment to education, the percentage of the national budget for education has increased significantly (Table 20.1), from 13.6 per cent in 2000 reaching a peak of 19.8 per cent in 2004 but currently down to 16.4 per cent in 2010.[22] Even though the recurrent budget for education has been declining in terms of percentage of the government national budget, it still continues to increase in absolute terms. Standing at $198 million compared to $276 million for defense and security, the MoEYS's budget in 2010 covers the recurrent expenditures on the salaries, operating costs, special programmes activities and other services delivered. Donor funding has provided materials and capital expenditure for projects such as school infrastructure, new equipment, renovation and major repair of buildings. More sustainable

FIGURE 20.3

Rectangular Strategy of The Royal Government of Cambodia

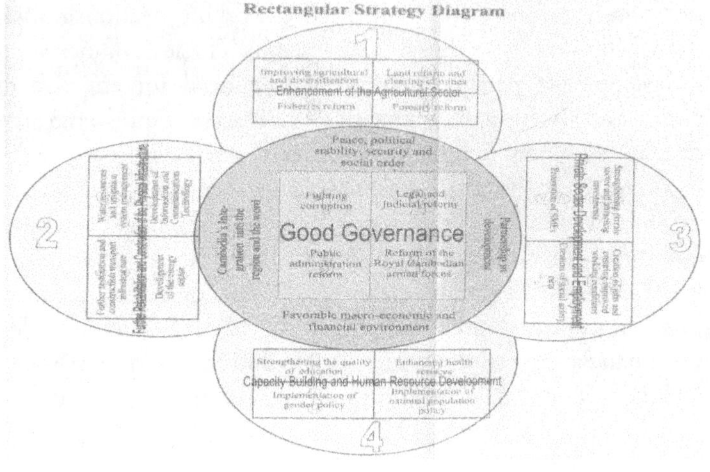

development can only happen with significant stakeholder involvement and strong government/donor endorsement to providing quality education for all. (See Table 20.1)

TABLE 20.1
Public Expenditure on Education as Percentage of National Budget, 2000–2010

2000	2001	2002	2003	2004	2005	2006	2007	2008	2009	2010
13.9%	17.6%	18.2%	18.3%	19.8%	18.5%	18.3%	19.2%	18.1%	17.0%	16.4%

Source: MoEYS, 2000–2010

With the strong support of its international partners Cambodia has made steady and continuous growth in the education sector.[23] These partnership arrangements have proven to be successful in instituting mechanisms for formal strategic education reforms. Since elementary schools are like the root of education, most of the external support and funds have been directed to the basic education sub-sector. UNICEF and a few others have supported secondary education and the World Bank has promoted higher education.[24] But in spite of these movements forward, little attention has been given to either science or research. These two areas are instrumental in contributing to a better quality education, responding to the socio-economic challenges and meeting international development targets including all of the Millennium Development Goals.[25]

Cambodia has developed a constructive working relationship with the international community in the education sector. The scale of intervention by various development partners underlines the need for effective donors' coordination and selection of donors' strategic intervention. To move towards better donors' alignment and harmonization, the Education Sector Working Group was created in 2001 to coordinate aid effectiveness and development results in the education sector. Given the amount of aid and the number of donors, aid coordination has played a very important role for both policy consistency and implementation efficiency. As part of mutual accountability for results and improved aid effectiveness, the MoEYS is responsible for all sources of financial support for education, including external assistance. The role of MoEYs is crucial in reallocating financial resources to the areas or populations where it is most needed.[26]

MANAGEMENT STRUCTURE OF EDUCATION AND EDUCATION SYSTEM

Through the Education Law in December 2007, Cambodia has embarked on another new era of leadership and ownership to develop a comprehensive long-term vision on how to educate its children, how the schools should look in the future and how the government will support education. This law puts strong emphasis on education system reform in line with the Constitution and relevant international laws. It administers all educational activities across the whole education system in Cambodia, both public and private. This education law provides more options for all parents so that their children can get the best quality education possible. It also invests in teaching practices that have been demonstrated to work. In short, it aims to foster a conducive environment in which every child can learn and succeed.

The administrative hierarchy and education management consists of four levels, namely national or central (MoEYS), provincial or municipal (Provincial and Municipal Departments of Education), the district or khan level (District Office of Education), and local school level. The government is working towards decentralization that aims to achieve better results in term of administration, management and practices. Schools will play an important role of this decentralization reform. The education system in Cambodia is comprised of public and private education and includes formal, non-formal and informal.

The formal education structure has Pre-School, 6 years of Primary Education, 3 years of Lower Secondary Education, and 3 years of Upper Secondary Education Students. In Cambodia, the pupils attend either morning or afternoon classes with morning shift: Monday through Saturday 7:00am–11:00am and afternoon shift: Monday through Saturday 1:00pm–5:00pm. (See Table 20.2)

The non-formal education program plays an important role in providing equivalency, literacy and life skill programs.[27] It aims to provide a new chance and opportunity for all citizens who do not have access to formal education to continue their study and to improve the quality of life. According to UNESCO, in 2008, 55,160 adults (64 per cent female) became literate and more female than males were enrolled in these literacy programs. Even with this increase, the non-formal education programme showed slow progress due to declining budget allocation from 13 per cent in 2006 to 5.4 per cent in 2007, low staff capacity, lack of human resources and little community support.[28] In Cambodia, the literacy rate for persons 15-years old and above in 2008 was 77.6 per cent, while 77 per cent of adults aged 15 and above who

TABLE 20.2
Education Structure: Approximate Starting Age and Duration

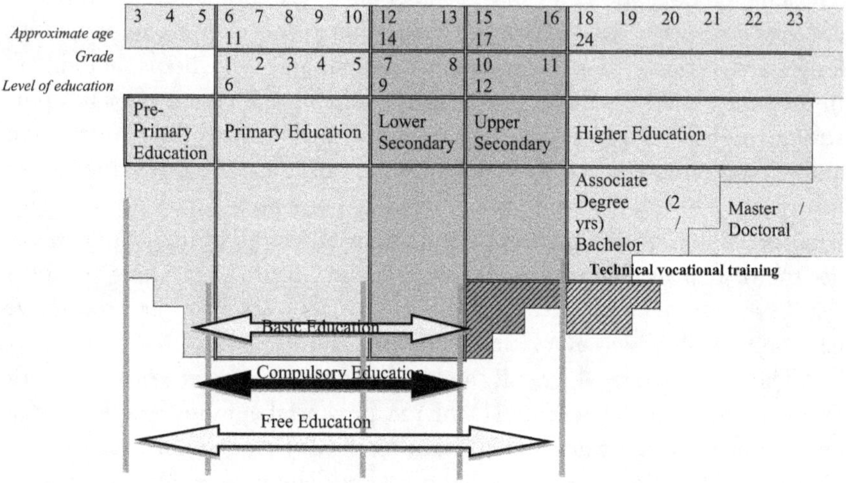

Source: UNESCO Secondary Education, 2008. Regional Information Base: Cambodia Country Profile.

are illiterate depend on manual labour in farming or production of goods.[29] Attention from the MoEYS and donor countries is seriously needed to develop and strengthen the non-formal education programs especially in support of literacy education for youth and adults.

ACCESS TO BASIC EDUCATION

According to the MoEYS Education Strategic Plan 2009–13, the total number of primary schools, lower secondary schools, and upper secondary has increased significantly from school year (SY) 2005–06 to school year (SY) 2009–10 (Table 20.3 below). This positive outcome reflects the commitment of MoEYS to bring schools closer to where citizens reside. (See Table 20.3)

The MoEYS also reported the total number of students in primary school has decreased from 2,558,467 in SY2005–06 to 2,239,757 (47.8 per cent female students) in SY2009–10 due to the fact that population growth rate that has decreased from 2.8 per cent to 1.5 per cent.[30] The total number of students in lower secondary school has decreased as well from 588,333 in SY2005–06 to 585,115 (47.8 per cent female students) in SY2009–10.

TABLE 20.3
Number of schools in SY 2005–2006 and SY 2009–2010

	School Year 2005–2006	School Year 2009–2010
Primary Schools	6,277	6,665
Lower Secondary	911	1,172
Upper Secondary	252	383

Source: MoEYS Education Strategic Plan 2009–2013

However, the total number of students in upper secondary school has increased from 204,925 in SY2005–06 to 323,583 (43.5 per cent female students) in SY2009–10. The net admission rate (NAR) and the Net Enrolment Rate (NER) at the primary school level are on track to achieve the 2015 Cambodia Millennium Development Goals targets. Table 20.4 outlines the achievements made by the MoEYS in SY2009–10 against SY2005–06. (See Table 20.4)

According to the Education Management Information System, the transition rate from primary to lower secondary recorded in 2008/2009 was 78.4 per cent which is again far below the 90 per cent target. The transition rate in the remote areas was down to 60.5 per cent compare to the rural rate of 76 per cent and the urban area figure of 92.6 per cent. This points to the urgent need for investing more resources in the remote areas and rural areas with specific policies providing remedial classes, expanding child-friendly school initiatives, providing more scholarships to students from poor families, strengthening school support committees for more community involvement, and eliminating all school informal fees. Given the recent rate of progress, the Education For All goal for 9 years of basic education target cannot be reached. The major challenges are to improve the primary school flow rates as well as transition rates to lower secondary school.[31]

In summary, as a result of the government's universal education policy, primary and secondary school attendance has increased significantly in recent years but access is still far from universal, especially from poor and destitute households, the hardest to reach, notably the disabled children, the ethnic minorities and out of school youth. A good number of children in remotes areas are not in school, with many never having enrolled. The main obstacle to children's access in urban, rural and remote areas is poverty. The United Nations Human Development Report in 2006 estimated 34 per cent of Cambodians live on less than $1 per day. Most importantly, the poor are significantly rural. In 2004, 91.6 per cent of the nation's poor were living in

TABLE 20.4

Actual Achievement against Target for Equitable Access to Education

Indicator	Actual SY2005–2006		Target SY2009–2010		Actual SY2009–2010	
	Male	Female	Male	Female	Male	Female
Net enrolment rate						
Nationwide	91.3%	81.7%	96%	96%	92.4%	92.7%
Primary: urban	91.3%	89.7%	97%	98%	92.2%	92.2%
Primary: rural	91.7%	90.1%	94%	95%	95.3%	95%
Primary: remote	83.7%	80.1%	94%	93%	n.a.	n.a.
Lower Secondary (LS) Nationwide	31.3%	30.4%	43%	45%	32.6%	34.6%
LS: urban	50.1%	50.3%	69%	71%	49.1%	50.5%
LS: rural	28.6%	27.4%	40%	41%	29.4%	31.5%
LS: remote	6%	6%	15%	15%	n.a.	n.a.
Upper Secondary Nationwide	11.3%	9.9%	18%	17%	19.4%	19.4%
Number of Students in Public/ Private Higher Education Institutions	90,607	29,000	162,000	57,700	145,265	51,596

Source: MoEYS Education Strategic Plan 2009–2013

rural areas and in 2007, this rose to 92.7 per cent (Ministry of Planning, 2010). As the students moved on from lower secondary education to the upper secondary education, they showed a very high dropout rate (Table 20.5: Percentage of Dropouts by Grade 7–12 and Geographical Area 2006–07). The survival rate from grade 1–12 for 1996–2008 was only 11 per cent. The family financial constraints, the need for students and especially girls to help out with household chores, the cost burden to pay for private classes and bribes to teachers, and the lack of understanding on the value and importance of education are some the main reasons for the low grade 12 completion.[32] (See Table 20.5)

TEACHER TRAINING AND DEVELOPMENT

Cambodia has achieved tremendous improvement in rebuilding its educational system. According to the MoEYS Education Achievements in SY2009–10, there were 27 training institutions providing all level of training. Currently, there are about 82,820 teachers (43 per cent female) in a total of 10,115 schools that serve approximately more than 3,248,479 students countrywide.[33] In 2010, there were 4537 teacher trainees (51.4 per cent females) who completed the training course.[34]

Although new teachers have been developed and trained, a myriad of challenges remain in rebuilding the entire teacher education and training system. The teacher education level remains low and the quality of teacher education and training needs to be seriously improved to deliver quality education.[35] The bulk of primary school teachers have only post-primary education. Currently, about 34.5 per cent of teachers in remote areas, and 6.4 per cent in rural areas have not studied beyond the primary level according to UNESCO National Education Support Strategy. The educational requirement

TABLE 20.5

Percentage of Dropouts by Grade 7–12 and Geographical Area 2006–2007

Area	Lower Secondary			Upper Secondary		
	Grade 7	Grade 8	Grade 9	Grade 10	Grade 11	Grade 12
Urban	14.8%	7.6%	14.3%	8.6%	3.0%	14.9%
Rural	23.1%	23.1%	26.3%	19.2%	15.0%	27.4%
Remote	21.4%	19.4%	22.7%	17.9%	15.7%	22.2%
Total	21.3%	19.3%	22.7%	14.6%	9.1%	20.9%

Source: Education Management Information System (EMIS), MoEYS, from 2007–2008

for entry into teacher training college for training at primary level is grade 12, or grade 9 for placement to remote areas. Secondary training requires grade 12 for lower secondary, and for upper, grade 12 plus a university degree. The low level of qualification raises concern of insufficient knowledge of the teacher-training curriculum. The high pupil-teacher ratio further aggravates the low teacher qualification with an average of 50 students per class at primary level, 25 at lower secondary, and 32 at upper secondary.[36]

While most teachers have completed pre-service training, in-service training that includes periodic workshops on spheres of pedagogy has remained insufficient and professional development has been limited. Only 15 per cent of lower secondary teachers attended in-service training sessions during 2005/2006.[37] In term of teacher supply, remote areas are constantly faced with a shortage of skilled teachers. There is also a serious shortage of trained teacher trainers and a limited pool of experienced professional teachers to monitor and evaluate student teachers during teaching practice. As another example, MoEYS still has to produce 5000 new teachers as targeted to meet the growing demand.[38] Teachers' placement and promotion can also be improved. The procedures for placements and promotion processes should be well-defined and regulated to ensure transparency and objectivity in decision. To further improve teaching and learning, teachers' social and financial statuses can be further upgraded and standardised. The most important school-based factor in a child's education is teacher quality. Investing in teacher is indirectly investing in children and their future. The MoEYS, together with the development partners, must invest in teachers' training and development. Here are some of the recommendations to improve teachers' motivation:

- Pay teachers more at a level appropriate to the cost of living and linked to inflation. Providing teachers with a wage which allows a livelihood with honour and dignity is the most important factor to improve quality education.[39]
- Eliminate corruption and nepotism in the work place.
- Improve leadership at the ministry, provincial, district, and school level.
- Abolish all school informal fees as stated in the Constitution.[40]
- Reinstate the Merit Based Performance Initiative.[41]
- Develop an incentive to retain the most competent teachers.

HIGHER EDUCATION

Ensuring high quality basic education for all remains the priority of the government, but in the long term, the development of quality higher education will be a key to economic growth and sustainable development.[42] Furthermore, higher education is often cited as a potential contributor to the reduction of poverty, inequality, and other broader social ills. Cambodia has witnessed the swift and substantial expansion of higher education institutions (HEIs) during the last decade.[43] This growth was attributed to the demand for higher education created by the growing number of graduates from secondary education schools coupled with the government policy toward increased private sector participation. With the new government policy of public and private partnership, the first private higher education institution, Norton University, opened its doors in 1997. With this policy and the demand of the graduates, higher education in Cambodia has blossomed especially in the private sector, many of which schools claim to be high in quality.

At present, there are 33 public and 43 private HEIs offering associate degree to doctoral degree programs in nearly 100 fields ranging from foreign language, agriculture, business, health sciences, tourism, engineering to law and economics.[44] While higher institutions are mostly in Phnom Penh, some were established in 18 of the provinces to provide significant opportunities to the provincial people to access higher education. Along with the increasing number of higher education institutions, the MoEYS also pays attention to the quality and efficiency of education services by developing legal frameworks, strategic plan, standards and mechanism for monitoring and evaluation.[45] The Accreditation Committee in Cambodia (ACC) was established in 2003 and has successfully completed assessments of the foundation years in 41 high education institutions.[46] The Education Law of 2007 was put in place to provide direction to raising the level of human resources development to meet the needs of Cambodian development in the knowledge-based world.[47] Higher education is expected to play a major in producing quality human resources with full capacity in terms of morality, attitude, knowledge, and skills. These graduates will become the future leaders, key decisions makers, teachers, doctors, lawyers, managers, economists, entrepreneurs, artists, writers and intellectuals and will have the ability to respond more effectively to the challenges of poverty, socio-economic development, and social dissonance.

While there are signs of progress in term of numbers, much remains to be done in terms of the quality in higher education. In an article "Cambodia's Sinking Higher Education System" (*The Phnom Penh Post*, 20 April 2011), Tivea Koam and Colin Meyn point out some major issues of the rapid and uncontrolled expansion of HEIs and offer a recommendation to the government:

> If we take a serious look at what is actually being offered in the buildings of these "universities," it is easy to see that, more often than not, it is not

> what a modern academic would recognize as post-secondary education. This is the greatest stumbling block on the path to producing capable human resources in the Kingdom. These business institutions use the guise of academics to attract tuition money, and as such they count success in terms of the bottom line, ignoring the service of schooling they purport to provide and the country so desperately needs. Some higher educational institutions have very good policies on paper (like the government they work under), but this rarely results in good practice. Uniformly, cheating is not allowed in exams, but it still happens and students continue to resort to this sort of behaviour, believing it to be a legitimate strategy for scholastic success...Education drives progress in all parts of society. The government must begin to refuel Cambodia's empty tank or it will suck its own people dry.

The establishment of private universities is driven by market forces and commercial interests rather than purely academic goals. Additionally, most students who enter higher education institutions are unprepared for the rigorous study at the university level. They lack certain skills including, but not limited to, analytical reading, basic writing, independent study, critical skills, and problem solving. Major improvements must occur at the primary and secondary sector to create a better opportunity for students to enter higher education. According to one expert, "A number of students are content to pay for a degree and do not realize the benefit of a good education. Some students are scared of studying hard and think what they need is any degree, not quality. The final result will be joblessness." (AsiaOne, 2008). The effectiveness of higher education rests on that solid foundation provided by a quality primary education system.[48]

The rapid growth of the private higher education institutions also concerns all education stakeholders and policymakers with the issue of quality higher educational services. The Accreditation Committee of Cambodia lacks resources and expertise to provide quality assurance at the international level. Many so-called "universities" don't meet the national and regional requirement.[49] The teaching staff is both weak and insufficient in number. At the level of higher education, the proportion of lecturers with higher degrees is still very low.[50] Special attention needs to be given to faculty and staff development to strengthen their academic, research, and financial and administrative skills.

Research is also a vital component of higher education. Besides providing students with the best educational experiences, independent research plays an important role in the development of the country. It promotes creative thinking and autonomy to solve many potential problems. (Branchini, 2003)

Research across the board in all areas of intellectual exploration is limited due to funding and low salaries for lecturers. Most universities do not have a clear research policy with supporting institutional mechanism to promote the quantity and the quality of faculty research. This issue needs to be addressed in the Kingdom's higher learning institutions. The research culture needs to be created and reinforced through increased government funding and expanded partnerships among universities in Cambodia and abroad.[51]

Extensive improvement at HEI level is urgently needed in terms of providing quality higher educational services including teaching (lack of highly qualified lecturers), learning, research capacity building and quality assurance to the new generation of Cambodian scholars to be competitive regionally and internationally. (Chet, 2009)

THE CHALLENGES: ADDRESSING THE PROBLEMS OF EQUITY AND QUALITY EDUCATION

Cambodia is at a crossroads. While these recent gains in the education sector are unprecedented in term of school buildings, the overall increase in the number of students and number of new trained teachers, there is still an unfinished agenda. The Cambodian people are principally rural. The government has instituted a democratic system of quality education designed to meet the needs of the masses. However, there appear to be serious rural-urban quality gaps. It is also noticeable that the system of education in Cambodia emphasizes quantity over quality education.[52] The country still faces numerous fundamental challenges in the education sector. Without an educated and competent workforce, Cambodia cannot compete on an equal scale with its neighbours. Providing quality education for all is one of the most important developmental tools to combat poverty. The issues of equity and quality education remain the two main barriers to developing competent human resources. The fact that people have schools doesn't necessarily mean they have a quality education.

ADDRESSING THE PROBLEMS OF EQUITY

Schools are symbols of order and stability. Despite great progress in the expansion of access of education over the past decade, inequalities still exists mainly between remote, rural and urban areas. Today, Cambodia is still a country where a quality education is usually out-of-reach for thousands of children growing up in poverty and grime. The gender gap is also a major problem at all education levels.[53] Research done by the World Bank and the

United Nations has clearly found that there is no better investment more effective for achieving developmental goals than educating girls. In Cambodia, only 33 per cent of school-age girls are enrolled at lower secondary school, 11 per cent at upper secondary, and a larger gap at the university level according to the Education Management Information System.[54] A low level of education deprives women from using their full potential for social and economic development.

Several factors contribute to inequitable access to education. First, the low level of socio-economic condition affects the poor mainly in the rural areas. Cambodia has a high percentage of people living below the poverty line.[55] With poverty rising and income diminishing, many of them are forced to cut back on education spending and withdraw their children from school to help support the family's most basic needs.[56] The International Labor Organization estimates that 45 per cent of 5 to 14 year olds, or over 1.5 million children in absolute terms were economically active in the 2001 reference.[57] Second, a shortage of schools and the long distance between home and school prevent a large number of children access to basic education (Table 20.4). Access to secondary school becomes even more difficult with the low number of schools and the longer distance from home. Currently, there are 187 communes that don't have lower secondary schools.[58] A good number of existing disadvantaged schools, which have unsafe roofs and floor, and no drinking water or toilets, are located in those hard to reach areas. About two-thirds of 9,000 incomplete schools are in the rural area and remote areas.[59] Third, there is a serious shortage of qualified teachers in the rural and remote areas. To compound the problem, irregular practices permeate the education system such as illegal fees and payment for hiring, transfer, and promotion.[60] Fourth, government funding is another issue in promoting education opportunity. According to Southeast Asia Globe 2011 Foreign Business Survey, education spending in Cambodia constitutes just 1.6 per cent of Gross Domestic Product (GDP), equating to just $33 per capita, much lower than Thailand's 4 per cent and Indonesia's 3.5 per cent.[61] The Government of Cambodia allocates $1.50–$1.75 per student per year to each primary school for teaching materials and school operating costs.[62]

ADDRESSING THE PROBLEMS OF QUALITY

The two most powerful influences on children as they are growing up are home and the school. Quality education can give hope for a better future and a better life. According to the Hewlett Foundation's Global Development Program, working in a unique partnership with the Bill and Melinda Gates Foundation, citizens who can read, calculate, and think critically have better economic opportunities, higher agricultural productivity, healthier children, and better reproductive health and rights.[63] Improving the quality education in Cambodia can lead them to this path.

Providing quality education in Cambodia is in the hands of the MoEYS. The importance of training a capable and competent of teachers, schools principals or other educational staff cannot be stressed enough. Countless studies have proved that teachers are the most significant factor in any student's schooling. (Thompson, 2002) Teachers are fundamental to achieving the aim of quality education.[64] They play a very important role in forming the foundation of the students. They can make a significant impact in the lives of the students. Without good teachers, increasing enrolment and new classrooms all have limited value. Delivering quality education requires well-trained, highly motivated, disciplined and professionally competent teachers, school principals and all educational staff. Each individual student's interest and welfare should be nurtured to promote lifelong learning. The teaching and learning process should put students first as a subject not as an object and treat all learners as ends rather than means. (Strike and Soltis, 1998) Students must become active in learning. A good reading habit is a prerequisite for better learning. (Sadiman, 2004). To complement teaching and learning, a relevant curriculum that matches the need of students, community and workplace should be adopted. It is unrealistic to have quality education with low quality teaching and irrelevant curriculum.

Corruption and poor governance has a negative effect on quality education. The extremely low teacher salaries contribute to a vicious cycle that encourages students to bribe their way through school, and eventually use bribery to carry them through life. In the national educational system, Cambodians are educated in corruption early — students aged 6-years-old and up are forced and thereby taught that paying unofficial fees to supplement teachers' salary is a part of growing up.[65] Teachers demand that students pay school fee every day.[66] Eliminating systematic problems such as corruption, nepotism, and poor leadership with transparency and accountability will contribute to quality education. A school system, that is free of corruption, is characterized by the following (Heyneman, 2002):

- Equal access to educational opportunity.
- Fairness in the distribution of educational curricula and materials.
- Fairness and transparency in the criteria for selection and more specialized training.
- Fairness in accreditation in which all institutions are judged by professional standards equally applied and open to public scrutiny.
- Fairness in the acquisition of educational goods and services.[67]

- Maintenance of professional standards of conduct by those who administer education institutions and who teach in them, whether public or private.

THE ELEPHANT IN THE ROOM

Given the generosity of the donor nations and the hard work of educators, administrators and politicians there is one special challenge still facing the education system in Cambodia. It is the elephant in the room no one wants to discuss or even admit exists. It is quite simply the mindset of students and many others towards the value of education and critical thinking. Many students falsely view education as a necessary obstacle to overcome to obtain greater economic rewards. Learning is not important or particularly valued. What is important is to overcome that obstacle by any means possible. In the end we are left with a generation that can barely read and write.

As educators it is easy to fall into the trap of thinking if only we had better equipment, better classrooms, et cetera. While the building and equipment situation in Cambodia is not perfect and many schools lack many of the basics, this is not what is holding back teaching our children to read and write. It is this mindset, created in part by the utter devastation of the education system by the Khmer Rouge that learning is not to be valued. With this mindset it is difficult to advance our level of education and knowledge. Only when we can advance education can we advance the nation.

Our challenge as educators, administrators, politicians, citizens and parents is to change that mindset. It is an enormous challenge. The first step is we must agree that we have a problem. Then and only then can we begin to discuss solutions.

CONCLUSION

In Cambodia, education is a work in progress. There is doubt about the government's desire to improve the quality of education and provide equal access to all its citizens. However, if Cambodia is to take a great leap forward to improve its education system, it must translate those lofty goals into lofty actions by providing equity and quality education for the benefit of all Cambodian people, and not just for the privileged urban population.

Notes

1. Education Law, 2007, Article 18: Higher Education shall teach learners to have complete personality and characteristic and promote the scientific, technical, cultural and social researches in order to achieve capacity, knowledge, skill,

morality, inventive and creative ideas and entrepreneurial spirit to the development of the country.

2. UNESCO, *Education For All Global Report 2010*, Summary: Reaching Out the Marginalized.
3. Ministry of Planning, *National Strategic Development Plan 2006–2010.*
4. Personal fieldwork interview with the Khmer Rouge family survivors at Koh Thom, March 2011.
5. Documentation Centre of Cambodia.
6. <http://en.wikipedia.org/wiki/Education_in_Cambodia>.
7. <http://www.tc.columbia.edu/cice/Archives/2.1/21clayton.pdf>.
8. *Study on Governance challenges for Education in Fragile Situations*, Study Synthesis Report, Euro Trends 2009.
9. M.A. Martin. "Vietnamised Cambodia: A silent ethnocide". *Indochina Report*, 7, 1-31. 1986.
10. <http://en.wikipedia.org/wiki/Education_in_Cambodia>.
11. For a detailed discussion of political education during the occupation, see Clayton: *The shape of hegemony: Vietnam in Cambodia, 1979–1989.* Education and Society.
12. <http://www.seasite.niu.edu/khmer/ledgerwood/education.htm>.
13. The National United Front for an Independent, Neutral Peaceful and Cooperative Cambodia (FUNCINPEC) and Khmer People's National liberation Front (KPNLF).
14. Child Friendly School Retrieved from <http://www.unicef.org/education/index_focus_schools.html>.
15. *Teaching Matters*, 2008.
16. The Constitution of Cambodia.
17. The Constitution of Cambodia.
18. Education Law: Article 31, Right to access to education.
19. *Achieving Cambodia's Millennium Development Goals*, Ministry of Planning, 2010.
20. Study on Governance Challenges for Education in Fragile Situations, Euro Trends, 2009.
21. The Rectangular Strategy for Growth, Employment, Equity, and Equity in Cambodia addressed by Samdech Hun Sen, Prime Minister of The Royal Government of Cambodia on July 2004.
22. MoEYS Key Indicators, 2006–2010.
23. For more information on a summary of key development partner see *UNESCO National Education Support Strategy, 2010.*
24. World Bank: Higher Education Quality and Capacity Improvement Project, 2010.
25. *UNESCO National Education Support Strategy, 2010.*
26. UNESCO, 2010. Monitoring Report. Summary. Reaching the marginalized.
27. For more detail information see MoEYS, Policy on Non-Formal Education Equivalency Program, 2008.

28. *UNESCO National Education Support Strategy, 2010.*
29. MoEYS Key Indicators, 2006–2010.
30. General Population Census of Cambodia 2008 — National Report on Final Census Results, National Institute of Statistics update 2010.
31. *Achieving Cambodia's Millennium Development Goals*, Update 2010.
32. *UNESCO National Education Support Strategy, 2010.*
33. MoEYS Key Indicators 2009–2010.
34. *UNESCO National Education Support Strategy, 2010.*
35. *UNESCO National Education Support Strategy, 2010.*
36. MoEYS Key Indicators 2009–2010.
37. Teaching in Cambodia, 2008.
38. *UNESCO National Education Support Strategy, 2010.*
39. Teaching Matters, 2008.
40. Constitution of Cambodia.
41. *UNESCO National Education Support Strategy, 2010.*
42. Achieving Cambodia's Millennium Development Goals, Update 2010.
43. This term refers to both universities and post secondary institutions that offer higher education degrees.
44. *UNESCO National Education Support Strategy, 2010.*
45. MoEYS, *Education Strategic Plan, 2009–2013.*
46. World Bank, 2010.
47. Education Law, 2007, Article 18: Higher Education shall teach learners to have complete personality and characteristic and promote the scientific, technical, cultural and social researches in order to achieve capacity, knowledge, skill, morality, inventive and creative ideas and entrepreneurial spirit to the development of the country.
48. UNESCO *Reaching the Marginalized, 2010.*
49. *UNESCO National Education Support Strategy, 2010.*
50. Scoping Study: Research Capacities of Cambodia's Universities. The Development Research Forum in Cambodia, 2010.
51. *UNESCO National Education Support Strategy, 2010.*
52. Teaching Matters, 2008.
53. The Cambodia Daily, "Prime Minister Calls for More Girls to attend Schools", 25 March 2011.
54. Southeast Asia Globe, April 2011. Cambodia: A woman's touch.
55. Achieving Cambodia's Millennium Development Goals, Update 2010.
56. UNESCO *Reaching the Marginalized, 2010.*
57. *Achieving Cambodia's Millennium Development Goals*, Update 2010.
58. MoEYS, Progress of Suntuk declaration on One Commune, One Lower Secondary School, 2008.
59. *UNESCO National Education Support Strategy, 2010.*
60. *UNESCO National Education Support Strategy, 2010.*
61. Southeast Asia Globe, *Foreign Business Leaders Survey*, 2011.

62. The Challenge –Why Educate Cambodia. <http://www.schools4cambodia.org>.
63. For more information, check Quality Education in Developing Countries/ Hewlett Foundation. <http://www.hewlett.org/programs/global-development-program/quality-education-in-developing-countries>.
64. *Teaching Matters*, 2008.
65. For further information, see my article on "The Black Economy" in Cambodia in 2009.
66. *The Cambodia Daily*, "Teachers to Return to Classes after Overcharging Allegations", 8 December 2009.
67. For more information, see Stephan P. Heyneman, "Education and Corruption". Paper presented to the International Forum at the Annual Meeting of the Association for the Study of Higher Education, Sacramento, California, November 2002.

References

Publications

Benveniste, Luis; Marshall, Jeffrey; Caridad, Araujo. *Teaching In Cambodia. Human Development Sector East Asia and the Pacific Region*. The World Bank and Ministry of Education, Youth and Sport, Royal Government of Cambodia, 2008.

Cambodia, Ministry of Education, Youth and Sport. *Sector Support Project. Working together to provide education for all.* Phnom Penh, 2005.

———. *Reaching the People: Public Expenditure Tracking and Service Delivery in Primary Education*. Phnom Penh, 2005.

———. *Child Friendly School Framework*. Phnom Penh, 2005.

———. *Education Law*. Phnom Penh, 2007.

———. *Education Indicators and Statistics*. Phnom Penh, various years.

Cambodia, Ministry of Planning. 2010. *Achieving Cambodia's Millennium Development Goals*. Phnom Penh.

CAMFEBA: Youth and Employment: Bridging the Gap. A Study About Youth and Employer Perspectives on Education, Skills, Opportunities and the Future, 2008.

Chandler, David. *A History of Cambodia*. Chiang Mai: Silkworm Books. Third edition, 2000.

Chet, Chealy. "Higher Education in Cambodia". In *The Political Economy of Educational Reforms and Capacity Development in Southeast Asia*, edited by Yasushi Hirosato and Yuto Kitamura, 2009.

Development Research Forum in Cambodia. Scoping Study: Research Capacities of Cambodia's Universities, 2010.

FitzGerald, Ingrid; Sovannarith, So; Sophal, Chan; Sithen, Kem; and Sokphally Tuot. *Moving out of Poverty?*, Phnom Penh, CDRI, 2007.

Hinton, Alex. *Truth, Representation and the Politics of Memory after Genocide. in People of Virtue*, edited by David Chandler and Alexandra Kent. Copenhagen: Nordic Institute of Asian Studies, 2008.

Jennar, Raoul M. *The Cambodian Constitutions* (1995). Bangkok: White Lotus, 1995.

Kent, Alexandra and David Chandler, ed. *People of Virtue: Reconfiguring Religion, Power, and Moral Order in Cambodia Today*. Copenhagen: Nordic Institute of Asian Studies, 2008.

Sadiman, Arief. "Challenges in Education in Southeast Asia". Paper presented at the International seminar on "Toward Cross-border Cooperation Between South and Southeast Asia," Kaziranga, India, 2004.

Southeast Asia Globe. *Foreign Business Leaders Survey*, 2011.

Southeast Asia Globe, "Cambodia: A woman's touch". 2011.

Stephan P. Heyneman. "Education and Corruption". Paper presented to the International Forum at the Annual Meeting of the Association for the Study of Higher Education, Sacramento, California, November 2002.

Strike, Kenneth and Jonas F. Sotis. *The Ethics of Teaching*. Teacher College Press. New York, 1998.

Teaching Matters: A policy report on the motivation and morale of teachers in Cambodia. European Union and the World Bank. 2008.

Thompson, Julia . First Year Teacher's Survival Kit. Jossey-Bass. San Francisco. California UNESCO. EFA Global Monitoring Report. 2010. Summary. Reaching the Marginalized, 2002.

UNESCO. EFA Global Monitoring Report. Summary. The Hidden Crisis: Armed Conflict and Education, 2011.

UNESCO National Education Support Strategy. Cambodia 2010–2013.

Websites

<http://en.wikipedia.org/wiki/Education_in_Cambodia>

<http://www.tc.columbia.edu/cice/Archives/2.1/21clayton.pdf>

<http://www.moeys.gov.kh/>

Child Friendly School Retrieved from <http://www.unicef.org/education/index_focus_schools.html>

AsiaOne, 2008. <http://www.asiaone.com/News/Education/Story/A1Story20081005-91729.html>

ADB, Millennium Development Indicator 2007, MDG Table (<https://sdbs.adb.org/sdbs/index.jsp>)

ADB, Key Indicators 2009 (<http://www.adb.org/Documents/Books/Key_Indicators/2009/pdf/Key-Indicators-2009.pdf>)

Branchini, Bruce R. "Why Should Students Do Research?" (2003). Convocation Addresses. Paper 3. <http://digitalcommons.conncoll.edu/convo/3>

Challenge in Education in Southeast Asia: <http://www.seameo.org/>

Clayton, Thomas. Education under Occupation: Political Violence, Schooling, and Response in Cambodia, 1979–1989. 2002 Current Issues in Comparative

Education, Teachers College, Columbia University. Archives <http://www.tc.columbia.edu/cice/Archives/2.1/21clayton.pdf>

Human Development Report 2009: Cambodia. Available at <http://hdrstats.undp.org/en/countries/country_fact_sheets/cty_fs_KHM.html>

Quality Education in Developing Countries/ Hewlett Foundation. <http://www.hewlett.org/programs/global-development-program/quality-education-in-developing-countries>

Articles

Cambodia: Quality Basic Education For All. Human Development Sector Unit. East Asia and the Pacific Region. Report No. 32619-KH. January 2005.

Cambodia: Expanded Basic Education Program (EBEP) Phase II: 2006–2010. Review report of year 2009. UNESCO.

Cambodian Business Review, January 2010, volume 6, issue 1.

Clayton, Thomas. "Building The New Cambodia: Educational destruction and construction under the Khmer Rouge, 1975–1979". *History of Education Quarterly*, v 38 n 1 pp. 1–16 Spr 1998.

Griffin, Patrick. "Challenges Facing Education: Roles and Goals". Paper presented at the Linking Latitudes Conference. Hanoi , 13 April 2004.

Higher Education Quality and Capacity Building Improvement Project, The World Bank, 2010.

Im Sethy, Minister of MoEYS, Speech at the Graduation Ceremony, Paññāsātra University of Cambodia, Phnom-Penh, 17 January 2011.

Internal Report on the Cambodian Independent Teacher's Association National Survey 2011. Cambodian Independent Teacher's Association.

Martin, M.A. "Vietnamised Cambodia: A silent ethnocide". *Indochina Report*, 7, 1–31. 1986.

Pou Sovachana. "The Corruption Behind the Black Economy in Cambodia", *The Cambodia Daily*, 2 February 2010.

"Cambodia's Sinking Higher Education System", Tivea Koam and Colin Meyn, *The Phnom-Penh Post*, 20 April 2011.

"Prime Minister Calls for More Girls to attend Schools", *The Cambodia Daily*, 25 March 2011.

"Teachers to Return to Classes after Overcharging Allegations", *The Cambodia Daily*, 8 December 2009.

21

BUDDHISM IN CAMBODIA SINCE 1993

Ian Harris

INTRODUCTION

Buddhism has had a long history in the country we now call Cambodia. Inscriptional and archaeological evidence suggest that it was already well established by the fifth century of the Common Era (CE) when the lower Mekong appears to have become a significant entrepôt in the passage of Buddhist ideas and material culture from India to the Middle Kingdom. In the Angkorian period Buddhist influence waxed and waned, sometimes thriving in a syncretic nexus with Brahmanical beliefs and practices, at others playing an important role in the rituals of state. The zenith of this Mahayanist and Tantric state-supported Buddhism coincided with the reign of Jayavarman VII (c. 1243–95) and declined swiftly following the fall of Angkor in the first decades of the fifteenth century. From this point on, and largely as a result of rising Siamese influence in the region, a grassroots, village-oriented form of Theravāda Buddhism took hold, and this has continued to be the dominant religion until the present. However, Cambodia's Theravāda tradition never remained static. It underwent a small, Bangkok-inspired renaissance during the reign of King Ang Duang (1848–60), while its bureaucratic structures were modified and its educational facilities enhanced during the French colonial and early Independence periods.[1]

As is now well known, Buddhist institutions were dissolved during the Democratic Kampuchea era, many thousands of monks lost their lives, and religious practice, where it occurred at all, was entirely hidden from public gaze. With the demise of the Pol Pot regime and establishment of the People's Republic of Kampuchea [PRK] in early 1979, organised Buddhism gradually re-emerged, although for the next decade it was obliged to operate within a strictly socialist setting. This meant that the activity of the monkhood (*saṅgha*) was largely restricted to the patriotic, nation-building role assigned to it by the government.[2] Despite these restrictions there is good evidence that Buddhism rapidly regained its relevance at the popular level. This was most apparent in regard to a greatly felt need to perform funerary rites for those who had perished during the country's appalling upheavals. Knowing that relatives had not been properly cremated, thus effecting transition to a new form of rebirth, appears to have been a great psychological burden. It induced a "*sense of guilt for having survived*" amongst many, some of whom embarked on journeys to places they had lived during Democratic Kampuchea to collect the remains of the dead (Ledgerwood n.d., 33). This in turn, resulted in a massive burst in the building of funerary monuments (*chedey*) and a renewed emphasis on the annual day of ancestors (*pchum ben*).

With the breakup of the Soviet Union, and subsequent withdrawal of Vietnamese troops, a new spirit of religious toleration began to manifest itself. The April 1989 constitution of the State of Cambodia [SOC] restored Buddhism as the state religion, while Prime Minister Hun Sen apologized for earlier government "*mistakes*" in a series of talks around the country, and senior leaders engaged in acts of conspicuous Buddhist piety. In this new atmosphere, monk numbers grew rapidly, pagoda reconstruction burgeoned — mainly as a result of funds flowing into the country from an extensive Cambodian Diaspora — taxes on pagodas were abolished, and Buddhist education, including Pali schools, began to re-emerge.[3] As if to underline these dramatic changes, the Cambodian People's Party [CPP], an entity rapidly forged from the embers of the old Khmer People's Revolutionary Party, now claimed that the:

> ...citizens' honour, dignity and life must be protected by laws. The death penalty is abolished. Buddhism is the state religion with the Tripitaka[4] as basis of laws. All religious activities are allowed in the country. The traditions, customs and cultural heritage of the nation must be preserved and glorified,

as well as the traditions of all the nationalities living in the Cambodian national community.[5]

REBIRTH OF SANGHA INSTITUTIONS

When Samdech Norodom Sihanouk returned in November 1991, one of his first acts was to resume his traditional kingly duty as supreme patron of the *saṅgha*. During the People's Republic of Kampuchea (PRK) era, a single unified *saṅgha* of the Front (*renakse sang*) had been created to administer Buddhist monks. In December 1991, this *renakse sang* was dissolved and Samdech Norodom Sihanouk appointed chief monks (*sanghareach*) for each of the two pre-1975 monastic fraternities (*nikāya*). Venerable Tep Vong,[6] the old head of the *renakse sang*, became patriarch of the Mahanikay, the largest and most influential of the two groupings, while Venerable Bour Kry,[7] a prominent figure from the Cambodian community in Paris, was given charge of the Thommayut, a small reformist order of Siamese origins, created during the reign of Ang Duang and having close links with the royal family.

The reestablishment of the two old *nikāyas* seemed to imply that the Mahanikay and Thommayut would once again enjoy theoretical equivalence. Although this is likely to have been Samdech Norodom Sihanouk's intention, suspicion of the Thommayut among key ex-communists in the ruling Cambodian People's Party has ensured that this would never become a reality.

Originally from Battambang province Bour Kry had crossed into nearby Thailand, home of the Thommayut order, during the civil war period. In due course, he moved to France, living throughout the Democratic Kampuchea and PRK periods at Wat Khemararam in the eastern suburbs of Paris. This was where in the late 1980s one of Sihanouk's sons and future king, Norodom Sihamoni, was temporarily ordained under his tutelage. On his return to Phnom Penh, Bour Kry naturally took up residence at Wat Botum Vaddey, previously the headquarters of the Thommayut in Cambodia. One might have expected the order to have flourished from this point on, but this has been far from the case. Even today, the pagoda's Thommayut monks remain greatly outnumbered, physically isolated in a separate section of the compound, and occasionally discriminated against by resident members of the Mahanikay. This situation was not aided by the fact that Wat Botum is the residence of Ven. Noun Nget, currently number two in the Mahanikay hierarchy.[8]

Another indication that the Thommayut continues to excite official suspicion is the fact that Wat Botum's lay management committee is presided over by Hun Neang, Hun Sen's father and a staunch supporter of Noun Nget. Moreover, it has proved very difficult for the order to recover most of its pre-

1975 pagodas in other areas of the country. How far this is a result of an anti-Thai or anti-monarchic outlook amongst members of the ruling elite, or of simple maladministration by the Ministry of Religions and Cults, it is difficult to determine. In any case, ongoing frustrations mean that Bour Kry continues to spend significant portions of the year in Paris.

THE MINISTRY OF CULTS AND RELIGIOUS AFFAIRS

The Ministry of Cults and Religious Affairs was re-established in early 1992. Its initial goals were to reform the ecclesiastical structures that existed before 1970, to develop monk education and to re-establish the Buddhist Institute, a centre of traditional learning and research that had originally been founded by the French colonial authorities in 1930. This re-emerged in June 1992 and was initially funded by grants from two non-Khmer NGOs, the Heinrich Böll Foundation [HBF], an organization linked with the German Green Party, and the Japanese Sotoshu Relief Committee [JSRC].

BUDDHISM OPENS UP TO THE EXTERNAL WORLD

From this point on, and especially after the May 1993 elections, Cambodian Buddhism accelerated its engagement with the external world. During the PRK era, the government had ensured that such links only occurred with Buddhists in other socialist contexts. But the massive influx of foreign aid workers during the UNTAC period meant that the floodgates would now be definitively breached. NGOs, both international and local, were soon active, and by the early 2000s it was estimated that around US$80 million of international aid flowed through these organizations into the Cambodian economy every year. Their work began to impact on all levels of Cambodian life including medicine, human rights, banking, art and culture, the rewriting of laws, urban planning, environmental matters, women's issues, education, disarmament, de-mining, and so on. Religion was also significantly affected because many NGOs felt the need to channel their activities through reliable partners with influence throughout the country. As always, the *sangha* was well-placed to perform such a role. But this came at a cost.

Given its almost total destruction during the Democratic Kampuchea era, the Buddhist monastic order was only just emerging from its chrysalis. With little money available inside the country it became reliant on sources of patronage emanating from outside. The Khmer Diaspora community tended to support the rebuilding of individual pagodas while international organisations focused more on the re-establishment of institutions and the country's devastated intellectual, spiritual and literary patrimony. At the same time, it was potentially vulnerable to external manipulation, however well-meaning, particularly given the fact that most monks had only the barest grasp of basic Buddhist teachings and principles. It is in this light that we should consider the previously mentioned HBF's support for the foundation of the Association of Nuns and Laywomen of Cambodia [ANLWC]. As a result, nun numbers have increased continuously, one informed estimate suggesting a total of 10,000 nuns (*don chee*) in the country. (Löschmann 2000, 93) However, nuns continue to face some discrimination and gain meagre material support from the Buddhist laity, since they are not generally regarded as a fertile ground for merit making.

The Japan Sotoshu Relief Committee (JSRC), on the other hand, had initially been stung into taking a role in Cambodia following a number of criticisms in the *Asahi Shinbun*, a leading Japanese newspaper, that while Christian agencies had been involved in rebuilding the country, the Japanese seemed to be doing nothing for their Asian and Buddhist brothers and sisters. As a result the organisation became heavily involved in republishing materials relating to Buddhism and Khmer culture. It restarted *Kambuja Suriya*, the original house journal of the Buddhist Institute, in 1994 and presented the King with 1,200 copies of the complete 110 volume set of the Khmer Tripitaka for distribution to monasteries and libraries the following year. (de Bernon 1998, 880)

MAHAGHOSANANDA

Many of these forces crystallised in the Mahaghosananda phenomenon. Ven. Mahaghosananda was born in Takeo province around 1922 and had studied at the Buddhist University in Phnom Penh before travelling to India for post-graduate studies at the newly-established Buddhist University of Nalanda, where he came under the influence of Nichidatsu Fujii, founder of the Japanese peace-oriented Buddhist sect Nipponzan Myohoji.[9] In 1980, with concerns rising over the Cambodian refugee crisis on the Thai border, Mahaghosananda formed the Inter-Religious Mission for Peace in Cambodia with Peter Pond, a Christian social-activist. One of its aims was to identify, support and re-ordain surviving Cambodian Buddhist monks, and as a result, over thirty temples in Canada and the United States were established.

Mahaghosananda's encounter with Christianity and the values of the international community appear to have reinforced his earlier Buddhist-oriented concern for peace, reconciliation and social activism. As a result, he became an important spokesman for Engaged Buddhism. In his own words:

> ...we must find the courage to leave the traditional temple and enter the temple of the teeming human experience that is filled with suffering...it is important to remember that we carry our temple with us always. We are the temple.[10]

Mahaghosananda's rise to greater prominence came in April 1992, when he led a peace march (*dhammayietra*) of some 350 monks, nuns and lay Buddhists as they escorted around a hundred refugees from the camps back to their villages against a background of official opposition, for neither the Thai nor the Cambodian governments would give permission for the marchers to cross the border. By the time the marchers arrived in Phnom Penh, the numbers had swollen significantly and in recognition Samdech Sihanouk conferred the title Leader of Religion and Peace (*samdech sang santipheap*) on Mahaghosananda. *Dhammayietra* subsequently became annual events organized by the Centre for Peace and Reconciliation (CPR), a group that had originally been established on the Thai-Cambodian border close to the Site 2 refugee camp, although it would relocate to Wat Sampeou Meas, Phnom Penh, in due course. The CPR's actual founders were Bob Maat — at that time a member of the Society of Jesus, Liz Bernstein, and the Paris-based Mahanikay monk Ven. Yos Hut.[11] It was they who subsequently co-opted Mahaghosananda and this, in part, explains the government's hostility to the movement, which they regard as largely organized by foreigners. Indeed, many of the early marches were led by chanting Japanese Nipponzan Myohoji monks and, as late as 1997, the $27,000 necessary for the organization of the sixth Dhammayietra came mainly from "Christian and ecumenical foreign NGOs, International Organisations, and King Sihanouk." (Yonekura 1999, 86f)

Most *dhammayietra* have focused on specific issues, some of which have not been welcomed by the Cambodian authorities. Mahanikay patriarch Tep Vong had been involved in the early stages of organisation of the first *dhammayietra* but subsequently withdrew his support. It appears that he had been warned off from involvement in unpatriotic activity by the government.[12] The fourth march in 1995 was intended to raise awareness of the issues surrounding landmines, whilst in 1996, marchers sought to highlight the adverse impact of large-scale deforestation. A sixth *dhammayietra* the following year entered the remaining Khmer Rouge strongholds around Pailin, where it was greeted by Ieng Sary, Y. Chhien, the town's mayor, and other important Khmer Rouge defectors. Other more localized marches have been organized against prostitution in Phnom Penh's Toul Kork red-light district, and in support of stranded Vietnamese fishing families, a pariah group in contemporary Cambodia.

As a result of his leadership Mahaghosananda was awarded the 15th Niwano Peace Prize in 1998. The cash involved, amounting to 20 million yen, was used by the CPR to finance various Cambodian NGOs, although doubts about the financial probity of some senior staff began to surface at the end of the 90s, and attempts were made to decentralize the movement. These allegations, when combined with Mahaghosananda's success in promoting an international profile, his popularity in Cambodia, especially amongst young and well-educated monks, and the fact that he never permanently took up residence in the country, are the most likely reasons behind the government's antagonism. Indeed, following his death in the United States in March 2007, his supporters attempted to return his body to his homeland, but have been consistently blocked by the authorities.

OTHER FORMS OF SOCIAL ENGAGEMENT

Another close associate of Mahaghosananda, the previously mentioned Yos Hut, has experienced related difficulties. He has initiated projects to construct and maintain a hospital (begun in 1996) in his home district of Kampong Trabek, Prey Veng province, and a forest monastery, with associated educational and development-oriented features, on some 100 hectares of land nearby. This has provoked hostility between the local authorities and monks associated with this work that crystallized in the attempt to defrock Ven. Khot Khon, abbot of Wat Beng Bury, for supposed sexual misconduct and involvement in politics. The charge seems to have arisen after the visits of several FUNCINPEC officials, including Prince Sisowath Satha, to the monastery (*Phnom Penh Post*, 9 (12), 9–22 June 2000) and suggests a level of government (i.e. CPP) opposition to aspects of the engaged Buddhist agenda, particularly when it is linked with the activities of opposition parties and foreign funders.

A knowledgeable observer has noted that the post-1993 emergence of Buddhist non-governmental organizations (NGOs) has been a phenomenon in which "*Buddhist concepts are diluted, distorted and jargonised by contact with the discourse of human rights*" (Marston, 2009, 236). But Mahaghosananda and his followers have, nevertheless, spawned a variety of Buddhist developments that have drawn on an internationalist agenda. He once commented, somewhat anachronistically it seems to me, that, "*...the Buddha lobbied for peace and human rights*" (Mahaghosananda 1992, 70) and it is against this background that one should interpret the establishment of the Cambodian Institute of Human Rights [CIHR] in 1993. The CIHR, drawing explicitly on Buddhist ideas and practices as the prime context from which an examination of human rights can begin, has received funding from both the

European Community and the French government, and includes the training of teachers in an attempt "*...to instil the values of non-violence" in the younger generation* (Neou 2000, 305 & 309) It also encourages Buddhist monks and nuns to use traditional Cambodian methods of dispute resolution that rely largely on their respected status in the community, and to train in issues related to good governance so that they may become significant opinion-shapers. The CIHR also organizes "Culture of Peace" rallies that demonstrate obvious affiliation to the *dhammayietra* movement.

Another feature of the kinds of Buddhist activity supported by foreign patronage is the prioritisation of social engagement over the performance of traditional forms of religiosity. Premised on a distinction between "*useful*" and "*useless*" activities, strong emphasis is given to developmental, educational and other welfare-oriented enterprise over the performance of ritual and contemplation, both of which are deemed to be superstitious and a form of time-wasting self-absorption. The suppression of the individual will is held to be out of tune with the romantic spirit of self-development while the ideology of development, it is claimed, more helpfully leads to enhanced engagement with a global culture of consumption. Financial support from international NGOs, then, is given exclusively to forms of Buddhism moving in a modernist direction, but one of the more paradoxical aspects of this attitude is that it parallels the justification of Buddhist reforms that were forced through during the early Khmer Rouge and PRK periods.

This is a nice illustration of Charles Taylor's "*affirmation of ordinary life*", a potentially momentous move away from "the supposedly higher activities of "*contemplation*" in favour of ordinary living and production.[13] A few examples will suffice. Funding for a socially engaged and modernist "*development-oriented Buddhism*" has been promoted by the German-based Konrad Adenauer Foundation (KAF), a supporter of Santi Sena, a local NGO based at Wat Prey Chlak, Svay Rieng which works on forest preservation and related environment activity. Between 1994 and 1997, the KAF also funded the Buddhism for Development (BFD) organisation led by the former monk Heng Monychenda. The BFD, founded in 1990, originally emerged from Son Sann and Venerable Pin Sem's attempts to revive Khmer Buddhist culture, and provide it with social relevance, at the Rithisen refugee camp on the Thai border (Son Soubert et al. 1986). It subsequently launched a number of initiatives, including the training of Buddhist monks in rural development work, plus the establishment of rice and money banks, tree-nurseries and compost-making activities. The Gesellschaft für Technische Zusammenarbeit (GTZ), on the other hand, seeks to regenerate the moral influence of Buddhism in contemporary society, arguing that lay people engaged in activities such as tree-planting and road building is a form of generating religious merit. It has tended to work with local *wat* communities, especially in Kampong Thom.

PATRIOTISM AND THE TRADITIONALIST BACKLASH

The influence of international organisations promoting a modernist, socially engaged agenda was bound to induce a reaction. In this context, attempts to sideline or harass monks associated with the movement are an inevitable backlash. But a cursory study of the history of Buddhism in twentieth century Cambodia (Harris 2005, 105ff) also suggests that monastic traditionalists themselves are likely to oppose attempts at modernization quite vigorously.

Evidence that the modernists are not the only act in town is provided by a number of high profile monks closely associated with leading figures in the political and business firmament. Ven. Om Lim Heng (b.1964), *cau adhikār* of Wat Champuskaek, a short distance south of Phnom Penh, is a case in point. He appears to act as a quasi-official chaplain to Hun Sen who lives in the vicinity and many photographs, prominently displayed in the rather magnificent shrine halls within the monastery compound, and jostling with more customary Buddhist iconography, depict him in the Prime Minister's company. Om Lim Heng holds a senior position in the national hierarchy of the Mahanikay but his renown flows from a widespread belief that he possesses magical powers. He specialises in sprinkling water on his lay followers, a long-standing apotropaic rite that he has developed in novel ways. One of these is the use of a power hose to lustrate the luxury automobiles of his supporters. In consequence of the success of Om Lim Heng's religio-magical entrepreneurialism, Wat Champuskaek has become one of the wealthiest religious establishments in the land, with Hun Sen, for example, contributing US$110,000 dollars to the pagoda's US$600,000 building program, while associated figures, such as Hok Lundy [now deceased] and Moeung Samphan, a three-star general and father-in-law of Hun Sen's eldest daughter, have also been significant donors (*Phnom Penh Post*, 9 (6), 17–30 March 2000).

Ven. Daung Phang is an equally successful and well-connected representative of a more traditional monastic marketplace. But unlike Om Lim Heng he also has an ability to articulate his opposition to the modernists in rational terms. In essence, he sees himself as the guardian of traditional monastic practices (*boran*) that have variously been eroded by conflict and the influence of non-Khmer forces on the *saṅgha.* Originally the chief monk of Kroch Chmar district, Kompong Cham province, Daung Phang now resides at Wat Prek Barang, Kompong Luong, a short distance from the old capital of Udong and surrounded by numerous iconographical prompts hinting at his influential contacts. One of these is a nearby equestrian statue of King Ang Duang erected alongside National Route Five just north of the *wat*,[14] but when I last visited several years ago, the monastery precincts also displayed large and colourful posters of its chief monk in the company of influential politicians.

Daung Phang is said to have the power of prophecy as well as being adept at various magical practices. He has been instrumental in revivifying the annual monastic rite of probation (*parivāsa*). From the mainstream Theravāda perspective, *parivāsa* should be regarded a period of suspension and penitence for an individual monk who has infringed certain rules of discipline, but in Cambodia the practice may also refer to a collective monastic ritual of purification with specific emphasis placed on ascetic practices. The first time this ritual was performed after the Pol Pot period was at Wat Prek Barang, in February 1997, but not without controversy. It seems that the event invoked opposition from segments of the *saṅgha* who were lukewarm about the reestablishment of certain pre-1970s traditions, and when Daung Phang held a repeat of the rite the following year at Wat Champuskaek, he was sternly rebuked by Ven. Noun Nget, and the dispute becoming so heated that unsuccessful attempts to adjudicate were made by the Ministry of Cults (de Bernon 2000, 475f.). Nevertheless, Tep Vong was a major participant when *parivāsa* rituals were performed in 1999 and 2000. The latter was a particularly grand affair that took place within the precincts of Angkor Thom, and appears to have been designed expressly to establish a connection between the traditionalists, their patrons, and the ancient Angkorian state.

Traditionalist monks like Daung Phang tend to be quite critical of certain Buddhist practices, putatively imported from other regions of the Theravāda world. These, they argue, are incompatible with long-established currents of Cambodian spiritual praxis. In this way, they seek to draw strong connections between legitimate forms of the religious life and the fate of the Cambodian nation. From this perspective, imported practices are unpatriotic and likely to corrode the body politic, an outlook that meshes perfectly with the view of senior politicians whose careers were forged in the highly xenophobic Democratic Kampuchea and People's Republic of Kampuchea periods, when Buddhism itself was often regarded as a foreign religion with origins in India or Thailand. The most important of these imports is insight meditation (*vipassanā*), a widespread practice throughout Buddhist Asia that involves the cultivation of bare insight into the rising and falling of physical and mental phenomena, without the need for highly concentrated states of mind. Some modern Buddhist meditation teachers have claimed that by simply applying the three marks of impermanence, suffering, and non-self to these states, one will gain enlightenment. Traditionalists, on the other hand, insist on the need to avoid quick fix solutions on the path to *nirvana*. But the argument is not simply over the correct means to liberation, it is also about the preservation of distinctively Khmer rites and practices.

By the end of the 1990s, Ven. Sam Bunthoeun had become one of Cambodia's most prominent teachers of *vipassanā*. Born in Kandal province in 1957 and ordained in 1980, it seems that a keen interest in *vipassanā* had led him to set up a centre for lay and monastic practice at Wat Unnalom, Phnom Penh, apparently with the support of Tep Vong. When his following outgrew these premises he established the Buddhist Meditation Centre at the foot of Phnom Preah Reach Trop near the old capital of Udong,[15] an organization that was well supported by wealthy lay followers, many of whom were women. Mysteriously he was shot in broad daylight by at least two assailants at the entrance to Wat Langka, Phnom Penh on 6 February 2003 and died in hospital two days later.

Theories abound as to who was responsible for his death, a situation compounded by the fact that his assassins remain unidentified. Certainly, the incident had all the characteristics of a contract killing. Some believe that the execution was related to the fact that he opposed Tep Vong's edict prohibiting monks from voting in the July elections (Falby 2003).[16] But others are unconvinced because Sam Bunthoeun does not appear to have been politically active. Disputes with contractors involved in building the new Centre, or the suspicions of a jealous husband of a key female supporter, have also been advanced as possible motives, as has the astonishing growth of the Buddhist Meditation Centre of Udong, a situation that may have led to rivalry with other prominent monks trying to ensure that their pagoda is larger, better appointed and more luxuriously equipped than its competitors. But the fact remains that Sam Bunthoeun also represented a trend in Buddhist practice that, as we have seen, has powerful critics.

Although the two events are probably unrelated it is also worth noting that Sam Bunthoeun's demise occurred only a little over a week after the Phnom Penh anti-Thai riots of 29 January 2003 (Hinton 2006). Given his own commitment to practices deemed unpatriotic by opponents, another curious incident that occurred the previous year comes into clearer focus. In early 2002 a group of Thai missionary monks representing the highly influential but somewhat unorthodox Dhammakaya Foundation, a movement that has gained currency by promoting a meditational technique popularized by Ven. Sot (1884–1959), the late Mahanikay abbot of Wat Paknam Bhasicharoen, Thonburi, established a Phnom Penh base in the Soriya Hotel. In June the

Dhammakaya monks sent a letter of invitation for their opening ceremony to the Ministry of Religions which, in turn, alerted students at the Buddhist University and Suramarit Buddhist High School. As a result, on 8 June several hundred monks led by one of Tep Vong's secretaries set off on a well-organized demonstration, reaching the hotel in the late morning. The Thai monks were vigorously urged to leave Cambodia as soon as possible, with a possible threat of legal measures if they remained. They took the hint and returned to Bangkok.

POLITICISATION OF THE SANGHA

We have noted that the *saṅgha* was kept on a very tight leash during the PRK period and it would be unrealistic to assume that this situation changed dramatically after 1993. The natural conservatism of the rank and file *saṅgha* certainly meant that there was considerable backing for the restored monarchy and, to a certain extent, this translated into a corresponding support for FUNCINPEC. In a sense this could not be helped, but the situation could be monitored, and in some cases counter-acted, by the appointment of pagoda lay management committees dominated by CPP supporters. This was especially so in the large and influential monasteries of Phnom Penh where a disturbingly high proportion of young and reasonably well-educated monks were thought to pose a threat to the national concentration of power into fewer and fewer hands.

Such fears seem to have become a reality during disturbances over the outcome of the July 1998 elections and the authorities acted accordingly. Suspecting foul play, Sam Rainsy Party supporters had organized a number of rallies in late August and early September. At one of these, on 7 September a young monk was severely injured and "*disappeared*". On the following day three hundred monks, some holding posters denouncing Hun Sen led a march through central Phnom Penh. The organisers wanted to recover the body. They also intended to "*beg violence*" from the authorities, in other words to draw any aggression down upon themselves, and so defuse a potentially dangerous situation. But events spiralled out of control. On 9 September police allegedly shot two monks outside the US Embassy,[17] while two days later a young male body with shaved head and eyebrows was found floating down-river. The demonstrations subsided after another week but genuine fears that they were under police surveillance persisted among segments of the Phnom Penh monkhood. At one point twelve monks barricaded themselves into a room at the top of one of the buildings at Wat Unnalom and Tep Vong seems to have requested assistance from Hun Sen's bodyguard unit and military police supplied by municipal governor, Chea Sophara, to flush them out. "*Unnalom monks know how to run!*" was a common maxim at the time.

Another problem area concerns the presence in Cambodia of Khmer monks from Kampuchea Krom who tend to escape from the Mekong region of the Socialist Republic of Vietnam in reasonably large numbers during periods of repression.[18] One might have assumed that safe arrival on Cambodian territory would have brought an end to a monk's ordeal but this has not always so, particularly given the tendency of post-1993 governments to be very touchy about foreign influences. The case of Ven. Tim Sakhorn is instructive in this connection.

Although originally a native of An Giang province, Vietnam, Tim Sakhorn had been abbot of a pagoda just across the border in Kirivong district for a significant period. On the legally dubious grounds that he had been undermining Cambodian-Vietnamese amity by circulating literature and organizing demonstrations to highlight the plight of Khmer monks in Vietnam he was arrested by the Cambodian authorities and defrocked by a committee of senior Cambodian ecclesiastics on 30 June 2007. A letter authorizing his expulsion from the monastic order was signed by Tep Vong and Noun Nget and subsequently distributed to every pagoda in Kampuchea Krom. Tim Sakhorn was then handed over to the Vietnamese authorities. In November 2007 he was sentenced to one year in prison for contravention of Article 87 of the Vietnamese criminal code,19 the indictment stating that he had distributed materials about Khmer Krom history and politics with a view to inciting Khmer in Vietnam to protest about their treatment by the authorities. (Human Rights Watch 2009, 68–69)

PROSPECTS FOR THE FUTURE

Current rivalries between traditionalists and modernists are nothing new. Rather they are part of the enduring rough and tumble of Cambodia's religious history and not something confined only to the post 1993 period. In many respects the same may be said about political interference in and manipulation of the Buddhist monastic order. We certainly know that during the colonial period the French were concerned that monks had the potential to cause them difficulties and for these reasons they tried to prevent them travelling to Bangkok from where they might return with seditious ideas. Similarly, Norodom Sihanouk promoted social engagement for monks as a form of nation building during the Sangkum Reastr Niyum period of the 1950s and 60s.

But Cambodian Buddhism some three decades after the fall of the Khmer Rouge is in a significantly more fragile condition than it was under the French or during the early Independence period. For this reason we should remain concerned about its future prospects. In terms of numbers there are around the same number of monks today as there were in 1970 and this could be used to support the illusion of health. But in terms of learning and discipline the *saṅgha* remains in a rather sorry state. Lack of funds and bureaucratic interference has meant that the Buddhist University and the Buddhist Institute, although superficially centres of higher learning and research, are a shadow of their former selves. It is difficult to be more sanguine about individuals who work outside customary ecclesiastical structures, such as Heng Monychenda and his Buddhism for Development (BFD) organisation. The BFD has certainly played a significant role as a think tank exploring new ways in which Buddhist ideals and practices can be made to address Cambodia's future development. It has also been successful in attracting finance from the international aid community for the implementation of practical projects in the field. But this mode of existence, as we have already seen, underlines the BFD's distance from the levers of power. In such a situation those promoting socially engaged in Cambodia must continue to exercise whatever influence they possess from a position of marginality and hold firm to the Buddhist virtue of patience (*khanti*).

The present monastic hierarchy is composed largely of elderly monks who rose to prominence during the PRK and remain creatures of that rather xenophobic and paranoid thought universe. They are also locked into an increasingly unhealthy patron-client system with senior politicians, rendering them either incapable or unwilling to exercise the Buddhist-oriented moral advocacy so missing from public discourse today. But we recall the Buddha's final admonition: "*all conditioned things are impermanent*", and hope in time for the emergence of a new, more cosmopolitan generation of monks — supportive of higher learning, attuned to the needs of those striving to cultivate the contemplative life, able to establish a proper balance between spiritual pursuits and social engagement, and, most importantly, possessing the courage to speak truth to power — to replace the current gerontocracy. But this may be a very tall order.

Notes

1. For exhaustive coverage of the history of Buddhism in Cambodia, see Harris 2005.

2. For detailed discussion of the fate of Buddhism under the Khmer Rouge, as well as during the People's Republic of Kampuchea, see Harris 2007.
3. Pali is the language of the foundational texts of Theravāda Buddhism.
4. The Tripitaka is the threefold collection of Theravāda sacred writings.
5. *Kampuchea* no. 623 (21 October 1991): 3-4; quoted by Frings 1994, p. 363.
6. For biographical information, see Moung Ra and Chheung Bun Chhea. 2001. *Braḥ rāja jīvapravatti samtec braḥ mahāsumedhādhipatī Tep Vong* (Biography of Tep Vong). Phnom Penh: n.p.
7. For biographical information, see Ang Chouléan et Tan Yinh Phong. 1992. 'Le monastère Khemararam: espace identitaire de la communauté khmère' in Matras-Guin, J. et C. Taillard [eds.] *Habitations et habit d'Asie de sud-est continentale: pratiques er représentations de l'espace.* Paris: L'Harmattan, p. 292.
8. Ordinations into the Thommayut seem to have gathered pace since the early 90s. 150 monks were reported to have been ordained in early July 1992 alone (*PPP* 1(2), 24 July 1992). In November 1999, Ven Noun Nget supplied me with the following (very high) figures for Wat Botum: Mahanikay — c.600, Thommayut — c.200 — in November 1999.
9. For more biographical information, see my obituary of Mahaghosananda in *The Times* [London], 26 March 2007.
10. Quoted by Hansen 1988, p. 61.
11. Yos Hut was pursuing postgraduate studies in Paris when the Khmère Rouge took power in 1975. He subsequently worked for the United Nations Border Relief Organization on the Thai border and now resides at Wat Langka, Phnom Penh. He maintains close connections with the Cambodian Diaspora and the international community and is President of the Fondation Bouddhique Khmère which has offices in Cambodia and France.
12. My interview with Bob Maat. 11 Feb. 2001.
13. Taylor, Charles. 1989. *Sources of the Self.* Cambridge, MA: Harvard University Press, particularly Ch. 13.
14. Guthrie (2002, 68) provides some evidence that Hun Sen's donation to Buddhist temples, Pali schools in and around Udong is an attempt to draw parallels between himself and king Ang Duang.
15. The centre publishes a biography of Sam Bunthoeun plus a number of his *dhamma* books.
16. Monks actually have a constitutional right to vote.
17. One of them, Cheng Sokly subsequently had an AK-47 bullet removed from his body and survived. He reported witnessing the shooting of another monk in the back of the leg.
18. Kampuchea Krom means "Lower Cambodia". It designates traditionally Khmer populated areas in the Mekong delta, now located in the Socialist Republic of Vietnam [SRV]. Since the creation of the SRV, Khmer Krom Buddhists have sought to retain their cultural and religious identities. The Vietnamese Communist Party regards such activity in a very negative light.

For detailed discussion of the recent history of Buddhism in Kampuchea Krom, see Harris 2009.

19. Tim Sakhorn was released from prison on 28 June 2008.

References

de Bernon, Olivier. 'L'état des bibliothèques dans les monastères du Cambodge' in Sorn Samnang (ed.) *Khmer Studies: Knowledge of the Past and its Contributions to the Rehabilitation and Reconstruction of Cambodia — Proceedings of International Conference on Khmer Studies.* Phnom Penh, 26–30 August 1996 Two Volumes, Phnom Penh, 1998, pp. 872–82.

———. "Le rituel de la «grande probation annuelle» (*mahāparivāsakamma*) des religieux du Cambodge". In *Bulletin de l'École française d'Extrême-Orient* 87, no. 2 (2000): 473–510.

Falby, Peter. "To Vote or Not to Vote: Buddhism's Monks Debate their Rights". *PPP* 12 (11), 23 May–5 June 2003.

Guthrie, Elizabeth. "Buddhist Temples and Cambodian Politics". In *People and the 1998 National Elections in Cambodia*, edited by John L. Vijghen, pp. 59–74. Phnom Penh: Experts for Community Research, 2002.

Hansen, Anne, R. *Ways of the World: Moral Discernment and Narrative Ethics in a Cambodian Buddhist Text.* Unpublished PhD thesis, Harvard University, 1999.

Harris, Ian. *Cambodian Buddhism: History and Practice.* Honolulu: University of Hawai'i Press, 2005.

———. *Buddhism Under Pol Pot.* Phnom Penh: Documentation Centre of Cambodia (Documentation Series No. 13), 2007.

———. "Theravāda Buddhism among the Khmer Krom". In *The Khmer-Krom Journey to Self-determination*, edited by Daryn Reicherter and Joshua Cooper, pp. 103–29. Pennsauken, NJ: Khmers Kampuchea Krom Federation, 2009.

Hinton, Alexander. "Khmerness and the Thai 'Other': Violence, Discourse and Symbolism in the 2003 Anti-Thai Riots in Cambodia". *Journal of Southeast Asian Studies* 37, no. 3 (2006): 445–468.

Human Rights Watch. *On the Margins: Rights Abuses of Ethnic Khmer in Vietnam's Mekong Delta.* New York, 2009.

Kassie Neou. "Buddhism, Human Rights, Women's Rights and Democracy". In *Innovative Buddhist Women: Swimming Against the Stream*, edited by K.L. Tsomo, pp. 302–11. Richmond: Curzon Press, 2000.

Ledgerwood, Julie. n.d. "Buddhist Practice in Rural Kandal province 1960 and 2003: An Essay in Honour of May M. Ebihara". Unpublished paper.

Löschmann, Heike. "The Revival of the Don Chee Movement in Cambodia". In *Innovative Buddhist Women: Swimming Against the Stream*, edited by K.L. Tsomo, pp. 91–95. Richmond, Surrey: Curzon Press, 2000.

Maha Ghosananda (edited by Jane Sharada Mahoney and Philip Edmonds). *Step by Step: Meditations on Wisdom and Compassion.* Berkeley, Parallax Press, 1992.

Marston, John. "Cambodian Religion since 1989". In *Beyond Democracy in Cambodia: Political Reconstruction in a Post-Conflict Society*, edited by Joakim Öjendal and Mona Lilja, pp. 224–49. Copenhagen: NIAS Press 2009.

Son Soubert et al. *Buddhism and the Future of Cambodia*. Rithisen: Khmer Buddhist Research Centre, 1986.

Yonekura, Yukiko. 'Case studies of civil associations in Cambodia: Their advantages and limitations in the struggle for democracy'. Unpublished paper delivered at *Cambodia: Moving Towards a Better Future Conference*. Oxford, 5 June 1999.

22

MANAGING POVERTY IN CAMBODIA

Pou Sothirak

INTRODUCTION

In the past decade, Cambodia has undergone a remarkable political transformation and has been able to generate robust economic growth. However, the country still faces persistent poverty issues. Poverty in Cambodia has largely resulted from insecurity, inadequate opportunities, low capabilities, vulnerability, and social exclusion, according to the National Poverty Reduction Strategy (NPRS).[1]

Therefore, in Cambodia, the term "*poverty*" has become rooted in multi-faceted dimensions; it is not only associated with a lack of income by households or individuals to meet basic needs or achieve an acceptable standard of living, but also with exposure to vulnerabilities to outside forces and a lack of access to opportunities, as well as social inclusiveness that these individuals do not enjoy. It includes having insufficient food and nutrition, lack of shelter and clothing, no access to healthcare or education, and the lack of wealth-creating assets such as land and rural credit. In addition, among the root causes of poverty in Cambodia are protracted conflicts and isolation, inability to benefit from economic growth, and having no sense of representation in the social mainstream. The effects of the multi-dimensions of poverty are manifested through such symptoms as: hunger, inequality, low capacity, social exclusion, and corruption.

NEW PARADIGM

It is obvious that poverty is a stain on the nation's soul and its corrosive effects not only contribute to human misery but also deprives the country of resources that would otherwise contribute to the future wealth and well-being of the Kingdom. National pride demands that Cambodia moves beyond the status of a poor aid-dependent country near the bottom of the world league table to that of a nation that can sustain progress and lift its entire population out of poverty. To achieve this aim, a set of institutional and policy frameworks will be required and, of necessity, a recalibration of the mindset that tends to put emphasis on sustaining the perceived requirements of the state rather than responding to the demands of the citizens. Reducing poverty depends primarily on the principle that development is first about people, and the need to view government's actions and development assistance from this perspective. Accordingly, this short paper on "Managing Poverty in Cambodia" is written in the hope that it will serve both as a spur and as a template for further work. The ultimate aim is to create in the 21st Century a country where poverty can no longer impede the attainment of peace and prosperity for the nation, and all citizens can take equal advantage of a burgeoning national wealth.

THE SITUATION OF POVERTY IN CAMBODIA

The 2004 Poverty Profile of Cambodia put the poverty rate for rural Cambodia at more than 39 per cent, and out of the total number of the poor, 91 per cent lives in the rural areas. Unless major changes and more focus attention are made to address poverty, Cambodia may not be able to achieve the Cambodian Millennium Development Goal No. 1: "Eradicate Extreme Poverty and Hunger" (UNDP Annual Report 2009: 17), which is set to reduce the poverty level to 19.5 per cent by 2015.

For Cambodia as a whole, national poverty estimate has decreased gradually at a rate of 1 per cent per year from 39 per cent in 1993/94 to 34.7 per cent in 2004 and down to 30.1 per cent in 2007.[2] Whereas overall, a total of 20 per cent of all Cambodians live below the food poverty line in 2004,[3] Phnom Penh accounted for only 3 per cent compared with about 14 per cent in other urban areas and 22 per cent in rural areas. The estimated National Poverty Line for three regions in Cambodia is given in Table 22.1.

TABLE 22.1
National Poverty Lines by Domain 1993/4, 2004 and 2007
(Current riel per capita per day)

		1993/4	2004	2007
Phnom Penh	Poverty Line	1,578 (¢US63)	2,351 (¢US58)	3,092(¢US76)
	Food	1,185 (¢US48)	1,782 (¢US44)	2,445 (¢US60)
	Non-Food	393 (¢US15)	569 (¢US14)	647 (¢US16)
Other Urban	Poverty Line	1,265 (¢US50)	1,952 (¢US48)	2,704 (¢US67)
	Food	996 (¢US40)	1,568 (¢US39)	2,274 (¢US56)
	Non-Food	259 (¢US10)	384 (¢US9)	430 (¢US11)
Rural	Poverty Line	1,118 (¢US45)	1,753 (¢US43)	2,367 (¢US58)
	Food	882 (¢US35)	1,389 (¢US34)	1,965 (¢US48)
	Non-Food	236 (¢US10)	364 (¢US9)	402 (¢US10)
National	Poverty Line		1,825 (¢US45)	2,471 (¢US61)
	Food		1,442 (¢US36)	2,042 (¢US50)
	Non-Food		383 (¢US9)	429 (¢US11)

Note: 1994 exchange rate of US$1 = 2,500 riel, 2004 exchange rate of US$1 = 4,034 riel, and 2007 exchange rate of US$1 = 4,060 riel (Statistic Year Book of Cambodia 2008)
Source: SESC 1994, CSES 2004, and UNDP Current Status of Cambodian Millennium Development Goal (CMDG)

WHERE ARE THE POOR?

Most of very poor villages are located in the plateau and mountain areas of the north-eastern region next to Thailand, Laos and Vietnam, and in Kampong Speu province and Pailin. There, poverty rates can be as high as 52 per cent. The next highest concentration of the poor is found in the Tonle Sap zone, with poverty rates of nearly 43 per cent compared to 32 per cent in the plain and 27 per cent in the coastal zone. The Phnom Penh zone has a very low poverty headcount rate of only 4.6 per cent. For more details on where the poor are and how poor they are, see Figures 22.1 and 22.2 for the concentration of the poor by geographical zones and by province within Cambodia respectively; and Table 22.2: Poverty Estimates by Geographical Zones in Cambodia, 2004 and Table 22.3: Poverty Estimates by Province in Cambodia, 2004.

WHAT HAS BEEN DONE TO REDUCE POVERTY IN CAMBODIA?

Cambodia is known to be an aid-dependent country. The country received more than US$9 billion worth of ODA from 1992 to 2010. ODA has

FIGURE 22.1
Poverty Map by Geographical Zone

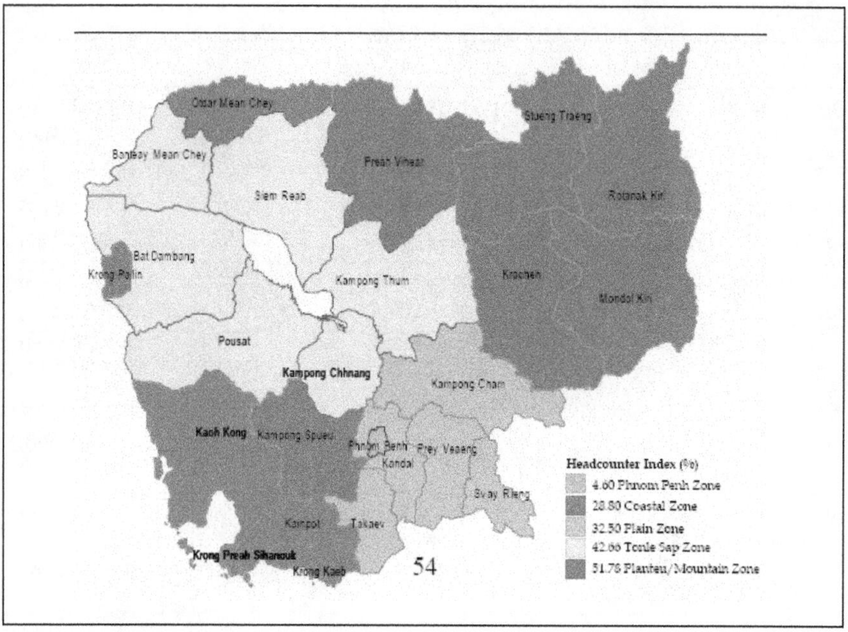

Source: Poverty Profile of Cambodia 2004

continued to play a fundamental role from the past to the present and will continue to do so for several years to come. For information on the donors ODA pledged to Cambodia from 1992 to 2010, see Tables 22.3 and 22.4.

To fight poverty and to make aid more effective in reducing poverty, the government launched a series of strategic documents, namely: the Socio-Economic Development Program (SEDP) I (1996–2000) and II (2001–2005), the National Poverty Reduction Strategy (NPRS) 2003–2005, and National Strategic Development Plan (NSDP) 2006–2010 (now extended for another three years until 2013). These documents describe strategies designed to coordinate government policies and spending towards the overall development objectives that can lower poverty incidence by half to 19.5 per cent by the year 2015.

The government reviews and monitors the progress of the NSDP annually to evaluate the poverty situation and the progress made to date and to assess the impacts of policies, and project intervention. It holds the view that by establishing good poverty monitoring systems, all stakeholders can keep track

FIGURE 22.2
Cambodian Poverty Map by Province 2004

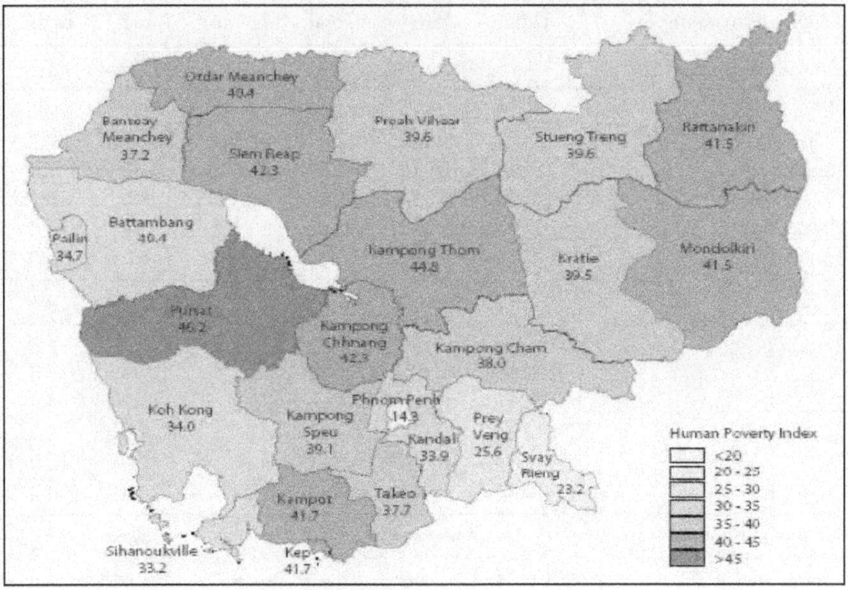

Source: Mid-Term Review 2008, National Strategic Development Plan 2006–2010

of poverty reduction targets and can improve policy intervention where necessary. According to the Mid-Term Review (MTR) in November 2008, the efforts to reduce poverty have achieved mixed results.

ACHIEVEMENTS AND SHORTFALLS

Cambodia achieved political stability and social order with strong macro-economic performance, and was able to manage inflation. Poverty has come down from 47 to 35 per cent from 1994 to 2004. Foreign direct investment has been growing significantly from US$121 million in 2004 to US$868 million in 2007. Gross foreign reserves increased from US$915 million in 2005 to US$2 billion in 2008 with double digit growth averaging about 11 per cent from 2004 to 2007. Most indicators in health care and education show signs of improvement (except the maternal mortality rate and dropout rate). However, these gains remained delicate as the high growth is narrowly based and undiversified, concentrated on a few urban-biased sectors such as garments, tourism and construction. This growth model of depending on

TABLE 22.2
Poverty Estimates by Geographical Zones in Cambodia, 2004

Geographical Zone	Urban	Rural	Total	Urban	Rural	Total
i) Headcount ratio		Index (%)			% of all poor	
Phnom Penh	1.11	8.92	4.60	1.9	1.1	1.1
Plains	13.74	32.86	32.07	8.9	42.3	39.7
Tonle Sap	28.21	45.38	42.80	46.3	36.2	37.0
Coastal	20.40	30.07	26.84	19.7	5.0	6.1
Plateau/Mountains	32.61	56.34	52.02	23.2	15.4	16.0
Cambodia	17.62	37.82	34.68	100.0	100.0	100.0
ii) Poverty gap		Index (%)			% of all poor	
Phnom Penh	0.16	2.54	1.23	1.1	1.2	1.2
Plains	3.00	7.64	7.45	7.4	37.9	35.4
Tonle Sap	8.51	12.79	12.15	53.1	39.2	40.0
Coastal	4.22	6.41	5.68	15.6	4.1	5.0
Plateau/Mountains	8.44	16.72	15.21	22.8	17.6	18.0
Cambodia	4.63	9.38	9.02	100.0	100.0	100.0
iii) Squared poverty gap		Index (%)			% of all poor	
Phnom Penh	0.04	1.06	0.49	0.7	1.3	1.3
Plains	0.93	2.64	2.57	6.1	35.4	33.0
Tonle Sap	3.46	4.94	4.72	57.3	41.1	42.4
Coastal	1.37	2.13	1.87	13.4	3.7	4.4
Plateau/Mountains	3.13	6.52	5.91	22.4	18.6	18.9
Cambodia	**1.75**	**3.63**	**3.34**	**100.0**	**100.0**	**100.0**

Note: The results refer to estimates using the poverty line base on full 12-month sample of 2004 covering whole of Cambodia.
Source: Knowles 2005, CSES 2004

external markets was quite susceptible to the 2008–09 global financial crises. Although the Government has been able to collect an increased amount of revenues, the ratio of revenue to GDP remained insufficient and well below the average of low-income countries. Only half of the children who attend primary school complete it, and dropout rates and repetition are very high; and governance remains weak, as confirmed by global rankings such as the World Bank's Doing Business and Transparency International.

THE BARRIERS OF POVERTY

The poor lack a wide range of economic and other resources. In general, the poor often face a variety of impediments which prevent them from gaining a foothold in society. They lack four major kinds of basic assets:

TABLE 22.3
Poverty Estimates by Province in Cambodia, 2004

Province	Poverty Headcount Index (%)	Poverty gap Index (%)	Square poverty gap Index (%)
i) Phnom Penh Zone	**4.6**	**1.23**	**0.49**
Phnom Penh	4.6	1.23	0.49
ii) Plains zone	**32.5**	**7.62**	**2.65**
Kampong Cham	37.04	9.28	3.34
Kandal	22.24	4.81	1.68
PreyVeng	37.20	8.09	2.65
Svay Reng	35.93	8.35	2.75
Takeo	27.71	6.31	2.09
iii) Tonle Sap zone	**42.66**	**12.09**	**4.74**
Banteay Meanchey	37.15	9.82	3.58
Battambang	33.69	7.94	2.65
Kampong Thom	52.40	15.55	6.23
Siem Reap	51.84	17.31	7.46
Kampong Chhnang/Pursat	39.57	10.35	3.78
iv) Coastal zone	**28.80**	**6.11**	**2.02**
Kampot	29.96	6.60	2.30
Sihanoukville/Kep/ Koh Kong	23.18	4.60	1.38
v) Plateau/Mountain zone	**51.78**	**15.47**	**6.22**
Kampong Speu	57.22	16.98	6.72
Other Provinces	46.11	13.20	4.98
Cambodia	35.13	9.19	3.45

Note: Other Provinces include the province of Kratie, Mondul Kiri, Preah Vihear, Ratanak Kiri, Stung Treng, Oddor Meanchey and Pailin. These and in two other instances, the estimates are provided in group of provinces due to limited number of samples to generate statistically significant separate estimates. The poverty estimated in this table is slightly different from the previous tables since these results are based on full 15-month sample of 2003/04 CSES whereas the earlier results are based on 12-month calendar year sample of 2004.
Source: Knowles 2005, CSES 2004.

- Physical and Human assets: Road networks, electricity, potable water for households to use and to improve their economic opportunity; health and nutrition needed for each person to sustain good physical condition, preventing disease and illness; education, skills and know-how for each individual to be economically productive, allowing oneself to raise productivity in business or farming output and the promotion of earning a decent living.
- Natural assets: equitably shared natural resources such as arable land, forestry, fishery that provide a base for wealth creation, needed by people in society.

TABLE 22.4
ODA Amount Pledged by Donors to Cambodia from 1992 to 2010

Meeting/Location	Date	Amount Pledged by Donors ($US million)
First Tokyo meeting	June 1992	880
First ICORC meeting, Paris	September 1993	120
Second ICORC meeting, Tokyo	March 1994	770
Third ICORC meeting, Paris	March 1995	520
First CG Meeting, Tokyo	July 1996	501
Second CG meeting, Paris	July 1997	450
Third CG meeting, Tokyo	February 1999	471
Fourth CG meeting, Paris	May 2000	548
Fifth CG meeting, Tokyo	June 2001	556
Sixth CG meeting, Phnom Penh	June 2002	635
Seventh CG meeting, Phnom Penh	December 2004	504
Eighth CG meeting, Phnom Penh	March 2006	601
First CDCF meeting, Phnom Penh	June 2007	689
Second CDCF Meeting, Phnom Penh	December 2008	951
Third CDCF Meeting, Phnom Penh	June 2010	1,100

Note: The donor pledges have been gathered by the author using the following sources:
1- For Tokyo meeting, ICORC and up to 7th CG meetings http://www.cdccrdb.gov.kh/cdc/8cg_meeting/dcr2004-2005/3-1-pledgeanddisb.htm> (accessed on 22 July 2009)
2- For 8th CG meeting: <http://siteresources.worldbank.org/INTCAMBODIA/Resources/293755-1141410443968/CG-Meeting.pdf > (accessed on 22 July 2009)
3- For 1st CDCF meeting <http://www.cdccrdb.gov.kh/cdc/first_cdcf/session5/press_conference_eng.htm> (accessed on 22 July 2009)
4- For 2nd CDCF meeting <http://www.cdccrdb.gov.kh/cdc/second_cdcf/session11/press_release_eng.htm> (accessed on 22 July 2009)
5- For 3rd CDCF meeting <http://www.cdccrdb.gov.kh/cdc/third_cdcf/press_release/press_release_en.htm> (Accessed 28 September 2010) And as reported by Phorn Bopha and Zsombor Peter, the Cambodia Daily Friday, 4 June 2010.

- Economic growth: sound economic policy frameworks that can be sustained and diversified to cover not only the urban but also rural sectors, such as agriculture and well-managed natural resource sectors. An economic policy that put people's well-being at the centre of development and guarantee the trickle-down effects to filter down to the poor, expanding their freedom and rights in society.
- Public assets: institutional supports such as an impartial judicial system, good governance and policing that underpin the peaceful and prosperous division of labour within the society, as well as a comprehensive Social

Safety Net program that protect and target the redistribution of growth and national resources to the poor, thus creating social harmony.

SUGGESTIONS ON HOW TO MANAGE POVERTY IN CAMBODIA

Focusing on the improvement of the government's efforts to reduce poverty with the collaboration of other stakeholders, this last section sets out the existing constraints and provides policy recommendations in a series of key areas to improve mainly the rural livelihood. It seeks to find feasible solutions to grassroots barriers and how government could reduce these barriers to sustain the livelihood of the poor. It concentrates on pro-poor policies that can intervene to achieve greater inclusion of the rural poor in government programs, more specifically, to: instil a top-down national commitment to reduce poverty (e.g. through effective implementation schemes); increase the national physical and human capital (e.g. public infrastructure, healthcare, education); share equitably the natural assets (e.g. arable land, forestry and fishery); diversify economic growth (e.g. make agriculture a viable sector); and empower the poor (e.g. through the practice of good governance and the provision of social safety net). Each of these policy recommendations is a key ingredient to poverty reduction, and to manage and improve the poverty situation in Cambodia in the 21st century.

1- COMMITMENT TO AN EFFECTIVE IMPLEMENTATION TO REDUCE POVERTY

Commitment to the task of reducing poverty is the first step in the right direction of making poverty history. The Government and all stakeholders need to embrace the goal of halving poverty by 2015 and ensure that this goal is achieved by endorsing the Millennium Development Goal's plan of action. Not only should the national government commit to those goals, but local governments at the provincial, district and commune levels should also adopt a committed mindset to the MDG in working together towards accomplishing both the aspiration and operational targets laid out in the country's policies and strategies to cut poverty.

Therefore, to ensure that the commitment is kept alive and the implementation is effectively carried on promptly, it is recommended that regular training courses on development cooperation on effective involvement in the Cambodian Poverty Reduction Strategy should be conducted for senior policy staff at the national and provincial level, including district chiefs, commune councils, and village chiefs. The World Bank should tap on its vast networks and expertise to design these training courses in order to mobilize all human capital and financial resources available at the national and provincial level and to focus on suitable and bold strategies to ensure that aid actually reaches the impoverished villages. Such training courses would insist that all apparatus of the Government working together with all donor agencies to honour their responsibilities to help the poor escape from poverty, as well as upholding their commitments to channel more investment in the poorest villages in Cambodia.

2. INCREASING THE NATIONAL PHYSICAL AND HUMAN CAPITAL

Key aspects of reducing poverty require the building up of national infrastructure and the long term investment in human resources. Schools, clinics, roads, ports, electricity, clean drinking water, and the like are the basic necessity to fulfil not only life's dignity and health, but also for economic productivity. As such, a strong component of poverty reduction should aim at building more schools and health centres as well as other essential physical infrastructures, such as rural roads and ensure universal access to affordable and reliable modern energy service for all people in the country. In addition, the Government and international donors should provide development interventions that would invest in long term development of human resources through the development of education and health care. These policy recommendations will make a difference between isolation and connectivity and deprivation and economic development.

2.1 Development of more rural roads

The Cambodian poor are often concentrated in remote communities in mountainous terrain without road-connections. Their poverty is aggravated due to geographical isolation and the high cost of motorized transport; most farmers in poor villages do not have adequate access to markets and face extremely limited mobility beyond their immediate communities. To address this issue, here are some recommendations:

- Continue to make substantial investment in the development of rural roads as a priority area of attention by increasing larger financial resources to this sector.
- Create an integrated road network of connections that reach from the impoverished communities to the cities and towns where economic activities and public services can be accessible by the poor.

- Improve the much needed rural roads that affect social and economic development in the countryside.
- Manage and maintain all existing roads more efficiently and ensure that there is no road tax levied illegally on the poor.

2.2 Development of adequate rural electricity

Today many of the poorest and most vulnerable communities throughout Cambodia still live without access to modern electricity. Only 10 per cent of rural Plateau/Mountain region and between 18 to 25 per cent in rural Plains, Tonle Sap and Coastal areas had access to electricity (WB's Equity and Development Report 2007: 80).

Due to this shortfall, it is virtually impossible for rural inhabitants to carry out productive economic activity or improve health and education. Thus Government should work collaboratively with development partners to identify and develop new approaches for extending access to modern energy to as many people as possible — especially in poor and remote areas — who remain off grid. The followings are some suggestions:

- Formulate innovative ways and secure necessary financing to provide affordable electricity, such as solar panels that can charge the batteries, small power plan that can generate electricity from the diesel-fired generators, or mini-hydroelectricity to provide the energy needed for various purposes; all these will enhance rural productivity, and improve comfort, safety, health, education and economy.
- The Government and key donors, such as the World Bank should consider adopting a practical electricity program that aim at easing poverty in the rural community similar to the "Access to Electricity program" created by the ABB[4] (Swiss based company specialized in power and automation technology). The main emphasis of this project is placed on working with local authorities to establish villagers' needs, and ensure that the electricity is affordable over the long-term. More information on this program can be found in a case study by the World Business Council for Sustainable Development.[5]

2.3 Development of pro-poor health care

The health status of Cambodia, when compared to other neighbouring countries in the region, remains far less favourable due to higher poverty incidence among the population. For this reason, Cambodia had the largest shares among all ASEAN countries in share of population below the minimum level of dietary consumption at 26.0 per cent in 2004 and mortality under 5 years old per 1,000 births. This was a serious situation at a high level of 91 in 2007, only better than Myanmar (see Table 22.5).

For the Cambodian rural inhabitants, suffering from ill health is considered the worse case that could ever happen. Sickness can push them into poverty very quickly, as they risk losing whatever savings they have or incurring debts that they cannot repay. Rural villagers consider ill health and diseases as being one of the reasons for their fall into poverty. The poorer communities remain vulnerable to ill health due to numerous factors such as severe malnutrition, lack of clean water and sanitation, inadequate health facilities, high costs of seeking healthcare, and lack of knowledge about good health practice. The followings are some recommendations to improve the health care situation in Cambodia, particularly for the poor and remote areas.

- Target public healthcare programs to provide more benefits to the poorest groups. This can be accomplished by directing programs toward areas where poorer people live or by identifying who is poor and therefore eligible for certain healthcare benefit.

TABLE 22.5
Poverty and Mortality among ASEAN Countries

	Population with income below $1 (ppp) per day (%)	Poverty gap ratio (%)	Population below minimum dietary consumption (%)	Mortality under 5 years old per 1,000 births (%)
Brunei				
Cambodia	40.2 (2004)	11.3 (2004)	26.0 (2004)	91 (2007)
Indonesia		2.2 (1996)	17.0 (2004)	31 (2007)
Laos	44.0 (2002)	12.1 (2002)	19.0 (2004)	70 (2007)
Malaysia	2.0 (2004)	0.5 (2004)	5.0 (2004)	11 (2007)
Myanmar			19.0 (2004)	103 (2007)
Philippines	22.6 (2006)	5.5 (2006)	16.0 (2004)	28 (2007)
Singapore				3 (2007)
Thailand	2.0 (2004)	0.5 (2004)	17.0 (2004)	7 (2007)
Vietnam	24.2 (2004)	5.1 (2006)	14.0 (2004)	15 (2007)

Note: Figures in parentheses indicate year
Sources: ADB, Millennium Development Indicator 2007, MDG Tables (https://sdbs.adb.org/sdbs/index.jsp)

- Based on the above eligibility list, targeting mechanisms should be designed to direct the health benefits to the poor. This should be a national scheme of subsidy to waive or scale back fees for the poor when they use public health services.
- Increase the availability and quality of health services. Ongoing efforts should continue to bring health services directly to poor people's doorstep. There should be an establishment of local family welfare assistants in districts and communes throughout Cambodia whose tasks are to provide health related information and education to poor, rural women and villagers in their homes where there are no health centre or hospital in the areas.
- Develop more reliable public-private partnerships. Given that many non-governmental organizations (NGOs) already work closely with the poor, the Government may opt to support NGOs to deliver health services to the poor and vulnerable segments of society, in fulfilling important services gaps.
- Create an incentive scheme for health providers to take care of poor clients. An introduction of 'health care stamp or voucher' should be contemplated based on a performance contract for health care providers (either public or private) to improve the efficiency and quality of a particular health service the government wants they deliver to poor clients. For example, a system of voucher should be given to poor women, in place of cash to obtain delivery and maternal and child health services.
- Donors should consider increasing more budget support for the Health Equity Fund scheme to increase the capacity of subsidizing medical services and reimbursement for food costs and transport for more than two million of Cambodia's poorest. In 2010, only about 700,000 patients received assistance from this scheme.[6]

2.4 Development of rural education

Access to education is also problematic in rural areas of Cambodia. There are fewer schools in remote localities and the long distance between home and school is another obstacle for village students. The shortage of teachers forces most school in the rural areas to reduce student time in school to only half a day. In addition, teachers are underpaid, so that most of them have to look for a second job in order to earn enough money to support their family.[7] Books and other educational tools are practically non-existent in the rural areas. As they lack basic education, many of the poor are often illiterate and have lower self esteem and as a result they lack empowerment. Poverty in Cambodia is definitely related to the lack of education. Education is one the best tool to break the generational chain of poverty and lead lives with opportunity, dignity and respect.

According to CSES 2007, the net enrolment rate in primary school in the rural area was recorded at 81 per cent. This rate drops to 25 per cent in lower secondary and eight per cent for upper secondary school. While most poor children spend more time in primary school, a significant proportion of them drop out before finishing. The progress toward achieving the goal of the nine-year completion of basic education for all is limited. The education quality either at primary, secondary or tertiary remains low. As the lack of education is undeniably related to poverty, and compared to other ASEAN nations, Cambodia was definitely lower in UNDP's Human Development Index at 136 in 2006, the lowest ranking; primary education completion rate at 85.1 per cent in 2007, only better than Lao PDR; and adult literacy rate at 76.3 per cent in 2007, slightly above Lao PDR[8] (see Table 22.6). For the improvement of this important sector, here are some suggestions:

TABLE 22.6

HDI, Primary Education, and Adult Literacy among ASEAN Countries

	Human Development Index			Primary Education Completion Rate (%)	Adult Literacy Rate (%)
	2000	2006	Rank in 2006		
Brunei	0.905	0.919	27	107.4 (2007)	94.9 (2007)
Cambodia	0.511	0.575	136	85.1 (2007)	76.3 (2007)
Indonesia	0.671	0.726	109	98.8 (2006)	91.4 (2007)
Laos	0.563	0.608	133	76.7 (2007)	73.4 (2007)
Malaysia	0.797	0.823	63	98.3 (2005)	91.9 (2007)
Myanmar	0.551	0.585	135	95.3 (2006)	89.9 (2007)
Philippines	0.725	0.745	102	93.8 (2006)	93.4 (2007)
Singapore	0.907	0.918	28		94.4 (2007)
Thailand	0.750	0.786	81	101.1 (2007)	91.4 (2007)
Vietnam	0.688	0.718	114		90.3 (2007)

Note: Figures in the parentheses indicate year

Sources: ADB, Key Indicators 2009 (http://www.adb.org/Documents/Books/Key_Indicators/2009/pdf/Key-Indicators-2009.pdf)

- Increase significantly the national budget for education. The national budget for education stood at only 1.6 per cent of GDP, according to UNESCO's 2008 statistic,[9] substantially lower than other countries in the region (Lao PDR 2.3 per cent, Philippines 2.6 per cent, Singapore 3.8 per cent, Indonesia 3.5 per cent, Malaysia 4.5 per cent, Thailand 4.9 per cent, and Vietnam 5.3 per cent,). The national budget for education in 2011 was set at US$223 million, representing about 9 per cent of the total budget of US$2.4 billion.[10] Unless the Government makes education a top priority and teachers can earn better wages, the children of poor family cannot hope to develop the needed knowledge and skills to help them get out of poverty.
- Develop education that is pro-poor by: building at less one elementary school in the rural areas where poverty levels are acute; ensuring that there will be enough teachers for these schools with adequate remuneration so as to encourage teachers to teach full time; providing school feeding program of one meal a day to allow poor children to attend school without interruption; equipping these schools with latest text books and other necessary pedagogic materials, include a setting up of a modest library with children's books and audio-visual capability; and ensuring equal access to primary education, especially take necessary steps to enrol girl students.
- Promote better quality in education by: adopting education as a number one national priority; improving existing school curriculum, developing good school administrators; producing sufficient qualified teachers who can teach all subjects, including moral and civic education; allocating more national budget to ensure proper functioning of elementary and secondary education, including the increase of monthly salary to teachers.
- Expand and improve technical training programs to the needy people by focusing on skills development curriculum.
- Develop an effective adult literacy classes for disadvantaged groups in a vocational training program, especially women to improve basic literacy, numeric knowledge, and other skills.
- Increase compulsory free education from 9 to 12 years. At present the constitution of Cambodia promulgates compulsory free education for nine years, guaranteeing the universal right to basic quality education. Enforcing longer periods of time for children to attend school will allow the next generation of Cambodians to achieve a brighter future. At present, the concerns in education are:[11] average primary completion rate stood at 78.6 per cent, primary level drop out 10.8 per cent, secondary drop out 21 per cent, grade 6 dropout rates in remote and urban areas

15.5 per cent and 9.1 per cent respectively, and secondary enrolment rate in remote and urban areas 29.4 per cent and 92.4 per cent respectively. Longer compulsory impose on education will also boost the participation rate in higher education where Cambodia still ranked poorly at just 1.2 per cent of the population enrolled, as compare to an average of 20.7 per cent in all the ASEAN countries.[12]

3. EQUAL SHARING OF NATURAL ASSETS

For Cambodia to address the problem of rural poverty effectively, viable policy and strict implementation on how to manage natural resources must be developed and strengthen to ensure the equitable distribution and utilization of the national assets among all citizens. While Government agencies and officials take a lead role in the formulation of resource management policy, local communities should be given important roles to play in identifying resources, defining development priority, choosing and adapting appropriate methods to extract or use natural resources, and taking part locally in the implementation of sound management practice. Clearly, poor households throughout Cambodia depend on natural resource to support their family.

The overarching constraint to common natural resources accessed by the poor are factors such as the increasing population, competing for access to commons forests and fisheries for food, and lacking sufficient access to land for agriculture. Over-exploitation of commons resources such as forestry and fisheries by big forest concessionaires and fishing-lot holders are constant threats to the poor's livelihood. Land grabbing and huge concession granted to farm-land holders are also seen as real intimidation in preventing the poor to produce as much food, by way of farming, to support their family. Out of these situations, conflicts are prevailing among the rural population and among the poor and the rich and powerful. In addition, bad governance also plays a role in aggravating the situation through a network of corrupt patronage whose de facto power exist at all levels of government.[13] Furthermore, CDRI's Moving Out of Poverty Survey (MOPS: 135–39) reveals the difficulties of life where villagers whose livelihood depend on natural resources need to cope with corruption, bullying and threats by authorities and powerful commercial interests.

Forest Issues

The poor face many constraints when it comes to exploiting forest resources for their daily sustenance. They lack protection and access to reserved forests for domestic consumption. Villagers who earn their living from a nearby forest are often harassed, intimidated, and deprived of access from the forest resource, while illegal companies and concessionaires are allowed to exploit the forest resource with the help from the forest authority and the military (MOPS: 136).

Deforestation is another main factor which contributes to the restriction of forest resources, via illegal and commercial logging and subsistence activities such as land clearing for agriculture and collection of fuel wood. From 1990 to 2005, Cambodia lost 2.5 million hectares of forest.[14] This severe degradation of the forest resources has occurred mainly because of commercial logging between 1994 and 1998, when large-scale forest concessions were granted. Although legal loggings were brought to a halt in 1999, illegal logging continues to deplete the forest without recourse of the law through over-exploitation, corruption and lack of a transparent monitoring process. One report[15] mentioned that due to funding constraint, an effective implementation of sustainable forest management could not be executed, while the forestry mismanagement happened due to corrupt practices among the police, local government, the forest administration, and the military. The illicit trade value is estimated at US$13 million a year, hence making illegal logging persistent.

Nevertheless, from 1999 Government has been more vigilant and had cancelled the agreement and suspended the concession forests of many companies. For those concessions remained in force, they are require by the Government to renegotiating the concession forest investment agreement and to re-planting the concession forest in accordance with technical specification for the conduct for sustainable forest management.[16] Moreover, the Government also has been promoting the concept of community forest management to enable local people to make forest management decisions and allow them to receive the benefits from that management.[17]

Land Issues

Since most of the poor make their living from land cultivation, landlessness is another major cause of poverty in Cambodia. As the numbers of rural inhabitants lacking land for farming are on the rise, from 13 per cent in 1997 to 16 per cent in 1999 and 20 per cent in 2004 (WB Poverty Assessment 2006: 85), issues such as land grabbing and conflicts arising from such activity are becoming more and more controversial. These situations are frequently the result of bad governance and corruption.[18] The poor are often victims of the middle-man acting on behalf of the rich and powerful people and companies to buy off or confiscate the poor's meagre land. The rural poor possess on the average 1.5ha of farming land, but 40 per cent of them only live off less than 0.5 ha (WB Poverty Assessment 2006: 84).

Land grabbing is a common cause for land disputes among poor families, who quarrelled with companies or powerful individuals who had obtained large land concessions from the local government. In June 2010, a joint statement by civil societies noted with concern that the incident of land disputes increased 36.5 per cent in 2009 compared to 2008 and 34.3 per cent by mid-year 2010 as compared to 2009. Violence against land activists often take the form of verbal threats, intimidation, serious assaults and killing, especially during the course of forced evictions. Most of the time, the affected parties are left without proper compensation and often targeted for arrest and imprisonment. It is rare that disputed cases of land grabbing are settled legally.

Another vital factor is that people do not have secure land titles. The challenge is for the state to provide all citizens, in particular to the poor, the right to land ownership. In Cambodia's countryside where about 85 per cent of the populations live, there are still numerous poor families without proper land titles. According to the WB Poverty Assessment 2006 (page 86), out of 4.5 million applicants for land titles received after 1989, only 14 per cent have been dealt with. However, in September 2009, the WB reported that the Government has managed to issue more than 1.1 million land titles to mostly poor villagers in rural communities.[19] Much of this success is due to government attempts to reduce poverty through land reforms based on a Land Management and Administration Project (LMAP) with the support from the World Bank and the governments of Germany and Finland.[20]

Recommendations

Promoting equal sharing of natural assets includes challenging goals such as improving food security through access to common resources such as fishery, forests, water and land, implanting sound judicial and legal institutions and access to justice for the poor, shaping the regulatory environment in which the required results can be attained, and enforcing good governance. To achieve these goals, policies must be designed and implemented with the active participation of local individuals, families and communities.

The policy that can produce best practices in natural resource management relies mainly on all stakeholders jointly identifying development parameters or constraints and participating in the decision-making process.

Natural resources such as forest, fisheries, water, land and minerals must be regulated properly to avoid illegal exploitation and should be made available for sharing equitably among all people while maintaining its productive cycle for use from generation to generation, hence promoting ecological sustainability. The following are some policy recommendations to consider, if natural resources are to be shared equitably among all citizen of Cambodia, especially the poor.

- Develop pro-poor natural resource policy that can ensure and encourage equitable use of natural wealth while pacifying internal conflict and promote the principle of conservation and self-sufficiency of resources consumption based on taking what is needed rather than accumulation of surplus or excessive individual gain. What should be avoid is the concept of planning and decision making at the government bureaucratic level that does not include the ideas and wishes of the local resource users.
- Promote the participatory approach for natural resource management in order to establish responsible, productive and sustainable management of forest, fisheries, water, land, and mineral resources with the local communities in order to meet local needs and stimulate local development. It should also promote private and community-based development activities in support of natural resource management, while at the same time pursues the objective of strengthening institutions and building local and regional capacity.
- The effectiveness to secure an equal sharing of natural resources must start with a practice of good governance to halt deforestation and illegal logging, fight against land deprivation (especially land grabbing), stop illegal exploitation of mineral resources, promote proper management of water resources through irrigation schemes and protect biodiversity, and ensure free access to common water and provide legal protection of people for their rights to fish for livelihood.

4. DIVERSIFYING ECONOMIC GROWTH

Cambodia's economy experienced dramatic slowness in 1997–98 due to the regional currency crisis, civil violence, and political infighting. Foreign investment and tourism fell off. Growth resumed and has remained within double digits averaging 11.1 per cent between 2004 and 2007, then dropped to 6 per cent in 2008 and there was hardly any growth in 2009, as the result of the global economic crisis.

During the period of high growth, tourism was Cambodia's fastest growing industry, with arrivals up from 1 million in 2004 to over 2 million foreign tourists in 2007.[21] Economic growth has been largely driven by expansion in the clothing sector as well. Clothing exports were fostered by the U.S.-Cambodian Bilateral Textile Agreement signed in 1999. The value of export of garment and textile products had increased from US$1.15 billion in 2001 to US$2.98 billion in 2008, over 60 per cent accounted for the USA.[22] The real estate and construction sectors were booming prior to the global downturn in 2007.[23]

Cambodia recorded a remarkable economic growth in the past, but this growth was not sustainable due to lack of diversification, depending mainly on garments, tourism and construction. Moreover, the recent global downturn has created severe strains on these sectors; hence growth dried up in 2009. What is more, according to a survey conducted by the Cambodian Economic Association of 15 villages in Cambodia during the first six months of 2009, it found out that 89 per cent of households reported multiple difficulties among the urban poor and poorest rural villages, where they faced substantial decreases in income, rising healthcare expenses, debt repayment burden, and high food prices. At the national level, the impact on employment was stunning with more than 63,000 garment workers laid off and about 100,000 jobs in the construction sector have disappeared. The survey also noted the impact of the crisis was more severe among the urban poor and tourist-dependent villages with 33 per cent of such households were affected by job loss and of that figure 3.7 per cent had at least one member lost their job.[24]

In sum, economic growth in Cambodia has proceeded in series of great surge of high growth, followed by a period of much slower growth. This up-down cycle was influenced greatly by internally generated factors such as political and security instability, lack of resources, inefficient institutional capacity, as well as external factors such as the regional financial crisis in 1997–98 and the 2008–09 global economic downturn.

Going forward, it is crucial for Cambodia to scale up economic progress, without which there will be no growth and poverty will continue. If there is no growth, the poor have no chance of getting out of the circle of misery. While economic progress is important and it is imperative for the country to forge ahead with stronger growth, the Government should try to ensure that the fruits of the country's economic growth are shared equitably among all Cambodians. The key question here is how to manage economic policy in a sustainable way with a pro-poor approach that can help alleviate the burden of many of the impoverish Cambodians?

The condition of Cambodia's poor has worsened due to the effects of the global crisis and lack of economic diversification. The closing down of garment factories, the suspension of construction sites and the slowdown in hotel and restaurant services have all aggravated the poor as they lose their jobs and have no income. The poor have suffered and will suffer the most, unless Cambodia can revitalize its economic policies to achieve the return to higher and more sustainable growth by properly managing risks, strengthening regional trade, tackling infrastructure limitation, and ensuring adequate investment in addressing constraints to agriculture development.

The poor need an economic policy that put the people's well-being at the centre of development and guarantee the trickle-down effect for prosperity. Below are some recommendations to be considered:

- Intensify the collaboration between Government and development partners and coordinate their actions to develop a more diversified economic policy that can serve as the foundation of potential engine for sustainable growth and poverty reduction over the medium and long term. This effort should concentrate on removing structural barriers in order to broader based growth beyond garments, tourism and construction to include the revitalization of the agricultural and mining sectors.
- As FDI is the key to economic growth, induce the private sector to participate fully in the economic activity. In so doing, make sure that the investment climate is conducive and efforts be made to reduce the cost of doing business by a set of effective regulations that are transparent, fair, competitive, with zero tolerance of corruption.
- Promote infrastructure development to cover the whole of the country adequately. This include the rehabilitation and reconstruction of the main, secondary and rural roads, upgrading the existing rail ways and expanding it to cover other part of the country, upgrading the airport in Sihanoukville, improvement of port services, expansion of a lower cost of electricity production and delivery network, building new bridges, irrigation system, and telecommunications. For some of these projects, the Government should strive to attract the private sector to invest in concessionary frameworks of public works, such as Build-Operate and Transfer (BOT).
- Liberalise trade and open up markets to reap the benefit of globalization and global trade with prospects of gain through sharper competitiveness and closer harmonisation. Engage in regional and bilateral trade agreements that can create new opportunities and allow greater access to widen market bases for Cambodian products.
- Rebalance trade to mitigate the risks arriving from the global crisis and strengthen regional trade to lessen the impact of unfavourable developments with the rest of the world. In the case of garment sector, Cambodia should explore other markets beside the USA, including enhancing garment trade with the EU, Japan, Australia, Middle East, Canada, and Africa.

- Undertake appropriate fiscal reform and apply prudent macroeconomic policy to enforce greater revenue collection and curbing inflation.
- Promote tourism sector by further improving tourism infrastructure, including the opening up more direct flights from America, Europe, and Japan.
- Capitalise on the development of agriculture as Cambodia has abundant arable land and water resource that can potentially be the base for the new growth sector. Major crop such as rice can be further encouraged for large scale production by improving irrigation system and up-grading rice farming technique.
- Make Cambodia a rice bowl of Asia by further expanding rice cultivation, increase export and gain access to new markets, such as China. According to the Government's projection, Cambodia is expected to produce 7 to 9 million metric tons of paddy from 2010 to 2015, resulting in the increase of export of paddy from 3.32 to 4.51 million metric tons and export of rice from 2.06 to 2.89 million metric tons.[25] Special attention must be given to assurance of a smooth and simple protocol on procedure and quality standard for exporting rice by ensuring consistency and good quality of rice, upgrading milling and storage technology and by injecting more financial investment into helping rice farmer to expand their production capacity.
- As pro-poor economic policy, remove several constraints that would allow locally produced goods greater freedom of access to market with minimum hindrance. Restrictions such as high transportation cost, border or road fees, poor access to local processing factory, and lack of market information should be addressed.
- Proactively promote small and medium enterprises (SMEs) as they contribute to solving both economic and social problems for the country. Smooth growth of this sector will be essential in promoting private sector development and employment generation. Government should make greater strides to remove some of the major hurdles SMEs are facing in term of the high cost of doing business.

5. EMPOWERING THE POOR

The poor need to be empowered so that they can be lifted out of poverty trap. They often must bear with poverty from generation to generation due to neglect or inability from the states in the exercise of theirs obligatory role to respect, protect, and fulfil the poor's most basic human rights in order that they can take part in all the mainstream activities in the society. The following two points are recommendations that can help strengthen the empowerment process among the poor, cutting across good governance and wide-ranging social safety net programs. These policies not only can promote fast and sustainable economic development but they can help to redistribute the growth and public resource to the poor more effectively, as well as ensure adequate social welfare protection to all citizens in need, thus creating social harmony for the nation as a whole.

Empowerment through good governance

The principle of governance has its main focus in the effectiveness of governments' actions in the delivery to their citizens a basket of public goods through their ability to execute economic, social, political and administrative authority to manage the country's affairs at all level. It is often seen as the ability to create and ensure political stability and legal environment conducive to sustained development whether it is economic or social. It is about the management of the development process, involving both public and private sectors, whereby the governments must implant proper functioning and capacity of the public sectors, as well as the appropriate rules and institutions that create the necessary framework for the conduct of both public and private business, and through such frameworks, the citizens can interact with government agencies and officials.

There exists political will in Cambodia to take governance to the next level. There are several governmental formulated documents which deal with the issue of governance. In these documents, numerous initiatives[26] to improve governance in several important areas are spelled out in efforts to promote development and social justice. Most if not all of these initiatives also addressed the root causes of poor governance and corruption. For instance, the Governance Action Plans I, approved in 2001, dealt with seven critical areas: public finance, military reform, land management, legal and judicial reform, anticorruption, public administration, and forest management. Whereas the National Poverty Reduction Strategy, approved in 2002, committed the Government to strengthen institutions and improving governance in four important areas: legal and judicial reform, administrative reform, democratization and local government and the fight against corruption. In the case of the latest government blue print called the National Strategic Development Plan (NSDP 2006–2010), approved in late 2005 and now extended to 2013, there are all-encompassing government initiatives to take the country toward an assured growth path. It has four principle pillars, including anti-corruption, legal and judicial reform, public administration reform, including decentralization, and reform of the armed forces, especially demobilization.

The Government views good governance as an essential tool to acquire transparency, responsibility, public participation, adherence to the rule of law and cooperation between government and civil society, which will lead to sustainable socio-economic development and social justice. The Government also admitted that corruption is the main symptom of weak governance. Studies have shown that corruption is widespread in Cambodian society with the judiciary, customs, tax authorities, health sector, education, road services and police being the worst affected areas.[27]

However, we have to accept that one of the main forces which drive poverty in Cambodia is the lack of good governance. To achieve good governance, Cambodia needs to continue and improve the development policy that is more broad based and pro-poor, invest more in physical infrastructure and promote human resource development, promote education, especially in the rural areas, provide adequate health care services, and ensure that the judicial system is well functioning, independent from political influence. In addition, we need to further improve the law enforcement and strengthen our national capacity to adapt to changes which take place at home, in the region, and around the world.

To ensure that citizens are empowered through the intervention of good governance, the Government should continue with fortitude to achieve the following:

- The prevalence of peace, internal security and political stability through abiding respect for justice, the rule of law, and human rights. The promotion of democratic establishment and civil society. The upholding of an independent and impartial judiciary in order to protect the rights and freedom of all Cambodian citizens.
- The strengthening the decentralization process by promoting good governance through processes of check and balance with focus on the rule of law and eliminating corruption.
- The provision of essential support for activities designed to genuinely empower and promote initiatives that focus on local community movement, while improving policy participation allowing grassroots people to participate.
- The assurance of an equitable, transparent, and accountable interface and mediation between citizens and marginalized people with the institutions which exercise power in the process of good governance.

- The opening up of the political space for the poor and the excluded people to freedom of information from an independent, responsible, accessible and effective media.
- The substantiation of rights of citizens and civil societies to question, to dissent peacefully, and to develop alternatives, through a process of critical engagement where the checks and balances can be assured in the application of governance between those who hold and exercise power and the citizens, particularly the poor and the excluded people.

The Development of a Social Safety Net

The social condition in Cambodia deserves a closer look. The many social challenges include an increased population, with annual rates of population increase at an average of 1.6 per cent from 2005–10 (Human Development Report 2009); 31 per cent of people or about 4 million people are still live under the poverty line (World Bank 2006's extrapolated figure for 2008 based on 1 per cent reduction per annum from 2004's figure of 35 per cent); 37 per cent of children under five chronically malnourished (Cambodia Demographic and Health Survey 2005); more than 300,000 households or about 1.7 million individuals, equivalent to 13 per cent of the population, were food insecure (World Food Program May–June 2008).

Internal and external shocks give rise to more concerns among rural population in Cambodia. The high cost of consumer and producer goods such as rice, meat, fish, fertilizer and oil — some of which doubled during 2008 — put intense strain on the cost of living among families who earn minimal income and have threatened food security among the poor throughout the country.

Other societal burdens include orphans and abandoned children, the disabled people and aged senior citizens. According to a country report on Social Protection and Disabilities of the 2nd ASEAN Go-NGO Forum in December 2007,[28] the number of orphans in 2010 was estimated at 7.8 per cent of all children. Orphans with HIV/AIDS might be at 27.5 per cent. The needs of these population groups overwhelmed the efforts of the Government. The Government also has to take care of huge numbers of demobilized soldiers, public servant retirees, and youth and adult unemployment.

Facing this range of burdens, the Government established a technical working group on food security and nutrition (TWG-FSN) whose responsibility is to determine the nature of existing safety net provision in

Cambodia and to identify policy, institutional and capacity gaps for developing a more systematic and integrated social safety net system.

While the Cambodian government and donors agree that social safety nets are important elements to sustain social, cultural and economic growth and the attainment of Cambodia's Millennium Development Goals, there have been insufficient allocations of resources and a lack of commitment to help provide: unemployment benefits to those who have lost their jobs, rice subsidy to those most affected by food shortages, conditional cash payment to poor families, comprehensive civil service pension, health insurance, free meals for school children, and food-for-work programs, just to name a few.

Improvement and concrete actions are required in the following propositions:

- Constructing a social safety net policy that can bring about social harmony and act as an effective agent in redistributing income and national resources to the poor. This requires the conducts of an appropriate strategy aimed at promoting long-term investment in socio-human capital, as well as physical infrastructure.
- Articulating a broad measure for a social safety net strategy that can underpin strategic change, linking the question of affordability and sustainability to social protection when economic indicators are worsening.
- Launching a social safety net program to address the importance of education, healthcare, community empowerment-employment creation, and rice-food subsidy programs.
- The national employment program should seek ways to broaden and sustain robust growth of the national economy, which is an important factor that can support social protection, so as to create enough jobs to reduce the existing unemployment — 275,000 new job seekers are expected to enter the labour market each year.[29]
- The Labour Law should be made more flexible and to support the introduction of better basic social insurance arrangements, so as to cover the vulnerable population's ability to cope with threats to income and livelihood.
- The social welfare funds should be created with an aim at providing adequate and continuing financial support to the destitute group of people such as the ageing, widows, and people with disabilities.

6. CONCLUSION

Efforts to reduce the levels of poverty are still inadequate, while Cambodia is striving to combat difficult barriers to ensure adequate infrastructures and upgrade human capacity, broaden access to health care, education and irrigation, promote the equal use of common natural resource, diversify the economy so as to become less dependent on Western markets, and give more voice to the poor so that they, too, can have the opportunity to participate in a more equal model of growth.

The best solution to manage poverty and help the poor get out of this misery requires strong commitment and successful Government intervention through a set of workable and practical policies designed to help the poor address four basic hurdles.

The first important obstacle to overcome is for the Government to provide basic goods and services through the development of rural infrastructures to the poor and most disadvantage group in the rural areas throughout Cambodia. The second difficulty is to ensure equal access to common natural resources for livelihood. The third impediment is for the Government to diversify the economy so as to create income and wealth among all population. The last stumbling block is for the Government to fulfil its social commitment to empower the poor.

Government has the responsibility to account for the fact that explains why and how people remain trap in poverty, only then the cycle of poverty can be broken. This is simply because the poor do not have the ability — by themselves — to get out of the mess, and therefore need a boost up to lift them out of poverty.

Notes

1. National Poverty Reduction Strategy (NPRS) 2003–2005, the Council for Social Development, 20 December 2002. <http://www.imf.org/External/NP/prsp/2002/khm/01/122002.pdf> (accessed 24 April 2009).
2. National Strategic Development Plan 2006–2010, Annex III for 1993/94 and 2004 figures, and the 2007 Cambodia Socio-Economic for 2007 figure.
3. Poverty Profile of Cambodia 2004, a publication of the Ministry of Planning in February 2006, the estimated food poverty line is 1,684 Riel (US$0.42) and the total poverty line is 2,124 Riel (US$0.53) in average 2004 Phnom Penh prices. The non-food allowance is 440 riel (US$0.10).
4. <http://www.abb.com>.
5. ABB: Access to Electricity program eases poverty, case study 2005, World Business Council for Sustainable Development <http://www.wbcsd.org/web/publications/case/abb_electricity_access_full_case_final_web.pdf> (accessed 31 May 2010).
6. Article by Alice Foster "Equity Funds Offer 700,000 Free Health Care", published in the Cambodia Daily, 29–30 January 2011.
7. For more information on the effect of low salaries of teacher s in Cambodia, see

the article by Bill Costello "Cambodia's Impoverished Education System", 13 June 2010 <http://makingmindsmatter.com/2010/06/13/cambodia%e2%80%99s-impoverished-education-system/> (accessed 15 September 2010).

8. ADB, Key Indicators 2009 <http://www.adb.org/Documents/Books/Key_Indicators/2009/pdf/Key-Indicators-2009.pdf> (accessed 15 September 2010).
9. See UNNSECO Statistic for Cambodia <http://stats.uis.unesco.org/unesco/TableViewer/document.aspx?ReportId=121&IF_Language=eng&BR_Country=4060&BR_Region=40515> (accessed 15 September 2010).
10. As reported by VOA News.com <http://www.voanews.com/khmer-english/news/cambodia/National-Assembly-Passes-24-Billion-Budget-110832964.html> (accessed 27 January 2011).
11. Cambodia-UNESCO Country Program Document 2009 -2010, Phnom Penh, January 2010 <http://unesdoc.unesco.org/images/0018/001865/186552e.pdf> (accessed 15 September 2010).
12. Cambodia Cultural Profile: Education <http://www.culturalprofiles.net/Cambodia/Directories/Cambodia_Cultural_Profile/-36.html> (accessed 15 September 2010).
13. See "Title through Possession or through Position? Respect for Housing, Land and Property Rights in Cambodia", a report done by The Centre on Housing Rights and Evictions (COHRE) <http://www.cohre.org/store/attachments COHRE%20Cambodia%20Report%202008%20Title%20through%20Possession%20or%20Title%20through%20Position.pdf> (accessed 30 September 2010).
14. See Cambodia: Environmental Profile <http://rainforests.mongabay.com/20cambodia.htm> (accessed 30 August 2010).
15. See Illegal-logging. Info: Cambodia <http://www.illegal-logging.info/approach.php?a_id=83> (accessed 30 August 2010).
16. For more detail on efforts of the Government, see Ibid, Agricultural Sector Strategic Development Plan 2006–2010, p. 11.
17. See a Press Release on "Cambodia Community-mange Forest Area to Expand Seven-fold", 2 December 2008 <http://www.recoftc.org/site/fileadmin/docs/Country_profile/Cambodia/Cambodia_2/RECOFTC_Cambodia_Press_Releasefinal.pdf> (accessed 9 September 2010).
18. Landlessness and land conflicts in Cambodia <http://www.landcoalition.org/pdf/07_r%5Bt_land_cambodia.pdf> (accessed 30 August 2010).
19. Statement from the World Bank on Termination by Royal Government of Cambodia of the Land Management and Administration Project <http://web.worldbank.org/WBSITE/EXTERNAL/COUNTRIES/EASTASIAPACIFICEXT/CAMBODIAEXTN/0, contentMDK: 22303344~menuPK: 293861~pagePK: 1497618~piPK: 217854~theSitePK: 293856, 00.html> (accessed 31 August 2010)
20. To learn more about the effort of the Government on Land Management and Administration Project, see WB's Enhanced Review Report, 13 July 2009 <http://siteresources.worldbank.org/INTCAMBODIA/147270-

1174545988782/22303366/FINALERMREPORT.pdf> (accessed 31 August 2010).

21. See Tourism Statistical Report 2008, Ministry of Tourism of the Kingdom of Cambodia <http://www.mot.gov.kh/kh/img_filesCambodia%20Tourism%20 Highlight%201993%20-%202008.pdf> (accessed 18 August 2010).
22. See Garment and Textile products exported statistic listed in the Garment Manufacturing Association in Cambodia <http://gmac-cambodia.org/imp-exp/default.php> (accessed 18 August 2010).
23. Ron Gluckman, "Cambodia Building Boom", October 2007 <http://www.gluckman.com/CambodianBuildingBoom.html> (accessed 18 August 2010).
24. A presentation by Ngo Sothath, Researcher at the Cambodian Economic Association "Impacts of Economic Downturn on Households and Communities in Cambodia" during the 34th Annual Conference of the Federation of ASEAN Economic Association, Phnom Penh, Cambodia, 15–16 December 2009.
25. See Royal Government of Cambodia's Policy Paper on the Promotion of Paddy Production and Rice Export, approved by the Council of Ministers in Phnom Penh on 25 July 2010, pp. 33–34.
26. NSDP 2006–2010, pp. 13–16.
27. Council of Development of Cambodia: Governance and Transparency <http://www.cdc-crdb.gov.kh/cdc/ngo_statement/governance_transparency.htm#top> (accessed 21 July 2010).
28. For more details, read: Cambodia Country Report on Social Protection and Disabilities, 2–3 December, Hanoi Vietnam <http://www.dac.org.kh/publications/download/Cambodia_Courtry_Report_2007.pdf> (accessed 3 August 2010).
29. US Department of States, Bureau of Economic, Energy and Business Affairs "2011 Investment Climate Statement — Cambodia" March 2011 <http://www.state.gov/e/eeb/rls/othr/ics/2011/157251.htm> (accessed 17 May 2011).

CAMBODIA'S FUTURE

23

THE MEKONG
Uncertain Future of a Great River

Milton Osborne

"Without doubt, no other river, over such a length, has a more singular or remarkable character"

Francis Garnier (1839–1873) explorer of the Mekong

When, at a meeting held in Phnom Penh in April 2011 the Lao government bowed to pressure from Vietnam and Cambodia and agreed to suspend until 2011 its decision to construct a dam at Xayaburi, a location on the Mekong River between Luang Prabang and Vientiane, the issue of the river's future was brought into sharp relief. For what was involved in the discussion that took place in Phnom Penh was an unresolved debate about how one of the world's great rivers would function in the future. Was it to continue as a major resource of food for the populations living in the Lower Mekong Basin or LMB (The area which drains into the Mekong in Laos, Thailand, Cambodia and Vietnam, but not Burma which 'tilts' away from the river)? Or was it to become a source of hydroelectric power, even if this meant destroying the combined bounty of fish and agricultural production that the Mekong has rendered up over thousands of years? At the time of writing, in June 2011, this issue remains far from resolved. In the text that follows, I have attempted to place contemporary developments in their historical context and to argue that embracing the second alternative — the development of hydropower as the choice for the future — carries with it risks of the most fundamental kind for the 60 million inhabitants of the LMB who are so reliant on the river.

THE RIVER AND ITS HISTORY

The Mekong, a name that is a contraction from the Thai Me Nam Khan, the 'Mother of the Waters', is frequently and correctly spoken of as Southeast Asia's longest river. For some 2,250 kilometres, or 46 per cent, of its total 4,900 kilometres length does indeed flow through Southeast Asia. But the other 44 per cent of its course runs through Chinese territory, since it rises high in the eastern plateau of Tibet, at an elevation of over 5,000 metres, and flows east and then south through Yunnan province. This is a fact of capital importance for contemporary discussion of efforts to exploit the river for hydroelectric power, as China has already constructed several dams on the river where it runs through Yunnan. Overall, in terms of its length, the Mekong is the twelfth longest river in the world. In terms of the amount of water that pours out of its several mouths in Vietnam's Mekong Delta into the South China Sea, it fluctuates between being the tenth or eighth largest river in the world by volume discharged.

These facts have only become widely known relatively recently, certainly by comparison with other great rivers of the world, such as the Nile and the Amazon. For although sections of the Mekong River were, of course, always known to those who lived beside it, it was not until the 1860s that the first scientific expedition surveyed its course from what is today southern Vietnam to the area in Yunnan province around the modern Chinese city of Jinghong. This was the French Mekong Expedition — the Commission d'Exploration du Mékong — led by Commander Doudart de Lagrée, but which is most closely associated with the memory of his second-in command, Francis Garnier. He, like Lagrée, was a naval officer then serving in the newly acquired French colonial territories in Indochina, and was both a man of action and the possessor of a lively intellect. It is to Garnier that we owe the most detailed account of the expedition's journey and its accomplishments.

Before the French expedition set out from Saigon (modern Ho Chi Minh City), in June 1866, Western knowledge about the river was both sparse and fragmentary. A Dutch expedition had travelled from Phnom Penh to Vientiane in the 1640s led by Gerritt van Wuysthoff, who wrote an account of this journey. But this account remained virtually unknown until the nineteenth century, and it was, in any event, not accompanied by useful maps. The famed 're-discoverer' of the great Angkor ruins, Henri Mouhot, appears to have been the first European ever to visit the royal city of Luang Prabang in Laos, in 1860, and in the course of doing so, left a limited map of his travel on the river from Paklai to that city. But, overall, the greater part of the river remained to be explored when the French party began their epic journey.

Spurred by the enthusiasm of Garnier and his young associates in the French colony of Cochin-china and based in Saigon, the government in Paris authorised the Mekong expedition in the hope that the river would provide a trade route into China. That this hope existed was remarkable since the members of the expedition knew that even before they left Cambodian territory, they would encounter rapids in the river that would inhibit navigation. Moreover, they also knew that there was a major set of waterfalls, the Khone Falls, located just above the modern border between Cambodia and Laos that would have to be traversed. One can only assume that in a decade which saw the construction of the Suez Canal, the explorers put their faith in the capacity of technology to overcome the obstacles they already knew existed.

In the event, the expedition was, in terms of hopes that it would provide a navigable trade route into China, a failure, for the Mekong was repeatedly punctuated by rapids after the explorers had traversed the Khone Falls. But in terms of heroic exploration over the course of nearly two years, it was a remarkable achievement. It was also an achievement marked by tragedy as the leader, Lagrée, died before the expedition ended while another member, Louis de Carné, died shortly after returning to France from an illness contracted in the course of his travels. During the expedition, the French explorers travelled no less than 5,870 kilometres on the Mekong and its tributaries, and 3,390 km. on foot beside it and in the regions through which it flowed. In the course of this often painful travel — at one stage the whole expedition was reduced to walking barefoot after their shoes wore out — 6,720 kilometres on and around the Mekong were mapped in meticulous detail, with Garnier responsible for no less than 5,060 kilometres of this task. However little about the expedition is remembered today, it was seen as one of the great examples of exploration in the nineteenth century. Indeed, the great British authority on exploration, Sir Roderick Murchison, the President of Royal Geographic Society and the man who decided that it was John Speke who had first reached the source of the Nile ahead of Richard Burton, was instrumental in seeing that Garnier was awarded the Society's Patron's Medal in 1870 for his ultimate leadership of the Mekong expedition. The French expedition was, in Murchison's words 'the happiest and most complete of the nineteenth century' — a striking example of the Victorian era's concept of happiness.

When, many decades later, a shipping service was established to link Saigon with the royal capital of Laos, at Luang Prabang, it took thirty-six days to make this journey. There were frequent changes of vessel according to the range of obstacles that were encountered and the changing level of the river during the year. And passage past the Khone Falls was only achieved as travellers bypassed the falls through the use of a short, narrow-gauge railway. The time required for this journey from Saigon to Luang Prabang was longer than it took Messageries Maritimes vessels to travel from Marseilles to Saigon. The limitations the Mekong imposed on those who had looked to use it as a trade route meant that, for more than a hundred years after Garnier and his companions had explored it, the river flowed from its source to the sea almost unchanged from how it had done for thousands of years.

Apart from its use for local travel and the unsatisfactory and time-consuming travel between the French possessions in Vietnam and Cambodia and Laos, it was uninterrupted by any dams or weirs. Even today, and only after major clearance operations between Jinghong in southern Yunnan and Chiang Saen in northern Thailand that were completed in 2003, has a section of the river become open to navigation above the Khone Falls on any regular basis. Even with these clearances between China and Thailand, navigation has had to be suspended during several dry seasons as the water level in the Mekong has fallen to the point where vessels could not make the journey.

PLANS TO EXPLOIT THE MEKONG FOR HYDROELECTRICITY

China

It is against this background that controversy now exists in relation to the proposed dam at Xayaburi. But the planned dam at Xayaburi is far from the first envisaged to be constructed on the Mekong after it flows out of China, as is detailed later in this article. Neither, if it is built, will it be the first dam constructed on the Mekong, since China embarked on a dam-building program in Yunnan province beginning in the 1980s. China has already brought four dams on the river into commission, with a further dam currently under construction. It has plans to build at least three more dams, so forming an eventual 'cascade' of no less than eight dams. China began its dam-building program in the 1980s but it was not until the mid-1990s, that there was a widespread awareness of what was taking place following the presentation of a paper at a conference held in Melbourne in 1996, which detailed developments in China up to that date. The reasons for this lack of general awareness reflected the limited amount of information on its activities released by Chinese authorities and, in particular, the remote and lightly populated locations within Yunnan province where the dams were constructed.

China's dams on the Mekong are, in order of completion, situated at Manwan, Dachaoshan, Jinghong and Xiaowan, with the latter reportedly commissioned in 2010 even if not all works at the dam have been completed. Meanwhile, construction continues on a site at Nuozhadu. All of the dams have been built to generate hydroelectricity and form part of a broader Chinese policy for the development of its underprivileged western provinces. While three of the dams so far completed are each commissioned to produce 1,500 MW, or slightly less, the fourth of the commissioned dams, at Xiaowan, is a massive dam capable of producing 4,500 MW and is the second largest dam ever built in China. Only the Three Gorges dam is larger than Xiaowan. Its dam wall is nearly 300 metres in height and its pond, or reservoir, when full will stretch back from the dam for 170 kilometres. The dam under construction at Nuozhadu will, when brought into commission, have an even greater generating capacity than the dam at Xiaowan, with a projected output of 5,500 MW.

Although the issue is hotly-contested, it appears to be the case that the Chinese dams have not, *so far*, had an irrevocable effect on the manner in which the Mekong functions, though it is almost certainly the case that there have been short intervals when dam works in Yunnan have affected the flow of the river downstream. This is set to change as the Chinese pursue their stated policy of using the dams in Yunnan to 'even out' the flow of the river. Doing this, Chinese officials have repeatedly stated, will be a desirable course of action which will minimise flooding in the Southeast Asian countries' wet seasons and raise the level of water in the river in the dry seasons. But the apparent desirability of such 'evening out' is misplaced. Flooding is an important part of the river's normal ecological character, ridding flooded areas of pests, and depositing rich nutrients in the sediments carried by the floods on agricultural regions, and combating salt water intrusion in the Mekong Delta. Changing the existing pattern of the river's flow will also have a negative effect on fish stocks in the river. In a 2007 study carried out by the World Fish Centre and the Cambodian National Mekong Committee, the following grave concerns were raised about the future impacts of the Chinese dams. If these dams function as is projected, the study concluded that the Chinese dam cascade would:

- alter the hydrology of the river and so the current 'flood pulse', the regular rise and fall of the river on an annual basis which plays an essential part in the timing of spawning and the [fish] migration pattern.

This will be particularly important in relation to the Tonle Sap in Cambodia, but will have an effect throughout the river's course;
- block the flow of sediment down the river which plays a vital part both in depositing nutrients on the agricultural regions flooded by the river and also as a trigger for fish migration — at present well over 50 per cent of the river's sediment comes from China;
- at least initially cause problems by restricting the amount of flooding that takes place most importantly in Cambodia and Vietnam;
- lead to the erosion of river banks.

In the light of these negative judgments, and the vigorous criticism levelled at the Chinese dams by NGOs, civil society groups, academics and independent scholars, it is a striking fact that the governments of Cambodia, Laos, Thailand and Vietnam have been reticent to indicate that they have any concerns about their great neighbour's actions. It is impossible not to conclude that in acting in this way the leaderships in Bangkok, Hanoi, Phnom Penh and Vientiane have placed their perceived concern not to complicate relations with China above what appear to outsiders as their own national interests.

Now, for the first time, as is apparent with the controversy surrounding the Xayaburi dam, the governments in the LMB have to address issues that will arise if any of the dams planned for the river below China actually come into being. In this regard, there seems some reason to believe, as suggested by Professor Phil Hirsch of the Australian Mekong Resource Centre that in pressing ahead with its dams China has, whether deliberately or not, provided a demonstration effect to its smaller neighbours of what might be done to exploit the Mekong's hydropower potential.

Earlier Plans for Dams in the Lower Mekong Basin

As long ago as the 1950s, plans were made for the construction of dams on the Mekong where it flows through the Lower Mekong Basin. Closely linked to Cold War politics and, after initial hesitation in Washington, with the firm support of the United States, plans were developed for a series of dams in Laos and in Cambodia. The dams were conceived to provide hydroelectricity and so to act as a major economic boost for the underdeveloped countries in which they would be built. But they were also planned as counter to what was seen as the aggressive advance of communist power following the 1949 victory of the Chinese communists and the 1954 partial victory of the communists in Vietnam. In short, economic development was to trump communist ideology. This was the era of general enthusiasm for big dams, so that the proponents of these dams did not appear concerned that one of the dams at Pa Mong, a little upstream from the Lao capital of Vientiane, would, if built, have resulted in the resettlement of some 250,00 people. Survey work for these planned dams took place in both Cambodia and Laos, but as the security situation deteriorated in conjunction with the spreading effects of the Vietnam War, none of the proposed dams were ever built.

The Vietnam War, its linked tragic aftermath in Pol Pot's Cambodia, and the unsettled circumstances of the 1980s put plans for dam construction in the LMB on hold until the mid 1990s. At that time, in 1994, a further set of proposals emerged for eleven dams on the Mekong's mainstream, with one proposed dam sited on or close to the southern extremity of Cambodia's Great Lake, the Tonle Sap. These proposals were put forward by a French state-owned company and a private enterprise in Canada. But, once again, external circumstances intervened to prevent these plans becoming a reality, as the Asian Financial Crisis of the late 1990s put paid to major construction of the kind envisaged. Although little attention was paid to the issue at the time, outside of a limited number of environmental groups, the proposals put forward at this period specifically noted that no research had been undertaken to evaluate the likely effects of the projected dams on fish in the Mekong.

THE MEKONG RIVER COMMISSION

The emergence of this last set of proposals for mainstream dams below China was followed shortly after, in April 1995, by the inauguration of a new body, the Mekong River Commission (MRC), designed to promote cooperation for the sustainable development of the river among the four countries within the LMB. A successor to the earlier Mekong Committee established in 1957, it has been a much misunderstood organisation and subject to often ill-informed criticism by advocacy NGOs which have not realised, or accepted, the limitations that have been placed on its mandate. Most importantly, the MRC does not have a mandate to sanction or prevent the construction of dams on the Mekong in the LMB. This remains the individual prerogative of the four member states: Cambodia, Laos, Thailand and Vietnam. Its Secretariat has provided very valuable research on the river in its many aspects, and most recently, as detailed below, it has played an important part in convening meetings to discuss the future of the river, in particular the likely effect of dams in the LMB. But it is important to remember that the MRC is not an organisation charged with governance of the Mekong. Moreover, and in relation to China, it has no authority whatsoever to play a role in relation to that country's actions. China is not a member of the MRC, neither, much less importantly, is Burma.

WHY DAMS ON THE LMB NOW?

Over the past three or four years, news about plans for dams on the LMB have emerged in a piecemeal fashion, and by 2008 it was apparent that no fewer than eleven dams and one water diversion project were being proposed for the LMB: nine dams in Laos and one diversion project, and two dams in Cambodia. In all cases, the dams being proposed were to be commercial operations, with capital provided either by construction companies or by state-backed commercial enterprises in China and Vietnam. This was a new situation involving, as it did, an abandonment of the previous assumption that major infrastructure such as dams would be financed by international organisations. So, as an example, the Xayaburi dam that has been the cause of such recent controversy is linked to the major Thai commercial company, Ch. Kamchang, while the proposed Sambor dam in Cambodia would be sponsored by the China Southern Power Grid.

Often described as 'run of the river' dams, those proposed for the LMB are far from the image that this term conjures up of minor obstructions sited in the river. To take the planned dam at Xayaburi as an example, its dam wall is projected to be 32 metres in height, and similar heights are envisaged for the other proposed dams on the Mekong below China, including, for instance, at Don Sahong. The dam walls have to be of such a height since otherwise there would not be enough water stored behind them to operate the turbines inserted in the dam walls below water level. More than incidentally, it is only because of China's dams and the planned 'evening out' of the Mekong's flow that sufficient water is projected to be maintained in the planned LMB dams throughout the year.

So this availability of water is one reason for the decisions that have been made in both Cambodia and Laos to consider building dams on the Mekong. But clearly other considerations are involved. Without doubt, there is the very real attraction of finding a way to earn foreign exchange from the production and export sale of hydroelectricity. This has a particular attraction for the Vientiane government because of its otherwise constrained economic prospects. The same is true, if to a lesser extent, for Cambodia. In both countries, it is also undoubtedly the case that the governments see in the planned dams an opportunity to extend electricity supply to a wider range of the population than is currently the case. There is probably another factor that should be noted. This is the inclination which appears to be present at the leadership level in both Cambodia and Laos which tends to regard fishing as an old-fashioned activity, in contrast to the modernity associated with the production of hydropower.

Finally, if far from exhaustively, there are reasons to believe that many officials in both countries are poorly informed on the negative consequences that will flow from the construction of dams in the LMB. On the basis of personal experience, I can cite cases of officials who simply did not believe that it would be impossible to mitigate the effects of the dams on fish migration, by one means or another. Yet all evidence indicates that mitigation is, indeed, not possible, as discussed below.

LMB TRIBUTARIES

In addition to plans for dams on the mainstream of the river, plans also exist for the construction of dams on tributaries of the Mekong. Limitations of space in this article mean that a full coverage of the various dams planned on the Mekong's tributaries is not possible. Nevertheless, it would derelict not to draw attention to the fact that proposed tributary hydroelectric dams carry with them the same risks to fish catches as those in the mainstream. In this respect, the proposed construction of the Sesan 2 dam, which would block fish migration on two of the most important Mekong tributaries in Cambodia, the Sesan and Srepok Rivers, is a matter for deep concern.

THE DANGERS TO FISH MIGRATION AND AGRICULTURE POSED BY LMB DAMS

The key concern associated with plans for dams on the Mekong below China stems from the river's vital role as a source of food, whether from fish caught in the river or from the agricultural and horticultural activity that depends on the river for irrigation. In relation to both these issues it is almost impossible to overstate the importance of the Mekong to the populations of the countries that form the LMB.

Put simply but accurately, the Mekong is at the heart a vast fluvial system that is among the richest source of freshwater fish in the world, with an annual catch of wild fish taken from the Mekong River system conservatively valued at time of catch at US$2 billion, and close to US$5 billion at retail prices. This is a greater value than the total freshwater catch for the whole of West Africa. In Laos alone the value of fish taken from the Mekong and its tributaries is estimated by the World Fish Centre at between US$56 million and US$100 million, with wild fish amounting to 78 per cent of the country's total fish production. Perhaps even more striking is the role fish play in the diet of the countries in the LMB. In Cambodia, as the most notable example, nearly 80 per cent of the Cambodian population's animal protein intake comes from fish taken out of the Mekong River and its associated systems including the Tonle Sap. Were the availability of fish, as the source of protein, to be seriously diminished, there is no possibility that they could be replaced at an acceptable cost by other sources such as poultry, pork or cattle.

Central to understanding why building dams on the Mekong in Cambodia and Laos is such a bad idea is the fact that such a large proportion of the fish found in the river are migratory in character. Of the approximately 900 species indigenous to the freshwater reaches of the river over 80 per cent are migratory. Some of these fish travel many hundreds of kilometres in the course of their migrations, which can involve travel from above the Khone Falls in Laos to the Cambodian Great Lake and back again. There are even reported instances of fish travelling from as far away as the Mekong Delta to above the Khone Falls.

Dams built in the LMB would dramatically and negatively affect these migrations. For there is general agreement among scientists that building dams would interrupt existing fish migration patterns and so reduce the size of fish catches. This is because no current means exist that can be used to mitigate the effects of such dams: neither fish ladders nor fish 'elevators,' nor fish passes — artificial rivers, around dams. Adding to concern is the fact that two of the proposed dams are located in particularly critical sites on the Mekong, at Don Sahong in Laos at the Khone Falls, and at Sambor in Cambodia, a little to the north of the provincial town of Kratie.

Despite the vast quantities of water that pour over the Khone Falls, migratory fish are able to make their way from below the falls to the calm water above through a series of channels at certain times of the year. But only one channel, that known as the Hou Sahong Channel, is used by migratory fish throughout the year. Yet it is at this channel that plans have been developed to build the Don Sahong dam. Since there seems no reason to believe that mitigation will overcome the fact that such a dam will block migration, the negative impacts from the dam effects will be felt by populations dependent on fish catches both above and below the proposed dam. A similarly negative outlook is associated with the proposed Sambor dam in Cambodia. This dam is planned for a section of the Mekong that is an essential part of the Middle Mekong Migration System, and as such, and without any mitigation, it will block much of the most important migration of fish between the Khone Falls and the Tonle Sap lake. Indeed, as long ago as 2003, the Sambor site was identified 'the worst possible location' for a dam on the Mekong in Cambodia.

The effects of dams blocking fish migration would be immediate as fish could not move to spawning areas and so would not spawn; young fish could not access nursery or feeding areas and those that passed through hydroelectric turbines would be killed. These effects would be apparent with 1–2 years for small fish and 2–5 years for larger species. Since dams result in a wide range of changes to river's hydrology — changed daily and seasonal flows, sediment trapping and altered water temperatures — these would affect fish that normally would move downstream of dams but which would now be confined to what would have become artificial lakes. The effects of such changed circumstances would ultimately be just as insidious as the more dramatic blocking of migratory species.

The dangers posed by the dams to the Mekong's fish catches represent the most dramatic of the effects likely to occur. But the long-term effects of dam construction in the LMB on the agriculture and horticulture along the river are also a matter of considerable concern. Nowhere is this more the case than in the Mekong Delta, Vietnam's most productive agricultural region. The region contributes more than 50 per cent of Vietnam's agricultural component of Vietnam' GDP, which makes up some 19 per cent of the country's total GDP. Clearly, any reduction or alteration of the Mekong's existing water flow in the delta will pose serious problems for Vietnam. At the same time, the role of the Mekong in providing irrigation elsewhere along the river's course will be endangered by alterations effected by the planned dams. In particular, the vital horticultural production along the Mekong's banks would be heavily affected.

WARNINGS OF DANGERS

Although the MRC is prevented from instructing its members how they should act, in the light of growing interest, and controversy, sparked by plans to build dams on the mainstream of the Mekong in the LMB, the MRC Secretariat in 2009 commissioned a report on the environmental implications of the proposed dams. On 15 October 2010, the MRC released the Final Report on the Strategic Environmental Assessment (SEA) of the planned dams prepared by ICEM Australia (International Centre for Environmental Management). The report was an uncompromising rejection of the desirability of building dams on the Mekong, stating, most importantly, in its main recommendation 'that decisions on mainstream dams should be deferred for a period of ten years with reviews every three years to ensure that essential deferment-period activities are being conducted effectively'. And, adding as a concluding point, the recommendation that the 'Mekong mainstream should never be used as a test case for proving and improving full dam hydropower technologies'.

The SEA provides a wealth of evidence in support of its conclusions. While acknowledging that there is potential for electricity production, it makes clear that the social impact of the dams would be very great indeed. To take fisheries alone, the SEA concludes that the 'loss of inland fish production would have major implications for food security given the dependency of the LMB region on fish as a source of protein'. It also states that 'replacing capture fish production by aquaculture production is not realistic', and addressing the issue of mitigation of the effects of dams on fish migration, the SEA states unequivocally that 'fish passes are not a realistic mitigation for Mekong mainstream dams'. The SEA's emphasis on this point reflects the increasing realisation, even among advocates for the mainstream dams, that fish ladders and fish 'elevators' are not realistic answers to the barriers that dams would pose to fish migration.

While the estimate made by the SEA of the number of people who would be directly affected by the construction of all of the proposed dams, as the result of necessary relocation, are of the order of 107,000, once account is taken of indirect effects of those living within a 15 kilometre corridor of the river, the numbers jump to no fewer that 26.9 million for Laos, Thailand and Cambodia, and 14 million in Vietnam.

PUTTING XAYABURI ON HOLD

Throughout 2010 and as it became apparent that the Lao government was likely to give approval for the construction of a dam at Xayaburi, public opposition to such a decision grew ever more vocal, and for the first time it included critical comment from elements of the Vietnamese government. In September 2010, the Lao government formally notified its intention to proceed with construction, so sparking further widespread opposition to its plans. Against this background and at the meeting convened by the MRC in Phnom Penh on 19 April 2011, the governments of Cambodia and Vietnam indicated their firm opposition to construction of the Xayaburi dam. In Vietnam's case, its representatives drew on the SEA to recommend that there should be a deferment of all plans for mainstream dams for ten years. Thailand's position was less clear-cut, as its representatives withheld outright opposition but indicated that their government was concerned about the effect the proposed Lao dam would have on downstream countries. In the face of this opposition, and presumably taking particular account of the position adopted by Vietnam, its long-time ally, the Lao representatives at the meeting agreed to suspend any action on the Xayaburi dam until October 2011, when the issue will again be discussed under MRC auspices.

WHAT NOW?

It is far too early at the present time of writing to conclude that the issue of dams on the mainstream of the Mekong in the LMB is resolved and that none will be built. Suspension of construction at Xayaburi was and is important; both in relation to that dam but also for the demonstration effect its construction would have in relation to the other planned dams along the Mekong's course. But as noted previously in this paper, there are other planned dams that should be regarded as posing a greater threat to the Mekong's ecology and so to its vital role for fish and irrigation. We cannot be sure, at this point, that the opposition that Cambodia displayed in relation to Xayaburi will necessary be replicated in relation to Sambor. Moreover, even if no dams are built in the LMB, the effects of the Chinese dam will begin to have an effect over the next decade and beyond.

For more than a decade, I have been concerned to present a balanced account of contemporary issues associated with the Mekong River. My overriding concern has been the manner in which far too often environmental and ecological issues have been ignored in the planning and action that has taken place, first in China and now in the countries along the Mekong below China, in favour of presumed economic benefits. This tendency has all too often failed to take account of the Mekong's vitally important role as a source of sustenance for the populations that lie along its course — both in terms of its almost unparalleled capability to supply fish to these populations and through its role in supporting agriculture. Whether or not there will ever be a body that will be empowered to exercise control of development of the Mekong may be a matter of debate, though I regrettably think it is unlikely.

Regarding the Mekong in its total character, rather than simply in terms of a resource to be exploited for hydropower, is essential for the wellbeing of more than 60 million people in the Lower Mekong Basin (LMB). In my Lowy Institute Paper No. 27/2009 entitled, The Mekong: River under Threat, I evaluated the potentially huge social and environmental risks for the Mekong River and the millions who depend on it for their livelihood of planned dam projects in Laos and Cambodia. The mighty Mekong River is a key area of global importance as the governments of the LMB seek a balance between economic development and social and environmental sustainability, with effective political cooperation between them. For the moment, it is far from certain that these challenges are being met.

It is now too late to stop China from continuing to construct its dams. But allowing the river to run free of dams in the LMB remains a possibility. For the governments in Laos and Cambodia to ignore the conclusions of the SEA would be to change the character of the river forever and to turn it, at best, into a series on unproductive lakes — not quite the drainage ditch of worst imaginings, but a threat to the livelihood of their people who have been sustained by the Mekong over time immemorial.

BIBLIOGRAPHIC DETAILS

The Mekong is a river with which I have been associated for more than fifty years. The preceding article is a distillation of my writings on the Mekong, mostly over the past decade. In particular, the article draws on the range of writings that I have published since 2004 in association with the Lowy Institute for International Policy, Sydney.

Material relating to the exploration of the Mekong and early efforts to use it for trade with China may be found in my books, *River Road to China: The Search for the Source of the Mekong, 1866–1873* (originally published in 1975 and reprinted in 1996 and 1997), and *The Mekong: Turbulent Past, Uncertain Future* (2000; updated edition 2006).

Detailed documentation for contemporary developments relating to the river up to and including 2009 may found in my following Lowy Institute publications: *River at Risk: The Mekong and the Water Politics of Southeast Asia*, Lowy Institute Paper 02, 2004; 'The Water Politics of China and Southeast Asia II: Rivers, Dams, Cargo Boats and the Environment,' Lowy Institute Perspectives, 2007; *The Mekong: River Under Threat*, Lowy Institute Paper 27, 2009. These three publications are available at no charge on the Lowy Institute website <http://www.lowyinstutute.org>.

Since publishing *The Mekong: River Under Threat*, in 2009, I have regularly commented on developments associated with the Mekong and plans to build dams in the LMB in the Lowy Institute blog, 'The Interpreter': <www.lowyinterpreter.org>.

As will be apparent from any internet search, there is now a very large amount of material available dealing with Mekong issues, and I do not intend to replicate that information in this brief note. I do however draw attention to two important and recent articles: one by Professor Phil Hirsch, to which I referred in the text, 'The Changing Political Dynamics of Dam Building on the Mekong,' published in Water Alternatives, 3 (2), 2010: <http://www.water-alternaatives.org>, and a recent article by Dr Ian G. Baird, 'The Don Sahong Dam', *Critical Asia Studies* 43, no. 2 (2011): 211–35, 2011.

THE MEKONG

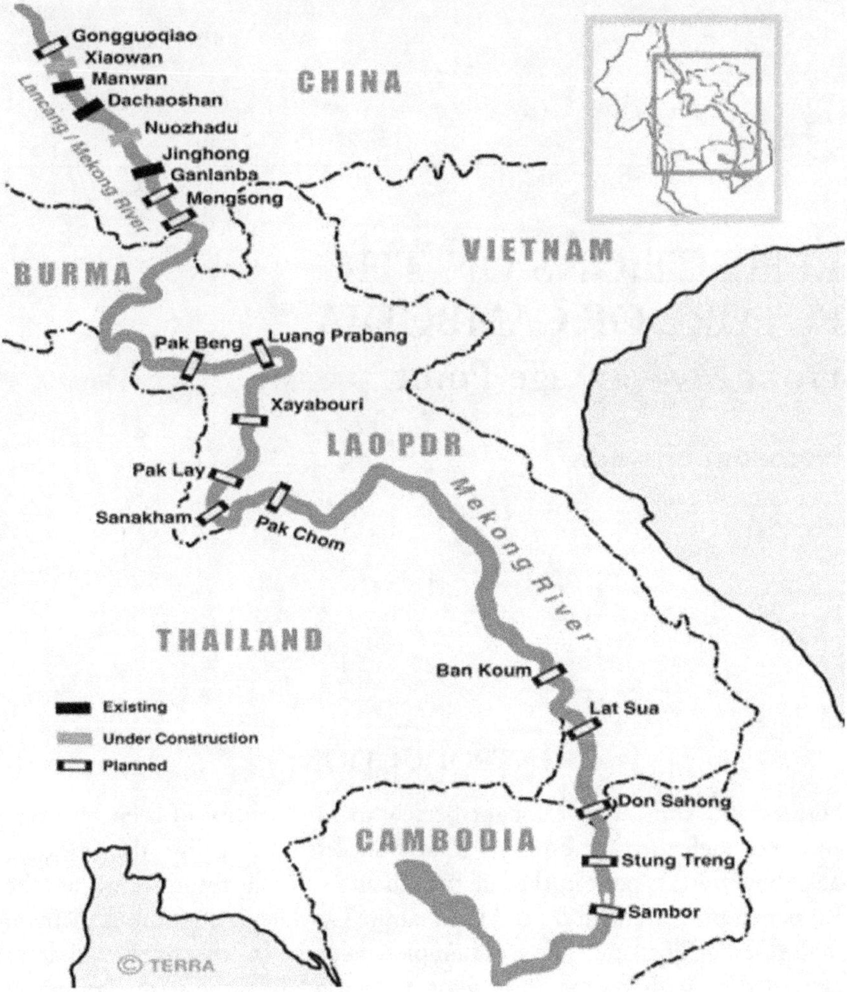

Hydropower dams:
Completed, under construction and proposed on the Mekong River
Sources: Towards Ecological Recovery and Regional Alliance (TERRA) <http://www.terraper.org> and International Rivers <http://www.internationalrivers.org>

24

REFLECTIONS ON THE FUTURE OF CAMBODIA
From My Vantage Point

Norodom Sirivudh

INTRODUCTION

Historically, Khmers have fought fiercely to gain control of their territory, and then defended it, but not always successfully, against the invading neighbours. At its peak in the late twelfth and early thirteenth centuries, the Khmer empire extended from the Annamite Cordillera in southern Vietnam to the Gulf of Thailand. The great temples, palaces and other public buildings erected during that time at Angkor are national symbols; the towers of Angkor form the central design of the national flag. The Khmer Empire later declined from the early thirteenth century. Over the next five centuries, Cambodia steadily contracted as neighbouring Siam (Thailand) and Annam (Vietnam) expanded. Although the Khmer Empire has collapsed, the spirit of being hard working and creative has always stayed with the Cambodian people. Angkor Wat has become the modern symbol of the Khmer civilization and identity.

Global realpolitik and ideological differences pushed Cambodia into the flames of war and armed conflict in the 1970s. Our historical and cultural heritage and values were massively destroyed during the Khmer Rouge period. We almost lost much of our national identity and strength. Now after decades of peace and stability, beginning in the 1990s, we are re-discovering who we are and our roots. We are a hard working people with a capacity for great innovations, but we need the right political and economic systems to fulfil our potential.

Globalization and regionalization has taken the centre stage of the world political economy. Cambodia has integrated herself with the region and the world with strong courage and commitment. We also believe that through such processes of regional integration and cooperation, Cambodia can develop and progress from a developing country to one of the developed countries. Many challenges lie ahead, but as long as we accept the truth and speak the truth, then we can find ways to overcome those challenges.

This paper attempts to shed some light on the past development of Cambodia and share my personal views on the prospects of Cambodia's development path. For Cambodia to be successful, we need to generate agents of change. The future generation of leadership determines the future of Cambodia. I have strong hopes that they will bring Cambodia to a higher position in the region and the world in terms of economic growth, social welfare, and social justice. We have gone through and learned much experience through different regimes. What we have found is that we really need leadership at all levels with wisdom, integrity, and which earns respect from people. Due to political sensitivities, I have to write simply and carefully, and trust that readers can understand the limits of discussion.

DEFINITION OF GOOD GOVERNANCE

When talking about good governance in Cambodia, we need to understand it in a comprehensive way. We need to emphasize the roles played by the state, the civil service, the international donor community/development partners, NGOs, research institutes and think tanks, the middle class and the people. These actors collaboratively design and make a strategic plan for the good governance and development in Cambodia.

As far as "good governance" is concerned, I personally believe that we all understand what it is and how it works. To put it simply, Good Governance exists when there is peace, prosperity, stability, socio-economic progress, justice, rule of law, anti-corruption and equality. To recognize the effects of bad governance is not difficult. Several indicators of Bad governance are: absence/lack of transparency and accountability, corruption, absence/lack of judiciary independence, absence/lack of law enforcement, absence/lack of social justice, high poverty rate, deepening discrepancy between the rich and the poor, and absence/lack of protection and respect of human rights and democratic principles.

INTERNATIONAL DEFINITION OF GOOD GOVERNANCE

The World Bank first used the term "good governance in a 1989 publication. Later in 1992, in a Report entitled Governance and Development, the Bank explored the linkages between the two sectors. The World Bank in 1992 defined Governance as "Development Management". It focused on 3 key aspects:

A. Form of political regime-thus, democracy;
B. Process by which authority is exercised-constitutionally and with respect for the rule of law;
C. Capacity of Government to design, formulate, implement policies, and to discharge functions. The Key Traits of good governance include: transparency, accountability, institutional pluralism, the participation of citizens, rule of law and independent judiciary, and a strong civil society. The World Bank's Worldwide Governance Indicators (WGI) Project reports aggregate individual governance indicators for 212 countries and territories over the period 1996–2007, for six dimensions of governance: Voice and Accountability, Political Stability and Absence of Violence, Government Effectiveness, Regulatory Quality Rule of Law, and Control of Corruption. The diagram below shows a schematic representation of good governance. (See Figures 24.1 and 24.2)

POLICY MAKING

Another way of looking at governance is to state that Governance is the art of policy making and implementation. It defines the way in which Governments and their regulatory authorities exercise power and care in their handling of state affairs and in managing the economic, political, socio-cultural and environmental resources which are entrusted to them. A critical assessment of Governance thus includes key issues such as abuse of power, accountability, transparency, rule of law, corruption and mismanagement of resources and policies, issues of stability and security, peace and war; and in general, the issues of public welfare. Other key issues involved include: democracy, free and fair elections, freedom of choice, freedom of voice, assembly, movement, individual rights, collective responsibility, social discipline, minority rights

FIGURE 24.1
Schematic Representation of Good Governance

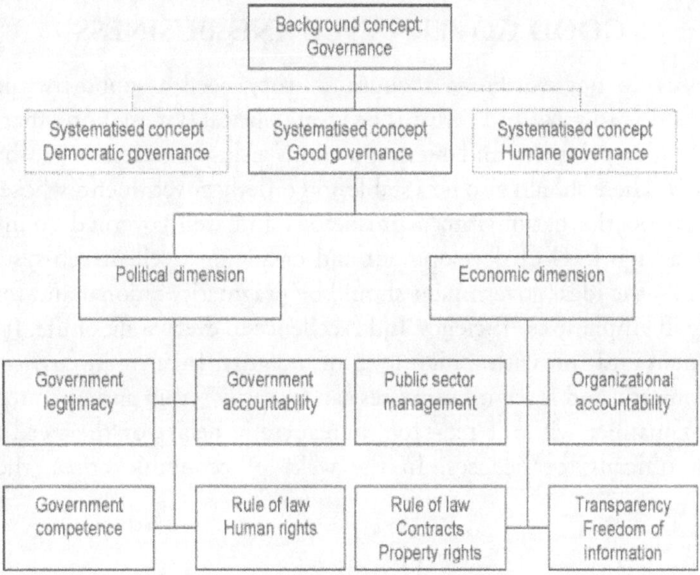

FIGURE 24.2
Components of Good Governance

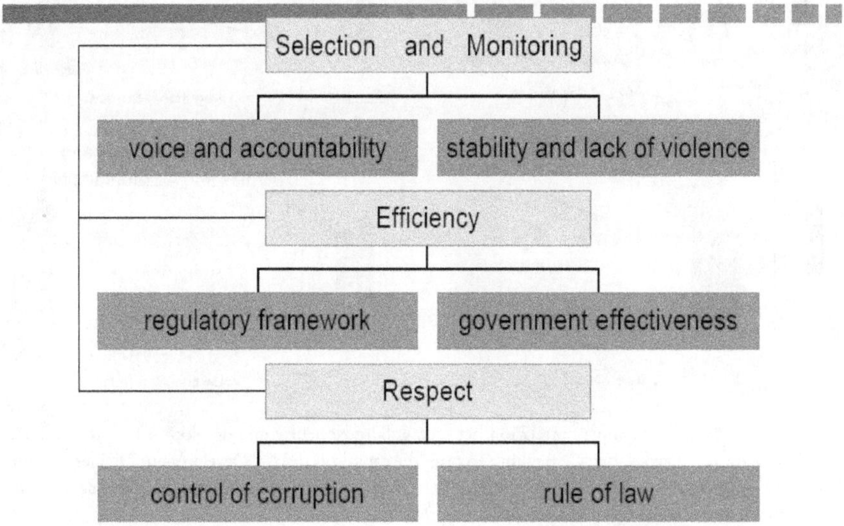

and protection, and racial and religious harmony. There are economic dividends from ensuring good governance, as shown below. (See Figure 24.3)

GOOD GOVERNANCE AND BUSINESS

Businesses do not exist in a vacuum — they need a supportive political infrastructure to grow and thrive. The ideal political system is one that enacts laws, decides priorities and sets regulations using a rational, pro-business approach. There should also be a stable and orderly government, whose vision is to develop the nation into a prosperous and well-governed country. To achieve a high level of development and create an excellent eco-system for businesses, the ideal government should be pragmatic, rational and forward-looking. It emphasizes efficiency and excellence in every walk of life. It is very transparent and run with a high level of integrity. In such an environment, both domestic and foreign businesses can be easily set up and operated in an efficient manner without red-tape, bureaucratic delays or the need to pay corrupt officials for licenses. In the wake of economic crises, the ideal

FIGURE 24.3
The Economic Development 'Dividend' of Good Public Governance

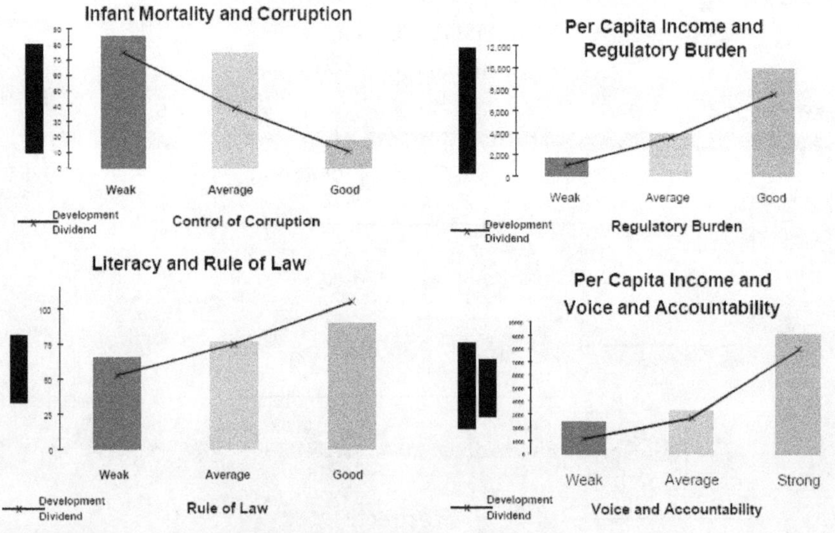

Note: The bar depict the simple correlation between good governance and development outcomes. The line depicts the predicted value when taking account the causality effects ("Development Dividend") from improved governance to better development outcomes. For data and methodological details visit <http://www.worldbank.org/wbi/governance.

government responds rapidly and decisively. It reviews its policies and programs and takes measures to restore stability as quickly as possible. Even with non-economic crises, protective and preventive measures are swiftly taken.Such an ideal government should possess the following traits:

- Thinking Ahead: the ability to perceive early signals of future developments;
- Thinking Again: the ability and willingness to rethink and remake current policies so that they perform better;
- Thinking Across: the ability and openness to cross boundaries to learn from other countries and institutions new ideas & practices;

Thus, Governance in a broader context refers to the rules, institutions, and networks that determine how countries and organizations function; the continuous learning and dynamic adaptation and innovative change results in adaptive efficiency — which is a country's ability to create productive, stable, fair and flexible institutions. Furthermore, dynamic governance does not happen by chance; it is a result of a deliberate leadership's intentions and ambitions to structure socio-economic interactions and to achieve national goals.

DEMOCRACY AND GOOD GOVERNANCE

Now, I shall briefly discuss democracy and good governance. They are deeply inter-linked, one cannot survive without the other. It is more than just electoral system. Democracy as a political system, is firstly, a system which ensures a peaceful power succession, and which:

- Ensures the fair distribution of public goods and services;
- Helps to resolve disputes and conflicts between interest groups;
- Helps protect the interest and well being of minorities;
- Promotes accountability and transparency of government to the people;
- Enables the rule of law, ensures justice and equality;
- Ascertains the will of the people;
- Meet the aspirations of the people;
- Helps strengthen public institutions;
- Enhances changes in society.
- Institutions: In order to avoid the problems of the rule of man- no matter how wise and benevolent a great leader is, he/she will pass away- institutionalization is necessary to systematize knowledge and practices in a democracy. The figure below shows the schematic traits and operational functions of institutions. (See Figure 24.4)

FIGURE 24.4
Schematic Traits and Operational Functions of Institutions

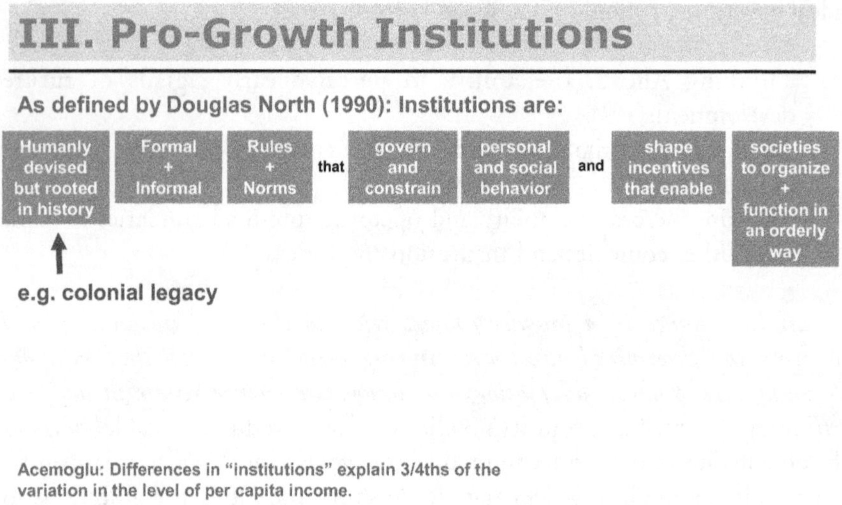

III. Pro-Growth Institutions
As defined by Douglas North (1990): Institutions are:
Humanly devised but rooted in history
Formal + Informal
Rules + Norms
that
govern and constrain
personal and social behavior
and
shape incentives that enable
societies to organize + function in an orderly way
e.g. colonial legacy
Acemoglu: Differences in "institutions" explain 3/4ths of the variation in the level of per capita income.

HUMAN RESOURCE DEVELOPMENT AND GOOD GOVERNANCE

Governance can only be as good as the civil service personnel administering services to the people — their professionalism, the ethos of service to the people. Briefly, Human Resource Development or HRD is defined as the training, education and developmental learning experiences which are organised to enhance human performance. The development of skills is a critical factor in human development. Thus, education and training are key factors in HRD- this includes proper funding. Examples of HRD and good governance include the following: the computerization of the entire civil service; secondly, setting up a proper Civil Service College to train officials. HRD is most effective when supported by a package of policies. Thus HRD should be accompanied by complementary policies in the sectors of governmental competence, infrastructural development and economic development. With proper HRD and good governance, there will be development dividends from such features, as shown below. (See Figure 24.5)

THREE ASPECTS OF GOOD GOVERNANCE

In general, Good Governance needs wise leadership and a strong/effective civil service:

FIGURE 24.5
Development Dividend from Good Governance

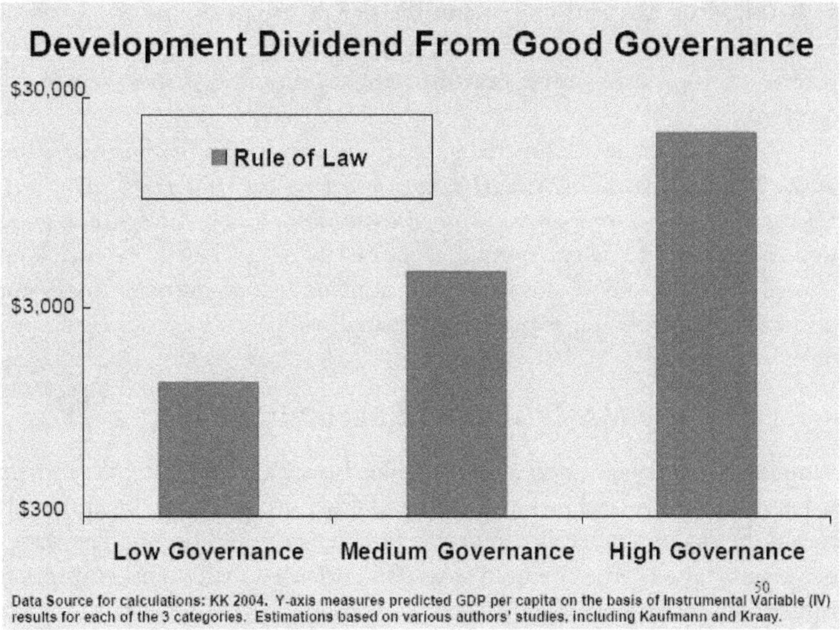
Development Dividend From Good Governance
$30,000
$3,000
$300
Rule of Law
Low Governance
Medium Governance
High Governance
50
Data Source for calculations: KK 2004. Y-axis measures predicted GDP per capita on the basis of Instrumental Variable (IV) results for each of the 3 categories. Estimations based on various authors' studies, including Kaufmann and Kraay.

- Political expertise: the degree of state commitment to people's welfare; also, the exercise of political power to manage state affairs;
- Technical expertise: Involving issues of efficiency in public management and nation building;
- General features: includes leadership determination process; legitimacy via free elections; transparency; accountability; participation; protection of human rights; dependability and predictability; capacity of institution building; responsiveness to changes; partnership between people/public/private sectors.

GOVERNANCE COMPARED TO DRIVING AUTOMOBILES

I personally prefer to compare governance to "driving a car". To drive a car, we need to have at least three components: destination/vision, mechanism (civil service), process (governance); and one driver (or leader) with of course the driving license (or Mandate of the People). To be a leader, we need the legitimacy, wisdom and ability and to motivate the people, we need to get their confidence and trust. Legitimacy is required for driving the nation. A good driver must have a clear destination or vision. A good driver must be aware of, recognize, and understand the signals, especially the red lights or warning signs of dangers, then take actions appropriately and in a timely manner. A good driver must bear the responsibility in case there is a traffic accident.

There is an ancient Chinese saying: *If you are planning for one year, plant grain; If you are planning for 10 years, plant trees; for 100 years, plant men (Human Resource Development through Education).* Good drivers, like good leaders need to be talent-spotted, educated and developed, exposed and trained. Leadership does not happen by accident; good governance does not operate haphazardly but is carefully prepared.

MANAGING MISBEHAVIOUR

Running a country well is in some ways like driving a car well. In the car there is a dash-board which shows all signals and other necessary instruments/tools to run the car, and especially important are the gears and brakes. The leader of a country also needs systems of checks and balances, such as anti-corruption regulations, incentives for good performance, indicators of economic progress and financial health. Driving a car in Cambodia is very challenging, given there are so many motorbikes, small roads, and lack of respect of traffic rules. The big and luxurious cars seem to have more privilege on the road. Of course, much depends on the drivers' behaviour. There are some cases where the drivers just run away after they commit a traffic accident. The drivers must be made responsible for the safe driving. The police and courts have to arrest and bring to justice those irresponsible drivers. Governing a new and reborn country like Cambodia, which was re-established after the UNTAC-supervised general elections in 1993, is also a sensitive and delicate enterprise.

GOOD GOVERNANCE IN CAMBODIA

This paper examines economic reforms and governance issues in Cambodia from the early 1990s. Good governance is the core of every successful national construction. Cambodia's 1993 Constitution provides for the separation of powers and an independent judiciary. It also enshrines Cambodia's adoption of a market economic system. The National Assembly enacts laws and the King promulgates them.

Part 1: Economic Reform

The 1993 Constitution stipulates that Cambodia is a multiparty, liberal democracy in which the Cambodian people are masters of their country and exercise their powers through the national assembly, senate, government, and courts. All citizens have the right to establish associations and political parties. The constitution incorporates the rule of law and human rights as enshrined in the Universal Declaration of Human Rights.

Cambodia's economic system is based on a market economy. The state has five main roles in the economy: 1. collect taxes, determine the national budget, and manage the monetary and financial system. 2. controls, uses, and manage state properties (natural resources). 3. promotes economic development. 4. protects the environment and oversee the management of natural resources. 5. protects the consumers.

Regarding the promotion and protection of the private sector, the government has adopted and implemented laws and regulations such as the 1994 Law on Investment, the 1995 Law on Organization and Functioning of a Council for Development in Cambodia and the Cambodia Investment Board, and the 1997 Law on Taxation. Moreover, a Public-Private Partnership mechanism was established to maximize mutual benefits and understanding between the two sectors.

These economic reforms together with efforts to maintain fiscal and monetary discipline, have enabled the government of Cambodia to keep the exchange and inflation rates stable and enhanced macroeconomic stability.

The government is rebuilding Cambodia's legal infrastructure with new laws that aim to combine the best of the pre-1975 civil law and common law traditions. Since 1993, the National Assembly has adopted many new laws to support the development of a modern market economy.

Some of the major economic reforms were:

- Virtually eliminating the divergence between the official and parallel exchange rates
- De-collectivizing a commercial banking system and a central bank
- Eliminating most non-tariffs barriers and streamlining tariffs
- Adopting a liberal foreign investment law
- Privatizing most state-owned enterprises
- Promoting regional and global integration

Below is a chart which explains the need to develop certain features to ensure high and sustained economic growth for all countries. (See Figure 24.6)

FIGURE 24.6
The Common Characteristics of High, Sustained Growth

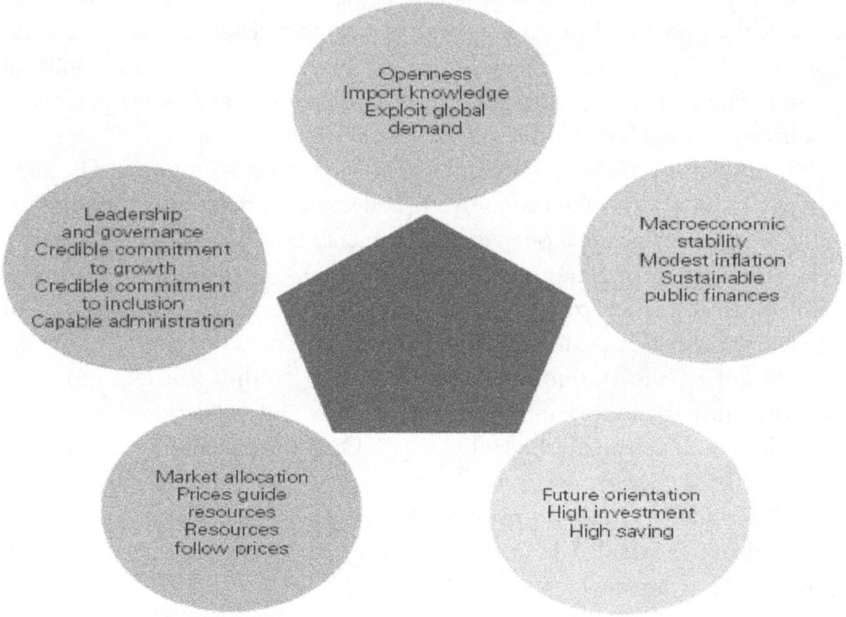

MISMATCH OF SECTORS

I use the analogy of a human being to explain the situation of Cambodia. Mr Cambodia is abnormal, given he has a small head, big stomach, and small legs. The structure is not sustainable and is very fragile. In order to assist Mr Cambodia to stand and walk, we need to increase the head-size, reduce the stomach, and strengthen the legs. The head here refers to the intellectual leadership and human resources while the stomach refers to the big administration with the lack of efficiency and transparency. The legs form the private sector. We cannot develop without the participation and support from the private sector.

State owned enterprises (SOEs) were privatized in two phases, between 1991 to 1993, and after April 1995, when new privatization regulations were approved. During the first phase, ministries privatized their own enterprises. They negotiated their own terms of sale or lease of assets and brought the resulting revenues directly into their own budgets. After April 1995, the central government tightened the privatization process, increasing its control over the process. The private sector has grown strongly, from a minuscule base, since the comprehensive program of economic stabilization and reforms were introduced in 1993. A highly competitive small business sector has emerged.

Part 2: Agricultural Reforms

Agriculture is the main element in economic development and employment. With a large flat arable land and about 80 per cent of the total population living in the rural areas, Cambodia has a comparative advantage in developing the agricultural sector. Prolonged civil war and armed conflict has damaged the irrigation system and road infrastructure in the rural areas. The reconstruction process is ongoing with dynamic support from the international donor community and the private sector.

A series of agricultural policy reforms was undertaken. Important agricultural reforms include agricultural collectives and privatizing agricultural land, removing price controls on most agricultural inputs and outputs, and eliminating licensing requirements for imports and exports of agricultural products, except logs. Most commodity prices are market determined and influenced by international trade.

In 2010, the government has issued a rice policy with quite clear directions. With the ambition to increase milled rice exports, the government has made efforts to invest in this sector and find the markets for Cambodian agricultural products. In realizing the vision of agriculture development, the government has adopted a three-pronged strategy — *productivity enhancement, diversification and agricultural commercialization* (from subsistence to commercial agriculture) — through the implementation of a package of interrelated measures: (1) infrastructure building and enhancement (roads, irrigations, energy/electricity and information and communication technologies (ICT); (2) improvement in the provision of extension services and agricultural inputs; (3) land management reform; (4) finance; (5) marketing; (6) farmer organizations; and (7) institutional building and coordination. In the current context, agricultural commercialization has become more dynamic in the light of global economic changes due to increasing food demand and prices. This trend bears some implications on, and revives the impetus of, paddy rice and other crops production in Cambodia, which have the potential for further higher growth.

Part 3: Industrial Reform

Manufacturing industry in Cambodia is still at the very preliminary stage in which only light industries with low technology have been developed and established. Cambodia is pursuing more export oriented rather than import substitution industrial development policy. Textiles and apparel are the top export oriented manufacturing in Cambodia. Other light industries, especially food and beverage, are focusing on local rather than foreign market. The food industry in Cambodia has great potential to expand their market to the region, especially China and Japan, as long as they can increase mass production with low costs and high quality.

Small and medium enterprises (SMEs), which make up approximately 95 per cent of all enterprises and account for almost half of all employment, are the backbone of Cambodian economy. The Royal Government of Cambodia has emphasized the important role of SMEs in economic growth and poverty reduction in its Second Socio-Economic Development Plan and National Poverty Reduction Strategy. The Prime Minister has also emphasized the importance of SMEs as part of the Government's 'Rectangular Strategy' for economic development.[1] In 2009, the total number of small and medium factories and handicrafts registered with MIME (Ministry of Industry, Mines and Energy) is 35,560 establishments. This figure shows a growth rate about 8.4 per cent compared to 2008. In term of product value, this sector is estimated to have a growth rate of about 9.3% compared with the value in 2008.[2]

According to the Cambodian Ministry of Industry Mines and Energy, it is noted that Small and Medium Sized Enterprises (SMEs) account for more than 80 per cent of the whole Cambodian manufacturing industries. Such firms form about 82 per cent, and deal with beverage, food and tobacco (as of 2006). There are 25,455 establishments of food, tobacco, and beverage industry. The small and medium size factories showed a remarkable growth rate in 2009. This is mainly due to the sector's close links with agriculture and domestic markets. The most significant growth is observed in the food and beverage sector.

Part 4: Regional and Global Context

Cambodia became a member of ASEAN in 1999. Although Cambodia is the youngest member in the ASEAN Family, Cambodia has committed itself to integrate fully with ASEAN and also to meet the deadline of the ASEAN Community construction by 2015. Cambodia is the first least developed country member in the World Trade Organization (WTO) in 2004. Through this membership, Cambodia could attract more export oriented FDI.

The Cambodian economy has strongly integrated with the regional and global economy since early 2000 after Cambodia became a member of ASEAN in 1999 and WTO in 2004. Regionalization and globalization have assisted Cambodian economic development through export led growth, better economic structure and growing tourism services. Cambodian economy has performed well in the last decade. The real annual GDP grow was at an average of 9.5 per cent.

ASIAN FINANCIAL CRISIS (1997–98) AND THE GLOBAL ECONOMIC CRISIS (2008–09)

The Asian Financial Crisis started from Thailand, and spread to other countries in the region. Cambodia was not really hit hard by the crisis since Cambodia did not really enter into regional and global production and consumption networks. But it adversely impacted much on the Cambodian tourism industry. The global economic crisis of 2008-09 has contracted the Cambodian economy in all sectors at different levels. The most hit industries are garments and tourism. It has had an adverse impact on Cambodian economy since the end of 2008. The GDP fell to 6.8 per cent in 2008 and was estimated to plunge further to 0.1 per cent in 2009. But Cambodia recovered from the crisis in 2010 when GDP growth hit 5 per cent and was expected to increase to 6 per cent in 2011. (See Figure 24.7)

FIGURE 24.7
Cambodia's Real Growth Rate

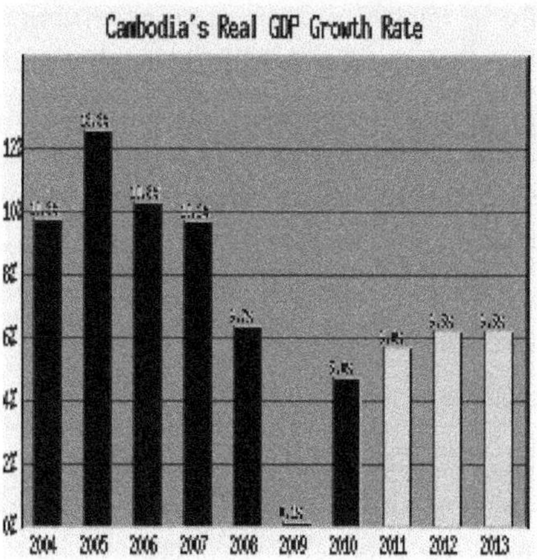

Source: Ministry of Economy and Finance, <http://www.mef.gov.kh/>

MEKONG RIVER AND CLIMATE CHANGE

Cambodian livelihoods depend greatly on the Mekong River, for instance in fisheries and irrigation. Any change in the flow of the river has a direct impact on Cambodia. The construction of dams in the upstream parts of the river will have a large impact on Cambodia, if there is no concerted and coordinated effort to cope with its impacts. Similarly, Cambodia has felt the impact of global warming and climate change. Unpredictable seasonal changes hamper the productivity of the farmers because most of Cambodian farmers rely on the rain and the weather for their crops production.

Regional production network and Regional markets

Cambodia has not yet fully integrated into the regional production networks. What Cambodia should do next is to integrate Cambodian enterprises and businesses into regional markets. How to create linkages to regional markets and production for the regional growth is being discussed within the government, and implemented to some extent, especially during this time of global economic crisis.

Part 5: Domestic Challenges

Poverty and Vulnerability Rate still high

Although there is good progress in poverty reduction in Cambodia of about one per cent per year, the poverty rate is still high, at about 30 per cent of Cambodian people live on less than one dollar per day. The lack of social safety nets, especially in health insurance, employment compensation; and retirement pension funds make Cambodia vulnerable to internal and external shocks. Landlessness and land disputes are the main challenges for socio-economic development in the country. The forced resettlement without appropriate compensation and other supports is putting huge difficulties on the livelihood of the victims. Some farmers have lost their land due to land grabbing.

Environmental Degradation

The most serious environmental issues in Cambodia are water pollution and deforestation. The toxic waste from the factories is damaging the quality of the water. Tonle Sap Lake, the biggest lake in Southeast Asia, is being threatened by the pollution caused by plastic bags. The Mekong River is being threatened by the construction of dams. Deforestation is another concern. According to various reports, much of the Cambodian forest has been seriously destroyed. The government has taken assertive actions to stop this. Hopefully, deforestation could be dramatically reduced and reforestation starts.

Part 6: Good Governance: The Key to the Future

We need to acknowledge the reality that Cambodia has been developed remarkably for the last decade under the leadership of Prime Minister Samdech Techo Hun Sen. However, we started from a very low base. Now the top challenge is how to maintain such high growth rates? In order to sustain economic growth and poverty reduction, we need to always reform and improve the governance structure. Corruption and red tape are considered the biggest obstacles for development. We accept that the government has a willingness to reduce corruption or even to fight corruption but the speed of implementation speed is not yet good enough.

Looking at the governance issues in Cambodia, I would like to focus on three main issues: Gas, Red signs, and Navigators.

Gas

There are some driving forces both international and external, contributing to the implementation of good governance. These include:

- Harmonious society: Cambodia has never experienced conflicts between its different ethnic or religious groups.
- Political commitment: Cambodian government has shown clear determination to maintain peace, stability and develop the country through holistic or comprehensive approaches.
- Good governance has been emphasized in the national development strategy.
- Young population with optimism: Cambodia is one of the oldest countries in the region in terms of history, but it is the youngest country in the region in terms of average population age (about 65 per cent of the total population is aged below 30 years old).
- Cambodia has been actively integrating herself into the regional arrangements or institutions such as Greater Mekong Sub-regional

Integration and ASEAN Regional cooperation and integration processes.
- After Cambodia became the first least developed country in the World Trade Organization (WTO) in 2004, Cambodia has strongly integrated into the international economic cooperation and interdependence. Cambodia has been preparing to become a member of the Asia Pacific Economic Cooperation (APEC) in the near future.

Navigators

International donor community/development partners, civil society organizations, scholars and researchers are cooperating and collaborating with the Cambodian government in directing destination and identifying the roadmap and stumbling blocks to overcome. Without the navigators, the driver cannot lead and drive smoothly to reach the goal. More support and cooperation should be given to the navigators.

Red Signs

Nothing is perfect. Good and bad, opportunities and challenges, achievements and problems are always together. As a human being, we cannot avoid making mistakes but the worst mistake is the ignorance of the reality or truth.

Here I would like to share with you some of the realities in Cambodia.

- There is a widening gap between rich and poor and between urban and rural areas
- Poverty rate is still relatively high compared with ASEAN member countries (about 30 per cent of Cambodians living below the poverty line, which means less than one dollar per day).
- People participation in the development policy is still limited
- Lack of human resources especially in the field of engineering and natural science

Part 7: The Way Forward

At the Macro-level

- Pro-poor development strategy needs to be more seriously implemented (rural infrastructure development needs much more attention, rural

business enterprises particularly small and medium enterprises requires greater supportive efforts from the Royal Government and development partners).
- Invest more on education especially in the field of natural science and engineering at the tertiary level and improve more basic education in the rural areas by developing both hard and soft infrastructure.
- In order to fight corruption, it requires an increase of the salary of the government officials to a sufficient level.
- Make further concrete steps towards the real partnership between Government and the Private Sector, between government and the civil society organizations.

At the Micro-level:

- Further integrate the values of transparency and accountability into Cambodian management and governance culture and behaviour. Singapore can be a partner of Cambodia in this endeavour.
- Advance leadership skills for the current and future generation of leadership by introducing short term leadership training programs, especially to the government officials.

CONCLUSION

Firstly, thanks to robust economic reform and privatization plus regional and global integration, Cambodia has gone through rapid growth in the last decade with an annual average rate of about 7 per cent. Good governance has become the core reform in which anti-corruption and transparency have been dealt with. However, Cambodia still has a long way to go to totally reduce its poverty and realize fair development. Further domestic reform and regional integration can bring Cambodia to a new level of development. Strengthening public institutions and competition capacity of the private sector will definitely help Cambodia to reap more benefits from regional and global economic dynamism. Cambodia can jump to the service industries only by incorporating a knowledge economy and producing a more high skilled labour force.

Secondly, good governance covers a whole spectrum of programs and policies which reinforce each other and provide synergy. The Key aspects of good governance include: Leadership; Institutions; Human Resource Development; Civil Service; Change and Adaptability. Good policy making includes due process, efficient and proper implementation, constant monitoring, frequent consultations and feedback, adequate resources and personnel. The capacity to change is crucial for sustainable growth-countries must not become fossilized, as seen in the Middle East, and be unable to adapt in a fast-changing world.

Notes

1. Sub-Committee on Small and Medium Enterprise (July 2009).
2. Ministry of Industry, Mines and Energy (2009).

INDEX

www.ingramcontent.com/pod-product-compliance
Lightning Source LLC
Chambersburg PA
CBHW021843020426
42334CB00013B/162
* 9 7 8 9 8 1 4 3 7 9 8 2 3 *